A CAPITOL IDEA

A Capitol Idea

Think Tanks and US Foreign Policy

DONALD E. ABELSON

McGill-Queen's University Press
Montreal & Kingston • London • Ithaca

© McGill-Queen's University Press 2006

ISBN-13: 978-0-7735-3115-4   ISBN-10: 0-7735-3115-7
Legal deposit third quarter 2006
Bibliothèque nationale du Québec

Printed in Canada on acid-free paper

This book has been published with the help of a grant from the
J.B. Smallman Publication Fund, Faculty of Social Science, The
University of Western Ontario.

McGill-Queen's University Press acknowledges the support of the
Canada Council for the Arts for our publishing program. We also
acknowledge the financial support of the Government of Canada
through the Book Publishing Industry Development Program (BPIDP)
for our publishing activities.

Library and Archives Canada Cataloguing in Publication

Abelson, Donald E
  A capitol idea : think tanks and US foreign policy / Donald E.
Abelson.

Includes bibliographical references and index.
ISBN-13: 978-0-7735-3115-4   ISBN-10: 0-7735-3115-7

1. United States – Foreign policy. 2. Research institutes – United
States. 3. Political planning – United States. 1. Title.

E744.A214 2006   327.73   C2006-901446-9

Typeset by Jay Tee Graphics Ltd. in Sabon 10/13

*To the memory of my mother, Estelle Abelson, who lived long enough
to see her son's dreams come true, and to my father, Alan,
who continues to instruct me on the finer points of life;*

*To my children, Rebecca and Seth,
whose lives are but a dream; and*

To Monda, who has given me inner peace

Contents

Preface   ix
Acknowledgments   xvii
Acronyms   xxi
Introduction   3

1   Lights, Camera, Action: Policy Experts and Presidential Campaigns   23

2   From Generation to Generation: The Origin and Evolution of American
Think Tanks   43

3   Theorizing about Think Tanks: Competing Visions and Conceptual
Approaches   97

4   Open for Business: Think Tanks and the Marketplace of Ideas   110

5   Something Is Missing: Think Tanks and the Study of Foreign
Policy-Making   127

6   Finding Their Way: In Search of Policy Influence   147

7   Is Anybody Listening? Assessing the Influence of Think Tanks   163

8   Think Tanks at Work: The Debate over National Missile Defense   182

9   A Hard-Fought Battle: 9/11, the Bush Doctrine, and the War of
Ideas   201

Conclusion: Think Tanks, Foreign Policy, and the Public Interest   225

APPENDICES

1 Profiles and Budgets of Selected American Think Tanks   235

2 Government Positions Held by Staff at Selected Think Tanks   239

3 Conferences, Workshops, Seminars, and Congressional Testimony on Missile Defence and the War on Terror Provided by Selected Think Tanks   259

4 Print Media Coverage, Television Exposure, and Congressional Testimony, January 2001–January 2005   273

5 Selected Publications on Missile Defence and the War on Terror from American Think Tanks   282

Notes   303
Works Cited   337
Index   359

Preface

For more than a decade, I have been preoccupied – or as some of my colleagues and students have observed, obsessed – with American think tanks and their role in the policy-making process. This preoccupation resulted in the publication in 1996 of *American Think Tanks and Their Role in US Foreign Policy*, which, among other things, chronicled the evolution of think tanks in the United States and highlighted the various strategies they rely on to enhance their visibility. In examining the transformation and behaviour of think tanks in the United States since the late 1800s and early 1900s, the book made two central observations. First, despite the widely held perception of think tanks as objective, scientific, and non-partisan scholarly institutions detached from the political process, many contemporary institutes have made and continue to make a concerted effort to influence public opinion and public policy. Rather than debating the advantages and disadvantages of various domestic and foreign policies from the comfort of their book-lined offices, think tanks, particularly those more advocacy-oriented, prefer becoming active participants in the political arena. In short, they have become vocal participants in the public dialogue. Second, although think tanks share a common desire to shape the way the electorate and policy-makers think about policy issues, the resources that institutes have at their disposal significantly influence how, where, and when they participate in public policy. Like corporations, they endeavour to employ the most effective strategies to market their product. As historian James Smith observed with some regret, think tanks have become all too savvy at competing in the marketplace of ideas. By marketing ideas like commodities regularly traded on the New York Stock

Exchange, they have sacrificed much of their integrity, a price, according to Smith, that traditional policy research institutions can ill afford to pay.[1]

In this book, I build on these observations by providing a more detailed examination of how a select group of American think tanks have attempted to influence two important and controversial foreign policies: the development and possible deployment of a national missile defense system and the ongoing initiatives of the Bush administration to wage war against terrorists and the states that harbour and nurture them. The latter case study includes the efforts of think tanks to influence public attitudes and the policy direction of the Bush administration with regard to homeland security before and after September 11, 2001, the war in Afghanistan, and the toppling of Saddam Hussein's regime in Iraq. These two contemporary case studies, which will be examined in chapters 8 and 9 respectively, offer much-needed insight into how and under what conditions think tanks can help to shape public attitudes and beliefs about emerging policy issues. They will also demonstrate how they have become involved in the policy-making process and the nature and extent of their impact.

The literature on think tanks and public policy has, for all intents and purposes, hit a roadblock. Although they have traced the growth and development of hundreds of think tanks in the United States and in other advanced and developing countries, few scholars have attempted to assess their impact or influence.[2] Despite countless studies on the involvement of interest groups, unions, multinational corporations, transnational organizations, environmental groups, religious associations, and dozens of other non-governmental organizations in the policy-making process, which, interestingly enough, do not adequately address the issue of policy influence, little progress has been made in understanding what, if any, impact think tanks have had in shaping public policy.

Scholars who study think tanks, as well as those who work at them, acknowledge how difficult it is to measure their influence. As David Ricci, a political scientist at Hebrew University, noted in his book *The Transformation of American Politics: The New Washington and the Rise of Think Tanks*, "I looked closely at what think tanks are doing, from books to seminars to briefings to breakfast meetings. I also asked fellows and managers to tell me what results they thought their activities would produce. The more I saw and heard, the more I understood that no one can know precisely what is happening in this drama."[3] Ricci's observations, which most scholars who have closely monitored think tanks would consider axiomatic, are based on the year he spent conducting research at the Brookings Institution. But even for scholars who have toiled at think tanks for most of their career, determining how much of an impact their institutions have had in shaping public policy is an exercise in futility. Some, including the American Enterprise Institute's David Frum, are even more blunt about why scholars should not waste time trying to assess the impact of think tanks over the short, medium, or long term. Asked what tangible or intangible indicators he would consider useful in evaluating the influence of think tanks, Frum responded, "None. You can't measure influence."[4]

Despite Frum's contention that policy influence cannot be measured, think tanks continue to make grand claims about how much influence they wield. For instance, in its 2003 annual report, AEI, perhaps unbeknownst to Frum, claimed, "Some [AEI scholars] entered the administration of George W. Bush in 2001 – but many others remained at AEI, where their work achieved a level of recognition and *influence* that would have astounded and gratified the founders of [AEI]."[5] In terms of its visibility, the report added, "AEI's standing in the national media is unmatched by that of any other policy research institute. The work of AEI scholars is cited more frequently and is published far more often in the leading U.S. newspapers and public affairs magazines then the work of scholars at other national think tanks."[6] The contributors to the report did not feel compelled to provide data to support their claims that AEI generated more media exposure than any other think tank, an assertion easily contradicted by several media databases, nor did they bother to explain how their influence was felt inside the Beltway. Perhaps Frum was right.

Although think tanks will undoubtedly portray themselves in the most favourable light, it is disconcerting that most scholars who study their behaviour have not been more critical in challenging their claims of influence. Ignoring the many methodological obstacles often encountered in assessing policy influence, those involved in this field of scholarly inquiry have, for the most part, been content to make sweeping assertions about which think tanks do or do not wield political influence. These unfounded observations are often based on the size of institutes and their budgets, their ideological orientation, the nature of their ties to high-level policy-makers, and the corporations, foundations, and philanthropists that provide generous funding. Scholars and journalists generally assume that if think tanks have multimillion-dollar budgets and hundreds of staff members and are more conservative in their thinking, they must have influence. Conversely, it is widely believed that if think tanks do not possess these attributes, they are destined to languish in obscurity.

It is not surprising that these kind of observations continue to make their way into the mainstream media and into much of the academic literature. It

is even less surprising that these claims are made in the promotional literature distributed by think tanks. After all, it makes sense that the more
money think tanks have, the more people they can hire. With a larger staff,
they can afford to devote more time and energy to influencing policy-
makers and the public. Moreover, since the vast majority of corporations
and philanthropists in the United States are more inclined to support conservative causes than those embraced by more liberal organizations, it follows that conservative think tanks must enjoy more political influence. In
American politics, it would be foolhardy to suggest that money and
influence do not go hand in hand. Or would it?

If the preceding discussion reflected the nature of the policy-making process and the types of think tanks that played a pivotal role in it, there would
be little need to continue our inquiry about the role these institutions play in
shaping public policy and public opinion. We would simply have to peruse
the annual reports of hundreds of American think tanks to identify those
with the largest budgets and staff resources and, after compiling this information, announce which think tanks enjoyed the most influence. Since only
a fraction of the two thousand or more think tanks in the United States have
millions of dollars to draw on, our work would be accomplished in short
order. Unfortunately, annual reports detailing revenues and expenditures in
tables and pie charts and newspaper articles listing who's hot and who's not
in the think tank world provide little insight into how these organizations
interact with different target audiences to achieve their goals. Discovering
which think tanks have the largest bank accounts is easy; identifying those
that exercise the most policy influence is, as Ricci, Frum, and others have
noted, problematic. Following the "trail of money" may have helped Carl
Bernstein and Bob Woodward to track down the culprits involved in the
Watergate scandal, but it is unlikely to provide political scientists with the
answers they require to assess the role and impact of think tanks. A more
nuanced understanding of policy influence and how it is achieved is necessary to account for how and under what conditions think tanks shape public policy. In undergraduate political science courses, students are often
taught that influence is a process which inevitably affords individuals and
organizations an opportunity to convince policy-makers to make decisions
they otherwise may not have been inclined to or, alternatively, to persuade
them to forego making decisions they otherwise would have. As much as
some scholars stress the importance of distinguishing between power and
influence, it is equally important to draw a distinction between different
types of influence. In so doing, we can better evaluate the contributions that
think tanks make and where in the policy cycle their impact is felt.

The purpose of this book is to impress upon those interested in non-governmental organizations generally and in think tanks specifically that we can no longer afford to make sweeping and unsubstantiated observations about institutions that have become permanent fixtures on America's political landscape. Think tanks in the United States – whether they are located on Washington's Massachusetts Avenue, a popular destination for public policy organizations, or overlooking the Pacific Ocean, as RAND does – were created with specific goals and interests in mind. At the very least, we can begin to make more informed observations about the behaviour of think tanks and how some of them have attempted to influence key foreign policy debates.

It would be so much easier for scholars studying think tanks and other non-governmental organizations that participate in the policy-making process if the amount of influence these groups claim to have could be verified. However, the world that think tanks inhabit and in which policy-makers make critical policy choices is not always easy to discern, making the study of policy influence inherently problematic. The policy-making process, as several scholars have noted, rarely follows a logical, linear, and predetermined path. Not unlike an obstacle course that new military recruits must learn to navigate, many barriers must be overcome by policy-makers and non-governmental organizations seeking to influence public policy. At times, think tanks can successfully weave their way through the policy-making process and have a desired impact. At other times, despite their best efforts, they may not be able to convince policy-makers to follow their advice, a painful lesson learned by several think tank directors as they have sought to increase the visibility and prominence of their institutions.

In studying policy-making in the United States, it has become commonplace to portray America as a highly pluralistic, decentralized, and fragmented country in which thousands of governmental and non-governmental organizations seek to influence the nation's political agenda. As Arthur Bentley, David Truman, Theodore Lowi, and other students of political pluralism have noted,[7] we cannot expect, nor should we assume, that all groups competing in the political arena will be able to achieve their goals. Although public policy may indeed reflect the outcome of group competition, as pluralists would instruct us, some interest groups, unions, and other non-governmental organizations will, for a host of reasons, enjoy a more dominant voice than their competitors. The same can be said about think tanks seeking to become more entrenched in the policy-making community. In some instances, a handful of think tanks, or perhaps even one, may play a critical role in influencing the direction of public policy. There are several think tanks, such as the Brookings Institution, the Hoover Institution, and the Heritage Foundation, that have taken credit, and rightfully so, for making important contributions to various domestic and foreign policy issues. However, in other instances, think tanks have barely left a mark on an administration's policies, a failure often admitted by those institutions that have tried to penetrate the highest levels of government but have come up short. Confronted by policy-makers in the White House who might not be inclined to solicit the advice and expertise of think tanks (or act on it even if it is requested), most policy institutes have turned their attention to other target audiences, including Congress, the bureaucracy, and the media, to convey their ideas. Indeed, for most think tanks, it is educating, informing, and at times lobbying members of Congress (although few, for legal reasons, would admit to doing so) that has become their main priority.

If we recognize that there are a multitude of domestic and international factors that may enhance or undermine the efforts of think tanks to assert policy influence, it is essential to make some observations about these organizations before determining the most useful methods to assess their impact. To begin with, it is important to understand that no two think tanks are exactly alike. Think tanks vary enormously in terms of staff size, budgets, funding sources, research programs, areas of specialization, and ideological orientation. Some inside and beyond the Beltway, including the Heritage Foundation, the Brookings Institution, the Carnegie Endowment for International Peace, the Cato Institute, the American Enterprise Institute, RAND, the Hoover Institution, and a select group of other prominent organizations, attract millions of dollars each year, have extensive publication programs, and have large staffs capable of organizing numerous conferences and seminars. Moreover, because of their visibility and stature in the policy-making community, most of these think tanks enjoy close ties with major media outlets and distinguished policy-makers.

However, these and other think tanks that frequently make the headlines are not representative of America's think tank community. The vast majority of think tanks do not resemble the Brookings Institution or the Heritage Foundation, which in the 2003 fiscal year enjoyed a budget of approximately $50 million. Most have even less in common with RAND, the Santa Monica–based think tank known for its expertise in defense and security studies. With a budget of over $200 million, a staff of more than a thousand, and close and lasting ties to the Pentagon, RAND is in a class by itself. Even a cursory review of *The Think Tank Directory*,[8] a comprehensive listing of policy institutes in the United States, reveals that the majority of these organizations have budgets barely reaching $1 million and approximately a dozen staff members, hardly competition for America's elite think tanks.

Given the enormous diversity of the think tank population, scholars realize that it is extremely difficult to define the organizations which they have come to study. Other than acknowledging that think tanks tend to be independent, non-profit, tax-exempt, and non-partisan organizations (not to be confused with non-ideological) engaged in the study of public policy, scholars are hard pressed to isolate other institutional characteristics that make these organizations unique. Moreover, since interest groups and other non-governmental organizations have begun to devote more time and resources to studying policy issues and making recommendations to policy-makers, it has become even more frustrating for scholars to identify think tanks. As James McGann, of the Philadelphia-based Foreign Policy Research Institute and an astute student of think tanks, observed, " I know one when I see one."[9]

McGann's method of identifying think tanks may not adhere to rigorous scientific standards, but it accurately reflects how scholars have come to analyze a group of organizations that have long been credited with influencing public policy in the United States. Scholars, journalists, and policy-makers may not be able to agree on what a think tank is, but they understand that strong ties exist between policy-makers and public policy institutes, a term often used synonymously with think tanks. The challenge for those studying think tanks is to determine how they become involved in policy-making and the extent to which they have been able to shape and mould the attitudes and beliefs of prominent policy-makers in each branch and at every level of government.

Since all think tanks in the United States do not enjoy the same resources, it is reasonable to conclude that they may not have the same priorities. Despite sharing a common goal to influence public opinion and public policy, think tanks, not unlike other organizations in the policy-making community, must think strategically about how to employ their resources most effectively to achieve their desired goals. For instance, some believe that attracting media exposure is the most effective way to influence public attitudes about such pressing issues as homeland security and the war in Iraq. As a result, they invest considerably more time and resources submitting op-ed articles to newspapers and granting interviews to the press than to writing book-length studies for policy-makers that may go unread. Alternatively, for think tanks that prefer to work more closely with bureaucratic departments and agencies to hammer out the details of specific policy initiatives or those that simply want to establish broad policy networks to help plant ideas in the minds of experts and policy-makers, attracting media exposure may be less of a priority. In short, faced with limited resources and an increasingly competitive environment, think tanks must carve out a niche.

Presidents of think tanks, not unlike policy-makers throughout government, realize that it often takes months, if not years, for ideas to be translated into concrete policy decisions. In the process, numerous individuals and organizations will seek to leave their imprint on government policy. If the ultimate goal of think tanks is to simply propose ideas and leave it to policy-makers to decide if they want to act on them, then what happens during the policy-making process is less important. Yet, as this study will demonstrate, think tanks have a vested interest in shaping public policy, not just observing the policy-making process unfold. Simply put, they make a concerted effort to influence policy over the short, medium, and long term.

In the pages that follow, a clearer picture as to why these interesting and complex organizations deserve closer scrutiny will emerge. It is my hope that this book will, at the very least, generate discussion and debate about the role American think tanks play in foreign policy and how we can better understand their impact. Ideas, as so many historians, philosophers, and political scientists have reminded us, do matter. So too do the organizations that try to shape our national conversation.

Acknowledgments

Jackie Robinson, the legendary infielder of the Brooklyn Dodgers who broke baseball's colour barrier in 1947, once remarked, "A life is not important, except in the impact it has on other lives." Over the course of researching and writing this book, I have thought a lot about Robinson's poignant observation and how often we take for granted the people who have had a particularly positive and lasting impact on our lives. I have been very fortunate, both personally and professionally, to be surrounded by people who have enriched my life, and I wanted to take this opportunity to express my gratitude. Each of them has, in his or her own way, helped me to achieve my goals.

First and foremost, I would like to thank my parents, Alan and Estelle Abelson, for a lifetime of encouragement, love, and support. My mother passed away while I was writing this book, but while she was alive, her interest in my well-being and in my research never wavered. My memories of her continue to be a great source of comfort and inspiration. She was more than my mother; she was my confidant, my ally, and, most importantly, my friend. I miss her deeply. My father, who like me, is convinced that on the seventh day G-d created baseball, has always been my greatest teacher. His words of wisdom and his insights on so many important topics relating to history, politics, and sports continue to give me much food for thought.

I would also like to thank my three sisters, who, whether they are aware of it or not, contributed to the completion of this book. Each of them taught her younger brother some of life's most important lessons. From Lynn, I learned the value of perseverance; from Joan, the confidence to stake out and defend my position; and from Karen, the importance of maintaining a sense of humour. I will always be indebted to them.

Writing by its very nature is a solitary endeavour, and it often helps to have some distractions along the way. Thankfully, I could always count on my children, Rebecca and Seth, to pull me away from my desk. Whenever they made their way into my study, I knew exactly what they were thinking: why write about a boring and stuffy topic like think tanks when you can play catch, run around outside, or watch Scooby Doo? Good point.

When I returned to my desk, I often sought the advice and wise counsel of Monda Halpern, a professor in the Department of History at the University of Western Ontario and the person with whom I share my life. From the time Monda convinced me to write a new book about think tanks and US foreign policy, she devoted considerable time and energy to improving the organization and content of my manuscript. I benefited greatly from her input, but I have benefited even more from her love, friendship, and kindness. I am so thankful to have her in my corner.

A number of other people deserve to be acknowledged. Monda's twin sister, Sonia, an art historian, decided to make her contribution to political science by suggesting the title for this book, a considerable improvement over what I had in mind. I am grateful for her helpful intervention. And I am eternally grateful to several of my former students and research assistants who worked tirelessly to compile critical information for this study. Shauna Cade, Issam El-Hourani, Daniel Hambly, Ryan King, Andrew Quinlan, and Brian Whitmore went out of their way to help me prepare the manuscript for publication. Words cannot possibly express my gratitude to them or to Christine Wall of the Centre for American Studies at Western. Among other things, Christine used her well-honed computer skills to format the many tables included in the book. In short, her work proved invaluable.

Since 1993 I have had the good fortune of teaching in the Department of Political Science at the University of Western Ontario. During this time, I have been able to draw on the expertise of several of my colleagues, who have done their utmost to point me in the right direction. For making suggestions and for allowing me to bounce ideas off them, I would like to thank Carol Agocs, Ian Brodie, Adam Harmes, Charles Jones, Kiera Ladner, Nigmendra Narain, Andres Perez, Elizabeth Riddell-Dixon, Andrew Sancton, Veronica Schild, Laura Stephenson, Richard Vernon, Marty Westmacott, and Bob Young.

I am also grateful to Elizabeth Hulse for copy-editing my manuscript. Her considerable talent helped to bring the text to life. Finally, I would like to thank Philip Cercone of McGill-Queen's University Press for supporting my work on think tanks and for giving me the time I needed to complete this book. I appreciate everything that he and his staff have done to make *A Capitol Idea* a reality.

Acronyms

ABM	anti-ballistic missile
AEA	American Enterprise Association
AEI	American Enterprise Institute
ASSA	American Social Science Association
CAP	Center for American Progress
CCF	Chicago Civic Federation
CFR	Council on Foreign Relations
CRB	Commission for Relief in Belgium
CSE	Citizens for a Sound Economy
CSP	Center for Security Policy
CSIS	Center for Strategic and International Studies
DLC	Democratic Leadership Council
FEC	Federal Election Commission
GOPAC	"Grand Old Party" Action Committee
GPALS	global protection against limited strikes
IGR	Institute for Government Research
ISP	Institute for Policy Studies
MAD	mutual assured destruction
NASA	National Aeronautics and Space Administration
NCF	National Civic Federation
NGO	non-governmental organization
NMD	national missile defense
NORAD	North American Aerospace Defense Command
PAC	political action committee

PNAC   Project for the New American Century
PPI   Progressive Policy Institute
SDI   Strategic Defense Initiative
UCS   Union of Concerned Scientists
WMD   weapons of mass destruction

A CAPITOL IDEA

Introduction

As long as there have been rulers, there have been advisers trying to influence them. Motivated by ambition, power, and a profound desire to leave their mark on history, political advisers, or policy experts, as they are commonly called, have gravitated to those entrusted with the authority to govern. The relationship between political leaders and their sometimes trusted advisers has long been a subject of interest to historians, political scientists, philosophers, psychologists, and of course playwrights. Scholars intrigued by the complex bond that often exists between those holding power and those intent on sharing it have gained much-needed insight from the many Shakespearean plays that closely follow the emergence and often tragic decline of leaders, including Macbeth, King Lear, Julius Caesar, and Hamlet. Some scholars, including Niccolò Machiavelli, the Renaissance political theorist, have drawn on their own experience as advisers to lay the groundwork for future leaders.

In the United States the relationship between political leaders and policy advisers, though at times tragic, is nonetheless critical in understanding the development and execution of public policy. By providing their expertise to members of Congress, the Executive, and the bureaucracy, policy advisers play a vital role in formulating and injecting ideas into the policy-making process. Policy-makers in the United States continue to solicit the advice of experts from universities, interest groups, professional and business associations, corporations, law firms, and other organizations where policy research is conducted. However, in addition to relying on their inner circle of advisers, policy-makers are increasingly turning to scholars from think tanks to help identify, develop, shape, reinforce, and implement policy ideas.

For close to one hundred years, as chapters 1 and 2 will document, think tanks have made their presence felt throughout Washington's policy-making community. Whether in testimony before Congress, in private meetings with the president and senior White House staff, or across the table from bureaucrats, policy-makers and think-tank scholars have exchanged ideas about some of the nation's most pressing concerns. In recent years, scholars and journalists have paid particularly close attention to the interaction between policy-makers and policy advisers during presidential campaigns and transitions when those aspiring to occupy the White House, or those determined to remain in it, turn to think tanks for timely and relevant advice.[1]

The list of presidents and presidential candidates who have established strong ties to leading think tanks continues to grow. Many historians are familiar with the policy experts who assembled to advise Woodrow Wilson, an academic with little patience for and even less faith in unelected policy advisers. There are also several historical accounts of the relationship between Franklin Delano Roosevelt and his so-called brain trust[2] and the small but enthusiastic group of scholars, including Richard Neustadt and Arthur Schlesinger, who contributed their intellectual resources to assisting the Kennedy administration. Until recently, few scholars have tracked the involvement of think tank scholars in subsequent presidential administrations. For example, to varying degrees and at different times, Jimmy Carter and Ronald Reagan drew on the policy expertise available at some of the nation's most prominent think tanks.

Although the visibility and prominence of think tanks in Washington's decision-making labyrinth appeared to fade temporarily during the administration of George Bush Sr, who, not unlike Woodrow Wilson, claimed to have little need for or interest in policy experts, think tanks have attracted considerable attention inside the Beltway over the past decade. President Clinton's close ties to a handful of small Democratic think tanks, including the Progressive Policy Institute and the Economic Policy Institute, as well as former speaker of the House Newt Gingrich's personal and professional association with the Heritage Foundation, the Hoover Institution, and the American Enterprise Institute, led to renewed speculation about the growing influence of think tanks in American politics.

After Texas governor George W. Bush announced his run for the presidency in 1998, this speculation reached new levels when he surrounded himself with a handful of conservative think tanks willing to advise him on critical foreign policy issues. However, political scientists and historians have only recently begun to explore the complex role that think tanks play in presidential elections and in the policy-making process more generally. Hundreds of studies have documented how interest groups, foreign governments, public advocacy coalitions, and other non-governmental organizations lobby government officials to pursue policies compatible with their institutional interests. By contrast, little scholarly attention has been devoted to studying how think tanks seek to influence America's political agenda. Several studies have detailed the institutional histories of prestigious American think tanks, but the efforts of these institutions to become firmly entrenched in Washington's decision-making network have not as yet been fully explored.

Given the extensive ties between think tanks and government departments and agencies, as well as the frequency with which their members are appointed to high-level government positions, it is essential to acquire a better and more complete understanding of how they become involved in the policy-making process. Think tanks, as pluralists remind us, represent but one set of actors competing for power and prestige in the marketplace of ideas, a fact often lost on those who make sweeping assertions about their impact. Nonetheless, as this study will demonstrate, think tanks, particularly those closely aligned to a presidential administration, represent a strong and at times decisive voice in the political arena. By publishing brief or full-length studies on a wide range of policy issues, inviting decision-makers to conferences and seminars, providing commentaries on network newscasts, establishing liaison offices to develop and maintain contact with members of Congress and the Executive, serving on various presidential boards, commissions, election task forces, and transition teams, and giving testimony before congressional committees and subcommittees, think tanks have become permanent fixtures in the policy-formation process. Though not generally considered to be part of the formal structure of the American government, for decades they have managed to operate effectively within its parameters.

As McGann and Weaver[3] and Stone and Denham[4] have documented in their comparative studies of think tanks, organizations engaged in policy research have become firmly ensconced in the political fabric of many nations. They can be found in virtually every developing and developed country in the world and have emerged in significant numbers in many newly formed democracies, most notably in Eastern Europe.[5] According to a recent estimate, there are over four thousand think tanks worldwide, half of which are located in the United States.[6]

While think tanks have taken root throughout the Western world, those in the United States are in many ways unique. What makes them distinctive, besides their sheer number, is the frequency with which their scholars gain access to virtually every level and branch of government. They do so because, unlike in parliamentary democracies, for example, where there is very little turnover in the senior ranks of the civil service, in the United States a "revolving door" facilitates the movement of think tank scholars in and out of government departments and agencies. When a new administration comes to power, the president not only hand-picks his inner circle of policy advisers but must fill thousands of positions in the bureaucracy. Many of these are filled by academics in think tanks looking to add government experience to their resumés. As some policy practitioners have observed, think tanks often serve as "holding tanks" where policy experts congregate in the hope of being recruited into senior government positions.[7] Once they have spent a few years in the State Department, the Pentagon, the National Security Council, or one of countless other departments, they often return to think tanks to write about the policy issue or issues in which they have been engaged. As Ivo Daalder of the Brookings Institution recently noted, after spending a year or more in government, policy experts look forward to returning to think tanks to "de-brief" themselves and other experts in their fields: "It gives them an opportunity to think and write about what they have done and learned."[8]

In addition to the revolving-door phenomenon, which will be discussed more thoroughly in chapter 4, the absence of a strong party system in the United States affords think tanks innumerable opportunities to share their ideas with elected officials. Again, unlike in parliamentary democracies such as Canada and Great Britain, where party unity is strictly enforced, members of Congress are free to solicit and consider policy recommendations made by think tanks and other non-governmental organizations without worrying that the direction they might consider moving in will somehow undermine their party's mandate.[9] Moreover, since members of Congress, unlike their counterparts in the German Bundestag, do not have the luxury of relying on party-based think tanks or foundations to provide them with policy advice, they must by necessity turn to the external research community for expertise.[10] Given the time constraints imposed on members of Congress and the reality that very few of them possess a detailed understanding of the various policy issues on which they have to vote, they have an incentive to listen to think tanks, which are all too eager to share their knowledge. These and other features of the American political system have contributed to an environment in which dozens of so-called non-partisan think tanks descend upon the nation's capital to promote what they believe is a "capitol idea." From missile defense to the war on terror, think tanks rarely hesitate to make their views known. They are competing among themselves for the attention of policy-makers and the public and are waging full-scale battles in the war of ideas.

Breaking with the traditions established by Robert Brookings, Andrew Carnegie, and other founders of early twentieth-century think tanks, who were determined to insulate their scholars from partisan politics, several contemporary research institutions, often described as advocacy think tanks because of their ideologically derived policy agendas, have consciously avoided erecting a barrier between policy research and political advocacy. Rather than promoting scholarly inquiry as a means to better serve the public interest, a goal ostensibly embraced by think tanks in the Progressive Era, advocacy think tanks such as the Heritage Foundation and the Institute for Policy Studies have come to resemble interest groups and political action committees by encouraging decision-makers, through various channels, to implement policies compatible with their ideological beliefs and those shared by their generous benefactors. Even the revered Brookings Institution, a think tank widely perceived as a scholarly, objective, and research-driven organization whose studies are regularly cited in the academic community, has become more conscious of marketing its products. According to Michael O'Hanlon, a defense and security specialist at Brookings, "the golden age of Brookings ended in the mid to late 1980s" when senior administrators and trustees "realized that the Heritage Foundation was cleaning our clock." As a result, O'Hanlon added, "we are encouraged to place less emphasis on producing long books and more emphasis in getting our ideas out in a timely fashion."[11] In addition to publishing shorter monographs, Brookings pays close attention to attracting media exposure. Three years ago, it went so far as to build its own television studio to allow its scholars to gain access to the airwaves on short notice.

The purpose of this book, as noted in the preface, is to challenge students of American politics and public policy to think more critically about the nature of think tanks and their impact in promoting and shaping important policy issues. Understanding how and why these institutions have emerged in significant numbers in the United States is relatively straightforward. The more difficult task is to determine the extent to which they have influenced the content and outcome of key policy decisions. To do so, it will be necessary, as noted, to isolate particular policies in which they have been actively engaged. In drawing on different theoretical approaches that enable scholars to isolate those think tanks which have been most relevant to particular policy debates, we can begin to evaluate the nature of their contributions.

In a recent book, *Do Think Tanks Matter?* I argued that measuring the influence of think tanks, either directly or indirectly, presented formidable methodological obstacles. Not only is it often difficult to trace the origin of an idea to a particular individual or organization, but assessing how much influence think tanks have had in altering the behaviour of policy-makers, journalists, and what scholars call the "attentive public" is even more problematic. Media citations, appearances before congressional committees and subcommittees, publications, and a host of other indicators of influence may allow scholars to identify those think tanks most active in certain policy discussions. However, such measurements tell us little about what, if any, impact these particular inputs have had in shaping specific policy decisions. As a result, I concluded that, in the absence of detailed case studies which explore the interaction between a select group of think tanks and policy-makers, it is virtually impossible to arrive at any definitive conclusions. The answer to my seemingly simple question Do think tanks matter? remained elusive.

By examining the efforts of a small group of think tanks to inform, educate, and in the final analysis, influence the attitudes of policy-makers and the public about two important contemporary foreign policies – the development and deployment of a national or theatre missile defense, or what Frank Gaffney, the president of the Center for Security Policy, calls simply "missile defense," and the ongoing war against terror – more concrete observations about the impact of think tanks can be made. Indeed, in these two instances, it will become apparent that not only have a handful of think tanks specializing in foreign and defense policy played a critical role in framing the parameters of these vital debates, but there is clear and compelling evidence that they have had a discernible impact in shaping the political agenda of the nation. Several other organizations in the ever-expanding marketplace of ideas have sought to have their voices heard, but there is no doubt that a small but well-positioned network of think tanks have been centre stage.

The importance of providing detailed case studies to highlight the participation of think tanks in the policy-making process cannot be overstated. Without a closer examination of the various channels that think tanks rely on to reach their intended target audiences, scholars and journalists are forced to speculate about the nature of their involvement. Invariably, such theorizing leads to unsubstantiated and at times unfounded observations about what think tanks have and have not been able to achieve. At the same time, it is imperative for scholars constructing case studies to resist the temptation to make general observations about think tanks and the many target audiences they are trying to influence. As this study will illustrate, the success of think tanks in shaping public policy can be influenced by a host of domestic and external factors, many of which are beyond their control. In some instances, their success in influencing specific policy debates may have little to do with the way institutes are managed and the quality of their policy recommendations. On the contrary, some think tanks may be able to exercise considerable policy influence because a political event, such as the terrorist attacks against the World Trade Center and the Pentagon on September 11, 2001, has made their ideological agenda more palatable.

The ability of think tanks to shape both the policy-making environment and specific policy decisions also depends heavily on the willingness of policy-makers to rely on the information and knowledge they are provided with in a timely and responsible manner. How policy-makers "use "information has been a topic of considerable scholarly debate in recent years and has led to several theories about the ability and willingness of policy-makers to draw on policy research. As some scholars have suggested, since the world that policy-makers inhabit is so different from the one policy researchers occupy, we should not be surprised that policy research has had a limited impact on public policy. Policy-makers and policy researchers do function in very different environments, but their worlds often intersect. In fact, it is because think tanks understand the nature and dynamics of both worlds that they are able to respond to many of the demands placed on policy-makers. The various strategies that think tanks rely on to supply information to policy-makers and the many reasons why policy-makers may or may not be receptive to their ideas will be explored in chapter 5.

Before we delve into more-detailed discussions about think tanks, policy-makers, and foreign policy, it is essential to shed some light on the diverse nature of the think tank community in the United States. Recognizing the similarities and differences between think tanks will enable scholars to construct a more useful conceptual framework within which to study these complex organizations. It will also enable them to keep track of the behavioural characteristics of think tanks in which they are in agreement and those that have generated little consensus.

STUDYING THINK TANKS

A Google search of the term "think tank" regularly locates approximately 4.5 million entries. Many of these highlight the work of prominent think tanks, including the Brookings Institution and RAND. Those using this search engine or one of many others available on the Internet can locate the Web sites of virtually every think tank in the world. The same search, however, reveals countless other uses of the term "think tank." Interestingly enough, a recent search uncovered a series of rock and roll albums that were neatly displayed in a "think tank." Another entry discussed a "think tank" that had been constructed to allow visitors to study the behaviour of orangutans and other primates at Washington's National Zoo.

When the term "think tank" was coined in the United States during World War II, it was intended to describe a secure room or environment in which military planners and policy-makers met to discuss wartime strategy. It is unlikely that the subject of orangutans or favourite rock and roll albums served as the basis for their discussions. Still, like many other words or phrases used originally to describe a specific place, event, or phenomenon, "think tank" has come to mean different things to different people. Among other things, the term can and has been used to describe world-renowned research institutions, places that exist in cyberspace, exhibits at public institutions, personal hobbies, and ideas for projects that have or have not come to fruition. Therefore it should not be surprising that there is little consensus on what constitutes a think tank or the criteria employed to identify them. Other than acknowledging that think tanks (if we are indeed talking about research institutions) are independent, non-profit, tax-exempt organizations engaged in the study of public policy, scholars have been unable to agree on an inclusive definition that would accurately describe what they are and the activities in which they are engaged. After we have surveyed the think tank landscape in the United States, it is understandable why scholars have experienced so much difficulty defining these organizations.

Since think tanks vary considerably in size, financial resources, staff composition, ideological orientation, areas of specialization, and research programs, no single definition can adequately describe a typical think tank. For instance, some elite think tanks, including the Brookings Institution, the Hoover Institution, and the Heritage Foundation, employ between 150 and 300 people and have annual budgets in excess of $30 million. Others, including RAND, have even larger financial resources. Courtesy of the United States government, RAND's budget exceeds $200 million. By contrast, the vast majority of American think tanks are considerably smaller in scope and have modest budgets. For example, the Center for National Policy and the Economic Policy Institute employ between one and two dozen people and operate on less than $2 million a year.[12] The Project for the New American Century, which continues to generate considerable media attention for its perceived alliance with the administration of George W. Bush, is even smaller. It has an operating budget of $600,000 and four full-time staff members.[13]

Think tanks differ in other important respects as well. One of the most obvious differences is the priority they place on research. Although think tanks portray themselves as institutions providing expertise in a number of domestic and foreign policy areas, they do not share the same commitment to scholarly research. For instance, in 2003 the Brookings Institution allocated 70 per cent of its budget to pursue research in three main areas: governmental studies, foreign policy studies, and economic studies.[14] In 2002 the Heritage Foundation spent 40 per cent of its budget on research, a significant increase from the 15.3 per cent it had set aside for this function in 1989.[15] Several other institutes devote considerably less time and resources to the study of public policy. Consequently, while some think tanks continue to see themselves mainly as research institutions, others have assumed different roles in the policy-making community. As noted, advocating policy positions, rather than engaging in long-term research projects, has become the main activity for many contemporary think tanks. Yet, regardless of their priorities, organizations perceived as engaging in policy research are often referred to as think tanks.

Given the tremendous diversity of think tanks in the United States, it is unlikely that scholars will agree on how to define these organizations. It is even less likely that they will agree on how to measure their influence. Nonetheless, it is possible to identify different types of think tanks that have evolved in the United States since the turn of the twentieth century in order to isolate some of their distinct characteristics. To this end, several typologies or classifications have been constructed to help make sense of the many kinds of think tanks that inhabit the policy-making community. Two of the most frequently cited classifications were constructed by Kent Weaver and James McGann. According to Weaver, there are three main types of think tanks in the United States, which he refers to as universities without students, contract research organizations, and advocacy think tanks.[16] McGann identifies seven types of think tanks: academic diversified, academic specialized, contract/consulting, advocacy, policy enterprise, literary agent/publishing house, and state-based.[17] Even Weaver and McGann acknowledge that these methods of classification do not account for every think tank in the United States, and through a recent collaboration, they have modified their earlier typologies.[18] Other scholars, including Diane Stone, have suggested using typologies that differentiate between think tanks which she labels old guards and new partisans. I and others have noted that some consideration should also be given to vanity and legacy or candidate-based think tanks. The important distinctions between these and other types of think tanks will be discussed throughout the study.

As research institutions specializing in domestic and foreign policy issues, think tanks have often been portrayed as disinterested observers of political affairs. Committed to scholarly research and determined to provide their expertise to decision-makers, early twentieth-century think tanks such as the Brookings Institution, the Russell Sage Foundation, and the Carnegie Endowment for International Peace were rarely viewed as organizations engaged in partisan politics. But as this study will make clear, think tanks have undergone a fundamental transformation in the decades since World War II, from institutions that were primarily committed to providing impartial advice to government officials in order to serve the public interest to organizations that devote considerable time and resources to becoming leading advocates for a host of domestic and foreign causes. The causes or issues that some think tanks are committed to, including less government intervention, free market capitalism, and a strong national defense, are clearly outlined as part of their mandate.

In some academic and policy-making circles, think tanks, like university departments and research centres, are still regarded as "ivory towers" where scholars pursue their research in relative isolation, that is, in an elite and insular environment rarely subjected to public scrutiny. Despite this commonly held perception, it does not appear that think tanks are committed to distancing themselves from the public or from the political arena. On the contrary, though many of the studies they produce may appear to be divorced from reality, individuals affiliated with these institutions are acutely aware of their role in the policy-making process. Some think tanks located outside the nation's capital, such as the Hoover Institution, may prefer to distance themselves from the vicissitudes of Washington politics, but others have made a conscious decision to position themselves close to the country's leading power-brokers.

As think tanks become more actively involved in both the policy-making and the political process, observers of American politics are finding it increasingly difficult to differentiate between think tanks and other types of non-governmental organizations, such as interest groups and political action committees (PACs), which are created specifically to lobby government officials. Moreover, as interest groups and industry associations devote more of their resources to research in order to enhance their credibility in the eyes of decision-makers, the boundaries that used to separate think tanks from other non-governmental organizations are beginning to crumble. Still, there are some noticeable differences between think tanks and interest groups that should be highlighted.

Unlike interest groups, which are comprised of like-minded individuals intent on influencing specific public policy issues, think tanks are rarely created to address a specific concern such as gun control or the protection of old-growth forests. They are established to provide expertise in a number of policy areas and are not limited to focusing on any one issue. Moreover, it would be naive to suggest that scholars working at a think tank are like-minded. Although they may share similar ideological views, their approaches to a wide range of issues can and do differ dramatically. In addition, while interest groups constantly seek to increase their membership base, think tanks have a far less direct connection to the public. Through their publications and frequent appearances on network newscasts, members of think tanks attempt to inform the public about the potential repercussions of various government policies. And for fundraising purposes, think tanks often enlist the support of direct-mail consultants to identify segments of the electorate most likely to support their work. But unlike interest groups and political parties, which help to bring together individuals to express their concerns to elected officials – what political scientists refer to as an aggregation and articulation function – think tanks do not try to serve as a conduit between the public and government. On the contrary, rather than taking their cue from the public, they try to impose their ideas on the electorate and on policy-makers.

There are other important differences between interest groups and think tanks, most notably in relation to elections. One of the most common strategies interest groups and PACs rely on to exercise influence is to make donations to congressional and presidential candidates. Through donations of hard money to incumbents and challengers, regulated by the Federal Election Commission, interest groups and PACs attempt to solidify their ties to elected officials. In exchange for helping to finance their campaign, interest groups hope to generate more political support for their organization. Think tanks, by contrast, are prohibited from donating money to political campaigns. Under chapter 501 c(3) of the Internal Revenue Code, think tanks, as non-profit, tax-exempt organizations, must remain non-partisan. Although members of think tanks can and have provided policy advice to congressional and presidential candidates, they must be careful not to violate the restrictions imposed on them by the Internal Revenue Service. In short, interest groups and PACs are in the business of giving money to attract support for their cause or causes. To put it bluntly, they seek to use their influence to deliver votes to those candidates who share their concerns. By contrast, think tanks are in the business of raising money to help advance their institutional mandates. They do not seek to deliver votes or to directly influence the outcome of elections but to share their insights with different target audiences. Think tanks measure their success, in part, not by keeping track of how many Republicans, Democrats, or Independents occupy seats in Congress, but by how receptive members of Congress, the Executive, and the media are to their ideas.

More than a decade ago, Joseph Peschek observed in a provocative and much needed study on think tanks, or what he termed "policy planning organizations," that scholars had long neglected the important role these institutions played in the policy-making process.[19] As he pointed out, a handful of books outlining the institutional histories of such prominent think tanks as the Council on Foreign Relations and the Brookings Institution were available to scholars who happened to browse through outdated think tank catalogues. Written by staff who had observed first-hand the evolution of their think tanks, these studies offered little more than a tribute to the work of the organization and the key figures who were ultimately responsible for transforming it into a prestigious research institution. Other than a small number of books and a smattering of academic articles that made occasional references to think tanks, the literature on this topic remained sparse. Acknowledging this lack of scholarship, Peschek claimed that unless political scientists began to focus more on the "subtle levels of [policy-making where] identifying and defining problems, shaping public understanding of issues, and constructing a political agenda" occurred, the significance of think tanks and their impact would be overlooked.[20] His admonition has not been ignored. Since the publication of his 1987 study, several books and articles have chronicled the history of think tanks in the United States and in other advanced and developing countries. James Smith's highly acclaimed book *The Idea Brokers*, published just four years after Peschek's seminal work, introduced scholars to the complex world of American think tanks and the many factors that influenced their development.

As the number of think tanks in the United States continues to grow, so too has scholarly interest in the inner workings of these organizations and their connections to the policy-making community.[21] Of particular interest to scholars has been the strong ties between think tanks and recent presidential administrations. Of more immediate interest have been the ties between think tanks and the Bush administration. Following the tragic events of September 11, 2001, several scholars and journalists began to speculate on what actions the Bush administration might take to combat global terrorism. To assist them in this regard, many began focusing on a seventy-six-page study entitled

Rebuilding America's Defenses, released by the Project for the New American Century (PNAC), a think tank founded in the spring of 1997 as part of the New Citizen Project. Released in September 2000, just two months before Americans cast their vote for the president, the PNAC study outlined in great detail ways to improve and safeguard America's strategic interests. Of the dozen or more key recommendations made, two in particular caught the eye of those interested in the Bush administration's emerging and controversial foreign policy: "to fight and decisively win multiple, simultaneous major theater wars" and "to develop and deploy global missile defenses to defend the American homeland and America's allies."[22]

What made these and other recommendations interesting to observers of American foreign policy was not so much the hard-line message being conveyed. After all, for decades, several policy experts in think tanks, universities, and government departments had been leading advocates of missile defense. Moreover, since the 1991 Gulf War, many Republicans and Democrats have insisted that the United States needed to take a stronger position against Iraq, North Korea, and other so-called rogue states, and quite possibly at the same time. The Clinton administration certainly did not conceal its antipathy toward Iraq. In the eight years Bill Clinton occupied the White House, US armed forces bombed targets in Iraq thousands of times.[23] What was interesting to foreign policy observers, including the foreign press, was who was conveying these ideas.[24] Among the over two dozen people who helped to draft and later endorse PNAC's statement of principles were Dick Cheney, President Bush's vice-president and former secretary of defense, Donald Rumsfeld, the current secretary of defense, and Paul Wolfowitz, deputy secretary of defense and a contributor to *Rebuilding America's Defenses*.

As the Bush administration's foreign policy goals began to unfold, even scholars and journalists not interested in conspiracy theories wasted little time piecing together how PNAC members serving in senior government positions had been able to convert the organization's recommendations into concrete policy decisions. The storyline that began to emerge hardly required the efforts of Robert Langdon, the Harvard symbologist who searches for the Holy Grail in Dan Brown's best-selling novel, *The Da Vinci Code*, to decipher. Once the close ties between PNAC and the Bush administration became clear, the rest of the story was simple. An inexperienced and untested president being forced to make critical policy decisions in the wake of unprecedented terrorist attacks on American soil does what most leaders in his position would. He relies on the advice of his close circle of seasoned foreign policy advisers, who just happen to have been members of the same think tank. The opportunity to leave a lasting imprint on the Bush administration's foreign policy becomes available, and Cheney, Rumsfeld, Wolfowitz, and others are perfectly positioned to influence the president. What else, several journalists asked, could explain why President Bush launched "simultaneous theater wars" in Afghanistan and Iraq? Moreover, what else could explain why, despite the technological limitations of a proposed national missile defense (NMD) system and the realization that, even if one were in existence prior to 9/11, it could not have prevented the terrorist attacks, has President Bush insisted on investing billions of dollars in this initiative?

On the surface, it makes perfect sense to conclude that PNAC has had a significant impact on the president's thinking. Key recommendations made by the organization either have been or are in the process of being adopted by President Bush, and it does not appear that Rumsfeld and other PNAC alumni have lost a strong foothold in the administration, despite the ongoing turmoil in Iraq. Furthermore, we should not be surprised if Bush continues to listen carefully to those, particularly in his inner circle, who may help him to wage a successful fight against global terror. After all, as the following chapter demonstrates, it is not unusual for presidents who enter the Oval Office with little to no federal government experience to surround themselves with experts from think tanks who can help to inform and educate them about the complex workings of Washington politics. For presidential candidates with a well-defined ideological agenda, it makes even more sense to seek the advice of like-minded policy experts who can help to market their ideas.[25]

However, as scholars studying the policy-making process have discovered, we cannot afford to assume that proximity to leaders guarantees policy influence. The fact that several members from a think tank happened to advise President Bush to wage war in Afghanistan and Iraq and continue development of a national missile defense does not mean that they had a profound impact on his thinking. Several policy experts from PNAC may have helped to reinforce the president's belief that he was doing the right thing by pursuing these initiatives, but the seeds for such actions appear to have been planted in Bush's mind by other individuals and events. For instance, it appears that years before securing the presidency, Bush thought that American interests could best be served by toppling Saddam Hussein, something his father fell short of doing during the Gulf War in 1991.[26] It is also conceivable that his strong belief in the foreign policy successes of the Reagan-Bush years and his father's continued commitment to strategic defense influenced his support for NMD. On a number of occasions during his first presidential campaign, Bush announced his intention to pursue missile defense.[27]

Put simply, while presidents place a great deal of trust in their advisers, they must ultimately pursue a path that is consistent with their values and beliefs. PNAC and other think tanks that have established close ties to the Bush administration have indeed played an important role. The question that remains is what role did they play and what impact have they had, a subject that we will return to later in this chapter and in the case studies to follow.

In his book *The Right Man*, David Frum, a former speech writer for President Bush and a fellow at the American Enterprise Institute, observes that President Bush surprised many Americans by his astute handling of foreign policy after the tragic events of 9/11. According to Frum, Bush entered the White House with considerable conviction and little in the way of practical policy experience, but he soon emerged as a leader capable of unifying a country during a period of immense fear and anxiety. The untested president had indeed passed what for many was the most important test – character. Ironically, it is Bush's character that has been subjected to intense scrutiny since the war in Afghanistan. With limited success in the oil industry, a failed run at the US Congress, and a short stint as managing general partner of the then fledgling Texas Rangers, Bush did not seem destined for a career in politics. Yet what he lacked in qualifications, he more than compensated for in perseverance. Against considerable odds, Bush defeated the Democratic incumbent, Anne Richards, in 1994 to become the forty-sixth governor of Texas. It was Richards who, anticipating an easy victory over the inexperienced son of the forty-first president, nicknamed him "Shrub." Over the next four years, the shrub grew in popularity and became the first governor in Texas history to be elected to consecutive four-year terms, securing re-election in November 1998 with close to 70 per cent of the vote.

As governor, Bush addressed several important issues, including education, crime prevention, and drug enforcement, and, according to some journalists, was adept at delegating much of his authority to subordinates. He learned to place trust in key advisers such as Karl Rove and Karen Hughes, individuals who understood his approach to politics and the agenda he wanted to pursue. Both Rove and Hughes would go on to assume key positions in the Bush administration. As Bush quickly discovered, being a successful leader did not mean he had to possess an encyclopedic knowledge of the issues that made their way onto his desk or become a "policy wonk," a term often used to describe those obsessed with the intricacies of policy issues.[28] A successful leader, according to Bush, who obtained a master's degree in business administration from Harvard University in 1975, was someone who understood the importance of being surrounded by intelligent advisers who could present a range of possible options for dealing with specific problems. Once the options were presented, it was up to the leader to make an informed decision.

Like many of his predecessors, including Jimmy Carter, Ronald Reagan, and Bill Clinton, who also made the transition from governor to president, Bush recognized that to advance his philosophy of "compassionate conservatism," he had to recruit policy experts who could shape, reinforce, and sell his vision of America. As we will discover in the following section, his decision to surround himself with some of the nation's best thinkers served him well on the road to the White House. Recruiting policy experts from some of the United States' most prominent think tanks had also played a key role in helping Carter, Reagan, and Clinton to strike a responsive chord with the American public. The extent to which these four presidents established ties to various think tanks is discussed below.

A MORE PERFECT UNION: PRESIDENTIAL CANDIDATES AND THE THINK TANKS THAT ADVISED THEM

In April 1998, Republican presidential candidate George W. Bush interrupted a fundraising trip for a gubernatorial candidate in Northern California to meet with several scholars from the Hoover Institution. The purpose of the meeting, which took place at the home of former secretary of state and Hoover fellow George Shultz, was to allow the governor of Texas to get acquainted with some of the nation's leading policy experts. Although Bush had little knowledge of the Hoover Institution or the work of its scholars before accepting Shultz's invitation, his friendship with Hoover fellow and economist Michael Boskin may explain why he gravitated toward the California think tank.[29] As a result of the almost four-hour meeting, Bush "engaged 12 or so Hoover fellows to advise his presidential campaign on issues from taxation to welfare to foreign affairs."[30] In addition to relying heavily on scholars from the Hoover Institution to help educate him on the intricacies of domestic and foreign policy issues, he enlisted the support of several other policy experts, including his top economic adviser, Lawrence Lindsey, former Federal Reserve governor and fellow at the American Enterprise Institute, and Robert Zoellick, who stepped down as president of the Center for Strategic and International Studies after only four months to advise Bush.[31]

Bush's decision to turn to some of the nation's most prominent think tanks for policy advice is not surprising. Indeed, it has become common for presidential candidates, particularly those who lack experience in federal politics, to establish close ties to such institutions. Eager to find candidates who can help to translate their ideas into concrete policy decisions, think tanks have frequently provided much of the intellectual ammunition that presidential contenders require to sell their message to the electorate. As Martin Anderson of the Hoover Institution points out, "it is during this period that presidential candidates solicit the advice of a vast number of intellectuals in order to establish policy positions on a host of domestic and foreign policy issues. Presidential candidates exchange ideas with policy experts and test them out on the campaign trail. It's like a national test marketing strategy."[32] In the following chapter, snapshots of the relationship between four presidential candidates and the think tanks that advised them will be provided. These are intended to reveal a pattern that has emerged in recent years where presidential candidates and think tanks have shared ideas which in some instances have served as the foundation for key policies introduced in presidential administrations. This discussion precedes the chapter on the historical evolution of US think tanks because it is intended to show that, with their newly acquired status, think tanks can now take advantage of the predictable electoral cycle in the United States to influence the discourse of the nation. Once it has been established that think tanks occupy a front-row seat in the political arena, we will then proceed to explain their rise to prominence and the various factors that have contributed to their proliferation.

In chapter 2 a historical overview of think tanks in the United States will be provided. By documenting their evolution, we can identify four distinct waves or generations of think tanks. Chronicling the development of think tanks in the United States will not only shed light on the diverse nature of the community but will help scholars to identify how these organizations have modified their behaviour to address the needs of policy-makers and the public. As noted, over two thousand think tanks exist in the United States, the majority being located at various universities. This study, however, will concentrate primarily on think tanks that function independently of universities and government – in other words, think tanks that operate in many respects like private corporations. Although several directories of think tanks have been produced, there is no consensus on how many "private" think tanks exist in the United States. Some scholars, including Kent Weaver, have estimated that approximately five hundred institutions fall into this category. Others have suggested that the number may be larger.

What is important, though, is not the exact number of think tanks on America's political landscape but how these organizations have become firmly entrenched in the policy-making process. By tracing the origins of think tanks in the United States since the turn of the twentieth century, we can develop a clearer picture of how and why these organizations have assumed an important voice in the policy-making community.

That think tanks have increased in great numbers in the United States over the past several decades is hardly a point of contention. Indeed, it is a phenomenon widely acknowledged among scholars in the field. What they disagree about is which theoretical approach or approaches can best explain their rise to prominence. In chapter 3 we will explore the various methods that have been employed to study the behaviour of think tanks in order to demonstrate what can or cannot be learned by adhering to a particular theory or paradigm. What we will discover is that no one theory can adequately account for how think tanks function in the policy-making world. Several theories, ranging from pluralism to statism, offer scholars a window through which to observe different aspects of think tank behaviour. As a result, it is necessary to draw on more than one approach to explain the many factors that may facilitate or frustrate the efforts of think tanks to become part of the policy-making process. This multi-faceted approach will be particularly important in explaining the findings of the case studies.

Once the competing theoretical approaches have been outlined, we can proceed to examine why think tanks in the United States are in many ways unique. To do so, chapter 4 will concentrate on the policy-making environment that has enabled them to establish such a strong foothold. In this chapter, considerable attention will be placed on the nature of the American political system and critical features of it that have permitted think tanks to expand their reach into different branches and levels of government. Comparisons to think tanks in countries such as Canada, Great Britain, and Germany will help to explain why American think tanks can and do take advantage of opportunities to influence policy-making in ways that are not available to their counterparts in other Western democracies. Despite the increased visibility of think tanks on the American political landscape, few scholars have made accommodation for them in their studies on decision-making. Chapter 5 will seek to explain why this is the case and how contemporary models and theories of decision-making can be modified to take adequate account of their presence.

In acknowledging that the highly decentralized and increasingly fragmented nature of the American political system provides fertile soil for think tanks to develop and grow, we must understand how these organizations have sought to exercise influence. In chapter 6 the various public and private channels of influence that think tanks rely on to convey their ideas to their intended target audiences will be explored. The strategies or channels they draw on range from submitting op-ed articles to major American newspapers to providing members of Congress with summaries of key policy issues currently being debated on the floor of the House and the Senate. How and why think tanks elect to employ certain tactics will be discussed in detail.

Identifying the many ways in which think tanks try to shape public opinion and public policy is relatively straightforward. What remains difficult, as noted, is how to assess their effectiveness or impact in achieving their goals. Chapter 7 will examine both quantitative and qualitative approaches to measuring policy influence. According to several think tank directors, the most obvious measurement of policy influence (and the easiest to track) is media exposure. Not surprisingly, think tanks with considerable resources spend a great deal of time and energy encouraging their staff to share their ideas with the print and electronic media. In short, for some think tanks, public visibility is equated with policy influence. As this chapter will discuss, data on media exposure, testimony before congressional committees and subcommittees, sales of publications, and Web site hits can help scholars to isolate those think tanks that appear most active in certain policy debates. However, such indicators only reveal part of a very complex story about the policy-making environment and the many factors that influence decisions made by policy-makers. Therefore it is imperative not to ignore the more subtle ways in which think tanks seek to influence policy. In this chapter we will also discuss why it is critical to provide a more nuanced understanding of influence and how it can be achieved.

The purpose of chapter 7 is to help set the stage for the two case studies that follow. Once readers have a better understanding of the methodological difficulties often encountered in assessing policy influence, it is useful – indeed, it is necessary – to examine how a select group of think tanks have sought to shape, mould, and reinforce the attitudes and beliefs of policy-makers and the public about important policy-issues. In chapters 8 and 9, two examples of think tanks at work will be highlighted. The first will concentrate on the efforts of think tanks to influence the debate over missile defense. This issue generated considerable controversy during the first term of the Reagan administration, and it continues to spark spirited exchanges between a group of think tanks that believe American security interests can best be served by constructing and deploying a system that would help to protect the United States from a nuclear attack and those that insist that such an initiative will, among other things, lead to another arms race. In the second case study, our attention will shift to an even more critical debate – the efforts of the Bush administration to take action against terrorists and the states that fund and harbour them.

On the basis of these two cases, a number of important observations about think tanks and their role in the policy-making process will be made. What will become apparent is that there is no single factor which can explain why think tanks succeed or fail in influencing public opinion and public policy. In some instances, such as missile defense, a small but vocal group of think tanks, including High Frontier, the Heritage Foundation, and the Center for Security Policy, have played a seminal role in convincing policy-makers to take necessary steps to fund research and development on this initiative. But as we will discover, scholars at think tanks are not the only individuals who have supported missile defense. Defense contractors, members of Congress, academics, and several journalists, to name a few, have contributed to this ongoing debate. Moreover, it will become evident that think tanks such as High Frontier were able to have such a significant impact on the debate over missile defense because they found in President Reagan a leader profoundly concerned about how little the United States could do to protect its citizens in the event of a nuclear attack. By contrast, when we investigate the debate over the war on terror, the opposite appears to be the case: President Bush's unwillingness to listen to ideas being circulated by individuals outside his inner circle has in some ways undermined the ability of think tanks to influence the direction of US foreign policy. Nonetheless, this failure has not discouraged think tanks from setting their sights on other target audiences to spread their ideas.

In my recent book *Do Think Tanks Matter?* I concluded that to learn more about the behaviour and impact of think tanks in the policy-making process, it was essential to focus on specific policy areas. How else, I remarked, can we begin to make inroads into a body of literature that has not adequately addressed the question of how to evaluate think-tank performance? In *A Capitol Idea* I begin the process of delving more deeply into this profoundly difficult question. By doing so, I hope to encourage scholars to think more critically about how to provide more insight into these interesting organizations that inhabit a complicated and complex policy environment. It is a journey worth taking.

CHAPTER ONE

Lights, Camera, Action: Policy Experts and Presidential Campaigns

To launch a successful presidential bid, candidates require not only a sufficient cash flow but also a steady stream of policy ideas that they can share with the American public. The former is often in short supply, particularly during the presidential primaries, when candidates must raise their own funds,[1] but candidates are rarely confronted by a shortage of policy ideas. Surrounded by political strategists, pollsters, media consultants, party loyalists, and lobbyists for various causes, they are inundated with advice. Despite being bombarded by information and advice from multiple sources, several presidential candidates have turned to think tanks to help develop, reinforce, and market their election platform. Why do candidates try to forge close ties to think tanks? And why are so many think tanks willing to offer their services?

To begin with, candidates, especially those with little or no experience at the federal level,[2] can tap into the wealth of knowledge available at some of America's most distinguished think tanks. Jimmy Carter, Ronald Reagan, and other presidential candidates who spent little time in Washington before assuming the presidency recognized the enormous benefits of relying on think tanks, which were home to many former high-profile policy-makers and leading policy experts. By drawing on experts at these organizations, candidates can not only obtain insights about the inner workings of Washington politics but also significantly enhance their understanding of policy issues. Moreover, by attending meetings at think tanks such as the Council on Foreign Relations, which includes several former policy-makers and prominent business leaders among its ranks, candidates can develop additional contacts in the private and public sectors that may prove invaluable as they travel the country soliciting support. However, even more important than the network of contacts that think tanks can offer is the credibility they can give to a candidate's ideas. Endorsement by leading economists such as Milton Friedman of the Hoover Institution or, better yet, having academics of such a high calibre providing advice can significantly enhance a candidate's platform. Candidates can also benefit from their visible association with think tanks that are in a position to reinforce the ideological underpinnings of their policy ideas.

The support and assistance of think tank staff costs candidates very little. Unless policy experts from think tanks take a leave of absence from their institutes to work on a campaign, which they are encouraged to do, they generally offer their services free.[3] In sum, for candidates, there are few costs and potentially enormous benefits in establishing an association with think tanks that can help them to strike a responsive chord with the electorate; for some think tanks, it can be extremely advantageous to align themselves with a winning presidential candidate. Not only does an election victory bring prestige and, at times, job offers, but a higher profile can translate into more funds from affluent donors. Although some candidates have relied more heavily on think tanks than others, a clear pattern is emerging. When candidates need policy advice from seasoned experts, they are certainly willing to meet and discuss issues with members of think tanks. And to the delight of many think tanks, candidates appear willing to rely on them as they embark on the long and often difficult road to the White House.

JIMMY CARTER AND THE SEARCH FOR POLICY ADVICE

When President Gerald Ford granted Richard Nixon "a full, free and absolute pardon" for "any and all crimes" committed during the Watergate scandal, it seemed even more probable to some that a Democrat would become the next president. Tainted by widespread corruption and unable to bring about an expeditious conclusion to the Vietnam War, the Republican Party failed to convince the American electorate that it could provide effective and responsible leadership. During the 1976 campaign, several prominent Democrats entered the presidential race, including Henry "Scoop" Jackson and George Wallace. But once Americans cast their votes, it was Jimmy Carter, a relatively unknown one-term governor of Georgia, who was sworn into office in January 1977.

Carter's rapid rise to power continues to baffle some political analysts, but his ties to prestigious policy research institutions in New York and

Washington, DC, may in part explain his ability to gain national exposure. By analyzing his dependence on a select group of think tanks for policy advice, we can identify those organizations that played a major role during and after his bid for the presidency. A closer examination of his association with a handful of prominent northeastern think tanks also reveals how research institutions seek to expand their networks of influence throughout the policy-making community.

Shortly after Jimmy Carter became governor of Georgia in 1970, he began to set his sights on the nation's highest office. It soon became apparent to Carter and his political and financial supporters that if he was to launch a successful presidential campaign, he would have to attract the attention of several well-known Democrats. Carter enjoyed the backing of many prominent leaders in Atlanta's business and policy-making circles, yet it was the support of leading academics, financiers, and journalists in the Northeast that he dearly coveted. According to Laurence Shoup, by gaining access to the "Eastern Establishment," Carter hoped to become part of the "national power structure" in the United States.[4]

As early as 1971, Carter became preoccupied with gaining national exposure. And through some of his close personal advisers, such as former secretary of state Dean Rusk, he met a number of individuals who were in a position to broaden his base of political support. Among the most influential contacts were David Rockefeller, chairman of the Chase Manhattan Bank, and Hedley Donovan, editor-in-chief of *Time* magazine. Following a *Time* cover story on Carter and the "New South" in May 1971,[5] Carter met with Donovan, who in turn introduced him to George S. "Benji" Franklin, a Rockefeller in-law and executive director of the Council on Foreign Relations. It was through one or more of these connections that Carter became known to David Rockefeller, who invited the governor to lunch with him at the Chase Manhattan Bank in November 1971.

Carter's southern disposition and Kennedy-style approach to state politics must have impressed Rockefeller, for when the latter decided to establish the Trilateral Commission in 1973, Carter was invited to become a member.[6] Zbigniew Brzezinski, who helped Rockefeller select individuals for the commission, maintained that Carter was asked to join because he seemed to share the organization's commitment to improving international economic relations: "we were very impressed that Carter had opened up trade offices for the state of Georgia in Brussels and Tokyo. That seemed to fit perfectly into the concept of the Trilateral."[7]

Carter's international economic initiatives appeared to coincide with the Trilateral Commission's mandate, but according to Barry Goldwater, the possibility of having one of its members occupy the Oval Office also appears to have influenced Rockefeller's and Brzezinski's decision. As Goldwater points out, Carter's invitation to join the commission was motivated by political as well as institutional interests: "David Rockefeller and Zbigniew Brzezinski found Jimmy Carter to be their ideal candidate. They helped him win the nomination and the presidency. To accomplish this purpose, they mobilized the money power of the Wall Street bankers, the intellectual influence of the academic community – which is subservient to the wealth of the great tax-free foundations – and the media controllers represented in the membership of the CFR [Council on Foreign Relations] and the Trilateral."[8]

David Rockefeller provides a very different account of why Carter was selected to be a member of the Trilateral Commission. In his memoirs, he notes,

We cast our nets widely in terms of membership and recruited labor union leaders, corporate CEO's, prominent Democrats and Republicans, as well as distinguished academics, university presidents, and the heads of not-for-profits involved overseas. We assembled what we believed were the best minds in America. The Europeans and Japanese assembled delegations of comparable distinction. The inclusion among the first group of an obscure Democratic governor – James Earl Carter – had an unintended consequence. A week after Trilateral's first executive committee meeting in Washington in December 1975, Governor Carter announced that he would seek the Democratic nomination for President of the United States. I have to confess that at the time I thought he had little chance of success.[9]

Goldwater and other Republicans recognized that a Carter victory would pay handsome dividends to the Trilateral Commission, which, through its published findings, was "hoping to influence the behaviour of our respective governments,"[10] but Carter also derived many benefits from participating in this organization. According to Shoup, "By becoming a member of the Trilateral Commission, Carter met and became friends with powerful upper class individuals who had contacts and influence where it mattered – in business, the mass communications media, in governments at home and abroad, in universities, in the associations and foundations. Jimmy Carter ... whom few people outside Georgia had even heard of in 1973, had become part of a group which could help him become President of the US."[11]

Few political commentators identified the close connection between Carter and the Trilateral Commission during the early 1970s, but by 1976 it became increasingly apparent that the Democratic presidential candidate was relying heavily on his Trilateral colleagues for policy advice. For instance, in June 1976 the *Los Angeles Times* described a "task force" that had helped the candidate prepare his first foreign policy speech, which began, "The time has come for us to seek a partnership between North America, Western Europe and Japan."[12] With several of his Trilateral advisers leading the applause, Carter emphasized the importance of encouraging closer cooperation between advanced industrial nations. In the ensuing months the Democratic candidate continued to espouse other foreign policy recommendations proposed by the Trilateral Commission. In fact, Carter's growing dependence on an elite group of Trilateral advisers, including Zbigniew Brzezinski and Cyrus Vance, convinced some campaign observers that "Carter's entire foreign policy, much of his election strategy, and at least some of his domestic policy [came] directly from the Commission and its leading members."[13]

It is difficult to determine the extent to which various Trilateral advisers influenced Carter's views on foreign and domestic policy, but there is little doubt that membership on the commission left a lasting impression on him. As Carter later noted, "In order to ensure the continuing opportunity for penetrating analyses of complicated, important, and timely foreign policy questions, there is an organization known as the Trilateral Commission. A group of leaders from the three democratic developed areas of the world meet every six months to discuss ideas of current interest to Japan, North America and Europe ... Membership on this commission has provided me with a splendid learning opportunity, and many of the other members helped me in my study of foreign affairs."[14]

Zbigniew Brzezinski, the Trilateral Commission's first director and later national security adviser to President Carter, agrees that the commission offered Carter an invaluable learning experience, but he denies that it advised him on domestic and foreign affairs.[15] Brzezinski has stated:

The commission did not play any role in advising [Carter] whatsoever. But I think the commission was of importance to him in two ways. One, it provided the framework for his generally first extensive exposure to international affairs. Prior to his membership on the commission, he had no exposure to international affairs. It was through the commission that he really became exposed to foreign affairs. Secondly, on the commission he met a number of people interested in foreign affairs, some of whom he recruited to work for him when he was making the appointments for his administration. I believe that someone once counted, I don't remember the exact number, but I sort of vaguely remember that up to eighteen senior appointees in his administration were from members of the commission.[16]

Brzezinski could not recall the exact number of Trilateral commissioners who were appointed by President Carter, but he stated that "all the key foreign policy decision makers of the Carter administration had served in the Trilateral Commission."[17] Rockefeller, on the other hand, was more emphatic: Carter "chose fifteen members of Trilateral, many of whom had served in previous administrations,"[18] further evidence of the revolving-door phenomenon referred to earlier. In addition to Brzezinski, several Trilateral members received appointments in the Carter White House, including Vice-President Walter Mondale, Secretary of State Cyrus Vance, Secretary of Defense Harold Brown, and Secretary of the Treasury Michael Blumenthal.

Carter clearly depended heavily on several Trilateral commissioners to fill key posts in his administration, but his search for policy advice did not end there. The president-elect also received advice from scholars at other think tanks, including, though by no means limited to, the Council on Foreign Relations. At his invitation, at least fifty-four members of the CFR joined his new administration. Among them were P.R. Harris, secretary of Housing and Urban Development (HUD) and Health, Education and Welfare (HEW); Philip Habib, undersecretary of State; Stansfield Turner, director of the CIA; D. Aaron, deputy to the national security adviser; and Donald McHenry, ambassador to the United Nations. Having assembled an impressive team of policy advisers from the Trilateral Commission and the Council on Foreign Relations, Carter finally turned to the Brookings Institution to complete his "brain trust," a term used, as previously noted, to describe the small group of experts who had advised President Franklin Roosevelt.

In recognition of the invaluable contribution that several Brookings scholars had made to the formulation of various governmental policies during previous Democratic administrations, Carter first approached the institution for advice in July 1975. During his brief visit, he attended two informal luncheons on foreign policy and economics and began to establish ties to many of Brookings's most distinguished residents. After his election victory, Carter invited several Brookings scholars to join his staff. In addition to Stephen Hess, who advised him on how to restructure his White House staff, the president appointed over a dozen other members of the Brookings Institution to administrative posts, including Charles L. Schultze, chairman of the Council of Economic Advisors; C. Fred Bergsten, assistant secretary of the Treasury for International Economic Affairs; Henry Aaron, assistant secretary of Health, Education and Welfare for planning and evaluation; Karen Davis, deputy assistant secretary of Health, Education and Welfare; Emil Sunley Jr, deputy assistant secretary of the Treasury; Barry

Blechman, assistant director of the Arms Control and Disarmament Agency (ACDA); Barry Bosworth, director of the Council on Wage and Price Stability; Henry D. Owen, special White House representative for economic summits; L.N. Cutler, White House counsel; L.W. Benson, undersecretary of State; Gerard C. Smith, ambassador at large; and Nancy H. Teeters, Federal Reserve Board.

With the support and advice of over one hundred policy analysts from three of America's most prestigious think tanks, Carter rose from relative obscurity to occupy the Oval Office. Although several factors contributed to his election victory, the vital role that think tanks played during his campaign cannot be overlooked. His dependence on think tank specialists did not end when he entered the White House. On the contrary, as the newly installed president sought to chart a new course for the United States in the latter half of the decade, he began to rely even more on his advisers for direction and guidance. While Carter solicited the advice of his top economic advisers to enhance America's position in the international economy, his preoccupation with resolving tensions in Latin America and the Middle East provided foreign policy analysts, both in and out of government, with remarkable opportunities to capture the president's attention. In fact, on several occasions, Carter's policies toward these particular regions appeared to be shaped and moulded by prominent members of Washington's think tank community.[19]

RONALD REAGAN AND THE THINK TANKS
THAT ADVISED HIM

While Carter depended on several prestigious think tanks in the Northeast to gain national exposure, his successor turned to other policy research institutions, including the Hoover Institution in his home state of California, to transform his set of conservative beliefs into a winning election platform. Reagan occasionally solicited the advice of policy analysts from prominent think tanks and universities during his tenure as governor of California,[20] but it was not until he launched his bid for the presidency in 1980 that he began to surround himself with some of the nation's most respected conservative policy intellectuals.

Ronald Reagan finished second to Gerald Ford at the 1976 Republican National Convention in Kansas City, Missouri, but he wasted little time preparing for the 1980 presidential campaign. As one of his campaign advisers observed during the candidate's return flight to California, Reagan stared out of the plane's window for a few seconds and then proceeded to write the following note on the back of a ticket to the National Convention, "We dreamed – we fought & the dream is still with us."[21] In those few words, he expressed his commitment to return to the campaign trail in the hope of securing the presidential nomination. And on 17 July 1980, in Detroit, Michigan, four years after his narrow defeat, Reagan won the Republican nomination by an overwhelming majority. One hundred and eleven days later he won the general election, and on 20 January 1981 Ronald Wilson Reagan became the fortieth president of the United States.

His sweeping victory over an increasingly despondent and frustrated incumbent is often attributed to the failure of the Carter administration to safeguard US economic and political interests in the international community. Carter's inability to prevent the overthrow of the shah of Iran, the installation of the Sandinista government in Nicaragua, the seizure of the US embassy in Tehran, and the Soviet invasion of Afghanistan did little to instill confidence in the electorate. Nonetheless, his foreign policy failures alone did not ensure a Republican victory. The ability of Reagan's advisers to translate a set of conservative beliefs into an appealing political agenda contributed to the outcome of the 1980 campaign.

Before Reagan's plane had even landed in southern California following his acceptance speech in Detroit, some of his campaign advisers had begun to map out a new strategy to promote their candidate's views on domestic and foreign policy. And just as Reagan had undergone a political conversion by leaving the Democratic Party to join the Republican cause after Kennedy's narrow election victory over Nixon in 1960,[22] his campaign team had to determine how to expedite the American electorate's conversion to conservatism.

For Martin Anderson, a senior fellow at the Hoover Institution and a key member of Reagan's inner circle of policy advisers, the most effective way to communicate his candidate's political agenda to the American public was to attract the support of some of the nation's leading intellectuals. Convinced that "ideas move nations"[23] and that policy ideas arise primarily in universities and think tanks,[24] Anderson set out to assemble an impressive team of academics who could promote Reagan's vision of America. As Anderson points out in his memoirs of the Reagan years, "As early as 1975, after I agreed to join his presidential campaign, I started a systematic effort to introduce the nation's best economists to Reagan. Most of them were selected from my personal file of leading policy experts I began collecting during Nixon's campaign in 1967. This was part of a more general effort to recruit an army of intellectuals to advise and counsel Reagan on the entire range of policy issues."[25]

After inviting such prominent economists as Milton Friedman, William Niskanen, and Murray Weidenbaum to join Reagan's campaign team, Anderson began to set his sights on creating several policy task forces to advise the candidate on domestic and foreign policy.[26] He had first recognized the importance of establishing policy task forces to advise presidential candidates when he was in charge of policy research for Nixon in 1968. He notes, "I learned that policy advisers from the intellectual world could be a tremendous asset to a campaign ... the very existence of a large group of distinguished intellectuals gave a powerful boost to the credibility of the candidate. In effect, those intellectuals were co-signing the ideas of the candidate."[27]

Anderson was in charge of organizing the domestic and economic policy task forces,[28] and Richard Allen, who had ties to Hoover, was entrusted with overseeing the foreign and defense policy groups. Reflecting on how his policy groups channelled information to Reagan, Allen later stated, "I had a total of 120 people; 80 foreign policy advisers and 40 defense and national security advisers. These people were typically specialists in the field, either academic specialists or retired or departed specialists from government, including people from the Pentagon and the Department of State, former diplomats and the like. [They] produced information, opinions, parts of speeches that would be included in the speeches of the candidate ... That's the way that part of the system worked. [The policy groups] were extremely useful in providing background information and general data."[29] Jeane Kirkpatrick, the American ambassador to the United Nations during the Reagan years, agrees with Anderson that the task forces were useful in bringing together policy experts to discuss a range of issues. According to Kirkpatrick, who served on one of the foreign policy task forces, the groups did not generate a great deal of paper work for Reagan, but "we did meet a few times over lunch to talk about different issues," which certainly was helpful.[30]

A press release issued by Reagan on 23 October 1980 documented the scope and function of the policy task forces: "Governor Reagan today announced the completion of 23 domestic and economic policy task forces with 329 advisers who have been asked to address the important issues that will have to be faced by a new administration ... These task forces join 25 foreign policy and defence working groups with 132 advisers that are examining, in detail, the major questions that relate to these two important areas."[31]

The active involvement of policy task forces during the Reagan campaign was commented on by Transition Team director Edwin Meese III: "Reagan's 1980 campaign had been served by policy task forces that comprised 'the largest and most distinguished group of intellectuals ever assembled for an American political campaign.' Nearly fifty groups, with over 450 advisors, studied numerous areas of foreign, defence, domestic, and economic policy and provided hundreds of recommendations."[32] By producing detailed studies on topics ranging from welfare reform to missile defense and by outlining several policy recommendations, the policy task forces had in effect established a blueprint for the incoming administration. As Martin Anderson points out, "When Reagan took power in 1981, the battle plan for what to do with that power was largely written."[33]

Two weeks before President-Elect Reagan took the oath of office, at a dinner in honour of the Hoover Institution's Board of Overseers, Meese elaborated on the important contribution the policy development teams had made in assembling information for the new administration: "We have already had a series of meetings ... with [the] Heritage [Foundation] and others to make recommendations to the new President-elect as to the course his administration should follow. By the time January 20th comes around, there will already be an agenda of initial action projects which will carry the administration through its first year of operation and which will set major and intermediate goals so that there will always be an eye on the blueprint of what the administration seeks to accomplish."[34]

The president-elect wasted little time rewarding advisers who had made important contributions to his campaign. Among those participating on Reagan's policy task forces who received high-level government appointments were Alan Greenspan, chairman of the Board of Governors of the Federal Reserve; Antonin Scalia, appointed to the Supreme Court; George Shultz, secretary of state; Caspar Weinberger, secretary of defense; William Howard Taft IV, deputy secretary of defense; Richard Allen, national security adviser; James Miller, chairman of the Federal Trade Commission and later director of the Office of Management and Budget (OMB); Edwin Harper, deputy director of the OMB; Murray Weidenbaum and Beryl Sprinkel, chairs of the Council of Economic Advisers (CEA); William Niskanen and Thomas Moore, CEA; Norman Ture and Paul Craig Roberts, undersecretary and assistant secretary for economic policy in the Department of the Treasury; Arthur F. Burns, ambassador to Germany; Darrell Trent, deputy secretary of transportation; Rudolph Penner, head of the Congressional Budget Office; and Martin Anderson, chief domestic and economic policy adviser.[35]

Of these, over half were members of think tanks before they joined the Reagan administration. Their institutional affiliations were as follows:

Richard Allen, the Center for Strategic and International Studies, the Heritage Foundation, and the Hoover Institution; Martin Anderson, Thomas Moore, and Darrell Trent, the Hoover Institution; Norman Ture, the Heritage Foundation; Caspar Weinberger, the Institute for Contemporary Studies;[36] Murray Weidenbaum, James Miller, and Arthur Burns, the American Enterprise Institute; and William Niskanen, RAND and the Institute for Defense Analyses.[37]

The number of individuals belonging to think tanks who decided to join the Reagan crusade is far more extensive. Between 1981 and 1988, close to two hundred members of America's leading conservative think tanks participated in the Reagan administration in a full-time consulting or advisory capacity.[38] Five think tanks in particular were well represented during the Reagan years: fifty-five scholars came from the Hoover Institution, thirty-six from the Heritage Foundation, thirty-four from the American Enterprise Institute, thirty-two from the Committee on the Present Danger,[39] and eighteen from the Center for Strategic and International Studies.[40]

When the complete records of the 1980 campaign at the Reagan Presidential Library become available, it will be possible to provide a more detailed examination of the relationship between think tanks and the Reagan administration; but a preliminary search of available materials indicates that some think tanks played a crucial role in the transition period following the 1980 election. Although several were actively involved in the campaign, few assumed more importance during the transition than the Heritage Foundation.

In the fall of 1979, in anticipation of a Republican presidential victory, Heritage president Edwin Feulner began to consider how his organization could assist in the transition to a conservative administration. After consulting several of his colleagues in the policy research community, he decided to launch an extensive research project to produce a study that could in effect serve as a manual for conservatives to follow in implementing domestic and foreign policy initiatives. According to Feulner, "our strong feeling was that people who came into the administration should have some source of information and guidance other than what you get from the incumbents that you replace."[41]

With the assistance of over three hundred academics, consultants, lawyers, and former government officials divided into twenty project teams, the Heritage Foundation produced an eleven-hundred-page "blueprint for the construction of a conservative government."[42] In its *Mandate for Leadership: Policy Management in a Conservative Administration*,[43] Heritage outlined two thousand proposals on issues ranging from how to streamline the government bureaucracy to ways to improve US national security. Delighted with the results of the foundation's year-long study, not to mention the outcome of the 1980 campaign, Feulner presented a copy of the document, still in manuscript form, to Edwin Meese III at the Hay-Adams Hotel in mid-November 1980.[44] After scanning the extensive report, Meese said the *Mandate for Leadership* study was very impressive and the Reagan team would "rely heavily on it."[45] It is "one of the most meaningful and best things that President Reagan and those associated with him will have to guide them in the next few years."[46] According to Meese, "President Reagan gave a copy of the book to each member of his cabinet and directed them to read it."[47]

In his memoirs of the Reagan years, Meese, currently the Ronald Reagan Fellow in Public Policy at the Heritage Foundation, stated that the *Mandate for Leadership* study was largely responsible for the growing influence of the Heritage Foundation: "This major accomplishment put Heritage 'on the map' as far as Washington decision makers were concerned. Indeed, many leaders in the federal government were appointed from among the Heritage staff and the contributors to *Mandate for Leadership*. [As well,] Edwin Feulner provided expert advice to the new administration in varying capacities."[48] Meese's overwhelming endorsement of the Heritage study may in part explain why it appeared on the *Washington Post's* best-seller list for three weeks in early 1981. It may also explain why observers of Washington politics began referring to the study as the bible of the Reagan administration; even a year after *Mandate for Leadership* was released, journalists and policy analysts were speculating on the extent to which President Reagan's domestic and foreign policies were influenced by the publication.

However, few individuals paid more attention to how closely government officials followed the policy recommendations outlined in the Heritage study than Edwin Feulner, who estimated in early 1982 that more than 60 per cent of Heritage's proposals had been adopted by the Reagan administration.[49] In flaunting this statistic, Feulner neglected to explain that a number of the policy recommendations included in his organization's study did not originate there but had been developed and refined by other policy research institutions over several years. According to Glenn Campbell, former director of the Hoover Institution, many of Heritage's recommendations were extracted from an earlier Hoover publication, *The United States in the 1980s*.[50] Even former Soviet president Mikhail Gorbachev was convinced that several of the Reagan administration's policies were borrowed from the Hoover Institution's three-and-a-half-pound study. Waving a copy of the publication in front of Secretary of State George Shultz and Robert McFarlane, Reagan's third national security adviser,[51] Gorbachev shouted, "We have read this book and watched all its programs become adopted by the Reagan administration."[52]

Notwithstanding the disagreement over where the majority of policy recommendations outlined in the Heritage study originated, it is difficult to ignore the integral role this organization played during Reagan's transition to power. As journalist Bernard Weinraub points out, "Working from an out-of-the way, white brick building in north-east Washington that once housed a Korean grocery and a halfway house for drug addicts, a group of little-known academics and congressional aides ... emerged as a major force in Ronald Reagan's transition to the presidency."[53]

The *Mandate for Leadership* study had propelled the Heritage Foundation into the national spotlight, and from its new headquarters located just two blocks from the Capitol Building, the "feisty new kid on the conservative block," as President Reagan called it,[54] continued to shape America's political agenda. By 1984 Heritage's clout in Washington's policymaking community had grown to the point that *New Republic* columnist James Rosenthal, writing about the impact of *Mandate for Leadership II*, commented, "Heritage helps shape what people in Washington talk about after they read the morning paper. It helps set the agenda."[55]

Riding the new wave of conservatism that was quickly sweeping across the United States, the Heritage Foundation soon became immersed in Washington's decisionmaking establishment. While several liberal policy research institutions were simply concerned with remaining afloat during the Reagan years, the Heritage Foundation, with the financial support of a growing number of individuals and corporations, including Joseph Coors, Richard Scaife, and Edward Noble, began to transform itself into one of Washington's leading think tanks. Yet despite its increasing visibility and overt desire to shape the political agenda, it did not monopolize the attention of decision-makers. By making their way through Washington's policy-making labyrinth, members of the Center for Strategic and International Studies, the Committee on the Present Danger, the Hoover Institution, and the American Enterprise Institute were also able to advise key government officials on a host of domestic and foreign policy issues in various capacities.

Like his predecessor, Reagan surrounded himself with some of the nation's most distinguished scholars. By so doing, he not only broadened his base of intellectual support throughout the academic community but, more importantly, attracted those individuals who could translate his conservative beliefs into a set of viable policy options. In the process of advancing Reagan's political mandate, several think tanks that previously observed the mechanics of government from the sidelines became firmly integrated into the decision-making network; as active participants in the political arena, many took advantage of new opportunities to shape governmental policies. The extent to which various think tanks were ultimately responsible for influencing American foreign policy during Reagan's terms in office is difficult, if not impossible, to measure. But there is no doubt, as the case study on missile defense reveals, that some think tanks, including the Heritage Foundation, played a seminal role in shaping the Reagan administration's attitudes about the importance of protecting the territorial integrity of the United States against ballistic missiles.

Interestingly enough, despite the growing presence of think tanks during the Reagan years, their role, particularly in the executive branch, began to diminish when George Bush assumed the presidency in 1989. Unlike Reagan, Bush did not invite dozens of academics from think tanks to participate in his 1988 or 1992 presidential campaigns; nor did he rely heavily on them to fill high-level positions in his administration. On the contrary, he made a concerted effort to insulate himself from think tanks that had established and maintained close ties to his predecessor. As Annelise Anderson, a senior fellow at the Hoover Institution and former adviser to Bush, points out, "President Bush wanted to climb out of Reagan's shadow and [therefore] distanced himself from most Republican experts attached to Reagan. He also treated neo-conservatives much like President Carter did. They both discounted their importance as intellectuals ... In doing so, they excluded a lot of intellectual firepower, people like Jeane Kirkpatrick, Norman Podhoretz, and Irving Kristol, who had inspired and invigorated the Reagan administration."[56]

BILL CLINTON AND A PLACE CALLED THE PROGRESSIVE POLICY INSTITUTE

The visibility and prominence of think tanks in Washington may have appeared to fade temporarily during the Bush years, but when Arkansas governor Bill Clinton announced his bid for the presidency in 1991, they began once again to attract considerable attention. As Clinton's campaign gained momentum, journalists started to monitor the individuals and organizations that were advising Clinton. What they discovered is that Clinton, like Carter and Reagan, had established close ties to a handful of think tanks.

In the winter of 1991, few Democrats on Capitol Hill or, for that matter, throughout the United States could have predicted that the Republicans' decade-long reign in the White House would soon come to an end. Enjoying unprecedented popularity in the polls, largely as a result of the overwhelming support for the US-led coalition to "liberate Kuwait," President Bush appeared destined to win a second term in office.[57] As a former Washington insider and long-time resident at a think tank confidently remarked at the time, "Jesus Christ could run on the Democratic ticket and he still wouldn't beat George Bush."[58] Nonetheless, as the growing frustration and concern of American voters over worsening economic conditions overshadowed their initial enthusiasm for Operation Desert Storm, Bush's political future no longer seemed assured. In fact, in the ensuing months it became apparent that unless he could convince the American public that an economic recovery plan for the United States constituted an integral part of his vision for a "new world order," the Oval Office would soon have a new occupant.

Anxiously anticipating a Democratic victory on election day, a handful of think tanks began preparing blueprints for the next administration. Modelling their ambitious research projects on the Heritage Foundation's *Mandate for Leadership*,[59] they outlined a series of recommendations for the next president to follow on issues ranging from health care and educational reform to international trade agreements and defense procurement programs.[60] By the spring of 1992, as Bill Clinton began to accumulate enough delegates to secure the presidential nomination, it appeared to many think tanks that if they were to have any discernible impact on shaping his campaign platform, they would have to capture the governor's attention.

For Clinton, the five-term governor of Arkansas, who easily secured his party's nomination at New York's Madison Square Garden in July 1992, there was little question as to which think tanks and policy advisers he would turn to for advice throughout his campaign and during his transition to the presidency.[61] Dozens of academics, interest groups, business leaders and representatives from a range of non-governmental organizations conveyed their ideas to Clinton in the months preceding the November election. But it appeared to many journalists covering the campaign that Clinton would rely predominantly on the Washington-based Democratic Leadership Council (DLC) and on its policy arm, the Progressive Policy Institute (PPI), to develop his election platform.[62] Unlike Carter and Reagan, Clinton appeared to spend little time developing his contacts in the think tank community. Nonetheless, he clearly acknowledged the valuable role these organizations could play in identifying emerging issues and made sure that he tapped into those institutions that shared a similar political philosophy. For

Clinton, it was not necessary to embark on an extensive tour of the think tank community. He understood what he was looking for and latched on to an organization whose experts he had come to know.

As one of the forty founding members of the DLC, created in 1985 following Walter Mondale's humiliating defeat in the 1984 election, when he only managed to win his native Minnesota, Clinton recognized how critical it was to revitalize the Democratic Party. Throughout his association with the DLC, which included a brief stint as its chairman from 1990 to 1991,[63] he, along with approximately three thousand other members,[64] invested considerable time and energy to move the Democratic Party from the left to the centre of the political spectrum, the principal mandate of the DLC. In an attempt to broaden the party's base of political support by appealing to disillusioned voters, particularly in the southern and western regions of the United States, Clinton participated in the creation of the PPI in 1989 to convince Americans that Democrats, like Republicans, could successfully compete in the marketplace of political ideas. By the 1992 election, the PPI was prepared to spread its message across the country, and fortunately for the institute, it found the right messenger. According to Joel Achenbach, "After creating the DLC, their next move was to create an idea arm, the PPI ... The solution was to come up with new ideas, and find someone to embody them – which happened when Clinton became chairman of the DLC and then carried the group's agenda into the presidential campaign."[65]

Clinton did far more than carry some of the PPI's policy ideas into the campaign. Once in office, he tried to translate several of the institute's suggestions into concrete public policies, often with the assistance of a handful of staff members from the DLC and the PPI who had joined his administration.[66] Several administration policies, including reforming America's health-care system, linking student aid to national service, helping communities to cope more effectively with crime, demanding that welfare recipients perform a variety of community services, and injecting an entrepreneurial spirit into the federal government, are among the many program initiatives that bear a striking resemblance to the recommendations made by various contributors to the PPI's study *Mandate for Change*.[67] Some of these ideas had been advocated by other individuals and organizations, but few institutions in the 1992 campaign offered a more comprehensive guide to reforming government than the PPI.

In addition to drawing heavily on the recommendations made by the DLC and the PPI, Clinton consulted formally and informally with several other individuals to solicit their advice on a wide range of policy initiatives. For instance, during the Clinton-Gore Economic Conference, held in Little

Rock, Arkansas, on 14–15 December 1992, Clinton invited some of the nation's leading economists, corporate executives, and labour leaders to address the economic problems confronting the United States.[68] In a less formal setting he also mingled with several hundred members of America's elite during the now-famous Renaissance Weekends, held at Hilton Head, South Carolina, over New Year's.[69] When scholars have an opportunity to delve into the records of Clinton's 1992 presidential campaign, his association with think tanks inside and beyond the Beltway may reveal an even greater dependence on policy experts. However, what is clear is that he was no stranger to the world of think tanks and paid close attention to those experts who promoted ideas that he could take with him to Washington.

PLANTING NEW IDEAS: GEORGE W. BUSH AND HIS QUEST FOR THE PRESIDENCY

The involvement of think tanks in the campaigns that propelled Carter, Reagan, and Clinton to office reveals one of the most visible channels that think tanks rely on to shape the policy direction of incoming administrations. It also demonstrates how candidates can benefit from the considerable policy expertise available at some of America's leading policy institutes and the potential rewards those institutes can earn by being so closely linked to a winning campaign. This reciprocal benefit may explain why George W. Bush, a newcomer to federal politics, unlike his father, who had spent years in Washington, enlisted the support of policy experts from several think tanks to help shape his policy ideas.

As a US congressman, former director of the CIA, ambassador to the United Nations, vice-president, and president of the United States, George Bush was the consummate Washington insider. By contrast, his first son, George W. Bush, had little first-hand experience with the types of issues he now must confront as president. In the Texas state legislature in Austin, Bush junior became familiar with a host of local concerns, including education, health care, the environment, and transportation,[70] but as president, he required insight into a multitude of domestic and international issues that he had little knowledge of before assuming office. Like Carter, Reagan, and Clinton before they declared their intention to run for the presidency, Bush possessed a limited understanding of foreign affairs, a fact not lost on several journalists and political opponents. In fact, his inability to pass a journalist's pop quiz on foreign policy in November 1999 raised serious concerns about his intellectual grasp of America's international priorities.[71]

In an attempt to allay concerns about his ability to lead the world's remaining superpower and to promote the United States' economic interests in the twenty-first century, Bush assembled a team of over a hundred policy experts, many from the Hoover Institution,[72] to advise him on economic, foreign, and defense policy. During his campaign, he also set up policy advisory committees on issues such as education and technology to help deepen his knowledge of domestic policy issues. Bush's team of economic advisers was headed by Lawrence Lindsey of the American Enterprise Institute, who served as chairman of the National Economic Council.[73] Joining Lindsey, who would return to the AEI in 1993, were several prominent economists, including John Taylor, a Hoover fellow who had also served on President George Bush's Council of Economic Advisers; Harvard economics professor Martin Feldstein; J.D. Foster, executive director of the Washington-based Tax Foundation; and R. Glenn Hubbard of Columbia University's Business School.[74]

Bush's thirteen-member educational policy advisory committee was also well stocked with experts from several leading think tanks. Among those who agreed to take time away from their institutes to assist Bush were Lynne Cheney, a senior fellow at the AEI and wife of Dick Cheney, and her colleague Lynne Munson; Williamson Evers, a senior fellow at the Hoover Institution; and Diane Ravitch, who holds research posts at the Brookings Institution and the New York-based Manhattan Institute for Policy Research.[75]

The foreign policy and defense policy teams Bush assembled were even more impressive, reading, as James Kitfield observed, "like a Who's Who of the Reagan and Bush foreign policy establishments."[76] Heading the foreign policy brain trust were Condoleezza Rice, then Bush's national security adviser,[77] who, in addition to being a fellow at the Hoover Institution, had also served in the National Security Council under President George Bush; Rice's colleague at Hoover, former secretary of state George Shultz; and Vice-President Dick Cheney, a former secretary of defense. Other prominent defense and foreign policy analysts included former Pentagon and State Department official Paul Wolfowitz; the dean of the Johns Hopkins School for Advanced International Studies, Richard Perle; former assistant defense secretary and director of the American Enterprise Institute's Commission on Future Defenses; and former president of the Center for Strategic and International Studies and US trade representative Robert Zoellick.[78] These and a handful of other foreign policy experts became known as "the Vulcans," a small but closely knit group of former high-level policy-makers who would constitute Bush's inner circle.[79]

From most accounts, the Vulcans have had a significant impact on Bush's thinking about a host of foreign policy issues, such as his decision to wage war in Afghanistan and Iraq. Indeed, according to several think tank scholars, including Ivo Daalder of the Brookings Institution, once one gets beyond his former and current top-level advisers, including Secretary of Defense Donald Rumsfeld, Deputy Secretary of State Paul Wolfowitz, Secretary of State Colin Powell, Deputy Secretary of State Richard Armitage, National Security Adviser Condoleezza Rice, Vice-President Dick Cheney, and a handful of others, the Bush foreign policy-making process is "a very, very, very closed system."[80] It has therefore been particularly difficult for think tanks, including PNAC, to convince the administration to listen to their ideas, a subject that will be pursued more closely in the case studies to follow. There is no doubt, as Bob Woodward has revealed in his book *Plan of Attack*, that Bush's inner circle of advisers have played a critical role in shaping his policies. It is also apparent that during his first campaign for the presidency, Bush relied heavily on his battle-hardened team of experts for advice. Particularly in foreign policy, where he admitted on the campaign trail that he had much to learn, policy experts were well positioned to articulate their views to a novice hungry for ideas. As Bush stated in an interview with the *New York Times* during the campaign, "I may not be able to tell you exactly the nuance of the East Timorian situation, but I'll ask people who've had experience, like Condi Rice, Paul Wolfowitz, or Dick Cheney. I am smart enough to know what I don't know, and I have good judgement about who will either be telling the truth, or has got some agenda that is not the right agenda."[81]

According to Tim Adams, a veteran of George Bush's administration who organized a briefing for the Texas governor on technology, the president's management style is in many ways similar to President Reagan's. Rather than trying to become an expert on most policy issues, he prefers to delegate authority to his inner circle of advisers. As Adams observes, "[George W. Bush] believes a chief executive should set out principles, a vision of where you want to go, and then surround yourself with very smart people and listen to them and work with them."[82] For Governor Bush and later President Bush, there was much to be gained and little to lose by developing an extensive network of policy experts. While he is under no obligation to accept anyone's policy advice, he has at his disposal dozens of leading economists, political scientists, and former policy-makers who can give substance to his vision of how America should be governed. They are attempting to do just that.

The relationship between presidential candidates and think tanks reveals more than a convergence of interests between individuals elected to govern and organizations intent on influencing their conduct. It illustrates, among other things, that think tanks are committed to shaping public policy and public opinion and have been able to gain access to the highest levels of government. But as this chapter has shown, focusing on presidential campaigns as a channel of influence offers readers little more than a brief glimpse into the behaviour of think tanks. To acquire a more complete understanding of how they have evolved and how they have come to play a more active role in American foreign policy, it is critical to establish a proper historical and theoretical context. This will be provided in the following two chapters.

CHAPTER TWO

From Generation to Generation: The Origin and Evolution of American Think Tanks

In an address at the University of Passau, James McGann, an expert on and consultant to think tanks, noted that over four thousand think tanks exist worldwide, a number which, he remarked, is quickly approaching five thousand.[1] Of these, approximately half are located in the United States. Interestingly enough, McGann observed, the majority of American think tanks were created in the past twenty years. This a far cry from the situation that existed at the turn of the twentieth century, when only a handful of think tanks were beginning to make their presence felt.

The purpose of this chapter is not to chronicle the origin of hundreds of think tanks in the United States but to illustrate how these organizations have evolved since the early 1900s. What becomes abundantly clear is that as each generation or wave of think tanks emerged in the United States, the complexion and nature of the policy-making community changed. Indeed, as the think tank population began to grow and as think tanks became more aggressive in marketing their ideas, the relationship between policy experts and policy-makers took on a very different dynamic. No longer content waiting for policy-makers to react favourably to a report or study they published, think tank scholars and the institutions that employed them discovered ways to establish a stronger voice. In time, as we will observe, policy-makers began to take notice.

By focusing on four distinct periods or waves of think tank development – 1900–45, 1946–70, 1971–94, and 1980–2004 – it is possible to highlight the different types of think tanks that inhabit the policy-making community as well as the many factors that have influenced their development. The

Figure 2.1 Annual budgets of selected American think tanks (in millions of dollars)

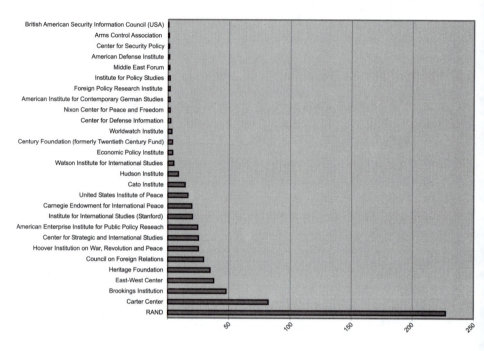

chapter begins by discussing the typology or classification of think tanks that will employed in this book to describe the think tanks that have emerged in the United States. The four waves of think tank growth will then be examined. Finally, to further highlight the significant diversity within the think tank community, a brief profile of some of the most prominent American foreign policy think tanks will be provided (see also fig. 2.1 and tables A1.1 and A1.2 in appendix 1).

CLASSIFYING THINK TANKS

Since there is no consensus among scholars as to what constitutes a think tank, Kent Weaver, James McGann, and others[2] have, as noted in the introduction, constructed various typologies or classifications to identify different types of organizations that typically fall under the rubric "think tank." In so doing, they have not only helped us to distinguish between different types of policy institutes; they have also helped us to identify the key motivations and institutional traits associated with each generation or wave of think tanks. Drawing on these and other classifications that are well suited to the American think tank experience, we can begin to observe how these organizations have transformed themselves over time and how they have come to play a more active role in the policy-making process. Although scholars employ different typologies to study think tanks and often label them in different ways, they generally agree that distinctions can and should be drawn between think tanks that are more research-oriented and those that assign a higher priority to engaging in political advocacy. They also agree that distinctions can be made between think tanks according to how they are funded and the clients or target audiences they are intended to serve.

In the discussion below, I draw heavily on a typology constructed by Weaver – a typology that serves as a useful point of departure to probe more deeply into the often confusing and complex world of think tanks. While Weaver's classification of three main types of American think tanks raises some interesting methodological questions, it goes a long way in setting out, in very general terms, the kinds of think tanks found in the policy research community. It is for this reason and this reason alone that his typology has been adopted.

Universities without Students

In one of the first classifications of think tanks, Weaver identified three types of organizations that populate the policy research community. At the top of the food chain or hierarchy of think tanks, particularly for purists, are think tanks that he refers to as "universities without students." These institutions are generally large by think tank standards (approximately fifty or more scholars) and are composed of academics whose primary interest is to research and write scholarly studies. Many of these scholars have worked in universities but prefer the seclusion of think tanks, where they are not expected to assume teaching and administrative responsibilities. Other scholars, especially those more "conservative" in their leanings, have sought refuge in these and other types of think tanks where they have felt more welcome. According to Ambassador Jeane Kirkpatrick, a long-time resident of the free market–oriented American Enterprise Institute, since universities in the United States are overwhelmingly liberal, many conservative scholars have been forced to find a more hospitable and congenial environment in which to pursue their research.[3] Not surprisingly, they have been attracted to think tanks that can both satisfy their research interests and nurture their ideological beliefs. Such institutions, whether liberal or conservative, function much like universities in the sense that their principal mission is to promote a greater understanding of important social, economic, and political issues confronting society. They are, to put it simply, in the business of disseminating knowledge. Unlike in universities, however, the seminars and workshops they offer and the studies they produce are generally intended for policy-makers, not students. Ironically, most of the hefty studies published by research-oriented think tanks find their way into university classrooms and libraries, not into the briefcases of policy-makers. Supported in large part "by funding from the private sector (with varying mixtures of foundation, corporate and individual funding),"[4] scholars working at these institutions regard book-length studies as their primary research product. However, as noted by Brookings scholar Michael O'Hanlon, the emphasis on book-length studies is beginning to change. The Brookings Institution and the Hoover Institution, two of the largest private research institutions in the United States, are among the few think tanks that would likely fall into this category.[5]

Government Contractors or Specialists

What distinguishes government contractors from Weaver's first category of think tanks is not so much the type of research they conduct (although some of what government contractors do is confidential) or the type of researchers they employ (most have PhDs) as it is their principal client and primary source of funding. Think tanks such as RAND and the Urban Institute, two of the leading government contractors in the United States, were created to serve specific needs of policy-makers. As will be discussed later in this chapter, both receive large sums of government money in order to provide advice on how to address key foreign and domestic policy concerns confronting the nation. As government contractors, these types of think tanks enjoy privileged access to federal departments and agencies, but this does not guarantee that they will be able to influence government policy. Indeed, there are several examples where the policy recommendations made by RAND and other contractors have clearly been at odds with the wishes and political concerns of members of Congress and the Executive. In these and other instances, government contractors have little control over how their advice will be received. However, government contractors generally acknowledge that their major concern is to offer sound and informed advice to their clients, not to influence how the clients use the information with which they are provided. This is not to suggest that government contractors willingly distance themselves from the reports they produce. On the contrary, it means that since they are almost entirely dependent on government funding, unlike other types of think tanks, they cannot afford to be perceived as having a political agenda. They must, at all cost, maintain their institutional legitimacy and integrity. It is also important to distinguish between large government contractors such as RAND and the Urban Institute which receive millions of dollars each year in government funding and the hundreds of other think tanks that are beneficiaries of limited pools of federal and/or state funding for specific projects. Unlike the former, which have a secure source of funding, smaller government specialists must compete among themselves to keep afloat. As many directors of think tanks have acknowledged, government funding can be both a blessing and a curse. Therefore it is critical for think tanks to generate revenue from multiple sources, a subject that we will return to later.

Advocacy Think Tanks

Since the early 1970s, the most common type of think tank to emerge in the United States and in other Western democracies, including Canada and Great Britain, has been what Weaver refers to as the advocacy think tank. Advocacy think tanks, as the name implies, "combine a strong policy, partisan or ideological bent with aggressive salesmanship and an effort to influence current policy debates."[6] They place greater emphasis on producing brief reports for policy-makers than book-length studies and employ a number of strategies to solidify their ties to members of Congress, the Executive, and the bureaucracy. Moreover, to influence public opinion and public policy, advocacy think tanks, including the Heritage Foundation, place a high premium on gaining access to the media. Their staff frequently appear on network newscasts and political talk shows to share their insights on a wide range of current policy issues, and op-ed articles submitted by their scholars regularly appear in major American newspapers.

Some Additions to Weaver's Typology

In addition to relying on Weaver's typology, we should add a fourth and possibly a fifth category – vanity or candidate-based and legacy think tanks. Vanity or candidate-based think tanks are created by aspiring office-holders (or their supporters) to generate ideas that the candidate can later draw on during his or her campaign. The advantage of creating a think tank for this purpose is that it allows candidates to circumvent federal campaign finance laws which limit the amount of money individuals and political action committees can donate to congressional and presidential candidates. By establishing a chapter 501, (3) non-profit, tax-exempt, non-partisan organization, candidates can attract considerable sums of money that are not regulated by the Federal Election Commission. It is, to put it bluntly, a win-win situation for candidates and their supporters. Those willing to donate to a candidate's think tank receive a charitable receipt that they can claim on their income tax form, and candidates in turn can benefit from the policy expertise made available to them. Examples of vanity or candidate-based think tanks include Ross Perot's United We Stand and Bob Dole's short-lived think tank called Better America.

Legacy think tanks are research centres created by former presidents and cabinet secretaries intent on leaving their mark on public policy well after leaving office. There are several examples of such think tanks, including the Carter Center, the Nixon Center for Peace and Freedom, and the James A. Baker III Institute for Public Policy at Houston's Rice University. These centres are frequently, but not always, part of a presidential library.

PROCEEDING WITH CAUTION: THE LIMITS OF THINK TANK TYPOLOGIES

Classifying generations or waves of think tanks according to specific institutional criteria may allow scholars to distinguish one type of think tank from another. Nonetheless, it is important to consider some problems that can arise in such classification. To begin with, since some organizations possess characteristics common to more than one type of think tank, they could conceivably fall into several categories. For instance, while few scholars would likely encounter difficulty distinguishing between the work of the Brookings Institution and the Heritage Foundation, these two institutions engage in similar activities. They both conduct research on a wide range of domestic and foreign policy issues and recognize the importance of marketing their findings. The main difference is the emphasis they place on pure research and political advocacy. To argue, then, that the Brookings Institution functions like a university without students and Heritage conducts itself like an advocacy think tank would, on the surface, be misleading. Each of these institutes could conceivably be classified as both a research institution and an advocacy think tank.

This potential problem cannot be overstated. How scholars and journalists classify institutes can and does have a profound impact on the way different think tanks are perceived in the media and by the public. Referring to the Brookings Institution as a world-renowned policy research centre provides the organization with instant credibility. It creates the impression, rightly or wrongly, that the institution produces objective, scholarly, scientific, and balanced research. Conversely, labelling the Heritage Foundation and the American Enterprise Institute, for example, as well-known advocacy think tanks implies that they are more committed to advancing their ideological agenda than to pursuing scholarly research. In short, the implication is that the views and recommendations of "research institutions" should be taken more seriously than those of "advocacy think tanks."

The problem of classifying think tanks incorrectly may become more pronounced as these organizations adopt similar strategies to convey their ideas. Like chameleons constantly changing their complexion to suit new environments, think tanks frequently alter their behaviour to become more competitive in the marketplace of ideas. To enhance their profile, some think tanks created in the early decades of the twentieth century now rely on strategies employed by newer waves or generations of institutes. Moreover, some newly-created institutes have looked to older generations of think tanks for ideas on how to manage their operations. In short, despite the increasingly diverse nature of the think tank community in the United States, it is becoming more difficult to isolate distinctive institutional traits.

Distinguishing between the different types of think tanks that currently inhabit the policy research community in the United States may lead scholars to describe some institutes incorrectly. Unfortunately, given the various methodological problems often encountered in classifying think tanks, this problem may be unavoidable. Nonetheless, typologies can be useful in identifying the kinds of think tanks that surfaced during particular time periods. As this chapter will illustrate, think tanks associated with each of the four waves of development possessed certain defining characteristics. It is these characteristics that allow scholars to identify when a new wave or generation of think tanks began to emerge on the political landscape.

THE ORIGIN OF AMERICAN THINK TANKS: REFLECTIONS ON RESEARCH INSTITUTIONS, 1830–1945

Few historians and political scientists disagree about the origin of political parties and labour unions in the United States, but there is little consensus on when the first think tank was created. While some maintain that prototypical think tanks were established during the early 1900s, others contend that the seeds of contemporary institutes were planted well before the end of the nineteenth century. According to Paul Dickson, who wrote the first major study on think tanks in 1970,[7] there is evidence to suggest that research institutions began to advise the US government as early as the

1830s. Dickson maintains that the relationship between think tanks and government "started in 1832, when the Secretary of the Treasury, confronted by pesky steam boilers that kept exploding in American steamboats, contracted with the Franklin Institute of Philadelphia for a study of the problem. Since then, the government has been paying for more and more outside brainpower each decade."[8]

Dickson selects 1832 as his point of departure to study the government's growing dependence on think tanks to resolve various political, economic, social, technical, and security problems, yet he fails to offer any justification for beginning his analysis at this particular date. Moreover, since he neglects to provide any documentation to support his chronology of the earliest think tanks, it is questionable whether the Franklin Institute was indeed the first organization that provided scholars with an opportunity to share their research findings with government officials. Furthermore, since several major educational institutions existed in the United States before 1832, including Harvard University (1636), Yale University (1701), Princeton University (1746), Columbia University (1754), and Brown University (1764), it is not only conceivable but highly probable that government officials solicited the expertise of individual academics or the departments with which they were affiliated. In other words, the absence of autonomous, non-profit research institutions with their own facilities prior to 1832 cannot by itself be used as a barometer to measure the interaction between intellectuals and government. Whether in the hallowed halls of prestigious universities and think tanks or in the labyrinth of conference rooms on Capitol Hill, scholars have discussed and debated public policy issues with government officials for over two hundred years. While academics during the seventeenth and eighteenth centuries may not have consciously regarded themselves as members of a particular association or institute, by sharing their views and insights with colleagues and government leaders, they performed many functions characteristic of contemporary think tanks. Consequently, to suggest that the origin of think tanks coincides with the construction of physical headquarters to house intellectuals would be misleading.

The development, refinement, and dissemination of ideas did not begin with the creation of the Franklin Institute, as Dickson argues, but preceded the founding of the American republic. However, like many studies that followed the publication of his pioneering work, Dickson devotes only passing reference to the historical evolution of think tanks before proceeding to analyze in detail such high-profile research centres as the Rand Corporation (now known as RAND) and the Urban Institute. To be fair to him, it is difficult to determine with any degree of certainty which organization, association, or political movement deserves to be regarded as the first think tank. Still, it is possible to shed light on those organizations that may have served as models for such venerable policy research institutions as the Brookings Institution, the Carnegie Endowment for International Peace, and the Council on Foreign Relations.

Published two decades after Dickson's sweeping overview of American think tanks, James Smith's informative study on the emergence of policy experts in twentieth-century America fills in many of the historical gaps left by his predecessors. Though Smith agrees with Dickson that the origin of contemporary think tanks can be traced to the nineteenth century, he argues that it was not until six months after the Civil War ended that academics began to take the first steps toward creating independent research organizations. According to Smith, when approximately one hundred people, including writers, journalists, educators, scientists, and government officials, met at the Massachusetts State House in Boston in October 1865 to discuss ways to improve the economic and social well-being of individual states slowly recuperating from the ravages of war, intellectuals began to recognize the benefits that could be derived by sharing their expertise.[9]

Meeting under the auspices of the newly formed American Association for the Promotion of Social Science (later shortened to the American Social Science Association, or ASSA), delegates at the State House modelled their organization on a British group established in 1857 "to investigate, advise, and lobby for social reform."[10] By committing themselves to fulfilling the ASSA's mandate, individual members sought not only to promote social reform and to raise the professional standards of social scientists but to extend their influence beyond the classroom.[11]

The ASSA continued to provide an important forum for social scientists and government officials to discuss and debate public policy issues in the decades following its creation. It also contributed to the establishment of other, more specialized professional organizations, such as the American Historical Association, founded in 1884, and the American Economics Association, incorporated in 1885.[12] Other national professional associations emerged during the latter half of the nineteenth century as the number of university-trained experts increased. As a result, further developments toward establishing close links between policy analysts and public officials were forged.

For William Domhoff, the author of several books on the formation and composition of policy elites in the United States,[13] the creation of professional associations played an important role in fostering closer ties between social scientists. He argues that it was the establishment of two business reform organizations near the turn of the twentieth century that enabled research institutions to gain access to the policy-making community. According to Domhoff, the Chicago Civic Federation (CCF), founded in 1894, and its successor, the National Civic Federation (NCF), established in 1900, were among the first research institutions to establish formal institutional links with local, national, and federal government departments.

Growing disillusionment with widespread corruption and mismanagement in municipal affairs, as well as concern over the assassination of Chicago mayor Carter Harrison Sr, convinced a group of community leaders to form the CCF. Building on their experiences as members of various business reform groups, the founders, who included financial, labour, and academic spokespersons, established the organization as a "non-sectarian, non-political group working to advance Chicago's municipal, philanthropic, industrial and moral interests."[14]

In the ensuing years, the CCF managed to achieve many of its stated objectives. It established several standing committees to investigate various problems in local government, including election fraud and voter registration, and recommended a number of useful reforms. In the late 1890s, however, some of its members were apparently no longer content to concentrate solely on municipal politics. Rather, they became preoccupied with expanding their efforts on a national scale. By 1899 the CCF had organized four national conferences on topics ranging from labour arbitration in 1894 to foreign policy in 1898.[15] Following a conference on trusts one year later, the CCF began planning for a National Civic Federation. It was at this juncture in the CCF's history that it virtually disappeared from national prominence. Taking its place was the newly created NCF.

Under the leadership of former CCF secretary Ralph Easley, the NCF attracted a large and influential membership composed of government officials, labour representatives, university professors, and reform-minded businessmen, including Andrew Carnegie, E.A. Filene,[16] Gerard Swope, V. Everett Macy, and George Perkins. According to James Smith, the NCF was "the proto-typical business research and policy organization" which was primarily motivated by one goal: "to promote legislation and to effect an accommodation of business and labour by steering a middle course between socialists in the labour movement and unreconstructed laissez-faire businessmen."[17] The NCF established itself as a major force in shaping domestic policy until the outbreak of World War I, but by the early 1920s it had become little more than a meeting place for business and labour leaders to discuss common concerns.[18] No longer was it regarded as an influential research institution that had left its mark on labour legislation. Although

Easley was largely responsible for the ascendancy of the NCF, it appears that his "militant anti-socialist propagandizing"[19] may also have contributed to its decline. As the CCF and the NCF rose and then gradually faded from national politics, other policy-planning organizations committed to improving the political, economic, and social well-being of the country were prepared to take their place.

In 1904 Richard Ely, an American-born, German-educated economist who was largely responsible for the creation of the American Historical Association, and the American Economics Association, and John R. Commons, an economics professor at the University of Wisconsin, combined their expertise to establish the Bureau of Industrial Research. With the assistance of a group of economists and statisticians and the financial support of several businessmen, including Andrew Carnegie, Ely and Commons produced a multi-volume study on labour and industry entitled *A Documentary History of American Industrial Society*.[20] Furthermore, in 1906 Ely joined forces with other economists and business reformers to create the American Association of Labor Legislation, "which sought greater uniformity of state and local laws, and ultimately federal legislation on workers' compensation, minimum-wage, and job-training proposals."[21]

Despite the diversity of research institutions that emerged in the first decades of the twentieth century, they appear to have shared two common characteristics. First, like many contemporary think tanks, organizations in the early 1900s could survive only with the continued support of generous benefactors. Second, while many turn-of-the-century research institutions attempted to transform policy-relevant research into governmental policies, some "tended to confuse the lines between disinterested investigation and political advocacy,"[22] a characteristic trait of advocacy think tanks created since the late 1960s. Yet for some policy experts such as John Commons, if research institutions were to maintain their intellectual credibility, they had to consciously avoid offering policy advice that merely satisfied their ideological agenda. Having been fired from Syracuse University for his allegedly radical positions, Commons was all too familiar with the many problems that could arise when academics attempted to masquerade as politicians. "I learned with Easley, as I had previously begun to learn with [other colleagues]," Commons noted, "that the place of economists was that of advisor to the leaders, if they wanted him, and not that of propagandist to the masses."[23] As Smith points out, "Commons believed that only practical experience could teach politicians how to filter the advisers' advice and that the politicians were accordingly free to use or reject that advice as they saw fit."[24] "They were leaders," Commons concluded. "I was an intellectual."[25]

In time, Commons learned to recognize the fine line between offering impartial policy advice and engaging in political advocacy. The creation of philanthropic organizations such as the Carnegie Corporation and the Rockefeller Foundation in the early twentieth century and their willingness to support many research institutions[26] also contributed to a more stable and permanent link between policy experts and government. By providing research institutions with several-million-dollar endowments[27] and hence long-term financial security, foundations allowed think tanks to devote more time to solidifying their ties to government officials. Moreover, unlike policy research institutions that continue to depend on the financial assistance of several corporations and private citizens, those supported by large endowments are less vulnerable to the partisan pressures of their donors. Although philanthropic foundations have on occasion refused to renew grants to research institutions,[28] financial endowments are difficult, if not impossible, to withdraw. The important and at times controversial relationships between philanthropic foundations and various research institutions will be examined accordingly.

The activities of the NCF, the CCF, and several other smaller research institutions deserve to be recorded in the early history of American think tanks, but it was during the first two decades of the twentieth century that the impact of policy research institutions began to be felt. Five think tanks, in particular, left a lasting impression on domestic and international politics prior to and in the aftermath of World War I:[29] the Russell Sage Foundation (1907), the Carnegie Endowment for International Peace (1910), the Institute for Government Research (1916),[30] the Hoover Institution (1919), and the Council on Foreign Relations (1921).

These organizations were established under different and often unusual circumstances, but each was formed for the purpose of providing an atmosphere in which to encourage scholars to investigate social, economic, and political issues. While these institutions attracted policy experts committed to a wide range of political beliefs, the organizations themselves were not intended to be transformed into ideological battlefields. At times, individual scholars overtly supported or opposed governmental policies, but the primary goal of these institutions was not to consciously interfere in the decision-making process but to provide an important source of policy expertise. Furthermore, the ability of these organizations to translate scholarly advice into concrete legislative and executive proposals appears to have depended as much on the quality of their research as on the extensiveness of their ties to government officials. A brief analysis of the origin and evolution of the aforementioned organizations will demonstrate how this generation of think tanks were able to become permanent fixtures in the policy-making community.

The Russell Sage Foundation

Though often overlooked in chronologies of early twentieth-century think tanks, the New York-based Russell Sage Foundation became the prototypical national research institution concerned with addressing and alleviating social problems. Established in 1907 by Margaret Olivia Sage in honour of her late husband, the foundation "helped shape social research, policy prescription, and public debate in the waning years of the Progressive Era, forging a new national arena for the discussion of policies."[31] The foundation set out to recruit researchers committed to resolving social problems, but "its goal was not knowledge for its own sake or basic social science research, but the application of research to the solution of social ills."[32] To fulfill its stated goal, many of the foundation's members believed it was necessary to confront social problems at home before addressing concerns on a national scale.

At the outset, the Sage Foundation devoted considerable attention to improving the administration of several local private charitable organizations so they could more effectively assist individuals in need. Moreover, by distributing hundreds of pamphlets, brochures, and articles on topics ranging from feeding infants to improving urban landscape, the foundation sought to educate the public about common health concerns. In addition, it examined many important social issues, such as the containment of tuberculosis and the working conditions of women. And on several occasions, it drafted model legislation on topics as diverse as loansharking and the juvenile court system.[33] While much of the foundation's work focused on short-term research projects, it also funded more extensive studies. Paul U. Kellogg's highly acclaimed six-volume study on Pittsburgh's industrial conditions represented but one of many long-term projects supported by the foundation.

As many of the social, economic, and political dimensions of their research became increasingly complicated, analysts at the Russell Sage Foundation began to communicate with a different audience. Scholars at the foundation remained committed to promoting the public good, but converting their research findings into government policy, rather than simply attempting to convey their ideas to ordinary citizens, became a top priority. According to James Smith, "as the metaphor of prevention lost its hold on social scientists, experts seemed less willing to attempt to communicate with the general public. Rather, they sought a new public role for themselves, not as doctors seeking to prevent and cure social ills, but as scientists of efficiency, experts in the techniques of institutional management."[34]

Moreover, as foundation researchers began to redefine their role and responsibilities as social scientists, they recognized the necessity of establishing closer ties to public officials. After all, if they were committed to reforming social welfare policies administered by government agencies and departments, they had to acquire access to those individuals who were in a position to implement changes. While the manner in which policy experts attempted to correct social problems changed, the Sage Foundation continued to strive for institutional objectivity. Unlike many think tanks created since the late 1960s which rarely conceal their political leanings, during its formative years, the foundation did not appear to overtly embrace a particular ideological orientation; nor did its researchers regard themselves as advocates of class or partisan interests. On the contrary, they perceived themselves as individuals relying on government channels to inform decision-makers and the public about the results and consequences of their research. According to Mary Van Kleeck, a prominent member of the Russell Sage Foundation for many years, "research was undertaken in the faith that the community itself must discover its own program of action."[35] More specifically, Van Kleeck and her colleagues "viewed themselves as neutral experts seeking facts that would raise the public to intelligent action."[36]

Relying on twelve to fifteen resident policy experts as well as a number of adjunct scholars at American universities, the Russell Sage Foundation continues to explore many aspects of social science research. With an endowment of $90 million based initially on a $10-million gift from its founder, the foundation spends approximately $4–5 million each year on research. The methods employed by social scientists at the foundation have become increasingly sophisticated, yet the goal of the institution has remained intact over its close to one-hundred-year history. The Russell Sage Foundation is America's oldest surviving research institution, but by 1910 it no longer held the distinction of being the only national policy research institution in the United States. Joining it in the policy research community was the newly created Carnegie Endowment for International Peace.

The Carnegie Endowment for International Peace

During his seventy-fifth birthday celebration on 25 November 1910, Andrew Carnegie (1835–1919), one of America's leading industrialists and philanthropists, announced the creation of the Carnegie Endowment with a

trust fund of $10 million. Acting on the advice of many of his pacifist col-
leagues, including Samuel Dutton, Edwin Mead, Hamilton Holt, and Secretary of State Elihu Root,[37] Carnegie became convinced that it was necessary
to establish an organization which would work for "the education of the
public for peace, to spread arbitral justice among nations and to promote
the comity and commerce of the world without the dangers of war."[38]

In making the announcement, Carnegie stated that the annual income
derived from the trust fund should be used in any way "appropriate to has-
ten the abolition of war."[39] Moreover, he directed that "when the establishment of peace is attained, ... the revenue shall be devoted to the banishment
of the next most degrading evil or evils, the suppression of which would
most advance the progress, elevation and happiness of man."[40] Turning to
the one person who was responsible for finally persuading him to establish
the endowment, Carnegie appointed Root, then a senator from New York,
president of the board of trustees. In the ensuing years, under the direction
of Root and his fellow board members, who included Nicholas Murray Butler, Henry Pritchett, Joseph Choate, James Brown Scott, Charles Eliot, John
W. Forster, Andrew White, J.G. Schmidlapp, Oscar S. Straus, and President
William Taft, who served as honorary president, a number of steps were
taken toward fulfilling the institution's lofty objectives.

By 1919 the Carnegie Endowment had established several divisions,
including International Law, Economics, History, and Intercourse and Education,[41] to examine the causes of war and to recommend various ways to
alleviate interstate conflict. Although the policy experts employed in these
divisions were by and large historians, political scientists, and economists,
their research was not intended to be digested solely by interested colleagues
or to be placed on dusty library bookshelves. On the contrary, as John
Frazier Wall points out, staff members at the Carnegie Endowment did not
lose sight of their responsibility to keep the public informed about the hor-
rors of war. The Intercourse and Education division, in particular, devoted
much of its resources to dealing directly with the public, "attempting both
to ascertain and to influence public opinion."[42] The institution also became
involved in establishing several international organizations and publicized
stories about human suffering in wartorn countries. The work of the Carnegie Endowment and its attempts to educate the public about the nature of
war did not go unnoticed. In the years following its creation, admirers
throughout the United States and Europe complemented Carnegie and his
research organization for their efforts. Paul S. Reinsch, professor of political
science at the University of Wisconsin and later Woodrow Wilson's minister
to China, praised Carnegie for assembling a board of trustees composed not

only of enlightened pacifists but of "men of action in both commerce and government."[43]

In addition to complementing the founder on the direction of the organization and its attempts to promote world peace, Reinsch encouraged the implementation of neutrality legislation in Congress and above all stressed "the necessity for working out an international code of law that meets the highest conception of equity and justice."[44] However, not all observers of the Carnegie Endowment's work were willing to pay a glowing tribute to its founder or to the work of his organization. In a letter to board member J.G. Schmidlapp in 1910, John Bigelow,[45] one of Carnegie's oldest acquaintances, stated:

Your brother peacemaker, Carnegie, reminds me of a verse that I learned at an early period of my life: "There was an old woman who lived in a shoe. She had so many children, she didn't know what to do." Carnegie seems to know no better what to do with his money than this old lady knew what to do with her children. He takes three columns of a newspaper to give you ten millions of money to spend to stop people from fighting, and gives not a single suggestion from beginning to end of what you are to do to accomplish this result, not even spanking. He gives you ten millions of dollars to promote peace, every penny of which was the Dead Sea fruit of a war tariff which he himself admitted was unnecessary and therefore oppressive, and he selects forty of the most conspicuous men of his acquaintance in the country, pretty nearly everyone of whom is a stand pat protectionist, and a red-handed partisan of war upon every commercial nation, including our own, to spend millions for peace, without the suggestion of a single step they were to take to accomplish it. Why could he not have said, "Use what is necessary to abolish the tariff and put the rest in your pockets" – for a riddance of the tariff would be a guarantee of peace, and your Board of Trustees would be functus officio.[46]

Bigelow believed that Carnegie's $10-million trust to establish an organization to promote peace was hardly a prudent investment and likely was only intended to generate further public adulation for its founder.[47] Yet whatever Carnegie's intentions, the Carnegie Endowment for International Peace has become an important and well-respected policy research institution in the United States. From its headquarters next to the Brookings Institution near Washington's Dupont Circle, it oversees an extensive research program on issues relating to international relations and US foreign policy. With the assistance of approximately forty full-time researchers and close to sixty staff members, the endowment publishes articles and books on a host of topics ranging from the proliferation of nuclear weapons in the Third World to the many social, economic, and political problems associated with illegal immigration to the United States. Moreover since 1970 the endowment, which has an annual budget in excess of $15 million, has published a quarterly magazine, *Foreign Policy*, which is recognized by the American Political Science Association and other professional organizations as a leading journal in the field of international relations.

In addition to devoting considerable resources to its expanding research program, the Carnegie Endowment has organized several special programs to allow academics, senior and middle-level officials of the executive branch, members of Congress, corporate leaders, and journalists to discuss and debate a wide range of global and regional concerns. Among the programs that have been established to date are Face to Face; the Mid-Atlantic Club; East-West Relations in Europe; Arms Proliferation in the Near East and South Asia Project; Immigration Policy Project; Trade, Equity, and Development; Post-Soviet Economies; and U.S. Leadership. The Carnegie Endowment's interest in the former Soviet Union became more evident in the spring of 1993 when it opened the Carnegie Moscow Center to accommodate "foreign and Russian researchers collaborating with Washington staff on a variety of topical areas and policy-relevant projects."[48]

Through these and other programs, the Carnegie Endowment provides not only a forum in which individuals can explore many contemporary public policy issues but an opportunity for its members to solidify their ties to key members in Washington's decision-making network. By interacting on a regular basis with members of Congress, the Executive, and other policymakers, it has been able to establish itself as an important research institution. Its success in acquiring a reputation as a respected think tank is often reflected in the regular appearances made by many of its scholars on network talk shows and newscasts.

The Institute for Government Research and the Brookings Institution

Unlike the Carnegie Endowment for International Peace, which was created for the specific purpose of promoting world peace, the Institute for Government Research (IGR) was established in Washington, DC, in 1916 to improve the overall management of government. By creating a national research institution composed of policy experts committed to enhancing the efficiency of government and the budgetary system, the founders sought not only to inject scientific rationality into the decision-making process but to prevent partisan politics from undermining the government's efforts to serve the public interest.[49] In short, by replacing the extensive and often pernicious influence of party machines with a cadre of neutral policy experts, the IGR attempted to reform and restructure the administration of government.

After serving on the Taft Commission on government administration in 1910 and observing the demise of its report in 1912, two of its members, Frank Goodnow, a professor of administrative law at Columbia University and later president of Johns Hopkins University, and William F. Willoughby, a statistician with the Labour Department, decided to continue their efforts to promote many of the recommendations outlined by the commission, including a proposal for a national budget system. By discussing the virtues of budget reform before a number of professional and business organizations such as the American Political Science Association and the US Chamber of Commerce, Goodnow and Willoughby began to generate interest in their message. Moreover, they attracted the attention of several business reform–minded individuals, and suggestions for a national research organization to perform a role similar to the New York Bureau of Municipal Research began to circulate.[50]

The idea of establishing a research institution to study the administration of the federal government eventually made its way to Jerome D. Greene, secretary of the newly endowed Rockefeller Foundation. After considering the idea, Greene sent a confidential letter to a distinguished group of nine corporate leaders asking them for their support in creating a research organization to "study the problems of administration and to interest the public in the solution of these problems."[51] Agreeing unanimously to support Greene's request, the nine formed a board of trustees for the new institute. In recognition of their efforts in launching a campaign for a national budget, Goodnow was later appointed chairman of the board of the IGR and Willoughby its first director. By 1915 the board had been expanded to provide a greater balance between liberals and conservatives. Still concerned about maintaining the institute's image as a non-partisan research organization, Greene recruited a number of prominent conservatives to sit on the board, including Arthur Hadley, president of Yale University, Cleveland H. Dodge, vice-president of Phelps Dodge, and Robert S. Brookings, a St Louis businessman and philanthropist who had served as a consultant to the Taft Commission.

Following its incorporation on 2 October 1916, the IGR, under the direction of Willoughby, began working toward fulfilling its first objective: "the establishment of a genuine national budget."[52] In January 1917 Willoughby, Goodnow, and Felix Frankfurter, who had recently been recruited to sit on the institute's board of trustees, met with President Woodrow Wilson to discuss the prospects of establishing a national budget system. During their meeting, Wilson, who, as noted earlier, was critical of the role of policy experts, asked Willoughby to submit a memorandum outlining the IGR's recommendations for budget reform. Furthermore, at the request of James N. Good, chairman of the House Committee on Appropriations, Willoughby was asked to assist in drafting a bill for a national budget system, which would later form the basis of the proposed Budget and Accounting Act of 1919.

Yet, despite the bill's passing both houses of Congress by an overwhelming margin, Wilson, who was in his second term, unexpectedly vetoed it. Arguing that some provisions of the bill violated the Constitution's separation of powers, the president refused to sign the legislation he had initially supported.[53] Frustrated by his decision but determined to convince the next administration to pass the Budget and Accounting Act, Willoughby met with President-Elect Warren Harding to discuss the bill. Moreover, in an attempt to generate additional support for the legislation, Willoughby hired a public relations specialist to place editorials and articles supporting the implementation of a national budget system in major newspapers throughout the United States.[54] By so doing, he appears to have undermined the non-partisan role of policy experts at the IGR. As Donald Critchlow points out in his sweeping history of the Brookings Institution, "A thin line divided partisan from nonpartisan, and nonpolitical from political activity. At this point in the IGR's history, these lines would be frequently blurred, contrary to institute rhetoric."[55]

Willoughby's tireless efforts finally paid off on 10 June 1921, when President Harding signed the Budget and Accounting Act. But despite playing an active role in shaping domestic legislation in the early 1920s, policy experts at the IGR continued to insist that their primary objective was to bring greater efficiency to government, not to interfere in the mechanics of the decision-making process. And to convince skeptics that the IGR was not a political institution but a policy research institution devoted to improving the administration of government, Willoughby and his colleagues launched an extensive research project to examine, in intimate detail, the organizational structure of several government agencies.

However, while the IGR had fulfilled its first objective, in the ensuing years it appeared to lack the direction and focus that ensured its earlier success. Indeed, to many it became increasingly apparent that "the IGR was an organization without purpose and without vision."[56] Notwithstanding the growing lethargy that plagued the organization in the early 1920s, some members of the board of trustees envisioned a new role for the institute.

Impressed by the ability of the IGR to contribute to greater efficiency in government, Robert Brookings recommended that policy experts begin to focus their energies on improving economic policy in the United States.

For Brookings (1850–1932), a self-made millionaire who had served on the War Industries Board,[57] the inability of government officials to appreciate the implications of major economic decisions during the war had demonstrated all too clearly the need for economists to provide expertise to political leaders. Sharing a distrust of partisan politics with many of his IGR colleagues, Brookings became convinced of the need to establish a non-partisan economic research institution and an affiliated graduate school "to collect objective data, to investigate economic problems, to evaluate current economic policy, and to develop a cadre of scientifically trained men to enter government administration."[58]

With a five-year grant of $200,000 from the Carnegie Corporation, Brookings established the Institute of Economics on 13 February 1922 and appointed University of Chicago economist Harold G. Moulton its first director. Under Moulton's direction, approximately thirty economists and political scientists at the institute were able to transform "Brooking's dream of a research institution into a viable organizational reality."[59] After securing additional funds and making arrangements with Washington University in St Louis to establish a joint graduate program, Brookings was able to incorporate the Robert Brookings Graduate School of Economics and Government on 24 November 1924.[60]

On paper, the Institute of Economics, the Robert Brookings Graduate School, and the Institute for Government Research existed as separate entities; in reality, they functioned as sibling organizations. By participating in joint research programs and conducting interdisciplinary seminars, staff members at the three institutes were able to create a stimulating environment in which to address and resolve many important public policy issues. In time, however, growing concern over the management of the graduate school and confusion surrounding overlapping administrative responsibilities convinced Brookings and the separate boards of trustees to merge the three institutions on 8 December 1927.

In creating the Brookings Institution, the founders continued to stress the importance of preserving an independent, non-partisan research institution.[61] In fact, to ensure the intellectual autonomy of policy experts, Robert Brookings prohibited the board of trustees from interfering in the research projects of staff members. Recognizing the achievements of the founding institutes while contemplating an expanding role for his new institution, he assigned the highest priority to providing impartial policy expertise. His commitment to insulating the Brookings Institution from partisan interests is reflected in the organization's charter:

[The Brookings Institution was established] to promote, carry on, conduct and foster scientific research, education, training and publication in the broad fields of economics, government administration and the political and social sciences generally, involving the study, determination, interpretation and publication of economic, political and social facts and principles relating to questions of local, national or international significance; to promote and carry out these objects, purposes and principles without regard to and independently of the special interests of any group in the body politic, either political, social or economic.[62]

Throughout its distinguished history, the Brookings Institution's philosophy and guiding principles appear, at least on the surface, to have remained intact. Through its research programs in Economic Studies, Foreign Policy Studies, and Governance Studies, over a hundred resident and non-resident scholars and visiting and guest scholars analyze, evaluate, discuss, and publish studies on a wide range of public policy issues. And according to Brookings president Strobe Talbott, ambassador-at-large during the Clinton administration;

We put the highest premium on the independence of our work and on doing it in a truly nonpartisan atmosphere. If there's one thing the Republicans, Democrats, and Independents here agree on, it's that no party has a monopoly on wisdom. A corollary of that independence and nonpartisanship is an institutional commitment to uphold, by our example, civility of discourse and debate as requirements for a healthy democracy. I believe extreme partisanship and attack politics increasingly threaten the health of our democracy. Brookings can be part of the solution to this problem, not just in what we do but in how we do it.[63]

The Brookings Institution, like many of its counterparts throughout the United States, professes to be policy-neutral. However, like all think tanks, its scholars and the studies they produce embrace a particular ideological orientation. As much as the Heritage Foundation is known for its conservative leanings, Brookings has a reputation for being more liberal or left of centre. This observation is not intended as a slight against either institute; it is simply a reality that cannot and should not be ignored. We should also recognize that as one of America's leading think tanks, the Brookings Institution has distinguished itself as a research organization which, for the most part, has remained faithful to the objectives outlined in its charter. Although it has undergone a number of structural changes since its creation, the guiding principles drafted by its founder have survived the passage of time.

The commitment of the Brookings Institution and other early twentieth-century policy research institutions to scholarly research reflects not only the vision of their founders but the desire of policy experts in the first decades of the 1900s to enhance governmental decision-making. For Margaret Olivia Sage, Andrew Carnegie, and his close friend Robert Brookings, government officials could develop and implement rational social, economic, and foreign policies if they relied on the advice of neutral policy experts instead of the opinions of individuals motivated solely by partisan interests. By so doing, public officials could more effectively administer government programs and policies. While some policy entrepreneurs established think tanks prior to and in the aftermath of World War I to improve the administration of government, others created research institutions with equally noble intentions in mind. Having observed the destruction caused by the war, Herbert Hoover set out to establish an organization in 1919 that would educate future generations about the causes and consequences of interstate conflict.

The Hoover Institution on War, Revolution and Peace

From its beginnings as a repository for documents and memorabilia on World War I, the Hoover Institution on the campus of Stanford University in Palo Alto, California, has become one of the most renowned think tanks in the United States. Its resident scholars are often portrayed as the loyal guardians of conservatism, willing to assist Republican administrations move even further to the right, but the organization was not initially created with policy-making goals in mind. On the contrary, while several Hoover scholars have played an important role in advising presidents and presidential candidates, including Richard Nixon, Ronald Reagan, Bob Dole, and more recently George W. Bush, Herbert Hoover (1874–1964), the thirty-first president of the United States, had as his primary objective in creating a research institution, not to recruit an elite group of influential policy experts, but to collect and preserve historical records.

Hoover's desire to build an institution dedicated to the study of war, revolution, and peace, can be traced to his experiences as head of the Commission for Relief in Belgium (CRB) during World War I. Appointed by the US ambassador in London to coordinate food relief efforts in wartorn Belgium, Hoover, a devout Quaker "motivated by humanitarian concerns,"[64] not only witnessed first-hand the devastation caused by war but, more importantly, recognized the necessity of educating future generations about the economic, social, and political ramifications of global warfare. While travelling across the English Channel on CRB business in late December 1914 or early January 1915, he read the autobiography of Andrew D. White, an eminent historian and diplomat who became Cornell University's first president. Inspired by White's obsession with accumulating historical documents on the French Revolution while studying in France during the 1850s, Hoover realized that he too was "in a unique position to collect fugitive literature" about another revolution.[65] According to George Nash, the author of a three-volume biography of Hoover,[66] "With the eagerness of a lifelong bibliophile, the decisiveness of an executive, and the assurance of a man of means, he resolved to undertake an audacious project similar to White's: the systematic collecting of contemporary documents on the Great War before they were lost to history."[67]

Before Hoover could seriously contemplate undertaking a project of such magnitude, he had to assemble a team of individuals willing to travel throughout Europe to collect vast amounts of documents. He also had to determine where these materials could be safely stored. For Hoover, there was little question as to where his collection of documents should be housed. Having graduated in 1895 from Stanford University, he had quickly established a reputation as one of the university's most generous benefactors. Therefore it seemed only natural for Hoover to look to his alma mater to maintain and preserve his collection. With the consent of Stanford University president Ray Lyman Wilbur and the board of trustees, Hoover's donation of $50,000 was accepted, and in 1919, arrangements were made to receive and catalogue materials on World War 1. And with the assistance of a handful of young Stanford graduates, Hoover set out across Europe to collect materials relating to the war. His ability to acquire a considerable quantity of important historical records led Wilbur to remark, "Hoover is the greatest pack rat of all time, whenever he leaves a ton of food, he picks up a pound of history."[68]

By 1922 the Hoover War Library, as it came to be called, contained 80,000 items, and as the collection grew, so too did Hoover's generous support. But as the War Library expanded in size and scope, he became concerned that his acquisitions might not be preserved as a single collection. His fears were not unwarranted. Indeed, on several occasions, Stanford library staff suggested that Hoover's growing collection be absorbed into the university library system. Moreover, frequent conflicts between the staff of the Hoover War Library and Stanford's head librarian, George T. Clark, over the maintenance of the war documents eventually convinced Hoover that it was necessary to construct a separate building to house his collection. His determination to protect the autonomous nature of the war collection can also be attributed to his desire to expand the role and function of the historical archive. In 1922–1923, after soliciting contributions from the CRB, Hoover revealed, apparently for the first time, "his deepening vision of a library that would function not just as a warehouse of books and manuscripts but as a centre for advanced research on contemporary history."[69]

In addition to expressing his desire to expand the scope of the Hoover War Library to include a research centre at Stanford, Hoover approached several private foundations in the early 1920s to support the creation of research institutes throughout the United States. According to Guy Alchon, "Hoover struck a technocratic bargain with the Carnegie Corporation, the Laura Spelman Rockefeller Memorial and the Rockefeller Foundation and the National Bureau of Economic Research to build a private association of planning and policy institutes across the country with an anti-statist outlook."[70]

In 1927 Hoover also launched several area research centres with the support of the Laura Spelman Rockefeller Memorial Fund. Among these were the Institute for Research on the German Revolution, headed by Ralph H. Lutz, and the Russian Revolution Institute, directed by Frank H. Golder and later by Harold Fisher. However, it was not until after World War II that area research centres began to proliferate, largely in response to the United States' expanding role in world affairs. Relying on Hoover's original initiatives and the generous support of the Ford, Rockefeller, and Carnegie foundations, hundreds of research institutes, world affairs councils, and foreign policy associations were created in the decades following the war.[71]

Hoover's commitment to building a network of policy research institutions throughout the United States rarely wavered, but it was the maintenance of the Hoover War Library that remained a priority. By the mid to late 1920s, however, his attention had shifted from expanding the library that bore his name to expanding his base of political support among the electorate. The Stanford-trained mining engineer and self-made millionaire from West Branch, Iowa, began to set his sights on the nation's highest office.

Hoover was not a stranger to the world of politics. He had served as secretary of commerce to Presidents Harding and Coolidge and run unsuccessfully for the Republican presidential nomination in 1920. Eight years later, according to presidential historian Robert Dallek, Hoover's "popularity and visibility easily won him the Republican nomination, and his campaign against Alfred E. Smith, the first Catholic to win a major party nomination, produced one of the greatest landslides in presidential history."[72]

Unfortunately for Hoover and the American people, the success he enjoyed in the public and private sectors did not carry over to his one tumultuous term in the Oval Office. One of America's least successful presidents, Hoover had a ringside seat to the stock market crash in October 1929 and the onset of the Great Depression. Moreover, despite playing such a pivotal role in creating research institutions that housed hundreds of academics across the United States, he ignored a petition signed by a thousand economists in 1930 urging him to veto the Smoot-Hawley Tariff, which imposed the highest tariff rates in US history. Intended to "protect struggling American businesses, [the bill] instead provoke[d] an international trade war that worsen[ed] the Great Depression."[73]

It was not until Hoover returned from Washington in 1933, after being defeated by Franklin Roosevelt and his promise of a New Deal, that he began to devote his energies to expanding the library.[74] Among the many activities of the library that Hoover encouraged or participated in directly was the creation of the Hoover War Library Publications series, which began in 1932, his last year in office. By 1935 nine documentary volumes had been published, and plans were made to distribute twenty-four volumes of documents on Hoover's European relief work in 1914–22. As Peter Duignan, a senior fellow at the Hoover Institution, points out, by the mid–1930s "Hoover's library was becoming a productive research centre."[75]

As the library's scope and functions were changing in the early 1930s, so too was the course of world history. After Adolf Hitler[76] and the National Socialist Party assumed power in Germany in 1932, a new crisis would soon engulf the international community. Once again Hoover believed that it was of the utmost importance to document this period in history. He and his colleagues took advantage of their contacts throughout Europe to gather and store important World War II documents.

To more accurately reflect the library's growing collections, its name was changed in 1938 to the Hoover Library on War, Revolution and Peace. And in early 1941 Hoover's desire to house his documents in a separate building was finally realized after two decades, when the Hoover Tower was completed. At the dedication ceremonies on 20 June 1941, he explained why he and his colleagues devoted so much time and effort to create this historical archive: "I suppose someone will wonder why all this trouble and expense to preserve these records ... If we assume that humanity is going to abandon the lessons of its own experience, the whole of this collection is useless, except to the casual visitor. But sometimes the voice of experience does call out to stop, look, and listen. And sometimes people respond to that call ...

The purpose of this institution is to promote peace. Its records stand as a challenge to those who promote war. They should attract those who search for peace. I therefore dedicate this building to those purposes."[77]

In the ensuing years, Hoover continued to work tirelessly on behalf of the Hoover Institution on War, Revolution and Peace, as it became known in 1956, and despite occasional conflicts with his staff and the trustees of Stanford University, he remained faithful to the goals and objectives of the institution. For him, the main purpose of the institution was "research, training of men in foreign affairs, and the development of scholarship and knowledge."[78] On countless occasions, Hoover emphasized that it was "not an ordinary library nor a 'packrat operation,' but a dynamic institution which sought to offer effective guidance for the future of our people and of mankind everywhere."[79]

Expanding on the purposes of the Institution, Hoover stated to a potential donor: As to war: "... to aid the defense of the U.S." As to revolution: the purpose is, "by research and publications, to protect the American way of life from evil ideologies and to reaffirm the validity of the American system." As to peace: "By research and publications to present the world's experience." He added that by publishing its documents "without comment or attempt at interpretation the institution could provide the raw materials upon which official action can be guided and historical studies can be founded."[80]

Hoover was convinced that his organization could play an important role in increasing public understanding about the causes and consequences of war, but he did not appear to assign a high priority to involving the Hoover Institution in the daily machinations of Washington politics. Since he often criticized the undue influence of pressure groups, it is not surprising that he portrayed the Hoover Institution as a research centre willing to provide scholars with access to its materials, rather than as an organization committed to influencing government officials on specific pieces of legislation. In fact, other than calling on some of his colleagues at the Hoover Institution to assume high-level positions in his administration, there is little evidence to suggest that there was a strong link between Hoover scholars and the US government between 1933 and 1960.[81]

In addition to preserving the Hoover Institution's intellectual independence by discouraging its involvement in partisan politics, Hoover wanted to ensure that the Stanford University board of trustees could not acquire unlimited administrative control over his organization. As early as 1930, he realized that Stanford's desire to limit the institution's autonomy would inevitably lead to serious tensions between the two bodies. As noted, Hoover was initially concerned about early attempts by Stanford's head librarian to oversee his war collection. He also became increasingly frustrated by Stanford's efforts to exercise greater control over the institution's staff and research projects. After several tense meetings with Stanford president Wallace Sterling in 1959, during which Hoover threatened, on more than one occasion, to withdraw his considerable financial contributions to the university, Sterling agreed to pass a resolution that would safeguard the Hoover Institution's administrative autonomy.

On 21 May 1959 the Stanford board of trustees issued a new agreement that in effect gave Hoover what he had fought for for so many years. An earlier resolution was rescinded and the Hoover Institution was no longer to be considered a separate division of the university, but was proclaimed "an independent institution within the frame of Stanford University."[82] Ironically, since 1960 Stanford, not the Hoover Institution, has attempted to protect its intellectual integrity by limiting what some faculty members consider to be the unethical involvement of a research centre in federal politics. While the two organizations have survived a stormy marriage for over eighty years, it is nonetheless important to examine the principal source of conflict in more detail.

When W. Glenn Campbell, a thirty-five-year-old Canadian economist with a doctorate from Harvard, became director of the Hoover Institution in 1960, he began to employ many of the marketing techniques he had developed as director of research at the American Enterprise Association (now the American Enterprise Institute) to enhance the visibility of the Hoover. Drawing on his skills as an academic and a policy entrepreneur, Campbell devoted most of his time in the mid–1960s and early 1970s to fundraising and expanding the research programs at the institution. He also relied on his personal friendship with then California governor Ronald Reagan and a number of other political leaders to strengthen the Hoover Institution's ties to the policy-making community. As noted in the introduction, when Reagan sought the Republican presidential nomination in 1976, he relied on several Hoover scholars for policy advice.[83]

Although resident scholars at Hoover welcomed the opportunity to share their expertise with policy-makers, their propensity to espouse conservative views during the turbulent decade of the 1960s was not well received at Stanford University. At the height of the Vietnam War, Campbell appeared before an angry crowd of students and faculty in front of the Hoover Tower not only to discourage them from breaking windows and storming the tower but to demand that they respect the academic freedom of the Hoover

Institution. Unfortunately for Campbell, this attempt to protect himself and the institution from the wrath of Stanford students and faculty members would not be an isolated incident. In the ensuing years, it became clear there would be little harmony between a liberal university and a conservative think tank located on its campus. It became equally apparent that Campbell would not be discouraged from transforming the Hoover Institution into one of America's most visible think tanks. A handful of Hoover scholars, including Martin Anderson, contributed policy ideas to the Nixon campaign in 1968, but it was during the Reagan years that the institution and its resident scholars enjoyed the greatest visibility. And it was during this time that tensions between Hoover and Stanford became even more pronounced.

When several scholars from the Hoover Institution became involved in the Reagan campaign in 1980, some students and faculty criticized the institution for its overt partisanship. Since the institution is considered part of Stanford University, its critics launched a campaign to persuade the board of trustees that it was unethical for a university research centre – not to mention illegal for a non-profit, "non-partisan" think tank – to participate directly in the political process. As noted above, according to the Internal Revenue Code, think tanks, as tax-exempt, non-profit organizations, are prohibited from publicly endorsing a candidate running for office. But according to some Hoover fellows, those criticizing their association with Ronald Reagan were not concerned about protecting the integrity of Stanford University and its affiliated centres. After all, several Stanford faculty members had advised John F. Kennedy during the 1960 campaign. They were, to put it bluntly, upset with Hoover scholars who were eager and willing to assist a Republican secure the presidency. As one Hoover scholar remarked, "there is an optical illusion at Stanford. The [Hoover] tower doesn't tilt to the right, the campus leans to the left." In short, what may have begun as a debate over academic freedom soon became a contest over political ideology.[84]

Despite the growing controversy at Stanford, the director of the Hoover Institution and his colleagues did not hesitate to assist Ronald Reagan in his attempts to become the fortieth president of the United States. In fact, the institution took great pride in publicizing its association with Reagan in several of its annual reports published in the early 1980s. The relationship between Reagan and the Hoover Institution was so strong that Reagan was prepared to build his presidential library at Stanford. However, as a result of a bitter conflict between Stanford faculty and the team of advisers assembled to negotiate the construction of the Reagan library, Ronald Reagan withdrew his offer and built his library in Simi Valley, California, where in the summer of 2004, he was laid to rest. While the involvement of the Hoover Institution and its scholars in the Reagan administration will be examined in more detail later, it is important not to misinterpret the primary objective of the organization. Hoover, as it is commonly known, is foremost a research institution that houses one of the most important historical archives in the world. Many of its critics have questioned and continue to question the partisan nature of this organization, but its contribution to the scholarly community cannot be ignored.

The Council on Foreign Relations

While Herbert Hoover was making plans to establish a library to educate future generations about the nature of war, an elite group of academics, lawyers, businessmen, and government leaders with a keen interest in international relations was gathering in New York to discuss and debate America's changing role in world affairs. Meeting once a month in the Metropolitan Club, the thirty participants, led by Nobel Peace Prize winner Elihu Root (1845–1937), the former secretary of war, secretary of state, US senator, and first president of the Carnegie Endowment for International Peace, established a special dinner club called the Council on Foreign Relations. The origin of the club meetings was recorded in the council's 1919 handbook:

In the late spring of 1918 a few gentlemen came together at a conference at the Metropolitan Club, New York, to discuss the most interesting and vital subjects concerned with the United States and its relations with the rest of the world. Two or three meetings were held, which showed that much could be learned and much good could be accomplished by such conferences, made up of people who were concerned in the world's affairs in a large way ... The object of the Council on Foreign Relations is to afford a continuous conference on foreign affairs, bringing together at each meeting international thinkers so that in the course of a year several hundred expert minds in finance, industry, education, statecraft and science will have been brought to bear on international problems. It is a board of Initiation – a Board of Invention. It plans to cooperate with the Government and all existing agencies and to bring them all into constructive accord.[85]

Although Root and his colleagues examined many important world issues, it was not until 1921, three years after the meetings at the Metropolitan Club began, that the Council on Foreign Relations was transformed from a monthly dinner club into a permanent research institution devoted to the study of foreign affairs.[86] Since then it has become a distinguished policy forum that has opened its doors to many of America's leading corporate and political leaders.

The idea of creating a non-profit, non-partisan research organization dedicated "to improved understanding of American foreign policy and international affairs"[87] emerged when twenty-one members of an elite group called The Inquiry[88] were invited to accompany Woodrow Wilson to the Paris Peace Conference in 1919. Frustrated by Wilson's refusal to accept their advice and disillusioned with many of the provisions included in the Treaty of Versailles, members of the American delegation began to discuss the prospects of creating a transatlantic research organization with their British counterparts. The two delegations were concerned about the lack of informed commentary on international affairs and agreed that it was necessary to "provide the material from which those who are most influential and who have the greatest amount of knowledge, comprehension and perspective in foreign affairs can form public opinion."[89] The newly proposed institute would, according to the British *Saturday Review*, represent "the revolt of the Peace makers against the Peace." It would gather "the young men in Paris [who] thought more, knew more, and learned more then the old men who actually signed the treaty."[90]

Despite agreeing to create a private research institution with branches in London and New York, the American and British delegates made little progress in achieving their objectives in the next two years. By June 1921, as anti-British sentiments grew more intense in the United States,[91] it appeared that a joint American-British research institution would no longer be politically feasible. Consequently, the Americans informed Lionel Curtis, a British proponent of the proposed research institution, that American public opinion would not permit them to go ahead. After telling Curtis of their decision, two members of the American delegation, Whitney H. Shepardson and Isaiah Bowman, asked Elihu Root if he would merge his Council on Foreign Relations with the body established at the Paris Peace Conference. With Root's consent, the two groups were consolidated and incorporated as the Council on Foreign Relations Inc. on 29 July 1921.[92]

Following its incorporation, the fifteen-man board of the council issued a statement reaffirming the goals of the institution: "The Council on Foreign Relations aims to provide a continuous conference on the international aspects of America's political, economic and financial problems ... It simply is a group of men concerned in spreading a knowledge of international relations, and, in particular, in developing a reasoned American foreign policy."[93] To contribute to a "reasoned American foreign policy," the council not only continued to meet on a regular basis to discuss and publish reports on various aspects of international relations, but decided to launch a quarterly journal in 1922 entitled *Foreign Affairs* to present the views and commentaries of distinguished political leaders and academics. The Council on Foreign Relations has since grown from a monthly dinner club comprised of a few dozen men to an organization with over 3,500 members nationwide. Its impressive membership list of corporate and political leaders[94] and its striking headquarters in the Harold Pratt House, a five-storey mansion on the corner of 68th Street and Park Avenue, has led some observers to describe it disparagingly as "the best club in New York," "the government in exile," and a "school for statesmen."[95] Membership in the council and its affiliates[96] is by invitation only, but in recent years the organization has attempted to make itself more accessible to the public. In its 1989 annual report, the CFR stated, "As a leader in the expanding community of institutions concerned with American foreign policy, the Council recognizes its responsibility to contribute to the public dialogue on significant international issues. All Council publications, and its journal, are available to the general public."[97]

The Council on Foreign Relations, by providing a forum for some of America's most influential citizens to discuss world affairs is often portrayed more as a meeting place for the elite than as a research institution committed to analyzing the changing nature of international relations. However, while it is difficult to ignore that many of the council's members have or continue to hold prominent posts in the US government or in the private sector, it is equally difficult to disregard the institution's contribution to scholarly literature. In addition to publishing one of the leading journals in the field, the Council on Foreign Relations has produced hundreds of studies since its incorporation,[98] many of which continue to generate debate in the academic community. Moreover, some of its research undertakings, including its renowned War and Peace Studies project (1939–45)[99] and its more recent work on terrorism, illustrate the important contribution scholars at the council have made and continue to make to providing policy expertise to government officials.

Recognizing from its inception that advising political leaders on foreign policy issues was one of its primary goals, the Council on Foreign Relations also sought to emulate other early twentieth-century research institutions by insulating itself from partisan interests. In its 1989 annual report the CFR reaffirmed its original commitment to protect the institution's intellectual autonomy. According to the report, "The Council shall not take any position on questions of foreign policy, and no other person is authorized to speak, or purport to speak for the Council on such matters."[100] This statement may have been included simply to protect the CFR's tax-exempt status under the Internal Revenue Code,[101] yet it reveals a distinguishing character-istic of think tanks created during the first decades of the 1900s. Unlike many advocacy think tanks that include similar statements in their publica-tions but nonetheless proudly reveal their political leanings, the Council on Foreign Relations appears genuinely committed to preserving its role as a non-partisan research institution. Critics of the council have referred to it both as a bastion of bolshevism[102] and as the protective guardian of Wall Street, yet its impressive membership list of prominent Republicans and Democrats seems to provide ample opportunity for the expression of diverse opinions and views. Furthermore, to ensure its status as an inde-pendent policy research institution, the CFR "has no affiliation with, receives no funding from, and does no contract research for the U.S. govern-ment or any other government."[103]

The Council on Foreign Relations' commitment to educating Republican and Democratic administrations about important policy issues reflects another common trait among early twentieth-century research institutions. The think tanks described thus far were created under different circum-stances and pursued a wide array of research projects, but their principal objective was to enhance governmental decision-making by offering politi-cal leaders informed advice on a host of public policy issues. In short, pro-viding a stimulating environment in which to conduct scholarly research, rather than indoctrinating policy-makers with a particular ideological posi-tion, inspired the creation of research institutions during the first decades of the twentieth century.

THE BIRTH OF GOVERNMENT CONTRACTORS AND SPECIALISTS: 1946–1970

As the Council on Foreign Relations and other research institutions con-tinued to advise decision-makers in the years after World War I and World War II, by the late 1940s a new generation of think tanks was beginning to appear on the horizon. Philanthropic foundations, corporations, and pri-vate citizens had played an integral role in establishing and supporting many think tanks created during the first decades of the twentieth century; after World War II the US government began to share the role of benevolent donor. Acknowledging the invaluable contribution of defence scientists dur-ing the war, the government recognized the enormous benefits that could be derived by funding private and university-based research and development centres. By tapping into the expertise of engineers, physicists, biologists, statisticians, and social scientists, government officials hoped to meet many of the new challenges confronting the United States as it assumed the role of a global hegemonic power.

The Rand Corporation

Leading the new generation of think tanks or government contractors was the Rand Corporation in Santa Monica, California, now known simply as RAND.[104] In late 1945, acting on the initiative of Arthur Raymond and Frank Collbohm, two engineers from the Douglas Aircraft Company, General Henry H. "Hap" Arnold, commanding general of the Army Air Forces (the Department of the Air Force was established in September 1947) and a popular figure on Roosevelt's Joint Chiefs of Staff,[105] proposed a $10-million contract with Douglas to fund Project Rand "for the study of V–1 and V–2 rocket techniques and other intercontinental air techniques of the future."[106] The new venture was greeted with enthusiasm, but over the next two years the relationship between the air force and Douglas soured. Concerned that the Douglas Aircraft Company was more interested in making profits than contributing to the defense of the United States, the air force supported the removal of Project Rand from Douglas.[107] Yet, despite the many formidable obstacles threatening the project from the beginning, the air force welcomed the creation of an independent, non-profit corporation committed to safeguarding American defense and security interests. With an initial capital investment of $1 million and close to $5 million in remaining funds from Project Rand, the Rand Corporation was chartered in May 1948 to "further and promote scientific, educational, and charitable purposes, all for the public welfare and security of the United States of America"[108]

Under the direction of Frank Collbohm, who left Douglas to become Rand's first president, a group of talented scientists, including Bernard Brodie and Herman Kahn, who would later go on to form the Hudson Institute, gathered at the ocean-front think tank to exchange ideas about how to protect and promote American national security interests during the nuclear age. Using systems analysis, game theory, and various simulation exercises, Rand scientists began to "think about the unthinkable." Faced with the prospects of a nuclear exchange, the Rand Corporation devoted itself in the early post-war years to advising the air force on how best to protect the United States against enemy attacks.[109]

RAND continues to receive the bulk of its $200-million-plus budget from the US air force, US army, and the Office of the Secretary of Defense,[110] but its research interests are no longer confined to defense and national security issues. As the largest think tank in the United States, RAND, through its

1,600 researchers and staff members, carries out research in a dozen major areas, including health care, civil and criminal justice, science and technology, and environment and infrastructure. Most of RAND's staff work in its Santa Monica headquarters or in its office in Washington, DC. Others are based at its Council for Aid to Education in New York City, RAND Europe in the Netherlands, or one of its smaller sites.

In addition to overseeing an extensive research program which has resulted in the publication of thousands of books, policy briefs, reports, and academic journals, RAND established it own graduate school in 1970 to help train future policy analysts. The RAND Graduate School stresses the importance of educating students to examine complex policy issues from a multidisciplinary perspective. RAND has also served as a prototype for other research and development organizations, including the Washington-based Urban Institute.

The Urban Institute

The Urban Institute, according to Paul Dickson, "had a typically long bureaucratic birth."[111] Although its conception can be traced to the Kennedy administration, it was not until President Lyndon Johnson put his weight behind the initiative that the prospect of creating a think tank which could address the many domestic problems plaguing the United States during the 1960s gained momentum. As noted in its 1998 annual report, "the Urban Institute got its start in 1968 as the brainchild of a blue-ribbon panel set up by President Lyndon Johnson to monitor and evaluate the Great Society Initiatives that sprang from some 400 laws that had been passed since 1964."[112] Johnson believed that the Urban Institute could bridge "the gulf between the scholar in search of truth and the decision-maker in search of progress."[113]

Answering the need "for independent analysis of government performance and for data-driven research on America's cities and their residents in the wake of widespread urban unrest," the Urban Institute devoted its early years to examining persistent domestic problems such as poverty, education finance, unemployment, urban housing shortages and decay, urban transportation gaps, and the need for welfare reform.[114] Since then it has greatly expanded its research program. With a staff of over two hundred and a budget exceeding $50 million, the Urban Institute conducts research in several areas, including education, population, health, and human resources. It is currently involved in research projects with partners in more than forty-five states and twenty countries. Although 85 per cent of its research agenda is financed by public agencies and foundations, the institute has made a concerted effort to broaden its base of support over the years. It lists dozens of private supporters as contributors. Moreover, the Urban Institute's $50-million endowment provides added financial security.

Like many think tanks created during the Progressive Era, the Urban Institute jealously guards its institutional independence. Despite relying heavily on government support, it has been able to insulate itself from outside interference. According to its former president William Gorham, the government has largely refrained from interfering in work that it has funded.[115] The Urban Institute continues to publish dozens of studies each year, and its staff are often quoted in the mainstream media.

The extent to which think tanks depend on federal funding varies considerably,[116] yet the continued dependence of some highly visible think tanks on government contracts may make them particularly vulnerable to political and budgetary pressures. As a result, although government contractors perform the same function as first-generation think tanks, their reliance on government grants and contracts may create the perception, rightly or wrongly, that their policy advice is slanted.

The growth of federally funded research and development organizations since the late 1940s and early 1950s not only altered the complexion of the policy-making community but once again reaffirmed the government's growing dependence on policy experts. As the many domestic and foreign policy issues confronting the United States became increasingly complex, members of the Executive and Congress increasingly looked beyond their individual departments and agencies for direction and guidance. As James McGann points out, "while it would seem that increasing the professional staffs of Congress and the executive branch and establishing think tanks within government would reduce the demand for independent policy research, just the opposite has occurred."[117]

Since many of America's leading economists and scientists were employed at prominent universities or independent research centres after the war, it made sense for government departments and agencies searching for policy expertise to provide these institutions with generous funding. But despite the close and growing ties between government contractors and the federal government, the policy-making community did not become dominated by federally funded research institutions in the post–World War II era. On the contrary, while a handful of government contractors such as RAND and the Urban Institute carved out important niches in the 1950s and 1960s, by the mid to late 1970s a small but vocal group of highly aggressive and ideologically driven policy research institutions known as advocacy think tanks began to make their presence known.

A NEW GENERATION OF THINK TANKS: FROM
POLICY RESEARCH TO POLITICAL ADVOCACY,
1971–1994

The Brookings Institution, the Council on Foreign Relations, and several other research institutions continued to devote considerable resources to examining public policy issues in the decades after the war. Their desire to provide impartial policy expertise (if this is indeed possible) to government officials in order to serve the public interest would not, however, be inherited by the next generation of think tanks. Indeed, while many of the newly emerging think tanks established credible research programs, their primary goal was not to pursue social science research but to advance their ideological agenda in the political arena. By relying on a variety of lobbying techniques to market their ideas, advocacy think tanks began to take root in and around the nation's capital. But why did such a massive proliferation of think tanks occur after World War II? More specifically, why did so many think tanks specializing in foreign policy emerge? A number of possible explanations are worth exploring.[118]

First, as a result of assuming the global responsibilities of a hegemonic power after World War II, the United States had to rely increasingly on policy analysts for advice on how to conduct its foreign relations. Moreover, as the American bureaucracy significantly expanded after the war, in response to growing domestic and foreign concerns, so too did the opportunities for policy experts to share their insights with government officials. According to Dr Dennis Bark, senior fellow at the Hoover Institution, the combination of these factors permitted such think tanks as RAND, the Council on Foreign Relations, and the Carnegie Endowment for International Peace to have "an enormous impact on US foreign policy" during this period.[119]

The considerable access these and other think tanks had to policy-makers during the first half of the twentieth century may very well have inspired the creation of other research institutions determined to leave their mark on US foreign policy. However, since many of the most prominent foreign policy advisers to presidents after World War II, such as George Kennan, Dean Acheson, Henry Kissinger, Zbigniew Brzezinski, McGeorge Bundy, and Dean Rusk, to name a few, gained national prominence while they were employed in universities or in the foreign service, it is difficult to argue that their success was the sole motivating factor for individuals to create dozens of think tanks in the post-war era.[120]

The impact of the anti-war and civil rights movements in awakening the public consciousness to political and social turmoil at home and abroad may have also contributed to the proliferation of think tanks. Not unlike interest groups mobilizing popular support against the Vietnam War, many so-called liberal think tanks, including, though by no means limited to, the Institute for Policy Studies, were created to provide scholars with an opportunity to challenge the underlying motivations of American domestic and foreign policy.[121]

Similarly, during the late 1960s and early 1970s, as several conservative academics were becoming increasingly disillusioned with what they considered to be a growing liberal bias among the faculty at American universities, an increasing demand for autonomous research institutions emerged. Dr Thomas Henriksen, senior fellow at the Hoover Institution, maintains that think tanks such as the Institute for Contemporary Studies (1972), the Heritage Foundation (1973), and the Cato Institute (1977) were founded to allow conservative academics to pursue their research interests in a more congenial environment, an observation consistent with statements made earlier by Ambassador Jeane Kirkpatrick.[122]

Generous corporate financing and tax exemptions for non-profit organizations have also provided an impetus for policy entrepreneurs, political leaders, and aspiring office-holders to create their own think tanks.[123] By establishing private think tanks as non-profit organizations and employing sophisticated direct-mailing techniques, founders of policy research institutions could, often with the assistance of prominent political leaders,[124] encourage corporations, philanthropic foundations, and private citizens to contribute thousands of dollars to support and advance their particular ideological and political perspectives on domestic and foreign policy issues. Contributing to the coffers of think tanks could also, according to some fundraising letters, provide corporate and private citizens with increased access to decision-makers.[125]

In addition to various tax loopholes and the growing desire of policy experts to pursue their research in a more hospitable environment, the proliferation of think tanks can be attributed to the declining role of political parties in the United States. As Kent Weaver, a senior fellow at the Brookings Institution and a professor of public policy at Georgetown University, points out, "Weak and relatively non-ideological parties have enhanced think tanks' role in several ways. The most important effect of the U.S. party system is that parties have not themselves taken a major role in policy development by establishing sizeable policy research arms of their own. Think tanks have helped fill this void."[126]

Unlike in Germany, where political parties have created their own political foundations to conduct policy research, in the United States, decision-makers in the White House and on Capitol Hill cannot draw on the expertise of party-based foundations, but must solicit policy advice from multiple sources. The absence of party research institutions and the decline in importance of political parties in the United States, combined with a highly decentralized and fragmented political system, have provided think tanks with considerable opportunities to market their ideas. The extent to which the institutional structure of the American government has enabled them to exercise policy influence will be explored in more detail in chapter 4.

The virtual explosion of advocacy think tanks since the early 1970s has not only contributed to the politicization of policy expertise but, perhaps more importantly, altered the relationship between think tanks and government. As more think tanks began to participate in the policy-making community, the strategies they employed to increase their visibility changed dramatically. In an environment where they now had to compete for the attention of policy-makers and the media, their priorities began to change. Providing policy-makers with timely and policy relevant advice, rather than engaging in long-term scholarly research, became the primary concern for this new generation of think tanks.

The Heritage Foundation, which recently celebrated its thirtieth year in operation, is often regarded as the prototypical advocacy think tank because of its unbridled desire and commitment to transform its institutional agenda into political reality. From its newly expanded stately office building, located minutes from Capitol Hill, the foundation has left an indelible mark in the policy-making community. A strong advocate of free market economics and an ardent proponent of missile defense, Heritage has played a key role in leading a new generation of think tanks. Political advocacy was previously frowned upon by more traditional think tanks, but Heritage has made it not only acceptable but, for some policy-makers, desirable. The foundation's success in marketing its ideas and the proliferation of other avowedly ideological think tanks in the latter half of the twentieth century can be traced to the creation of the American Enterprise Institute.

The American Enterprise Institute for Public Policy Research

Established in 1943 by Lewis H. Brown, president of the Johns-Mansville Corporation, to promote the virtues of "free-market economics in the face of a rising tide of Keynesianism,"[127] the American Enterprise Association (AEA) existed in relative obscurity for over a decade. Although Brown hoped his organization would effectively challenge the growing influence of the Brookings Institution, by 1954 the AEA only had four full-time employees and an annual budget barely exceeding $80,000. In an attempt to transform his organization from a small business association that analyzed economic policies for corporate clients into an influential policy research institution, Brown turned to the AEA's executive vice-president, William J. Baroody Sr.

Baroody, who had formerly served with the US Chamber of Commerce, shared Brown's vision of a research institution committed to promoting free market economics. And after becoming president in 1962, he took the first step toward restructuring and revitalizing the AEA by changing its name to the American Enterprise Institute (AEI), "so that it sounded less like a trade association and more like an intellectual centre."[128] Committed to promoting conservatism as the "dominant strain of thought,"[129] Baroody invented a new role for policy entrepreneurs – that of impresario of intellectuals.[130] As Sidney Blumenthal, a journalist and former adviser to President Clinton, points out, "AEI was his stage. Conservative thinkers would rehearse ideas there, and then present them to political leaders."[131]

Combining the skills of an advertising executive, a corporate fundraiser, and a political strategist, Baroody turned AEI from an insignificant business association into the "MGM of Washington think tanks."[132] By recruiting some of America's most prominent economists, political scientists, and former government officials, including Milton Friedman, Jeane Kirkpatrick, and the late Herbert Stein, he created a strong platform from which to promote the organization's conservative beliefs. However, unlike Robert Brookings and Andrew Carnegie, who sought to insulate their research institutions from partisan interests, Baroody took pride in publicizing AEI's mission. Guided by the belief that the competition of ideas is fundamental to the survival of a free and democratic society, he took several measures to ensure that AEI's conservative message would be heard. By inviting government leaders to participate in seminars, publishing books and periodicals, and encouraging resident scholars to solidify their ties to corporate leaders and public officials, he carved out an important niche for AEI in the policy-making community.

AEI's rise to prominence can be largely attributed to Baroody's vision and guidance, but it may also have been facilitated by the changing direction of political winds in the United States during the late 1970s. According to Patricia Linden, "It was the right idea at the right time, a period when the insistent voice of the neo-conservative think tanks began to invade opinion- and decision-makers' consciousness, and present formidable rivalry for research dollars as well. AEI's glittering lineup not only invigorated the organization with fresh ideas, it all but guaranteed lineage, attention, credibility and funding. The institute rocketed to prominence: a world-class organization peopled with multi-disciplinary star analysts whose wide-ranging views ... gave conservatism an intellectual depth."[133] In 1978, after devoting more than twenty years to transforming AEI into one of Washington's leading think tanks, William Baroody Sr stepped down as president and invited his son, William Baroody Jr, to guide the organization into the 1980s. A former press secretary to Melvin Laird, secretary of defense in the Nixon administration[134] and the principal architect of the Ford administration's Office of Public Liaison, Baroody Jr was well qualified to market AEI's basic philosophy. Under his leadership, the institute's research program was expanded to encompass governmental, social, and international affairs, and several former officials of the Ford administration, including the president himself, who became a distinguished fellow at AEI after leaving public office, were hired to further enhance the prestige and visibility of the organization. But like his father, Baroody Jr realized that unless AEI's ideas were properly marketed, the institution would be unable to exercise influence on Capitol Hill and in the White House. Consequently, in the ensuing years, he relied on his extensive experience in media relations to increase AEI's exposure in Washington. With the confidence of a prizefighter standing over his defeated opponent, Baroody extolled the virtues of marketing the institute's research products:

I make no bones about marketing ... We pay as much attention to the dissemination of product as to the content. We're probably the first major think tank to get into the electronic media. We hire ghost writers for scholars to produce op-ed articles that are sent out to one hundred and one cooperating newspapers – three pieces every two weeks. And we have a press luncheon monthly. [AEI] also produces a monthly television show on public policy shown on more than four hundred stations, a weekly radio talk show on more than 180 stations, and publishes four magazines (*Regulation, Public Opinion, The AEI Economist, Foreign Policy and Defense Review*), legislative analyses and books ... It's important for them [AEI scholars and government officials] to deal with public issues that permeate the environment in which they have to do business ... That's become clear to them.[135]

Baroody's preoccupation with marketing AEI and its products to policymakers and to the public began to generate concern among the organization's board members in the mid–1980s. The appointment of close to three dozen AEI scholars to government posts, boards, or commissions in the Reagan administration reflected the organization's growing visibility, but Baroody's inability to properly manage AEI's research program began to cause major setbacks. In addition to blaming him for mismanaging funds,[136] conservative critics argued that while the United States was moving comfortably to the right, AEI was drifting too far toward the centre of the political spectrum.

As the rising tide of conservatism swept across the United States in the mid–1980s, conservative foundations began to look to think tanks that were willing and able to promote ideas consistent with their mandate. For example, in 1986, fearing that AEI was not playing a leading role in the conservative revolution, two prominent organizations, the Olin Foundation and the Reader's Digest Association, withdrew their financial support from AEI and gave it to the Heritage Foundation claiming that the former had strayed too far from its rightward course.[137] Faced with increasing criticism from board members and corporate sponsors, Baroody was fired and eventually replaced by Christopher DeMuth, a former official in the Reagan administration.[138] After leaving AEI, Baroody admitted that "he created too rich a feast and served it too fast."[139] DeMuth appears to have learned from his predecessor's mistakes. Commenting on the primary goal of AEI, he stated, "We will continue to be a research institution rather than a marketing institution."[140] In AEI's 2003 annual report, DeMuth and Chairman Bruce Kovner once again stress the importance of AEI as a research institution. They note, "It was a year of unusual risks and opportunities in economic, health care, trade and regulatory policy. AEI responded with an outpouring of research, publications, and conferences of exceptional quality and influence – an apt tribute to the Institution's six decades of work at the center of policy-making.[141]

With a staff of over a hundred and an annual budget in excess of $24 million,[142] AEI conducts research in three main areas: Economic Policy Studies, Foreign and Defense Policy Studies, and Social and Political Studies. Each area is further subdivided into several program and policy areas. In addition to pursuing active research in these areas, which account for over 70 per cent of its budget, AEI has not lost sight of the importance of marketing its ideas, a subject that we will return to in chapter 4. It also understands the importance of increasing its visibility. In part, it has done so by hiring several former government officials and advisers, including Richard Perle, a member of the Pentagon's Defense Policy Board, former speaker of the House Newt Gingrich, Lawrence Lindsey, former chairman of the National Economic Council, Senator Fred Thompson, and David Frum, a former speech writer in the George W. Bush administration. As Jeffrey Gedmin, a former research fellow at AEI, points out, the institute "falls between two worlds,"[143] the secluded world of academic research and the real world of Washington politics.

Notwithstanding the many obstacles AEI has faced in its sixty-year history, it has left a lasting imprint on the policy-making community. From its beginnings as a proponent of free market economics, the American Enterprise Institute has paved the way for the creation of other advocacy think tanks in the United States. By transforming the role of think tanks from traditional non-partisan research institutions to vehicles for the expression of political beliefs, AEI is to a large extent responsible for paving the way for third-generation think tanks. As Burton Yale Pines, former senior vice-president and director of research at the Heritage Foundation, pointed out, "AEI is like a big gun on an offshore battleship. We are the landing party. If they hadn't softened it up, we wouldn't have landed."[144] Building on AEI's achievements in marketing its research findings, Heritage has taken political advocacy to new heights. In fact, for many observers of Washington politics, Heritage is the quintessential advocacy think tank.

The Heritage Foundation

Established in 1974 by Paul Weyrich and Edwin Feulner with $250,000 in seed money from the late Colorado brewer Joseph Coors, the Heritage Foundation rocketed from relative obscurity in the 1970s to become one of Washington's most visible think tanks during the 1980s. Emphasizing America's need to reassert its military resolve and demanding less government intervention in the economy, its conservative message was music to Ronald Reagan's ears. Heritage has continued to enjoy success in promoting its conservative beliefs to policy-makers in more recent presidential administrations and, as will be discussed, has had a profound impact in shaping critical policy issues. As Heritage Board chairman David Brown and Heritage president Edwin Feulner noted in the organization's 2003 annual report, "Thirty years ago, America ended its involvement in the Vietnam War ... 'Watergate' entered the national lexicon ... lines formed at gas pumps ... And the Heritage Foundation was born. We didn't make news back then. We barely made our payroll for our staff of 10. But it was the start of something that today animates the conservative movement, informs Washington policy-making and helps shape our country's future."[145]

For Feulner, Heritage's president since 1977, think tanks, like corporations, must properly market their products in order to capture the attention of their key target audiences, a guiding principle enshrined in the organization. "There's an old saying in business: 'Nothing happens until somebody sells something.' In the ideas industry, nobody sells like The Heritage Foundation. [Since 1974], we've marketed conservative policy solutions to those who make or shape national policy. Of course, dozens of Washington-based think tanks – and hundreds of special interest groups do the same. What sets Heritage apart is our 'sales departments' [Government Relations, Communications and Marketing, and External Relations], which are the best in the business."[146] While Feulner was well acquainted with marketing techniques, having graduated with an MBA from the Wharton School of Commerce and Finance at the University of Pennsylvania, the idea of establishing a think tank to provide decision-makers with timely, informative, and policy-relevant information did not take hold until he was employed as a congressional aide to Republican Philip Crane of Illinois in the early 1970s. As Feulner recalls, it was during a discussion with fellow aide Paul Weyrich that the idea for creating the Heritage Foundation surfaced.

Weyrich and I were having lunch together in the Senate Office building and he showed me a study that had the pros and cons on the SST [Supersonic Transport]. It was a good analysis, but it arrived on his desk the day after the vote took place. We both kicked that around and said, "Wouldn't it be great if there were an institution that delivered the kind of timely, useable policy analysis so that those of us working on the Hill could really make use of it?" I immediately called up the President of the organization to praise him for this thorough piece of research and ask why we did not receive it until after the debate and the vote. His answer: they did not want to influence the vote. That was when the idea for The Heritage Foundation was born.[147]

From the outset, Feulner realized that if his organization was to compete successfully in "the battle of ideas,"[148] it would have to provide decision-makers with up-to-date and digestible information on domestic and foreign affairs. That is why the Heritage Foundation specializes in distributing one-to-two-page summaries on a wide range of policy issues to each member of Congress. Aware that politicians rarely have the time, inclination, or patience to sift through a several-hundred-page study, Heritage built its research program around producing concise and timely reports. As Feulner points out, "We initiated and we specialize in the area of quick-response public policy research and in marketing academic works for public policy consumption."[149] Unlike research institutions that are reticent to distribute studies which could influence the outcome of congressional debates, the Heritage Foundation welcomes the opportunity to leave its mark on public policy. According to Feulner, "Our role is trying to influence the Washington public policy community ... most specifically the Hill, secondly the executive branch, thirdly the national news media."[150]

With the support of sixty resident policy experts and several adjunct scholars and an annual budget exceeding $30 million,[151] the Heritage Foundation is well placed to attract the attention of decision-makers. In addition to maintaining a comprehensive Web site, publishing books, articles, newsletters, a journal, and a variety of brief publications to express its views to government officials, Heritage relies on several other channels to strengthen its ties to the policy-making community. It invites government officials to participate in seminars and conferences, provides them with expertise through its close to a dozen Centers of Excellence, maintains close contact with members of Congress and the Executive through its liaison offices, provides a job-placement service to fill government positions with its personnel,[152] and on occasion recruits prominent politicians to endorse its fundraising campaigns. While many of the strategies adopted by the Heritage Foundation to influence the content of public policies are frequently used by other Washington think tanks, its decision to solicit the support of political leaders for fundraising purposes during the early 1980s continues to raise some eyebrows in the policy-making community.

In 1982, at the request of Edwin Feulner, Reagan presidential adviser and later US attorney general Edwin Meese III wrote a letter to potential Heritage donors informing them that in exchange for a tax-deductible donation of $1,000,[153] they would be allowed to join the President's Club. The club, according to Meese, would entitle them to "a series of meetings with the most senior members of the administration and Congress."[154] In his accompanying fundraising letter, Feulner added, "you will be provided with an access to Washington policy-makers which cannot be had at any price. I have no doubt that you will find your membership fee returned to you many times over."[155] Dismissing claims that he was directly asking people to give money to Heritage, Meese commented, "I am enthusiastic about the establishment of the Heritage Foundation President's Club ... [It is] a vital communications link [between the White House and those who support President Reagan, and] this administration will cooperate fully with your efforts."[156]

Despite Meese's explanation, several critics of the foundation argued that the fundraising campaign spearheaded by Feulner and Meese violated the organization's tax-exempt status under the Internal Revenue Code.[157] However, little was done to prevent the creation of the President's Club. Stating that it was formed simply to allow supporters of the Heritage Foundation to express their concerns to political leaders, Feulner expressed confidence in its success. Years later, the President's Club Executive Committee and the Young President's Club were also formed to strengthen ties between generous donors and senior-level policy-makers. And according to its 2003 annual report, the President's Clubs continue to be the most popular programs for Heritage supporters.[158]

The Heritage Foundation takes considerable pride in its ability to get the message out,[159] but flatly denies interfering in the decision-making process. As Herb Berkowitz, former vice-president for public relations, points out, "We're not allowed to endorse candidates, and we don't. We're not allowed to suggest to members of Congress how they should vote, and we don't. We are allowed to discuss items on the agenda of Congress. We do the same thing Brookings has been doing for years."[160]

Heritage's former vice-chairman, Dr Robert H. Krieble, agrees that Heritage does not interfere in the decision-making process, but that it has nonetheless played an important role in shaping such important policy goals and initiatives as deregulation of the marketplace, tax reform, the institution of cost-benefit analysis as the primary decision-making criteria for all government programs, the development of free enterprise zones, and the creation of the Strategic Defense Initiative (Star Wars).[161] Krieble confirms that, unlike disinterested research institutions in the early twentieth century, advocacy think tanks measure their success, not by the number of scholarly publications they produce, but by their ability to stimulate discussion and debate about important policy issues.[162]

Echoing Krieble's observations, Stuart Butler, vice-president, Domestic and Economic Policy Studies at Heritage, remarked: "It is naive, in the public policy area, to assume that people don't have an ideological predisposition toward things. Every economist subscribes to a school of economics ... Unlike other institutions that pretend ideological neutrality, we're conservatives, no bones about it. We don't pretend to be anything different from what we are."[163]

Although supporters and critics of the Heritage Foundation may disagree about the extent to which the institution participates in the political process, they generally agree that it has served as a model for other think tanks in the United States and throughout the industrialized world. Indeed, just as AEI served as an inspiration for the Heritage Foundation, so other think tanks look to Heritage to develop and deploy effective strategies to market their ideas. By taking advantage of the changing political climate in the early 1980s to market its research products, Heritage not only established itself as one of the dominant think tanks in the United States but, more importantly, paved the way for the creation of hundreds of advocacy institutions, including the Cato Institute, the Progressive Policy Institute, and Empower America, home to former secretary of education Bill Bennett and former

Republican vice-presidential candidate Jack Kemp. Advocacy think tanks continue to spring up throughout the United States. Among those that opened their doors in the past decade have been the Project for the New American Century, which will be discussed in more detail in the case study on terrorism, and the Center for American Progress (CAP), headed by John Podesta, former chief of staff to President Clinton. The CAP is affectionately known among Democrats as "the liberal Heritage."[164]

AND ANOTHER THING! PRESIDENTS, PRESIDENTIAL CANDIDATES, AND THEIR LEGACIES, 1980–2004

As advocacy think tanks such as the Heritage Foundation and the Cato Institute were beginning to make their presence felt in the late 1970s and early 1980s, other kinds of think tanks were starting to find their way in the policy-making community. Created by former presidents intent on leaving a lasting legacy well after stepping down from public office, a small but well managed and financed group of think tanks began to carve out their own niche in an increasingly congested environment. Although little has been written on so-called vanity, legacy, and candidate-based think tanks, their growing visibility deserves some attention.

After four or possibly eight years of being subjected to intense public scrutiny, most presidents in the latter half of the twentieth century have left public office in search of peace and seclusion. Given that every word they utter or facial expression they make is dissected and interpreted by journalists, scholars, and, interestingly enough, psychiatrists, it is not surprising that most former presidents dedicate themselves to a passion shared by millions of Americans – golf. As John Kennedy, Richard Nixon, Gerald Ford, Bill Clinton, and George Bush (both father and son) have demonstrated, it is often much easier to hit a golf ball off a tee than to field questions about controversial policy decisions. But for some presidents, including those named above, as important as it might be to pursue a recreational hobby, it is equally, if not more, important to leave a legacy.

As presidents prepare to leave the Oval Office, they are often asked how they want to be remembered. Will it be for a particular foreign policy achievement, such as convincing the former Soviet Union to tear down the Berlin Wall, or will it be for something less dramatic but nonetheless monumental, such as promoting universal health care? For most presidents, despite their best intentions, the legacy they begin to carve out in office is rarely completed when they leave. As a result, in recent years, several presidents have created what are termed vanity or legacy think tanks in the hope of encouraging scholars to pursue research in areas that they deem essential. Two think tanks that fall under this broad category are the Carter Center in Atlanta, Georgia, and the Washington-based Nixon Center for Peace and Freedom.

Founded in 1982 by former US president and Nobel Peace Prize winner Jimmy Carter and his wife, Rosalynn, the Carter Center, in partnership with Emory University, "is committed to advancing human rights and alleviating unnecessary human suffering."[165] With 150 full- and part-time staff members and a budget exceeding $36 million, the centre "seeks to prevent and resolve conflicts, enhance freedom and democracy, and improve health."[166] To this end, its researchers focus on issues ranging from election monitoring and conflict-resolution methods to refugee mental health and tropical diseases.

According to its Web site, the centre has, among other things, "strengthened democracies in Asia, Latin America, and Africa; mediated or worked to prevent civil and international conflicts; intervened to prevent unnecessary diseases in Latin America and Africa; and strived to diminish the stigma against mental illness."[167] The mandate of the Carter Center closely reflects the goals and dreams its founder brought to the Oval Office. Although Carter was unable to achieve many of his stated objectives while president, he has, through his non-profit, non-partisan research centre, been able to leave an indelible mark on domestic and foreign affairs. His involvement in many international and regional conflicts since leaving office has not been welcomed by some critics, including AEI's Steven Hayward,[168] but his efforts to bring peace to troubled parts of the world will no doubt be his legacy.

For Jimmy Carter, the cornerstone of American foreign policy should be a commitment to alleviate human suffering through development assistance, education, and health promotion. For Richard Nixon, on the other hand, policy-makers entrusted with guiding the United States through troubled waters must always treat its security and defense needs as the highest priority. Three months before his death in April 1994, Nixon, whose fall from grace continues to intrigue historians and political scientists, founded the Nixon Center for Peace and Freedom to "combine hard-headed pragmatism and fundamental American values."[169] Led by its president, Dimitri Simes, an adviser to President Nixon and former researcher at the Carnegie Endowment for International Peace, the Nixon Center's staff of close to a dozen people oversee four main programs: National Security Studies, Chinese Studies, US-Russian Relations, and Regional Strategy (Middle East, Caspian Basin, and South Asia).

The Carter and Nixon centres function in many respects like other contemporary think tanks that combine policy research and political advocacy. They frequently organize conferences and seminars, convey their views to the print and broadcast media, and publish their findings. The main difference is that their mandates closely resemble the interests and concerns of former policy-makers, not those of policy entrepreneurs intent on making an impact on public policy. It is also important to note that legacy or vanity think tanks are usually affiliated with a presidential library. As a result, these types of think tanks will likely proliferate, albeit in small numbers, over the next several years.

As noted in the beginning of the chapter, presidential candidates and members of Congress have also created think tanks or affiliated themselves with them. They do so not only to draw on the expertise of policy experts but also to circumvent campaign finance laws that impose limits on contributions. According to the Washington-based Center for Responsive Politics, a non-profit research group founded in 1983 to "track money in politics, and its effects on public policy,"[170]

Because the campaign finance law's restrictions kick in only when money is being donated for an election, no limits apply to contributions to non-profit organizations with which members of Congress are affiliated. Corporations, labor unions, and individuals may contribute unlimited amounts and, in some cases, receive tax deductions for their generosity. The problem? The same generous donors also have a way to gain access to elected officials without falling under the restrictions of the campaign finance law. Additionally, the affiliation of politicians with charitable organizations raises concerns that the organizations are engaging in electioneering activities on behalf of the elected official. Non-profit organizations can be used to support the research needs of a candidate, to prepare policy material for use in a campaign, and to give a candidate wide exposure by paying for travel or sponsoring forums at which the candidate appears.[171]

In recent years, several politicians have had their ties to think tanks closely scrutinized. For example, Senator Bob Dole established the Better America Foundation as a charitable organization in the early 1990s, but it soon became apparent that it was being used "as a think tank to promote Republican positions," including his own. As the Center for Responsive Politics points out, "In 1994, the organization spent $1 million on a television campaign spotlighting Dole."[172] After several Democrats complained that Better America was being used to support Dole's 1996 presidential election bid, the senior senator from Kansas closed down the foundation.

Dole's Better America Foundation was not the only organization targeted for supporting a politician's run for office. The GOP ("Grand Old Party") Action Committee (GOPAC) also came under intense scrutiny for several reasons, including its support for such high-profile Republicans as former speaker of the House Newt Gingrich. Despite its name, GOPAC did not register as a political action committee until May of 1991, well after it began funding congressional candidates. "Under the law, organizations are to be treated as political action committees when their major purpose is federal election activity." Since GOPAC failed to register initially as a political action committee, the Federal Election Commission (FEC) sued it, claiming that the committee's "election related activities, its promotion of Gingrich, and its goal of gaining a Republican majority in the House made the organization a political action committee."[173] Although GOPAC successfully defended itself against the FEC's allegations, the controversy raised several interesting issues regarding the relationship between think tanks and politicians. It also led to further speculation about the involvement of think tanks in the political arena, a subject that will be explored further in chapter 5.

In this historical overview, four distinct waves or generations of think tanks have been highlighted. Among other things, it has become clear that as each new generation of think tanks has emerged, it has not replaced previous generations but has found ample space to coexist. This is not to suggest that older think tanks have not been influenced by the development of more contemporary think tanks but, rather, that the newer organizations have been able to carve out their own niches. In the final section of this chapter, a more complete picture of foreign policy think tanks in the United States will be provided. The purpose here is not to offer an institutional profile of every think tank that lists foreign and defense policy as one of its areas of specialization but to identify those that have clearly emerged as key participants in foreign policy debates. Thus far, several think tanks that concentrate on foreign policy have been examined, including the Carnegie Endowment for International Peace, the Brookings Institution, the Hoover Institution, the Council on Foreign Relations, the American Enterprise Institute, RAND, and the Heritage Foundation. To this list, the following institutes should be added: the Center for Strategic and International Studies, the Center for Security Policy, the Project for the New American Century, and the Institute for Policy Studies. In later chapters, references will also be made to several think tanks that focus on particular regions of the world, including the Middle East Forum and the Washington Institute for Near East Policy.

THINKING ABOUT FOREIGN POLICY: A PROFILE
OF SELECTED FOREIGN POLICY THINK TANKS

The Center for Strategic and International Studies

The directory of scholars at the Center for Strategic and International Studies (CSIS) reads like a who's who in Washington's foreign policy-making community. Home to several former ambassadors, secretaries of defense, and national security advisers, CSIS is among the most respected defense and foreign policy think tanks in the United States. Some of its high-profile experts include Zbigniew Brzezinski, national security adviser to President Carter, Henry Kissinger, former national security adviser and secretary of state during the Nixon and Ford administrations, and his colleague James Schlesinger, former secretary of defense. Founded in 1962 by David Abshire, former assistant secretary of state for congressional affairs, and by Arleigh Burke, former chief of naval operations, CSIS has as its mission "to inform and shape selected policy decisions in government and the private sector by providing long-range, anticipatory, and integrated thinking over a wide range of policy issues."[174]

With close to two hundred policy experts, support staff, and interns and a budget in 2005 of $25 million, CSIS is well positioned to put its mission statement into action. The organization is led by John J. Hamre, formerly deputy secretary of defense during the Clinton administration. It convenes approximately seven to eight hundred meetings, seminars, and conferences with policy-makers and scholars in the United States and abroad each year and generates hundreds of media appearances. CSIS also publishes books, several journals, and conference papers. Its marquee publication is the *Washington Quarterly*. The centre conducts research on every region of the world and has programs that deal specifically with issues relating to technology and public policy, international trade and finance, and energy.

The Center for Security Policy

Founded in 1988 to "promote international peace through American strength," the Center for Security Policy (CSP) "specializes in the rapid preparation and real-time dissemination of information, analyses and policy recommendations."[175] With seven full- and part-time staff members and a modest budget, the CSP focuses its attention on a number of target audiences, including the US security policy-making community (the executive and legislative branches, the armed forces, and appropriate independent agencies), corresponding agencies in key foreign governments, the press, the global business and financial community, and members of the attentive public. The president of CSP is Frank Gaffney Jr, former deputy assistant secretary of defense for nuclear forces and arms control during the Reagan administration.

The CSP does not arrange or sponsor large conferences and events, nor does it oversee an extensive publications program. The reports and newsletters it produces are "typically short and highly readable."[176] It is best known for its work on missile defense, although it does conduct research on other defense and foreign policy-related issues, including arms control, information warfare, and homeland security. It also attempts to provide expertise on most regions of the world. With limited resources, the CSP has had to focus on what it does best – creating a "network of people and associations, including think tanks,"[177] that can discuss and debate critical security policy issues. Reflecting on the work of his organization, Gaffney recently observed, "I would like to think that, dollar for dollar, no other think tank has had a greater impact on security policy."[178]

The CSP's contribution to the security policy community has been acknowledged by important policy-makers, including Secretary of Defense Donald Rumsfeld, the recipient of the organization's Keeper of the Flame award.[179] On 4 March 2001 Rumsfeld observed, "Through the years, the Center for Security Policy has helped ensure a vigorous national security debate and, in so doing, has strengthened our national security, with energy, persistence and patriotism."[180] The CSP's contribution to American security interests has also been recognized by some of its staunchest critics, who, unlike Rumsfeld, paint a dire picture of how the organization has threatened global peace and security, a subject that we will explore in chapter 8.

The Project for the New American Century

Given the amount of interest the Project for the New American Century (PNAC) has generated since President Bush came to office in 2001, one might expect that, like the Heritage Foundation, it would occupy thousands of square feet of luxurious office space close to the main centres of political power. After all, where else would the think tank apparently responsible for creating a blueprint for the Bush administration's invasion of Afghanistan and Iraq be located? How about in a small suite of rented offices in a downtown building that houses the American Enterprise Institute and the *Weekly Standard*, a conservative magazine edited by William Kristol, the chairman of PNAC? With a budget of $600,000, PNAC can hardly afford an office building in Heritage's pricey neighbourhood.

Established in the spring of 1997 "to promote global leadership," PNAC employs four full-time staff members and a handful of interns, who, among other things, help to write and disseminate policy papers and issue briefs (two to four pages in length) to approximately two thousand journalists, academics, members of Congress, editorial writers, and think tanks every six weeks. This strategy, according to PNAC's president Gary Schmitt, a political scientist with a PhD from the University of Chicago, allows it "to make a case that is well-reasoned and brief. We have a much bigger voice than our size because we offer a vision that is clear and articulate."[181]

PNAC's vision, which was shaped by a 1996 *Foreign Affairs* article co-authored by William Kristol and Robert Kagan,[182] best-selling author of *Of Paradise and Power*, was clearly articulated in its "Statement of Principles" released in June 1997. It states in part:

American foreign and defense policy is adrift. Conservatives have criticized the incoherent policies of the Clinton Administration. They have also resisted isolation-ist impulses from within their own ranks. But conservatives have not confidently advanced a strategic vision of America's role in the world. They have not set forth guiding principles for American foreign policy. They have allowed differences over tactics to obscure potential agreement on strategic objectives. And they have not fought for a defense budget that would maintain American security and advance American interests in the new century. We aim to change this. We aim to make the case and rally support for American global leadership.[183]

What caught the eye of most journalists scanning this statement was not the organization's desire to advance what amounted to a "Reaganite policy of military strength and moral clarity" but the list of high-profile policy-makers who had offered their endorsement. As noted in the Introduction, among the original signatories to PNAC's principles were: Donald Rumsfeld, secretary of defense, Paul Wolfowitz, deputy secretary of defense, Lewis "Scooter" Libby, chief of staff to Vice-President Dick Cheney, and Cheney himself.[184]

When President Bush's strategy to promote and protect American security interests began to take shape in the months following the tragic events of September 11, 2001, the small and relatively obscure conservative think tank with powerful connections in the Bush White House was propelled into the national spotlight. Its September 2000 report entitled *Rebuilding America's Defenses* outlined a series of policy recommendations strikingly similar to the actions Bush was in the process of pursuing. Indeed, it appeared to several journalists, even those weary of conspiracy theories, that PNAC had laid the foundation for what became known as the Bush doctrine. However, as we will examine in chapter 9, while there is no doubt that PNAC has had an important impact in contributing to the debate on global terror, its influence in shaping Bush's post-9/11 strategy has, by its own admission, been greatly exaggerated.

The Institute for Policy Studies

Often regarded as Washington's think tank of the left, the Institute for Policy Studies (IPS) was founded by Marcus Raskin and Richard Barnett, two former staffers in the Kennedy administration. Convinced that steps had "to be taken to combat the over-militarized ways of thinking in foreign and national policy,"[185] Raskin and Barnett decided to establish their own institute, and with $200,000 in grants, IPS opened its doors in October 1963.[186]

Its fundamental purpose is to provide the country's most important social movements with the intellectual ammunition they require to transform "their moral passion into a sensible public policy." According to its Web site, IPS "serves as a bridge between progressive forces in government and grass-roots activists, and between movements in the U.S. and those in the developing world."[187] To this end, it oversees more than a dozen projects on such issues as ecotourism and sustainable development and peace and security. These projects are intended to stimulate public debate and to help social movements succeed.

IPS, like other advocacy-oriented think tanks, relies on several channels to influence political change. In addition to conveying its ideas to policy-makers and the public through the media, the institute has established links to several members in Congress and the executive branch. It has also advised several presidential candidates, including George McGovern, Jesse Jackson, Bob Kerrey, and Tom Harkin. IPS relies on other strategies as well. For instance, to better equip leaders of social movements to articulate their views to policy-makers, it created a Social Action and Leadership School for Activists (SALSA), where organizers can meet to discuss strategy. IPS also works closely with other national and transnational social organizations to mobilize opposition to various public policies. With a budget of over $2 million[188] (none of which is derived from corporations or government agencies) and a staff of approximately thirty, it does not enjoy the visibility of Washington's larger and better-funded think tanks. Nonetheless, because of its publications and networks with other non-governmental organizations, its views have not been ignored.

The history of think tanks in the United States reveals, among other things, how philanthropists, policy-makers, and policy entrepreneurs have created a diverse body of institutions that are capable and willing to assist the nation address critical policy issues. While there is no doubt that think tanks, like corporations, often assign a higher priority to advancing their own interests than the nation's, they have nonetheless played a key role in providing expertise and knowledge to policy-makers and the public. On this point, most scholars are in agreement. Indeed, if they did not recognize the contribution think tanks have made to shaping public policy, it is unlikely that these organizations would be attracting increased scholarly attention. Where they disagree is on how best to study the relationship between think tanks and the policy-makers and opinion leaders they are trying to influence.

In the following chapter, we will explore competing theoretical approaches to the study of think tanks. By comparing the various frameworks scholars have employed to make better sense of how these institutions have become entrenched in the policy-making process, we can better appreciate that no one theory can account for their rise to prominence. Rather, to understand think tanks and their role in public policy, we must tap into several different theories. Recognizing the contribution that various theories can make to our understanding of think tanks might be seen as "fence-sitting" to some scholars. After all, is it not more compelling to study organizations through one particular conceptual lens? Perhaps, but it is more prudent to evaluate what can be gained or lost by relying too heavily on one theoretical perspective. By doing so, we can construct a more appropriate framework within which to study the behaviour of think tanks and their efforts to influence the discourse of the nation.

CHAPTER THREE

Theorizing about Think Tanks: Competing Visions and Conceptual Approaches

As think tanks have come to occupy a more visible presence in both advanced and developing countries, scholars have employed various theoretical approaches to explain their role, significance, and impact in the policy-making community. In this chapter we explore what these approaches are and what steps can be taken to provide more-informed insights about their efforts to shape public opinion and public policy. In the process, we will demonstrate the strengths and limitations of each and suggest how they can be integrated more effectively. What will become clear is that it is necessary to move beyond the existing literature to develop a more useful and challenging conceptual framework within which to evaluate think tanks and their involvement in policy-making. It will also become apparent that we must resist the temptation to base our observations about think tanks on one particular theoretical approach. As we will discover, no single theory can adequately explain the behaviour of think tanks and their conduct in the policy- making community. With this proviso in mind, it is important to consider how think tanks have been studied and what assumptions scholars have made about their conduct in the United States.

Scholars who study think tanks or make passing reference to their influence tend to examine their behaviour from one of four competing perspectives. First, think tanks are treated as elite organizations that rely on their expertise and close ties to policy-makers to advance the political and economic interests of corporate and philanthropic sponsors. This approach has found its way into the literature on the military industrial complex and on iron triangles, concepts familiar to students of defense and security studies.

Second, think tanks are regarded as one of many groups in what has become an increasingly crowded marketplace of ideas. Think tanks, like interest groups, trade unions, human rights organizations, environmental associations, and other non-governmental bodies, are perceived as yet another set of actors vying for the attention of the public and policy-makers. Scholars who adopt this approach do not regard think tanks as elite organizations but see them as institutions, like those listed above, that are committed to influencing important policy debates. Third, a handful of scholars acknowledge the presence of think tanks and other non-governmental organizations in the policy-making community but suggest that, relative to the state's authority and autonomy, they play a very modest role in shaping public policy. This view of course assumes that individuals recruited from think tanks are not in a position to speak on behalf of the state, an assumption that can easily be challenged. Contrary to the assertions of scholars who argue that public policy is controlled and manipulated by elites and/or by special interest groups, those embracing the "statist paradigm" maintain that the state can and does act independently of various societal and bureaucratic pressures. In short, they suggest that rather than allowing outside forces to impose their agenda on the state, the president and his senior advisers ultimately determine the fate of the nation. And finally, there are those who focus less on the elite or pluralist nature of think tanks and their relationship to the state and more on the institutional structure and orientation of the organizations themselves. Scholars in this camp pay particularly close attention to the mandate and resources of think tanks and the many factors that influence the strategic choices they make to become involved at different stages of policy-making. It is to these various approaches that we now turn.

THINK TANKS AS POLICY ELITES

For several scholars, including Joseph Peschek, Thomas Dye, William Domhoff, and John Saloma, think tanks not only regularly interact with policy elites; they help to comprise the nation's power structure.[1] Particularly in the United States, where think tanks frequently serve as talent pools or holding tanks for incoming presidential administrations and as retirement homes for former senior-level policy-makers, they are portrayed as elite organizations that are both capable and willing to influence public policy. The multi-million-dollar budgets enjoyed by a handful of American think tanks and the many prominent and distinguished business leaders and former policy-makers who serve on their boards of directors and trustees help to reinforce this image. The close and intimate ties between corporate and philanthropic donors and several think tanks suggest to Marxists and elite theorists[2] that think tanks are indeed instruments of the ruling elite. The argument they advance is straightforward: in exchange for large donations, think tanks use their policy expertise and connections with key policy-makers to advance the political agendas of their generous benefactors. On the surface, this interpretation seems entirely plausible. After all, it is unlikely that corporations and philanthropic foundations would donate thousands, and sometimes millions, of dollars to think tanks that are acting contrary to their interests. Rather, they fund those that share similar ideals and concerns about the nation. However, it is important to question the type of return that donors expect on their investment. While it makes sense for philanthropic foundations to fund like-minded think tanks, it is less important for corporate donors to use think tanks to help them make contact with senior-level policy-makers. Through their sizable donations to congressional and presidential candidates, not to mention their personal friendships with dozens of politicians, corporations and heads of philanthropic foundations hardly need think tanks to introduce them to the world of politics. Moreover, since corporations can and do hire lobbyists to represent their interests on Capitol Hill, it is unlikely that they would turn to institutions such as think tanks, which are prohibited under the Internal Revenue Code from engaging in overt political lobbying. And since professional lobbyists have an incentive to work tirelessly on behalf of their clients, what can think tanks offer corporate America that lobbyists cannot?

The answer is simple: credibility and respectability. Corporations and philanthropic foundations turn to "elite" think tanks such as Brookings, the Carnegie Endowment, and the Hoover Institution, not so that they can take advantage of their political connections (although this could help periodically), but rather so that they can benefit from the access these and other think tanks have to the media, to universities, and to other power centres in America. But even more importantly, corporations and philanthropic foundations can take advantage of the reputation that think tanks have cultivated as scientific, neutral, and scholarly organizations to more effectively shape public opinion and public policy. Donating large sums of money to political campaigns may buy corporations access, but it does not necessarily buy them credibility. On the other hand, supporting think tanks that provide the media and policy-makers with a steady stream of information, expertise, and policy recommendations may allow donors to secure both. This outcome may in part explain why corporations and philanthropic foundations also lend support to several other types of research organizations and university departments that can draw on their credibility to influence both the policy-making environment and specific policy decisions.

By closely examining the interaction between the largest American think tanks and key officials in government, scholars may be justified in concluding, as some have, that think tanks play a critical role in influencing public policy. However, since very few institutes resemble Brookings, Heritage, or RAND for that matter, we must question the utility of employing an approach which assumes that think tanks, by their very nature and purpose, are well positioned and equipped to promote the interests of the ruling elite. We must also question whether, as non-profit organizations engaged in policy analysis, they should be treated as elites.

Elite theorists portray the political system as dominated by a select group of individuals and organizations committed to advancing common political, economic, and social interests, but it would be naive to assume that all think tanks have the desire or the resources to help advance an elite agenda, however that may be defined. Think tanks are in the business of shaping public opinion and public policy, but, as noted, they have very different ideas of how various domestic and foreign policies should be formulated and implemented. Several think tanks, for instance, may embrace the views of some elites who advocate free market solutions to economic problems. The Heritage Foundation, the Cato Institute, and the American Enterprise Institute, among others, would certainly favour such an approach. But there are many other think tanks, including the left-leaning, Washington-based Institute for Policy Studies, which have profoundly different views of how governments should resolve economic and social problems. Should think tanks that often oppose the interests of the ruling elite be considered part of the elite?

Despite some limitations, which will be explored in more detail below, adopting an elite approach to the study of think tanks has some advantages. As Domhoff and others have discovered,[3] examining the close and interlocking ties between members of think tanks and leaders in business and government can provide interesting and useful insights into why some policy institutes enjoy far more visibility and notoriety than others. Moreover, by keeping track of who sits on the boards of directors of think tanks, we may be able to explain why some institutes generate more funding than their competitors. Nonetheless, it is important to keep in mind that while members of think tanks frequently interact with high-level business leaders and policy-makers, their corporate and political connections do not necessarily allow them to exercise policy influence. Such ties may facilitate access to important officials in the Executive, Congress, and the bureaucracy, but their ability to influence public policy depends on a wide range of factors.

It is tempting for scholars to treat think tanks as policy elites because it enables them to make sweeping assertions about who controls public policy. But as appealing as this approach might be, it is also problematic since it tells us little about the ability or inability of think tanks to exercise influence at different stages of the policy cycle. It tells us even less about how to assess or evaluate the impact of think tanks in policy-making. In short, an elite approach assumes that with the right connections, think tanks can and will be able to influence public policy. Unfortunately, it offers little insight into how this will be achieved.

THE PLURALIST TRADITION: ONE VOICE AMONG MANY

Members of think tanks may occasionally travel in elite policy circles, but according to some political scientists, including David Newsom, they represent only one set of organizations in the policy-making community.[4] According to this perspective, which is deeply rooted in the American pluralist tradition,[5] think tanks, like interest groups, trade unions, and environmental organizations, compete among themselves in the political arena for limited resources. The gains achieved by one group or organization are frequently offset by costs incurred by others.[6] Since the government is perceived simply as a moderator or referee overseeing the competition between these groups, pluralists devote little attention to assessing government priorities. They view public policy, not as a reflection of a specific government mandate, but rather as an outcome of group competition.

Studying think tanks within a pluralist framework has its advantages. For one thing, it compels scholars to acknowledge that despite the widely held view that think tanks have become important actors in the policy-making community, they remain one type among many organizations engaged in the ongoing struggle for power and influence. This approach also serves as a reminder that think tanks, like other non-governmental organizations, rely on similar strategies to shape public policy, a subject that will be explored further in chapter 5. The pluralist approach, however, has serious weaknesses. To begin with, although pluralists assume that public policy is an outcome of group competition, they provide little insight into why some organizations are better positioned than others to influence public attitudes and policy decisions. Is it simply a matter of which groups have the most members, largest budgets, and greatest staff resources that determines who does or does not have influence? Or do other factors, such as the amount of money groups donate to political campaigns or the number of advertisements they can afford in the print and electronic media, offer better insight into which organizations are destined to succeed or fail in the political arena?

The major deficiency of the pluralist approach is not that it assumes that all groups can influence public policy, but rather that it cannot adequately explain why some do. Moreover, by treating think tanks as simply one group of the many voices in the policy-making community, pluralists overlook why policy institutes are often better positioned to shape government priorities than interest groups and other non-governmental organizations. Think tanks may indeed be part of the chorus, but they possess distinctive attributes that enable them to stand out. By identifying the differences between think tanks and other NGOs, (i.e., the privileged status of some think tanks), pluralists would have to acknowledge that all groups do not compete on a level playing field. Think tanks, by virtue of their expertise and close ties to policy-makers, may compete among themselves for prestige and status, but they do not necessarily compete with the hundreds of other participants in the policy-making community. In fact, in some policy areas, think tanks may face little competition at all.

Pluralists must also acknowledge that policy-makers often have a vested interest in influencing the outcome of group competition. Instead of behaving as referees, policy-makers representing various government branches and departments can and do rely heavily on organizations that will help them to achieve their goals. As we will discuss in chapters 8 and 9, at critical stages of the policy-making process, members of Congress and the Executive often turn to specific think tanks for advice on how to tackle difficult policy issues. At other times, they rely on different think tanks to help frame the parameters of important policy debates.

Marxists and pluralists disagree about the extent to which think tanks are entrenched in the policy-making process and the willingness of the state to embrace their ideas. However, both schools acknowledge that think tanks have the ability to play an important and, at times, decisive role in public policy, a position that has been questioned by proponents of state theory. While scholars employing the first two approaches isolate various societal and bureaucratic pressures to reveal how public policy is shaped and moulded, those advancing the so-called statist paradigm look no further than the state to explain who makes policy decisions.

IN THE NATIONAL INTEREST:
A STATIST APPROACH

As multinational corporations, media conglomerates, and powerful special-interest groups have established a strong foothold in the nation's capital, it is not surprising that we have lost sight of who ultimately is entrusted with protecting the national interest. It is not Bill Gates, Ted Turner, or leaders of other blue-chip companies who speak on behalf of the United States and take steps to promote its economic, political, and security interests. It is the president and the people who surround him who make decisions that are intended to serve the needs of the nation. To remind us of this fact, a handful of scholars, including Theda Skocpol[7] and Stephen Krasner,[8] have empha-sized the relative autonomy of the state in making difficult policy decisions. State theory, according to Aaron Steelman, advances the argument "that while the public can indeed impose some restraint on the actions of the bureaucracy and elected officials, the state retains a degree of autonomy and works according to its own logic."[9]

In his book *Defending the National Interest*, Stephen Krasner elaborates on the theory of statism. He notes: "[Statism] is premised upon an intellec-tual vision that sees the state autonomously formulating goals that it then attempts to implement against resistance from international and domestic actors. The ability of the state to overcome domestic resistance depends upon the instruments of control that it can exercise over groups within its own society."[10] For Krasner, it is the central state actors – the president and the secretary of state – and the most important institutions – the White House and the State Department – that control foreign policy.

If Krasner, Skocpol, and other proponents of state theory are right, what impact could think tanks possibly have in influencing state behaviour? Although one might assume that they would be relegated to the sidelines, Steelman suggests that state theory leaves ample room for think tanks to make their presence felt: "State theory can help explain the seeming anoma-lous cases of former think-tank staffers who enter government pledging to work for a certain set of ideas and then enacting policies that are quite dif-ferent. In some cases, these individuals have been co-opted by the system; in others, they are generally doing their best to reach their goal, however slowly or circuitously. But either way, the state itself is an important actor."[11]

There are several advantages to incorporating state theory into studies of think tanks. First, it helps to explain how think tank staffers can become directly involved in making key policy decisions. If we accept Krasner's argument that the president and the secretary of state and the two institutions they represent, the White House and the State Department, are the most important participants in the foreign policy-making process, it becomes very clear which think tanks have or do not have access to the highest levels of government. Rather than trying to monitor the efforts of think tanks to influence Congress and the media, scholars could simply explore the relationship between the president, the secretary of state, and their closest advisers. If it appears that members from think tanks have served in an advisory capacity or been recruited to serve in the White House or in the State Department, we could assume that they have had direct access to the policy-making process. After all, if the president and the secretary of state are the most influential participants in policy-making and often rely on think tank experts for advice, it would be logical to conclude that think tanks are in a position to influence policy decisions. Conversely, if there is little evidence to suggest that think tanks have gained access to the upper echelons of government, scholars could, according to state theory, conclude that they have had little impact in influencing state conduct. In short, state theory can explain both when think tanks have and when they have not been influential.

State theory is not without its limitations, however. It may be useful in explaining why some presidents such as Richard Nixon were able to insulate themselves from Congress and the American people.[12] But by the same token, it is less helpful in explaining why many recent presidents have gone to great lengths to consult with the public, members of Congress, foreign governments, international organizations, and a host of non-governmental organizations before making important policy decisions. President Bush's efforts in 1990–91 to secure an international coalition to deter Iraqi aggression is a case in point. Before deploying US armed forces to the Persian Gulf, Bush made sure he had the support of the United Nations and several of its member states, a strategy that his son considered but later abandoned prior to invading Iraq.[13] As the foreign policy-making process has become more transparent over time and as more governmental and non-governmental organizations have sought to become involved in shaping world affairs, proponents of state theory have had a more difficult time defending the relative autonomy of the state. They certainly have had difficulty explaining why the US Congress appears to have taken a more active interest in foreign policy.[14] In the final analysis, both advocates and critics of state theory acknowledge that the president makes decisions that can profoundly influence America's conduct in the international community. Yet, as we have witnessed in recent years, how presidents make policy decisions ultimately depends on their management style and their willingness to listen to their inner circle of advisers. State theory might help to account for the management of US foreign policy under President George W. Bush, but it might do little to shed light on how President Bill Clinton governed the nation.[15]

Thus far we have looked at three different theoretical approaches and how they can be employed to study think tanks. Before considering how it might be possible to integrate them more effectively, it is important to consider a fourth approach that has attracted considerable attention. Focusing on think tanks as a diverse set of organizations that have very different priorities and concerns, rather than as members of the policy elite, the state, or the broader policy-making community, this approach appears more promising. As we will discover below, a better understanding of how think tanks function at various stages of the policy-making process can allow scholars to make more informed insights about their role and impact.

DIFFERENT THINK TANKS, DIFFERENT PRIORITIES: AN INSTITUTIONAL APPROACH

There are three distinct institutional approaches to studying think tanks. The most common focuses either on the history of specific think tanks or on their evolution and transformation in particular countries. Several scholars have written institutional histories of think tanks, including the Brookings Institution, the Council on Foreign Relations, the Heritage Foundation, the Institute for Policy Studies, and RAND.[16] There are also a number of studies that have detailed the rise of think tanks in the United States, Canada, and other advanced and developing countries.[17] The obvious advantage of providing detailed histories of think tanks is that they offer a wealth of information on the nature and mandate of organizations, the research projects they have conducted over time, and the various institutional changes they have undergone. The main disadvantage is that many of these studies provide little empirical evidence to support or deny claims that particular think tanks have played a major role in shaping specific policies.

The second and more systematic institutional approach has concentrated on the involvement of think tanks in epistemic and policy communities.[18] These communities consist of individuals and organizations which, by virtue of their policy expertise, are invited to participate in policy discussions and deliberations with government decision-makers. The formation of policy and epistemic communities is often seen as a critical stage in policy formulation and regime formation. This approach has been undertaken by a handful of political scientists, including Hugh Heclo, Evert Lindquist, and Diane Stone, who regard think tanks as active and vocal participants in these communities.[19]

By examining think tanks within a policy and/or epistemic community framework, scholars can make several important observations. To begin with, by focusing on specific policy issues such as the abrogation of the ABM treaty or the drafting of the controversial Helms-Burton legislation, they can better identify the key organizations and individuals who have been invited to share their thoughts and ideas with policy-makers. In addition to determining which groups and individuals have participated in the "sub-government," a term used to describe the various non-governmental and governmental policy experts who coalesce around particular policy issues, this approach offers much needed insight into the nature of the policy-making process. Among other things, a policy or epistemic community framework compels scholars to delve far deeper into the process by which ideas make their way onto the political agenda and how policy experts draw on their knowledge to support or oppose government initiatives. Moreover, rather than treating policy decisions as an outcome of interest-group competition or as a reflection of elite interests, this approach requires scholars to think seriously about how policy decisions can be influenced through discussions between non-governmental and governmental policy experts.

There are other advantages to adopting this approach. Once the actors involved in the sub-government have been identified, it is possible to compare the recommendations made by participants to actual policy decisions. Access to minutes of meetings, personal correspondence, testimony before legislative committees, published recommendations, and other information may not enable scholars to arrive at definitive conclusions about which participants in a policy community were most influential. Nonetheless, these and other materials can offer additional insight into whose views generated the most support.

Given the involvement of think tank scholars in different policy communities, it is not surprising that this framework is frequently employed. It is important to keep in mind, however, that while this approach may be better suited to the study of think tanks than either an elite or a pluralist framework, it too has its shortcomings. Examining think tanks within a policy or epistemic community is useful in identifying which institutes are called upon to offer their expertise at an important stage in policy formulation. Unfortunately, it does not tell us what, if any, impact think tanks inside policy or epistemic communities or those operating outside the sub-government have in shaping public attitudes and the policy preferences and choices of policy-makers. In short, this approach may tell us who is sitting at the table when key issues are being discussed, but it cannot to tell us whose voices have struck a responsive chord with those in a position to influence policy decisions. Since we cannot assume that all or any important policy decisions are made inside specific policy communities – after all, politicians, not policy experts, cast votes in the legislature – a third group of scholars have begun to consider a more inclusive approach that can be used to study the involvement of non-governmental organizations in policy-making.

Recognizing that such organizations vary enormously in terms of their mandate, resources, and priorities, John Kingdon and Denis Stairs,[20] among others, suggest that rather than trying to make general observations about how much or how little impact societal groups have on shaping the policy-making environment and policy-making itself, scholars should examine how groups committed to influencing public policy focus their efforts at different stages of the policy cycle. Although Kingdon and Stairs do not write specifically about think tanks, they do examine how groups try to get issues onto the political agenda and how they attempt to convey their ideas to policy-makers throughout the policy-making process. This approach is well suited to the study of think tanks.

For Kingdon and Stairs, trying to determine which domestic and external forces shape public policy constitutes an enormous and at times overwhelming undertaking. In fact, as the policy-making community in the United States becomes increasingly crowded, it has become difficult, if not impossible, to identify those groups that have had a direct impact on specific policy decisions. As a result, instead of making generalizations about which groups have or have not influenced public policy, Kingdon and Stairs argue that not all organizations have the desire or the necessary resources to participate at each stage of the policy cycle: issue articulation, policy formulation, and policy implementation. Put simply, while most organizations attempt to shape the parameters of policy debates (issue articulation), others may be more inclined to enter the policy-making process at a later stage (policy formulation or policy implementation). Conversely, some organizations may be more interested in sharing their ideas with the public than in working closely with policy-makers to formulate or implement a specific policy.

By acknowledging that think tanks do have different priorities and mandates, we can construct a conceptual framework that allows scholars to make more insightful observations about the role and impact of think tanks in policy-making. At the very least, a framework that recognizes the diversity of think tanks and their distinct missions will discourage scholars from making sweeping and often unfounded observations about their impact.

The conceptual framework employed in this book, which is expanded on below, is based on a simple premise: think tanks in the United States represent a diverse set of organizations that share a common desire to influence public opinion and public policy. Because of their distinctive institutional characteristics, however, each think tank must make strategic decisions about how and where to make its presence felt. In other words, because think tanks vary enormously in terms of the resources they have at their disposal, they must assign different priorities to participating at various stages of the policy cycle. This consideration becomes particularly important in interpreting data, such as media citations and testimony before legislative committees, that can be used to evaluate think tank performance.

After examining the four different approaches that have been employed to study think tanks and their involvement in policy-making, we must ask one remaining question: Which approach or conceptual framework best explains their role and function? Unfortunately, there is no simple answer. As we have discovered, each approach encourages scholars to move in a different direction and to ask very different questions. Therefore the question that should be asked is not which theory best explains the role and function of think tanks, but which framework helps scholars to better understand a particular aspect or feature of think tanks. For instance, scholars concerned about the relationship between think tanks and corporations could benefit far more from drawing on the assumptions underlying elite theory than from tapping into pluralist theories of democracy. On the other hand, those interested in explaining why some think tanks seem more preoccupied with working on various policy initiatives than with grabbing the headlines would learn a great deal from Kingdon and other scholars of public policy.

To examine the efforts of think tanks to influence key policy debates, an integrated approach is required. This would draw on the observations made by each of the theories outlined in this chapter, but would not adhere rigorously to any one framework. Public policy and the process by which decisions are made is complex and can rarely be explained by one theory. The advantage of relying on multiple theories to explain the involvement of think tanks in public policy is that it offers scholars some room to test different hypotheses about when and under what conditions think tanks can have the greatest impact. The alternative is to select a theoretical framework that offers one particular perspective on the nature of think tanks and their relationship to policy-makers. For example, one could adopt Krasner's statist paradigm to explain why think tanks and interest groups have had a limited impact in influencing the Bush administration's efforts to combat global terrorism. Given the relatively small group of advisers that Bush listens to and the president's decision to invade Iraq with limited support from the international community, state theory might offer scholars the answers they need. However, the same theory would provide little insight into the debate over national missile defense, which has been kept alive for over two decades by a handful of think tanks, including the Heritage Foundation and the Center for Security Policy. Contrary to the central assumptions underlying state theory, successive administrations have succumbed to pressure from both societal and bureaucratic interests to construct and deploy a missile defense. Rather than looking to Krasner for answers to why this has occurred, scholars would likely benefit more by reading the work of C. Wright Mills and others who have written extensively about the military-industrial complex.[21]

In the final analysis, scholars must select a theory or theories that will help them to understand the information they have uncovered. They should not rush to find a theory and then hope to uncover empirical and statistical evidence to make it more credible. Such an approach may be of little comfort to those looking for a grand theory to explain what think tanks do and how they achieve influence. As many experts of American foreign policy and international relations have learned, as tempting as it is to construct one theory that will explain the complexity of world affairs, such an undertaking often becomes an exercise in futility.[22]

To avoid falling into the methodological traps some scholars have unintentionally set, this book will allow the facts to speak for themselves. Once the facts about the involvement of think tanks in two foreign policy case studies have been revealed, we can draw on the theoretical approaches outlined in this chapter to explain what has transpired. In short, before we rush to judgment about the elite or pluralist nature of think tanks and how they seek to influence American foreign policy, we need to observe their behaviour and carefully document how they have participated in critical policy discussions. To do that, we must first explore the environment that they inhabit and explain why the United States has provided such fertile soil for the growth and development of hundreds of think tanks. The policy-making process in the United States and the opportunities it affords to groups and individuals intent on shaping public policy will be the focus of the following chapter.

CHAPTER FOUR

Open for Business: Think Tanks and the Marketplace of Ideas

In "Federalist No. 10," James Madison, the Virginia statesman and fourth president of the United States, observed, "Among the numerous advantages promised by a well constructed Union, none deserves to be more accurately developed than its tendency to break and control the violence of faction."[1] For Madison, a faction referred to "a number of citizens, whether amounting to a majority or a minority of the whole, who are united and actuated by some common impulse of passion, or of interest, adverse to the rights of other citizens, or to the permanent and aggregate interests of the community."[2]

Although it is unlikely that Madison had think tanks in mind when he penned his famous essay for the people of New York in 1787, he undoubtedly would have regarded many of these organizations as factions "actuated by some common impulse of passion" that can and have acted in ways adverse to the nation's interests. To control the effects of faction or, in this case, to curb the influence of hundreds of think tanks, Madison would likely have prescribed the same remedy: create a republican form of government based on separate branches sharing power which, among other things, can prevent minority groups from seizing control of the nation's agenda. He writes: "If a faction consists of less than a majority, relief is supplied by the republican principle, which enables the majority to defeat its sinister views by regular vote. It may clog the administration, it may convulse the society; but it will be unable to execute and mask its violence under the forms of the Constitution."[3]

Madison's essay on controlling the effects of faction may have helped to allay, temporarily, the concerns of those suspicious of how individual rights and liberties could be safeguarded in a large and extended republic. However, it did little to discourage individuals and organizations representing a multiplicity of interests from taking advantage of a more fragmented and decentralized political system to impose their preferences on the electorate. As many anti-federalists anticipated, rather than providing a remedy for the "mischiefs of faction," the constitutional framework conceived by the founding fathers created innumerable opportunities for both the federal government and private interests to exercise undue political influence. Indeed, as we will discover in this chapter, not only have think tanks, interest groups, and other non-governmental organizations proliferated in great numbers, but they have, through various channels, become firmly entrenched in the policy-making process. Rather than simply commenting on the range of policy options available to decision-makers, think tanks have, in Diane Stone's words, sought to capture "the political imagination"[4] of the nation. Or, to be more blunt, they have made a concerted effort to capture the "political agenda" of the nation.

Think tanks, as discussed in chapter 2, can no longer be perceived as detached observers of American politics. On the contrary, they have a vested interest in participating, directly and indirectly, in the conversations taking place between power-brokers on Capitol Hill, in the White House, and in the sterile corridors of bureaucratic departments and agencies. As think tanks have undergone a transformation from institutions devoted to policy research to organizations more often committed to political advocacy, their priorities, not surprisingly, have changed. Although they may have "squander[ed] their potential influence"[5] in the process, a concern expressed by Andrew Rich, their ultimate goal has remained the same – to shape and mould American domestic and foreign policy.

The purpose of this chapter is to explore the world think tanks inhabit so that we can better explain why they are able to become active participants in the policy-making process. We begin by focusing on features of the American political system that have facilitated the access of think tanks to the executive and legislative branches of government and to the key agencies and departments involved in foreign policy. In the process, some comparisons will be made to similar institutions found in Westminister parliamentary systems and in countries such as Germany, where many think tanks, by virtue of their formal ties to political parties, are in a special position to influence policy-making.[6] Attention will also be paid to the various incentives policy-makers have to turn to think tanks for policy advice and why policy entrepreneurs and philanthropic foundations and private donors have played such a critical role in think tank development.

THE DISTINCTIVE WORLD OF AMERICAN THINK TANKS

There are aspects and features of every culture and society that are distinct. And in most of the social sciences and humanities, including anthropology, sociology, history, and political science, scholars have identified characteristics of nations and states that help to distinguish them from other members of the international community. Some of these differences relate to language, religion, geography, culture, government, architecture, food, and sport. In his classic account of the United States, *Democracy in America*,[7] Alexis de Tocqueville, a young, aristocratic French lawyer who came to America in the early 1830s to study its penitentiary systems, commented on several features of American society that he deemed noteworthy. These included the existence of a free press and the propensity of Americans to join associations.[8] Had he written his seminal study a century and a half later, he undoubtedly would have considered other things distinctively American, such as theme parks, fast food, and think tanks.[9]

At the turn of the twentieth century, think tanks had been established in Great Britain, Germany, and a handful of other countries, but it was in the United States that their presence began to be most strongly felt. As the Russell Sage Foundation, the Carnegie Endowment for International Peace, the Brookings Institution, and several other think tanks shared their insights on social, economic, and foreign policy with leading decision-makers, it became clear that they could, and most likely would, come to play an important role in the Progressive Era. In fact, as think tanks assumed more visibility and prominence in the political arena, some scholars, including James McGann, noted that, in many respects, they had become an American phenomenon.[10] When dozens of new think tanks emerged on the political landscape in the ensuing decades, there was little reason to challenge what had become a generally accepted observation. In the post–World War II era, think tanks were considered as American as hamburgers and apple pie. Yet in recent years, as the number of think tanks has skyrocketed throughout the international community, McGann and others have acknowledged that they are no longer uniquely American;[11] they have become a global phenomenon. Still, few would dispute that the United States, with more than half the world's think tanks within its borders, more than any other country, provides fertile soil for them to develop and grow. This conclusion begs an obvious question: Why, relative to other advanced industrialized countries, has the United States become a popular home for think tanks?

Have think tanks emerged in unparalleled numbers in America because there is a shortage of policy expertise in universities and in government? On the surface, this answer appears to make perfect sense. After all, if the research capacity in universities and in various government departments and agencies is insufficient to meet the policy needs of decision-makers, it might explain why hundreds of think tanks with specific areas of expertise have been created and why even more may be required. This is a theory that Steven Simon and Jonathan Stevenson, two think tank residents, believe warrants closer consideration. In their 2004–05 article in *The National Interest*, they argue that there are some policy issues, such as how to neutralize "a stateless, religiously inspired network of militants who seek to bring down great powers,"[12] that necessitate the development of think tanks which can think "outside the box." It is not that universities, government departments, and other institutions which engage in research and analysis are in short supply. Rather, it is that with respect to some policy concerns, including the war on terror, experts in universities and in government are not prepared or equipped to contribute to an informed and enlightened public policy.[13] This is why, Simon and Stevenson claim, institutions capable of thinking in new and innovative ways are required.

Their argument that additional think tanks may be required to better serve the interests and needs of policy-makers compels us to reconsider the response to our initial question. To explain why America, relative to other advanced Western democracies, has become a home for think tanks, we suggested that perhaps they have emerged in large numbers to compensate for the lack of policy expertise in the country. However, this does not seem to be the case. The faculty listings at American universities and colleges confirm that many of the brightest minds in the country reside in the hallowed halls of academe, where scholars tackle some of the most pressing concerns in the arts, humanities, social sciences, and sciences. Similarly, in every government department and agency, including the Executive Office of the President,[14] hundreds of policy experts armed with advanced degrees examine and analyze issues and trends that are of profound importance to members of Congress, the White House, and the electorate. In the process, they can draw on financial and staff resources that far surpass those available to even the most affluent think tanks in the country. If anything, there is an abundant supply of policy expertise in the United States.

Hundreds of think tanks have not taken root in the United States because of a perceived shortage of policy expertise. They have proliferated, if we follow the logic of Simon and Stevenson's argument, because of a lack of *specialized* expertise. New think tanks may be required to address the complex set of issues that have arisen in the post–September 11th world, just as think tanks were created before and after World War II to assist policy-makers confront a wide range of economic, social, and security concerns. What Simon and Stevenson are suggesting is not radically different from what Robert Brookings, Andrew Carnegie, and a group of engineers at Project Rand proposed decades ago.

The rise of think tanks is also closely associated with the type of expertise and services they offer and their ability to satisfy the needs of policy-makers, journalists, opinion leaders, philanthropists, and corporate and private donors in ways that other institutions engaged in research and analysis cannot. For example, unlike university professors, who in most instances must balance the demands of teaching, research, and administration, policy experts at think tanks have the luxury of concentrating on what they do best – monitoring, analyzing, and commenting on timely and relevant policy issues. Experts at think tanks often publish books and articles that stimulate discussion in the academic community, but they are concerned primarily with generating a range of research products that will be of immediate interest to policy-makers and to the public. They cannot afford, as their colleagues in universities often can, to invest five, ten, or even fifteen years on a research project. Moreover, most private or independent think tanks do not have the luxury of relying, as many academics at universities do, on government support for their research. Although a handful of prominent think tanks continue to draw heavily on government funding, many, including the vast majority of advocacy think tanks, look to philanthropic foundations, corporations, and private donors for assistance. Furthermore, like the institutes they fund, donors have a vested interest in influencing the political climate of the day. This in large part explains why so many advocacy think tanks have been created over the past several decades. They have struck a responsive chord with donors who are prepared to support their vision of how the United States ought to be governed.

Experts at think tanks understand the importance of responding to the needs of policy-makers and therefore make this a priority. They need not be reminded that securing a captive audience on Capitol Hill and/or in the White House can pay handsome dividends. By contrast, scholars at universities are rarely concerned about meeting the daily demands of policy-makers. Instead, they prefer to engage in long-term research in the hope that their findings, based on years of rigorous analysis, will help to advance the public interest. In short, scholars working at think tanks and universities have very different priorities, objectives, and timelines. This is why universities cannot be a substitute for think tanks and why think tanks cannot take the place of universities.

Rather than competing with each other, think tanks and universities have carved out their own niches in the knowledge industry. But what about government departments and agencies? Do they threaten the survival of think tanks? Apparently not. Despite being able to draw on extensive resources in the bureaucracy, policy-makers on Capitol Hill and in the White House often solicit "outside expertise." The absence of a permanent senior civil service in the United States, combined with a general distrust of government, may in part explain the reluctance of members of Congress and the Executive to rely exclusively on the bureaucracy for advice. Moreover, as Rich and others have argued, think tanks can provide many valuable services to policy-makers, not the least of which is offering ideological reinforcement for their political views, a service that bureaucrats cannot offer publicly.[15] Think tanks can also be of great assistance to congressional aides, who often do not have the time or the inclination to produce independent research for members of Congress. The opposite appears to be the case in Canada and Great Britain, where elected officials and their staff are more likely to heed the advice of public servants than to turn their attention to the external policy research community, although this pattern appears to be changing.[16]

The existence of a large and well-staffed bureaucracy has not rendered think tanks redundant. In fact, there are many bureaucratic departments that have established a close and enduring relationship to some of the nation's most visible think tanks. The Department of Housing and Urban Development (HUD), for example, enjoys strong ties to the Urban Institute, and the Department of Defense continues to provide the lion's share of RAND's $200-million-plus annual budget. Several other departments and agencies contract work out to think tanks.[17]

Turning to think tanks for their expertise can benefit bureaucratic departments in many ways. Not only can think tanks offering specialized expertise help departments to provide more informed advice to policy-makers, but soliciting an outside perspective can often reinforce or augment the work of government policy experts. In addition, relying on research-oriented (as opposed to more advocacy-motivated) think tanks that operate at arm's length to government can at times lend credibility and legitimacy to policy debates. This reinforcement becomes particularly important when departments and agencies come under fire for being overtly partisan.

By examining the differences between policy experts working at universities and in government and their counterparts in think tanks, we can begin to understand why there is a need in the United States for organizations capable and willing to offer independent policy expertise. Clearly, think tanks operating outside the formal parameters of government can assist policy-makers in ways that scholars in other environments cannot. But their distinctive institutional characteristics – for example, their ability to provide timely and succinct position papers – does not account entirely for why hundreds of think tanks have made their home in the United States.

The United States has not become their sanctuary because of an unlimited demand for both policy research and ideologically driven think tanks. It has become a sanctuary because, unlike political systems that actively discourage the participation of non-governmental organizations in the legislative process, the institutional structure of the American government invites them to become engaged in policy-making.[18] Put simply, the highly decentralized and fragmented political system enshrined in the US Constitution, combined with weak parties and considerable turnover in the upper echelons of the bureaucracy, provides think tanks with unparalleled opportunities to shape public opinion and public policy. This factor becomes particularly clear when administrations change and the revolving door between think tanks and government is in full swing. Supported by generous benefactors, inspired by policy entrepreneurs, embraced by a voracious media searching for controversial and provocative ideas, and lured by political power, think tanks have become permanent fixtures in the political arena.

THE LAND OF OPPORTUNITY: THINK TANKS IN THE AMERICAN POLITICAL SYSTEM

In a country where political power is dispersed among separate branches, where legislators are free to vote as they wish, and where a growing number of congressional and presidential candidates look to policy experts for advice, think tanks find themselves in an enviable position. Like foxes holding the keys to the chicken coop, they have found a captive audience. More specifically, they have identified multiple target audiences with whom to establish and maintain contact. These range from policy-makers assembled around conference tables debating policy options to journalists searching for a ten-second sound bite.

Faced with limited resources, the majority of think tanks, like interest groups, must think strategically about how and to what extent to become involved at various stages of the policy cycle. The various factors that influence their decisions will be considered in the following chapter, but in the section below, our attention will focus more generally on where in the political system think tanks try to make their presence felt and the many institutional and societal factors that have enabled them to become active participants in the policy-making community. We begin, as the US Constitution does, by looking at Congress, a favourite destination for many Washington-based think tanks.

A CAPITAL IDEA ON CAPITOL HILL

Edwin Feulner, the Heritage Foundation's charismatic president and resident visionary, is well known in Washington's policy-making community. A graduate of the University of Pennsylvania's Wharton School of Business and the University of Edinburgh, where he obtained a PhD, he is a leading figure in the conservative movement. In January 1989 President Reagan conferred on him the Presidential Citizens Medal for "building an organization dedicated to ideas and their consequences." Rarely shy about his institute's mission, Feulner has proclaimed that Heritage's role is to influence what goes on in Congress, in the White House, and in the media.[19]

With over two hundred researchers and staff members and an annual budget of $35 million, the Heritage Foundation extends its tentacles into virtually every branch, department, and agency of the US government. But as Feulner has acknowledged on numerous occasions, Congress is his institute's principal target. It is also the focus of attention for countless other think tanks that have tried to emulate Heritage's success. They realize, as Feulner did over thirty years ago when he and Paul Weyrich were working as congressional aides, that gaining access to members of Congress and their staff, as well as important committees and subcommittees, is critical in waging successful battles in the war of ideas. After all, it is Congress, not the president, that is primarily responsible for making legislation, and it is Congress that approves the nation's budget. Moreover, it is the responsibility of the Senate to confirm presidential appointments, including US ambassadors, cabinet secretaries, the directors of the CIA and FBI, the national security adviser, and other key officials.[20] And it is the Senate that has the authority to ratify or reject international treaties and to regulate trade and commerce. But even more importantly than exercising these powers, Congress is the key institution responsible for responding to the needs of the electorate, a civics lesson that think tanks have committed to memory. By establishing strong lines of communication with Congress, they can tap into a direct pipeline to the American people. For many think tanks, this pipeline is the life-support system they depend on to shape public opinion and public policy.

With so much power and responsibility at their disposal, members of Congress naturally attract the attention of think tanks, interest groups, lobbyists, and other NGOs. House and Senate staff members and advisers are also courted by think tanks eager to enlighten them about the costs and benefits of supporting or opposing proposed legislation. That is why some think tanks, including Heritage, maintain liaison offices with both houses of Congress to closely monitor current and emerging issues. Think tanks must also pay close attention to hearings organized by various congressional committees and subcommittees. Testifying before a high-profile congressional committee can offer think tanks a valuable opportunity to plant ideas in the minds of influential members of Congress who are looking either for a different perspective on important and controversial policy matters or for some additional reinforcement for their position. Even if think tank staff do not testify before a particular congressional committee, they can ill afford to lose sight of the recommendations being made. Providing timely and relevant policy advice, the mantra for think tanks, necessitates remaining informed about the issues policy-makers are thinking about and the steps they are considering taking to transform their beliefs into public policy.

For the various reasons outlined above, Congress remains an important and inviting target for think tanks. And by virtue of the weak party system in the United States, a system that encourages representatives and senators to support the wishes of their constituents and those of organized interests over the needs of their party, it is also a highly accessible institution. Since members of Congress, unlike members of the British and Canadian parliaments, are not bound by party unity, they need not be concerned that their association with particular think tanks or their endorsement of some of their policy ideas will undermine party cohesion. Rather than evaluating ideas emanating from think tanks in terms of whether they would be compatible with party interests and policies, members of Congress can evaluate them on their own merits. As Weaver argues, political systems with weak parties have not only opened doors for think tanks[21] but, in some ways, increased the demand for them.

AEI's David Frum, the Canadian-born and American-educated pundit whose conservative credentials and biting prose helped land him a speechwriting position in the first term of the Bush administration, agrees that the absence of a strong party system in the United States has resulted in a higher demand for think tanks. Quoting from Gilbert and Sullivan's HMS *Pinafore* – "I always voted at my party's call and I never thought of thinking for myself at all" – Frum wryly observes that "parties do not have a coherent call." He adds that in Congress and in the Executive "you have to think for yourself, and of course, most policy-makers find this physically impossible. [It is] impossible for any representative to think for himself on every issue, to do all the preparatory work on every issue that is going to come before him in the course of a legislative or executive career."[22] Moreover, according to Frum, in the United States "you have a tremendous need for incoming politicians in the executive and legislative branches to arrive with specific, not general proposals. They [policy-makers] must not only lay down general ideas about policy but actually devise and answer many of the specific and highly technical questions, and they need expertise ... So if you're an idea entrepreneur, as all national political leaders are, you can cast about and find expertise to help you in a way that no one else will."[23]

There are a handful of congressional research institutes or public think tanks, including the Congressional Research Service and the General Accounting Office, that members of Congress can rely on for "objective" information and data about the economy, the environment, and other important matters.[24] However, these institutions cannot be expected to provide policy-makers with the range of services that many private think tanks offer. They certainly cannot be called upon to support or advance their ideological goals. Although they can assist members of Congress to obtain more in-depth knowledge about a particular issue, public think tanks are not in the business of marketing ideas. In short, they can be found in the federal government directory, not in the burgeoning "advocacy think tank" section of the Yellow Pages.

For a brief period of time, members of Congress could turn to another government body for policy expertise. The Congressional Policy Advisory Board was established in March 1998 to allow experts to discuss several policy issues with the House leadership. Of the twenty-eight policy experts who comprised the board, twenty-one were affiliated with US think tanks, including the board's chair, Martin Anderson, a senior fellow at the Hoover Institution.[25] But while it appeared that the board had the potential to play an important role in advising members of Congress, it was disbanded with little notice or explanation in 2000.[26]

Yes, Mr. President: Inside the Oval Office

Congress may remain the principal target for many think tanks in the United States, but they also keep the White House clearly in their sights. The authority of the president to fill thousands of positions in the bureaucracy when he assumes power affords think tanks opportunities to influence policy-making in ways that their counterparts in parliamentary systems such as Canada and Great Britain cannot even fathom. As previously noted, the absence of a permanent senior civil service in the United States creates an incentive for think tanks to supply personnel for key positions throughout the bureaucracy. While a Canadian or British prime minister may elect to fill a handful of senior bureaucratic positions with career civil servants or faithful party members, the president can appoint close to ten thousand people. "By and large, everybody from deputy assistant secretary level and above is a political appointee."[27] In short, the president has the opportunity, not to mention the authority, to reward thousands of policy experts with government positions.

It is a familiar scene on NBC's *The West Wing*: The door to the Oval Office swings open, and the president finds himself surrounded by White House staff and a handful of policy experts exchanging ideas about an emerging political issue. After carefully outlining the major issues involved, the policy expert or experts who have been summoned to the White House leave the president and his inner circle of advisers to deliberate. With their arms folded and eyes fixed like a laser beam on the leader of the most powerful nation in the world, those who remain in the inner sanctum are left to shape the course of history. Although the events that unfold on *The West Wing* may not necessarily mirror reality, presidents often rely heavily on their trusted advisers, many of whom are recruited from think tanks, to address a wide range of policy concerns.

As noted in chapter 1, several presidents, including Jimmy Carter, Ronald Reagan, and to a lesser extent, Bill Clinton and George Bush, have turned to experts from think tanks for advice both during their campaigns and in their administrations.[28] Many think tank staff members have gone on to serve in senior positions in government, while countless others have assisted the president by participating on advisory boards or task forces. The strong ties that have been developed between think tanks and various administrations will be examined in greater detail in the case studies that follow, but what is important to understand is that think tank staff have much to gain by securing access to the White House. Indeed, by becoming one of the president's key advisers, as several think tank alumni have, they are in a position to exercise extraordinary influence.

The US Constitution may bestow upon Congress far more powers in the area of foreign policy than have been entrusted to the president,[29] but few scholars of foreign policy can afford to ignore the authority invested in the president as commander-in-chief. Particularly during times of crisis, Americans look to the president, not to Congress, for leadership. And it is during times of crisis that presidents look to their advisers before making critical policy decisions. As a result, it is important to understand who these advisers are and what experience they bring to office.

Making Their Way in Washington: Think Tanks and the Bureaucracy

Often referred to as the fourth branch of government, the federal bureaucracy in the United States has wide-ranging responsibilities that extend into virtually every aspect of society. Among other things, it has the authority to approve new pharmaceutical drugs, to inspect safety measures in the transportation industry, to protect the environment, and to grant licences to cable broadcasting companies. It is also responsible for overseeing and ensuring the national security of the United States.

As a matter of course, think tanks specializing in foreign policy and national security matters are aware of the mandate and jurisdiction of the key agencies and departments engaged in American foreign relations. They closely monitor the issues being explored by the Departments of Defense, State, and Homeland Security and, through their contacts, try to remain informed about key concerns in the CIA, the FBI, and the National Security Council. Think tanks, like interest groups, understand that if they are to have a long-term impact on policy-making, they must at the very least establish and maintain personal ties to policy analysts and advisers in the bureaucracy. They therefore make a point of sending their publications and other relevant information about their organizations to mid-level and senior staff in the bureaucracy and why they keep a detailed list of who occupies important positions in the foreign policy-making establishment. In short, think tanks want to keep as many lines of communication open as possible, and doing so means keeping track of who's who in the bureaucracy.

How successful think tanks are in penetrating various government departments is, as we will discover, difficult to measure. But as Howard Wiarda, a long-time student of foreign policy, notes, we must begin somewhere. "Government runs, in part, on the basis of memos. If a State Department or Defense Department official, or an analyst at the CIA or the National Security Council, has your study in front of him and open at the time he is writing his own memo to the secretary or the director or perhaps the president himself – if, in short, he is using your ideas and analysis at the time he writes his own memo – then you have influence. If your study is not open in front of him or, worse, you do not even know who the responsible official is, you do not have influence. It is as simple as that."[30] Assessing how much or little influence think tanks have in foreign policy is hardly as simple as Wiarda suggests, but he is correct in identifying the bureaucracy as an important channel of influence and one that warrants further consideration. In chapter 6 we will take a closer look at how think tanks seek to strengthen their ties to the bureaucracy and some factors that may impede or facilitate their access.

Thus far we have highlighted where in the American political system think tanks have sought to make their presence felt and why specifically they are attracted to these particular targets. While it is clear that they are interested in strengthening their ties to Congress, the Executive, and the bureaucracy, they also remain committed to increasing their media profile, a subject that we will accordingly examine.

Identifying principal targets or stakeholders with whom to share their ideas is not a difficult undertaking for America's think tanks. They understand that in a highly decentralized and fragmented political system – or what I have sarcastically described as a land of opportunity – think tanks can rely on multiple channels to influence public opinion and public policy. But they also understand that having good ideas does not guarantee success in the political arena. Influencing public policy, as we will discuss, requires far more than making policy-makers aware of the policy options they have at their disposal. Several factors, including the willingness of policy-makers and the electorate to embrace new ideas and the availability of resources to support additional government programs or initiatives, are among the many conditions that must be satisfied in order for individuals and organizations to exercise policy influence. Yet even before think tanks begin to concern themselves with the logistics of influencing public policy, they must secure access to funding so that they can research, publicize, and promote their ideas. To this end, they must, like major corporations in the United States, rely on strong leadership, a subject to which we will now turn.

A PENNY FOR YOUR THOUGHTS: POLICY
ENTREPRENEURS, PHILANTHROPIC
FOUNDATIONS, AND THINK TANKS

The important role that philanthropic foundations, corporations, and individual donors play in elevating the status of think tanks in the United States cannot be underestimated, nor can the contribution of so-called policy entrepreneurs to think tank development. As Abelson and Carberry point out in their comparative study of American and Canadian think tanks, "In the United States, independent policy entrepreneurs have provided important leadership in the formation of think tanks dedicated to providing information and advice to government. In Canada, on the other hand, such leadership is likely to come from the government itself or from senior public servants. This difference reflects both the incentives created by the institutional structure of each form of government as well as cultural understandings of the appropriate repositories of policy expertise."[31] John Kingdon's work on policy entrepreneurs, defined as "advocates for proposals or for the prominence of an idea," demonstrates how these individuals can have an important impact on policy issues: "their defining characteristic, much as in the case of a business entrepreneur, is their willingness to invest their resources – time, energy, reputation, and sometimes money – in the hope of a future return."[32] Why do policy entrepreneurs undertake these investments? They do so, according to Kingdon, "to promote their values, or affect the shape of public policy."[33] And there is some evidence to suggest that at least with respect to the private sector, these entrepreneurs are likely to be more prominent in the United States than in parliamentary systems such as Canada.

In their study of the environmental agenda in the United States and Canada, Harrison and Hoberg observed a difference in policy entrepreneurship between these two countries.[34] Among other things, they discovered that policy entrepreneurs in the United States played an important role in the promotion of certain environmental issues, particularly the effects of radon, and were able to facilitate its discussion on the political agenda. They also noticed that there was an absence of similar activity in Canada. Harrison and Hoberg note how the presence of policy entrepreneurship is, in a certain sense, tied to the institutional arrangements of each political system.[35] As in the case of think tanks, the highly fragmented nature of the American political system, combined with an absence of strong party unity, provides incentives to private policy entrepreneurs to help shape the political agenda. Conversely, the relatively closed and party-driven system in Canada offers few allurements to such entrepreneurs.

As noted in chapter 2, several think tanks in the United States owe their existence and, indeed, their success to policy entrepreneurs intent on contributing to the national conversation. Robert Brookings, Andrew Carnegie, and the Heritage Foundation's Edwin Feulner represent but a handful of such entrepreneurs who have created think tanks as institutional vehicles to advance a particular ideological agenda. This entrepreneurial spirit is also being expressed in the form of vanity and legacy-based think tanks in the United States.

By contrast, as Abelson and Carberry argue, there are few examples of think tanks in Canada that are the direct creation of *private*-sector policy entrepreneurship.[36] The Fraser Institute, under the initial guidance of British businessman Sir Antony Fisher, Patrick Boyle, and economists Sally Pipes and Michael Walker, Fraser's former executive director and now president of its foundation,[37] and the defunct Canadian Institute for International Peace and Security, which was inspired by former prime minister Pierre Elliott Trudeau's global peace initiative, are notable exceptions. On the other hand, the *public* sector has served as a viable source of leadership. Senior public servants, including Michael Pitfield and Michael Kirby,[38] played important roles in creating the Institute for Research on Public Policy, the Economic Council of Canada, the Science Council of Canada, and other governmental advisory bodies that provide policy expertise.[39]

The fact that major initiatives for creating Canadian centres of policy expertise generally arise from inside the government and not from the private sector, as in the United States, is not surprising. In part it reflects the different cultural understanding of the relationship between government and the provision of policy expertise in Canada. Private sector policy entrepreneurs have had a significant impact on the creation of the think tank landscape in the United States, while government has led the way in Canada. This role for governmental leadership in Canada is not unexpected, given the importance assigned to bureaucratic and party policy advice in the parliamentary process.[40]

The tendency for private, rather than public, endeavours in the United States is reflected in the country's extensive private and corporate philanthropy.[41] Several prominent American think tanks, including the Russell Sage Foundation, Brookings, Heritage, the Hoover Institution, and the Carnegie Endowment for International Peace, have benefited significantly from foundation funding and charitable donations. But these activities are not as prominent in Canadian society;[42] so policy institutes created and supported by individual and philanthropic actions are not as common. Instead, the government is more likely to take the lead in their development and sustenance.[43] In the United States the Ford, Rockefeller, and Carnegie foundations, among others, have long supported social science research, much of which has been conducted at think tanks.[44] The generous tradition of philanthropic support for think tanks in the United States has not taken root to the same extent in Canada. Consequently, the majority of think tanks in Canada must struggle to keep afloat.

Relying too heavily on philanthropic foundations and corporations can also prove to be risky. Like governments, which often insist that recipients of foreign aid make certain concessions, philanthropic foundations and large corporate donors must be satisfied that the organizations they are making grants to act in a manner consistent with their institutional mission. Failing to conform to the political agenda of philanthropic and corporate donors can, as the American Enterprise Institute discovered in the mid-1980s, have serious repercussions. When AEI president William Baroody Jr was unable to satisfy several right-wing benefactors, including the Olin Foundation and the Reader's Digest Foundation, the institute was committed to pursuing a truly conservative agenda, these and other like-minded donors withdrew their significant financial support. The result was that AEI was brought to the verge of bankruptcy.[45] Conversely, acting in the interests of affluent donors can pay handsome dividends for some think tanks. The Washington-based conservative think tank Citizens for a Sound Economy (CSE) discovered this after it began its campaign to derail a multi-billion-dollar federal plan to restore the Florida Everglades in 1998. For its efforts, CSE received $700,000 in contributions from Florida's three largest sugar enterprises, "which stand to lose thousands of acres of cane-growing land to reclamation if the Army Corps of Engineers plan goes into effect."[46]

In sum, think tank development in the American context is supported by several important cultural influences, including, but by no means restricted to, a pattern of philanthropy and the presence of independent advisers operating alongside the bureaucracy. This phenomenon has promoted policy entrepreneurship stemming from the private sector, with think tanks originating within society. The Canadian cultural context provides a different environment for think tanks, particularly with a bureaucratic ethos, which at times discourages external advice.

The picture that has been painted so far helps us to better understand why the United States, relative to other advanced Western democracies, has become a sanctuary for think tanks. The open nature of the American political system, combined with weak political parties and philanthropic foundations and policy entrepreneurs willing to support these institutions, has helped to pave the way for hundreds of think tanks. However, despite the growing presence of think tanks on America's political landscape, the literature on policy-making has, for the most part, failed to adequately address the role these organizations play. In flow charts and diagrams outlining the policy-making process, the role and responsibilities of the Executive, Congress, the National Security Council, the Pentagon, the State Department, the Central Intelligence Agency, and other intelligence-gathering agencies are clearly defined. Yet, interestingly enough, the involvement of think tanks has largely been ignored. In the next chapter we will explore how several scholars, drawing on traditional models and theories of foreign policy-making, have sought to explain America's conduct in world affairs. In the process, the various ways that think tanks can be better incorporated into studies of foreign policy will become apparent.

CHAPTER FIVE

Something Is Missing: Think Tanks and the Study of Foreign Policy-Making

Despite the growing presence of think tanks in the United States and their ongoing efforts to influence the policy preferences and choices of decision-makers, political scientists have been slow to recognize their involvement in the policy-making process. But as Joseph Peschek points out, given the propensity of scholars to explain policy decisions as either an outcome of intergovernmental politics or interest group competition, this neglect is not entirely surprising. "The acceptance of a split between 'private' and 'public' uses of power may help to account for this dismissive attitude. Political scientists who examine policy only as an outcome either of intergovernmental processes or of overt interest group pressure from outside the government will miss the significance of [think tanks] in the political process ,"[1] which, Peschek notes, is more strongly felt during the initial stages of the policy cycle, when the parameters of public debates are being framed.

Even if one were prepared to acknowledge that intergovernmental and interest group bargaining occur in separate policy domains,[2] it does not explain why so little attention has been paid to the contribution of think tanks to both political processes. As a matter of course, think tanks interact on a regular basis with officials in various levels and branches of government. Moreover, as we will examine in the following chapter, they rely on several different channels, many of them public, to communicate their ideas to those who occupy positions of power. Through their publications, conferences, and research programs, think tanks can also directly and indirectly support the mandate of interest groups, unions, trade associations, and corporations, a subject that we will return to in chapters 8 and 9. In short, scholars would be hard-pressed to *miss the significance* of think tanks even if they differentiated between the public and private uses of power.

It is more likely that they have downplayed or underestimated their impact in policy-making because, unlike those of interest groups, whose motivations and goals are relatively transparent, the role of think tanks is ambiguous and therefore more difficult to define. In other words, given the emphasis that interest groups place on influencing governmental policies, it is expected that they will draw on a wide range of lobbying tactics to achieve their goals. This, after all, is their raison d'être. It is hardly a well-kept secret that interest groups pressure, cajole, and manipulate the public and policy-makers to support their goals. By contrast, the objectives and priorities of think tanks are far less predictable and, as a consequence, are not always easy to discern.

At the turn of the twentieth century, some think tanks believed that the most effective way to advance both their institutional mandate and the public interest was to develop and foster an environment in which the pursuit of knowledge was the highest priority; achieving policy influence, though desirable, was of secondary importance.[3] Think tanks such as the Brookings Institution understood and appreciated the importance of bringing the scientific expertise of scholars to bear on issues of significant concern to those entrusted with overseeing the nation's interests. However, in what has become an increasingly competitive marketplace of ideas where individuals, non-governmental organizations, and even the media struggle to be heard,[4] the vast majority of think tanks seem convinced that neither their private concerns nor the broader public interest can be advanced unless they transform themselves into staunch advocates for various political causes, a trend that many scholars find disheartening.

To sum up, since think tanks can and do assume multiple and conflicting roles, making general observations about their behaviour, as we will discover in the case studies that follow, is problematic. Furthermore, because their involvement in policy-making is not as easily understood as the contribution made by interest groups, it stands to reason that they are often ignored. It is far simpler to pretend that think tanks do not exist or to assume that they play only a modest role in policy-making than to construct a conceptual framework which would allow scholars to evaluate their influence in policy development.

However, since scholars can no longer disregard the two thousand or more think tanks that have taken root in the United States and the active role many play in shaping public opinion and public policy, it is necessary to consider how these organizations can be incorporated into mainstream models, theories, and approaches to policy-making. In this chapter we will pay particular attention to foreign policy-making and the various methods that have been employed to explain the behaviour of the United States and its leaders in world affairs. Among other things, this analysis will allow us to consider what changes need to be made to give due consideration to the involvement of think tanks in the policy-making process. The chapter begins by discussing the basic framework scholars have relied on to study foreign policy-making. This framework divides the policy-making process into three distinct stages: policy inputs, throughput (or the black box of decision-making), and policy outputs. Following this discussion, several theories that have been developed to shed light on the inner workings of the policy-making process will be outlined. Finally, we will consider alternative approaches, some of which have been outlined in chapter 3, which may prove useful in studying think tanks and foreign policy-making.

THE STUDY OF FOREIGN POLICY DECISION-MAKING

In many respects, foreign policy analysis, or the study of foreign policy decision-making, is the cornerstone of international relations. It is by examining and dissecting the many domestic and external factors thought to influence the behaviour of leaders and states that we try to make sense of the mysterious and complex world of international affairs. In so doing, scholars engaged in this field of inquiry quickly come to the realization that analyzing foreign policy is at once both fascinating and immensely frustrating. Indeed, what could be more fascinating than tapping into the minds of world leaders who, through their actions and deeds, can and ultimately will shape the course of history? Alternatively, what could be more frustrating than not knowing for certain what factor or event or adviser, for that matter, influenced a leader's decision?

Unlike trying to follow step-by-step instructions to assemble a barbecue or a child's swing set, it is difficult, not to mention futile, for scholars to construct a pictogram to summarize how decisions are made. Decision-making, particularly when it involves matters of war and peace, cannot and should not be explained by translating human emotions into a simple formula, model, or equation. Although some scholars may treat foreign policy-making as a science, there is little about the process of making decisions that is scientific.[5] Those who study foreign policy, like those who make it, need to recognize that every issue and every situation is unique. They must understand, just as the late sixth-century Greek philosopher Hericlitus did, that you can never step in the same river twice. In other words, although there are some aspects of policy-making that remain relatively constant, such as the constitutional authority invested in Congress and the Executive, there are many other features that are in flux. The challenge is to construct an analytical framework for studying foreign policy-making that provides scholars with an opportunity to evaluate both.

It Is as Easy as 1–2–3 – or Is It?

In undergraduate survey courses in international relations, American politics, and US foreign policy, it is not uncommon for instructors to introduce the study of foreign policy-making by identifying three separate stages or phases of the policy cycle: inputs, throughput and outputs. Using boxes to denote these stages, the foreign policy-making process is often outlined as follows.

In box 1, labelled "Inputs," scholars identify the various organizations and individuals in the United States and from abroad that have a vested interest in influencing American foreign policy and who, through various channels, try to make their views and preferences known. Those that provide input into the foreign policy-making process may include academics, journalists, political parties, interest groups, lobbyists, political consultants, think tanks, foreign leaders, labour unions, multinational corporations, and defense contractors. However, to make the study of foreign policy more manageable, scholars often choose to closely monitor those individuals and organizations that are genuinely committed to influencing a particular foreign policy goal or action of the United States. Since it is impossible to keep

Figure 5.1 The foreign policy-making process

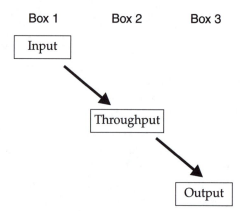

track of the thousands of groups and private citizens that try to share their insights about the virtues and pitfalls of American foreign policy, it is necessary to focus on specific policy issues.

Compiling a list of those that are in a position to provide significant input into the policy-making process is not as formidable a task as one might imagine. In fact, in most policy debates, a small but vocal cadre of interest groups, advocacy organizations, journalists, and policy experts quickly appear to stake out their positions. They articulate their concerns in newspapers, in opinion magazines, and on various Web sites and provide commentary on radio and television. At times, recognized experts in the field are also asked to provide congressional testimony, a further opportunity to market their message. Although some groups and individuals prefer to work behind the scenes to influence policy-makers, foreign policy analysts can in most instances identify the "usual suspects" in short order.

Simply put, the first stage of the policy cycle is one in which groups and individuals compete for the attention of the public and policy-makers by sharing their insights on policies being considered or implemented by the United States. In some respects, this stage closely resembles a compost in which materials are collected and stored for future use. Some of the ideas gathered at this stage are disposed of, but others are recycled and marketed by organizations and individuals who may be in a position to influence the attitudes and beliefs of decision-makers.[6]

Before delving into the contents of box 2, it will be useful to skip ahead to box 3 – policy outputs or policy outcomes. These are simply the decisions that leaders make on behalf of the state. This is by far the easiest and most transparent stage of the policy cycle. Students of foreign policy often spend their waking hours trying to explain how and why policy-makers arrived at particular decisions, but they need not invest much time in recording the actual policy decisions that have been made. After all, with respect to matters of conflict, conflict resolution, international trade, and other issues that fall under the auspices of foreign policy, leaders cannot conceal their decisions for long.

Thus far we have been able to describe, with little difficulty, what takes place in two important stages of the policy cycle. Unfortunately, to complete our three-step process, we must shed light on what transpires in box 2, or the "throughput" phase. It is the throughput phase, or what many scholars have dubbed the "black box of decision-making," that creates innumerable obstacles for those looking to connect policy inputs to policy outputs. As Kim Richard Nossal, a leading student of foreign policy, points out "Since the manner in which a state arrives at the decisions that shape its actual behaviour in international politics is unknown, the foreign policy decision-making process of states [is] commonly conceived of as a black box, the inner workings of which [remain] largely hidden from view and [can] only be guessed at until diplomatic historians ... get their hands on the diplomatic records for the period."[7]

Historians have the luxury of analyzing diplomatic records, diaries, letters, memos, and other important and relevant documents and the time and distance to situate them in a proper historical context. By contrast, political scientists who study foreign policy cannot always afford to wait for these records to surface; nor can they remain silent even when confronted with the black box of decision-making. Trained to comment on political affairs as they unfold, they have few alternatives but to construct theories and models that will allow them to peer inside the black box. In the following section, we will discuss some of the models and theories that have been developed to pry open box 2 and will assess their potential benefits and drawbacks. Among other things, we will discover that the study of foreign policy-making, while often illuminating, is inherently complex. Despite our best efforts to construct a grand theory that would explain the nature of foreign policy-making, there is no single theory or explanation that can account for the behaviour of leaders who occupy positions of extraordinary power.

PEEKING INSIDE THE BLACK BOX

The Rational Actor Model

For proponents of state-centric models of decision-making, the rational actor model serves as a useful starting point to explain the behaviour of states and leaders in foreign affairs. This model assumes that the state acts as a rational, monolithic, and unitary decision-maker. It also assumes that the state, drawing on perfect information, has the capacity to identify and select a course of action that will enable it to realize its strategic goals and objectives.[8] The process by which states select a course of action in response to a perceived problem is thought to be similar to how individuals make rational choices. Once they define their goals and objectives, the next step is to evaluate the various options they have at their disposal. It is assumed that, in evaluating their options, states assess the consequences of each particular action and, after careful deliberation, make a value-maximizing decision – that is, they select a course of action that will maximize their benefits and minimize their costs.

The rational actor model is attractive to many scholars because it offers a manageable and straightforward approach to the study of foreign policy-making. Unfortunately, several of the assumptions on which the model are based are questionable. To begin with, it is unrealistic to assume that states, particularly those founded on democratic principles, behave as unitary decision-makers. By treating the state as an individual capable of making rational choices, proponents of the rational actor paradigm attempt to explain what motivates particular policy decisions. Yet when the state is reduced to the level of an individual, the mechanics of the governmental process, not to mention the various individuals and organizations that participate in it, are virtually ignored. Political leaders may prefer to make decisions without external interference, but the various pressures imposed on them by policy advisers, political parties, individual departments, agencies, boards, interest groups, corporations, labour unions, and other non-governmental organizations often limit their ability to make independent policy choices. Moreover, in a highly decentralized and fragmented political system such as that of the United States, the government rarely has the luxury of speaking with one voice. Rather, as evidenced by several controversial foreign policies, including the Bush administration's decision to invade Iraq, the state speaks with multiple voices. In the case of Iraq, the president and his inner circle of advisers have staked out one position on the war, but many in Congress have articulated a very different vision of how and when the United States should engage in armed intervention. Periodically, the Supreme Court also weighs in on discussions about the president's constitutional authority to make war.[9]

It is also important to recognize that while the president occupies the nation's highest office, the government he represents is comprised of loosely allied organizations competing to advance their own institutional mandate. As Graham Allison demonstrates in his seminal work on the Cuban Missile Crisis,[10] although individual departments and agencies are in theory supposed to assist the government in formulating and implementing policies, they are often preoccupied with enhancing and promoting their own position in the bureaucratic hierarchy. And in the event that they are fundamentally opposed to specific governmental policies, they can take measures to frustrate the efforts of political leaders to pursue their preferred policy choices.[11] This possibility again suggests that it is difficult for the government to speak with one voice.

Secondly, the rational actor model is based on the assumption that in the process of assessing the advantages and disadvantages of a particular course of action, leaders have access to perfect information – in other words, all relevant information necessary to make value-maximizing decisions. If states had access to perfect information, leaders could make decisions based on the rational calculation of perceived costs and benefits. However, from time immemorial, they have adopted policies which, for all intents and purposes, have been clearly irrational. How can such actions be explained? According to Herbert Simon, a renowned authority on organizational behaviour,[12] the willingness of leaders to reduce the requirements for information – in other words, to settle for inadequate, unreliable, and often faulty information – in part explains why states are inclined to make irrational policy decisions.

While most theories of individual and organizational choice "employ a concept of 'comprehensive rationality' according to which individuals and organizations choose the best alternative, taking account of consequences, their probabilities, and utilities,"[13] Simon argues that the concept of "bounded rationality" more accurately reflects how individuals and organizations process information. This concepts argues that "the physical and psychological limits of man's capacity as alternative generator, information processor, and problem solver constrain the decision-making processes of individuals and organizations. Because of these bounds, intendedly rational action requires simplified models that extract the main features of a problem without capturing all of its complexity."[14]

In other words, Simon contends that since individuals are incapable of processing the volume of information necessary to make "rational" policy decisions, they have no alternative but to simplify the decision-making process.[15] Faced with time pressures and other constraints that undermine their ability to make rational choices, Simon maintains, leaders replace the goals of maximization and optimization with a process he refers to as "satisficing." More specifically, in making policy decisions, individuals do not consider all possible alternatives before selecting an appropriate course of action. Instead, they are thought to choose a solution that is "good enough," that is, one that will satisfy their immediate goals and objectives. As Simon points out, individuals and organizations "are happy to find a needle in the haystack rather than searching for the sharpest needle in the haystack."[16]

Simon's theory of bounded rationality not only sheds light on the limitations of the rational actor model but, more importantly, helps to explain why leaders often fail to fully appreciate the consequences of their decisions. Preoccupied with resolving immediate policy problems, policy-makers can lose sight of the long-term implications of their actions. As a result, despite the best intentions of leaders, their actions can prove to be very damaging.

Notwithstanding its limitations, the rational actor model can be used as a frame of reference for our discussion about how think tanks can be integrated into more formal theories of foreign policy decision-making. Assuming, as proponents of the rational actor model do, that decision-makers acting on behalf of the state assess the advantages and disadvantages of pursuing various options before making policy decisions, one would expect them to solicit and at times rely on many different sources of policy advice. Since few decision-makers possess expertise in every policy area, an observation by AEI's David Frum cited earlier, it is not surprising that they frequently turn to their inner circle of policy advisers for guidance. Moreover, as discussed throughout this study, presidents and presidential candidates, not to mention members of Congress and their staff, frequently invite input from think tanks as they begin the long and difficult process of developing and shaping specific policies.

In examining how think tanks formulate and transmit ideas to decision-makers, those employing the rational actor model can, at a minimum, evaluate an important source of policy expertise. Since think tanks constantly bombard decision-makers with information and advice on a wide range of issues, their efforts to frame the parameters of policy debates should not be overlooked. Even if proponents of the rational actor model insist that the state speaks with one voice, they should not ignore how the state discovered and gave substance and clarity to its voice. At times, policy-makers, including the president, assume public office with a profoundly clear vision of how America ought to be governed. For example, although he was often criticized for not paying close enough attention to how his policy goals would be implemented, Ronald Reagan was strongly committed to building a country whose economic and military prowess would go unchallenged.[17] John F. Kennedy and Bill Clinton, among others, also had a strong sense of what they wanted to accomplish in office.[18] But each of these presidents understood that the process of transforming his vision into reality required considerable input from hundreds of experts and advisers, many of whom were recruited from the nation's most prominent think tanks.

The rational actor model can make additional accommodation for the role of think tanks. As noted above, think tanks can and do assist policy-makers to better understand the costs and benefits of pursuing different courses of action. Many can also provide advice on how best to implement policy decisions. In short, those relying on a rational actor model to explain the nature of foreign policy-making need not abandon the assumptions on which this model is based in order take into account the involvement of think tanks. On the contrary, they need only ask very basic questions about those assumptions. If the state speaks with one voice, who helps to shape that voice? Moreover, if it is believed that the state has the capacity to identify problems and suggest appropriate courses of action, which types of organizations are in a position to assist in these endeavours? And if the state has the ability to make value-maximizing decisions, who is equipped to evaluate the state's perceived costs and benefits?

The answers to these and other related questions will undoubtedly lead to a closer examination of the many sources of foreign policy expertise in the United States. In pursuing this avenue of inquiry, scholars will discover something that Peschek and other observers of think tanks have known for some time – that think tanks can and do play a visible role at key stages of the foreign policy-making process. But as we will discover later, it is not only in the White House and on Capitol Hill that they make their presence felt. Several policy experts from think tanks have established close and lasting ties to dozens of government departments and agencies, an important channel of influence often overlooked by those studying the role of the bureaucracy in foreign policy.

BUREAUCRATIC MODELS OF DECISION-MAKING

Few scholars have made a more important contribution to the literature on bureaucratic decision-making in the United States than Graham Allison, former dean of Harvard's Kennedy School of Government. In his study *Essence of Decision: Explaining the Cuban Missile Crisis*, Allison reveals the inherent weaknesses of the rational actor model by constructing two alternative paradigms to explain how foreign policy decisions are made: the organizational process model and the governmental (bureaucratic) politics model. According to Allison, those who adopt the rational actor model tend to disregard two important features of the policy-making process: the extent to which bureaucratic departments limit the policy options available to political leaders[19] and the intense competition between government officials to advance their political and personal interests.

The rational actor model assumes that states will, as a matter of course, make value-maximizing decisions, but Allison argues that bureaucratic departments can and do constrain the policy options available to decision-makers. According to the organizational process model, in order to function properly – in other words, in order to maintain a manageable hierarchical system – individual departments and agencies must adhere to standard operating procedures. As a result, Allison suggests, they may at times not have the flexibility to alter their behaviour or to commit resources in such a way as to satisfy the goals and preferences of decision-makers. As he points out in his analysis of the events leading to the decision of the Executive

Committee (ExCom)[20] to order a naval blockade around Cuba, decision-makers strongly favoured an air strike but were forced to reconsider this option when high-ranking officials in the US Air Force raised concerns about the logistics of such an operation. Put simply, he argues that while political leaders may prefer to adopt a particular strategy, bureaucratic constraints may compel them to pursue alternative courses of action. This theory is particularly troubling to some scholars, including Stephen Krasner, who remains convinced that the president, not the bureaucracy, dictates how foreign policy is managed.[21]

The extent to which the bureaucracy undermines the efforts of political leaders to advance their goals in the international arena cannot be overlooked, nor can the desire of decision-makers to promote their own agendas in the policy-making process. Flow charts outlining the foreign policy-making process illustrate how the executive and legislative branches of government share responsibilities in international affairs, but they rarely reveal the political bargaining that takes place among key players in the Executive and Congress. For Allison, unless foreign policy observers acknowledge the political struggle among high-level decision-makers to promote their institutional and personal interests, they cannot possibly paint an accurate portrait of the decision-making process.

Unlike the organizational process model, the governmental (bureaucratic) politics model focuses on the competition between high-level decision-makers to advance their personal and political goals. The bureaucratic politics model views the policy-making process as a game involving players competing for the president's attention. According to Allison, "the Governmental (or Bureaucratic) Politics Model sees no unitary actor but rather many actors as players-players who focus not on a single strategic issue but on many diverse intra-national problems as well; players who act in terms of no consistent set of strategic objectives but rather according to various conceptions of national, organizational, and personal goals; players who make government decisions not by a single rational choice but by the pulling and hauling that is politics."[22] In this model, Allison attempts to demonstrate the chaotic and often ad hoc nature of the policy-making process. And in doing so, he reaches the conclusion, and rightly so, that success in the policy-making arena ultimately depends on a number of factors, including the relative importance of a select group of policy-makers in the bureaucratic hierarchy, the amount of expertise they possess in a particular area, and their ability to persuade colleagues to support their position.[23]

The organizational process and bureaucratic politics models focus on important and frequently neglected aspects of the policy-making process.

However, neither model takes into consideration the important role played by individuals and organizations operating outside the formal parameters of government that maintain strong ties to the bureaucracy. As organizations committed to influencing public policy and public opinion, think tanks, for example, have made a concerted effort to expand their influence throughout government. By developing their own areas of expertise and establishing contacts with officials in various departments and agencies, they have attempted to secure long-term access to decision-makers. As noted in the previous chapter, some think tanks such as RAND, the Hudson Institute, and the Urban Institute enjoy, by virtue of their contractual relationship with various federal departments, considerable access to the bureaucracy. Others, including Heritage, AEI, and Cato, are also committed to expanding their reach and influence into the fourth branch of government.

The involvement of think tanks in the bureaucracy could easily be incorporated into the parameters established by the organizational process and bureaucratic politics models. For instance, in his case study of the Cuban Missile Crisis, Allison could have considered the contribution made by scientists from the Rand Corporation in helping to develop American nuclear strategy during the 1950s and 1960s. This information may have been relevant in assessing the Pentagon's response to a nuclear threat from the Soviet Union and could in part explain why Defense officials in the Kennedy administration were prepared to dismantle American Jupiter missiles based in Turkey if Khrushchev agreed to remove missiles from Cuba.[24] The advise of think tanks, particularly those that enjoy close ties to bureaucratic departments, can at times be important in evaluating how decision-makers approach particular policy issues.

Similarly, since many high-level government officials come from and return to think tanks after leaving office – the so-called revolving-door phenomenon – it is impossible to ignore the strong ties between think tanks and the bureaucracy. As the chart in appendix 2 illustrates, dozens of scholars from some of America's most prestigious foreign policy think tanks have held a wide range of senior positions in government. Indeed, if we scan the biographies of several think tank scholars, it is difficult not to acknowledge the extent to which think tanks have gained access to the federal bureaucracy. In virtually every major department and agency involved in foreign policy, including the State and Defense departments, the CIA, and the National Security Council, scholars from think tanks have been well represented. By serving in various capacities in government, they are able to establish a wealth of contacts they can later draw on to transmit their ideas.

That is why think tanks are particularly interested in recruiting policy-makers who have served in government. They recognize, among other things, that developing and expanding networks inside the bureaucracy can pay handsome dividends. As we will discuss in the following chapter, several think tanks have made a concerted effort to establish a strong presence in the bureaucracy.

So far, we have examined briefly how the rational actor model and Allison's bureaucratic models of decision-making could be modified or expanded upon to allow scholars to pay due consideration to the role of think tanks. One need only glance at the table detailing the amount of experience think tank staff have in the federal bureaucracy to appreciate how these vital links to government may facilitate the access of think tanks to the major departments involved in foreign policy. Indeed, just as Graham Allison examined in painstaking detail how bureaucrats in various government departments reacted to the Cuban Missile Crisis, so scholars could undertake a detailed examination of how staff from think tanks rely on access to their previous employers to market their ideas to those in positions of power. Simply possessing knowledge of how information is transmitted within a government department or agency provides think tanks with an enormous advantage over their competitors and other NGOs whose employees may have little or no government experience. This underdeveloped avenue of scholarly inquiry could produce extremely interesting and worthwhile findings.

THE PSYCHOLOGY OF DECISION-MAKING

In addition to paying closer consideration to the strong ties between think tanks and the bureaucracy, scholars could benefit by delving more deeply into the psychology of decision-making, an area of foreign policy analysis that in recent years has attracted renewed scholarly interest. By doing so, they would discover that mainstream models and theories of decision-making need not be supplanted but simply supplemented to better understand how think tanks can and do participate in the foreign policy-making process.

Like Allison, John Steinbruner argues that the rational actor model alone cannot possibly explain why, throughout history, states and the leaders that represent them have pursued policies which defy rational behaviour. As he points out, "Japan's attack on the United States in 1941 is not easy to reconcile with analytic assumptions. Similarly, British decision-makers in 1941 apparently believed estimates about the destructive capacity of the German

Luftwaffe which should have made them much more interested in peace terms than they in fact were. The Egyptian Army's mobilization against Israel in May-June of 1967 was a risk whose outcome leaves doubts that the men who chose to take it were operating in accord with analytic logic[25] ... events such as these have generated doubts about the dominant paradigm."[26] To better explain how leaders make decisions, Steinbruner advances what he refers to as a "cybernetic theory of decision-making." According to Steinbruner, policy-makers rarely take decisions in the manner prescribed by the rational actor model. They do not rely on perfect information in their deliberations, nor do they even pretend to make value-maximizing decisions. Rather, they simply try to reduce the level of uncertainty in an environment that is often chaotic and unpredictable; policy-makers do so by learning to rely on their instincts. In making this argument, Steinbruner suggests that like a tennis player returning a serve or a person removing his or her hand from a hot element to avoid serious injury, political leaders, through years of experience, can learn to resolve policy problems instinctively.

Overwhelmed by information from multiple directions and sources, Steinbruner agrees, policy-makers cannot possibly digest all pertinent data before making critical decisions. Instead, they develop a highly structured and stable environment in which to address and examine policy issues. He states, "[the] decision maker possesses procedures for processing information which in fact generate decisions and outcomes, but psychologically he is not engaged in the pursuit of an explicitly designed result. The psychological effects of uncertainty are therefore held to a minimum ... The decision maker is assumed to have a small set of 'responses' and decision rules which determine the course of action to take once he has received information in which he is sensitive."[27] By establishing procedures and mechanisms to process information, Steinbruner claims, decision-makers can make rational policy decisions without considering all possible courses of action. In other words, contrary to the rational actor model, which assumes that individuals select a course of action that will maximize their goals and objectives, cybernetic theorists maintain that policy decisions are dictated by how decision-makers respond to certain types of information. "[D]ecision mechanisms screen out information which the established set of responses are not programmed to accept. That is, uncertainty control entails highly focused sensitivity. The cybernetic decision maker is sensitive to information only if it enters through an established highly-focused feedback channel, and hence many factors which affect the outcomes have no effect in his decision process."[28]

Steinbruner's cybernetic theory of decision-making is useful in explaining how decision-makers attempt to reduce uncertainty in their environment by screening out certain types of information. However, his contention that policy decisions are the result of programmed responses requires closer scrutiny. Individual leaders may prefer to immerse themselves in stable and protective environments, but the views they promote and the ideals they embrace may be influenced by a multitude of factors. For instance, surrounded by political advisers and policy experts from various government departments and think tanks, decision-makers may feel compelled to alter their preferred course of action. More specifically, although they may consciously establish mechanisms to absorb only a narrow range of information, how they react to that data may have less to do with programmed responses and more to do with who is providing that information and advice.

Decision-makers, unlike programmed machines, are not conditioned to respond in a predetermined manner. They may elect to ignore or discard information that they consider irrelevant, but it is difficult to argue that a small set of rules influence the formulation and implementation of policy decisions. Motivated by an intense desire to survive, decision-makers will try to adapt to their environment by determining the most effective ways to make rational policy choices. For some, this process may entail digesting as much information as possible before making a final decision. Presidents Carter and Clinton, for instance, were obsessed with absorbing every detail concerning a particular policy issue before arriving at a decision. Yet for other political leaders, Herbert Simon's concept of "satisficing" may be a more appropriate way to describe their decision-making style.

Steinbruner's cybernetic theory, like Allison's bureaucratic analysis of foreign policy-making, cannot provide a definitive explanation of how political leaders make critical foreign policy decisions. Nonetheless, his framework does allow for additional opportunities to observe how think tanks attempt to shape the policy environment inhabited by political leaders. Recognizing that decision-makers rarely have the time or patience to digest the amount of information necessary to make value-maximizing decisions, several think tanks have attempted to provide them with concise analyses of major domestic and foreign policy issues. As will be discussed in the following chapter, the Heritage Foundation has been particularly effective in this regard. By supplying elected officials and their staff with information that can easily be incorporated into briefing notes, memos, and speeches, Heritage has, in some respects, helped to reduce uncertainty in the decision-maker's environment. At the very least, it has been able to assist decision-makers to manage and process information.

As indicated in the beginning of the chapter, scholars who study American foreign policy have been slow to acknowledge the involvement of think tanks in the policy-making process. But interestingly enough, in other sub-fields of political science there has been a growing recognition that think tanks can and do play an important role in shaping public opinion and public policy. Particularly in the fields of public administration and public policy, where scholars pay close attention to the role of elites and interest groups, accommodation has been made for different types of non-governmental organizations, including think tanks, that have a vested interest in influencing the political agenda. In this final section, some consideration will be paid to alternative approaches that scholars may wish to consider in studying think tanks. Many of these approaches have been mentioned briefly in chapter 3 and will be expanded upon in the case studies included later in the book. The purpose here is to simply enrich our discussion about theories and models of decision-making by demonstrating that those who study foreign policy have much to learn from their colleagues in other sub-fields of the discipline. As the boundaries between domestic politics and foreign policy have become increasingly blurred, scholars have come to realize that straying into "terra incognita" – unfamiliar or foreign territory – may help them to better understand their own area of expertise. In this case, it may help students of foreign policy to appreciate more fully the extent to which think tanks have become integrated in the foreign policy-making process.

ELITE AND INTEREST-GROUP MODELS OF DECISION-MAKING

Political scientists who study foreign policy often take credit for developing and advancing theories of decision-making, but scholars in several other sub-fields, including comparative politics and public policy, have also made important contributions to this burgeoning literature. For instance, by examining the formation and conduct of policy elites, Robert Dahl and C. Wright Mills have made great strides in answering the age-old question of who controls public policy. Moreover, several other scholars, influenced by the works of Arthur Bentley, David Truman, and Theodore Lowi, have written extensively on how interest groups in pluralistic societies immerse themselves in policy debates.[29] Their work, as we will discuss below, is particularly relevant to the study of think tanks in policy-making.

In his classic study *Who Governs? Democracy and Power in an American City*, Dahl examines the behaviour of elites in New Haven, Connecticut, a city made famous by its most important occupant, Yale University. By identifying key leaders involved in political parties, public education, and urban redevelopment, he concludes that municipal politics in New Haven is not dominated by a homogenous group of policy elites but by several distinct groups which have developed expertise in different policy areas. His research indicates that leaders responsible for overseeing important community issues do not share the same goals and objectives. In fact, his study demonstrates that municipal organizations often engage in a bitter competition to advance their institutional interests.

Dahl's observations about the presence of multiple elites and their participation in the policy-making process sheds additional light on why organizations such as think tanks cannot be expected to play a dominant role in every policy debate. While some may take credit for influencing the overall direction of government policy, as Heritage did during the Reagan years, others such as RAND, AEI, and the Hoover Institution have identified specific government programs and initiatives in which they have been actively engaged. In short, we cannot assume, nor should we expect, that all think tanks will participate equally in every conceivable policy debate. As Dahl points out, elites do not necessarily share the same goals, objectives, and priorities. Why then would we expect elite organizations such as think tanks to behave as a homogeneous group? Think tanks differ enormously in terms of their areas of expertise. They also have vastly different resources on which to draw. This factor, as we will discuss in subsequent chapters, can and does influence profoundly how and where in the policy cycle they seek to have the greatest impact. This said, there is little doubt that think tanks, regardless of their mandate and resources, remain committed to influencing public policy.

The efforts of think tanks to shape America's political agenda would hardly have come as a surprise to the late C. Wright Mills, author of the acclaimed study *The Power Elite*. Written during the mid-1950s, a time in which Wisconsin senator Joseph McCarthy and the Cold War were becoming part of the national conversation, Mills's study argues that the American political process, particularly with respect to matters of war and peace, was being controlled largely by the military-industrial complex. According to him, policy-makers in Congress and the Pentagon, in cooperation with military and defense contractors and with the blessing of the president, formulated and implemented domestic and foreign policies that promoted their common economic, political, and security interests.[30]

Discussions about a military-industrial complex dominating the American political system did not likely earn Mills much favour among conservative policy-makers in the 1950s, but his work has taken on heightened

importance in recent decades. Particularly since the Vietnam War, scholars
on both the left and the right of the political spectrum have recognized the
need to better understand the intimate relationship between the president,
Congress, and the military. Some have also begun to consider the relationship between the military and the think tanks the Pentagon employs to identify emerging threats to America's national security interests.[31] The reliance
of the military on such think tanks as RAND and the Hudson Institute provides policy research institutions with considerable opportunity to shape
vital national security policies.

The Center for Strategic and International Studies, the Center for Security
Policy, the Hudson Institute, the Institute for Naval Analysis, RAND, and a
handful of other foreign and defense policy think tanks fall within Mills's
analytical framework. However, the majority of think tanks in the United
States do not specialize in defense studies and therefore should not be considered part of a military-industrial complex. Nonetheless, two other
observers of think tanks, William Domhoff and Thomas Dye, contend that
regardless of their areas of expertise, think tanks form an integral part of a
more extensive institution in the United States called the ruling elite. Composed of academics whose research is supported by corporations and philanthropic foundations, Domhoff and Dye argue, think tanks such as the
Brookings Institution and the Council on Foreign Relations play a vital role
in furthering corporate interests in the United States. In short, they contend
that think tanks should not be viewed as institutions committed to the
advancement of social science research but rather as organizations dedicated to furthering the economic interests of their corporate sponsors.[32]

After an examination of the list of corporations that support the
Brookings Institution, the Council on Foreign Relations, and other think
tanks, as well as the individuals who sit on their boards of directors, it
would be difficult to dismiss Domhoff and Dye's remarks. In fact, as some
observers have commented, many of these institutions are reserved for
members of the American establishment.[33] However, while it may be accurate to portray some think tanks as policy elites that are in a unique position
to advise decision-makers, it would be misleading to treat all think tanks in
this manner. Not unlike other non-governmental organizations competing
for power and influence in the political arena, some think tanks are better
positioned and equipped than others to exercise influence.

The intense competition in the marketplace of ideas has led some scholars
to treat think tanks as simply another type of interest group committed to
influencing public policy. Indeed, as noted in the Introduction, some think
tanks do share many of the behavioural traits of interest groups. But as the

following section will show, applying the group theory approach to decision-making will further reveal the fundamental differences between think tanks and interest or pressure groups.

In his study *The Governmental Process*, David Truman argues that the government does not pursue its own goals and objectives but merely serves as a referee moderating between competing interest groups. In other words, contrary to the assertions of elite theorists, who claim that elites by and large set the political and economic agenda, advocates of group theory contend that public policies simply reflect the outcome of interest-group competition. The process by which policy decisions are made therefore does not depend on the psychological characteristics of individual leaders, the close relationship between government officials, the military, and defense contractors, or the inherent constraints of bureaucracy. Rather, it depends on how effective interest groups are in exercising influence in the political arena.

In examining Truman's theory, we should not lose sight of his central argument regarding the role of government in the political process. If the government behaves as little more than an impartial referee ensuring that interest groups follow the rules of the game, what, if any, incentive would political leaders have to deliberate over policy issues? After all, if elected officials are expected to simply respond to interest-group pressure, why would leaders struggle over making critical policy decisions? Moreover, how can policy-makers ensure that interest groups and other non-governmental organizations compete on a level playing field when they depend on some of the participants for policy advice?

Contrary to Truman's assertions, the government and its leaders rarely behave as referees moderating between competing policy positions. In developing and formulating policy ideas, decision-makers do not remain on the sidelines; rather, they align themselves with groups and individuals with whom they share similar interests. Politics is often about forming alliances to achieve desired goals, and policy-makers and the various organizations and individuals that participate in the policy-making process understand the rules of the game. So do think tanks that understand how to survive and thrive in a world in which money, politics, power, and even ideas can be harnessed to shape the fate of the nation.

Those who study and observe American politics acknowledge that there is rarely a shortage of ideas being discussed and considered on Capitol Hill, in the White House, or in the dozens of government departments and agencies that comprise the bureaucracy. Good ideas may be in short supply, but suggestions and recommendations on how to improve the economy, the health-care system, education, transportation, and foreign policy are as plentiful as hot dogs on Opening Day. It is in this environment – an environment in which countless ideas and policy recommendations are being discussed and debated – that policy-makers are expected to make public policy.

While it is often tempting to focus on the normative questions surrounding policy decisions, this chapter has concentrated primarily on the study of foreign policy-making in the United States and some of the many models, theories, and approaches that have been employed to examine and assess America's behaviour in world affairs. More specifically, it has sought to explain why scholars have, for the most part, overlooked the involvement of think tanks in the policy-making process. Is it because those who study public policy are so concerned about differentiating between the public and private uses of power that they miss the significance of think tanks? Or is it more likely that think tanks have attracted little attention in the literature on decision-making because their role is not properly understood? Regardless of which explanation is more plausible, the result is the same – the efforts of think tanks to generate and transmit ideas to decision-makers have been largely neglected. But as indicated in our discussion about how to pry open the black box of decision-making, contemporary models and theories of foreign policy-making need not be supplanted to account for the increasingly active involvement of think tanks in the policy-making process. Rather, the parameters of these models simply need to be expanded or redefined to take into consideration how think tanks contribute to policy-making.

Think tanks, as noted, do not fit neatly into any one conceptual or methodological framework. That is why, as we will discuss in the case studies later in the book, it is difficult to generalize about their behaviour. Yet despite the methodological issues that need to be addressed in studying think tanks, we can no longer afford to ignore how they have become entrenched in the policy-making process. In the following chapter, our attention will shift to the many public and private channels think tanks rely on to shape public opinion and public policy. We must do so if we are to make any headway in evaluating the nature and extent of think tank influence.

CHAPTER SIX

Finding Their Way: In Search of Policy Influence

Think tanks are in the business of developing and promoting ideas, and like corporations in the private sector, they devote considerable attention to marketing their products. Unlike corporations, however, they do not measure success by profit margins but by how much influence they have in shaping public opinion and the policy preferences and choices of leaders. Unfortunately, for think tank directors and those who study these institutions, it is far simpler to read quarterly reports than to measure the performance of these organizations. In this chapter we lay the foundation for assessing the impact of think tanks by exploring the many channels that policy research institutes use to market their ideas. It is important to keep in mind that while think tanks in the United States have different areas of expertise, resources, and priorities, they tend to rely on similar strategies to exercise policy influence. However, not all think tanks are willing or able to rely on these strategies to the same degree. In other words, while generating media exposure is a preferred tactic for many think tanks, including the Heritage Foundation, AEI, the Cato Institute, and the Brookings Institution, it is not considered a priority for many smaller institutes, which are more committed to strengthening their ties to key policy-makers than to making the six o'clock news.

The chapter begins by highlighting the strategies think tanks generally employ to generate attention in the public arena and in important policy circles. Particular emphasis is placed on what has become the most visible method they rely on to exercise policy influence – gaining access to the media. Finally, as a segue to chapter 7, we will discuss briefly what steps need to be taken to provide more-informed insights about the nature and extent of think tank influence.

PUBLIC INFLUENCE

Though often portrayed as elite organizations where scholars pursue research in relative isolation, think tanks have become increasingly visible in the public arena. Indeed, as active participants in the marketplace of ideas, they understand the importance of competing for the attention of policy-makers and the public, not to mention the financial support of government agencies, individuals, and corporate and philanthropic donors.[1] While some of the strategies they rely on to exercise influence are concealed from the public, many can be easily identified. In fact, to varying degrees, think tanks in North America adopt some or all of the following strategies to influence policy-makers and the public:

- holding public forums, seminars, and conferences to discuss various domestic and foreign policy issues
- encouraging scholars to give public lectures and addresses
- testifying before committees and subcommittees of Congress or Parliament
- publishing books, opinion magazines, newsletters, policy briefs, and journals that have wide distribution
- selling audio tapes to the public which summarize key policy issues
- creating Web pages on the Internet which, among other things, allow visitors to download institute publications
- targeting the public during annual fundraising campaigns
- attracting media exposure

Holding public forums, seminars, and conferences is among the most common strategies think tanks employ to increase awareness about a particular domestic or foreign policy issue. Policy-makers, journalists, academics, and representatives from the private and non-profit sectors are regularly invited to discuss timely and often controversial issues before public audiences. At times, conferences are also arranged to generate exposure for a newly released study. A well-publicized and attended event on an important topic such as homeland security, terrorism, or the future of Iraq can benefit think tanks in many ways. In addition to taking credit for encouraging opinion-makers to discuss issues they have helped to identify, think tanks take advantage of these opportunities to educate those in attendance about the role of their institute and the work in which they are engaged. At times, think tanks may elect to co-sponsor conferences in order to attract even more attention. For instance, in May 2004 several think tanks, including the Brookings Institution, the Heritage Foundation, and the Progressive Policy Institute, participated in a one-day conference on "Restoring Fiscal Sanity," organized by the Virginia-based Concord Coalition. Representatives from these and other think tanks exchanged ideas with policy-makers, academics, and other policy professionals. In addressing the issue of fiscal sanity, keynote speakers Republican senator John McCain and Democratic senator Joe Lieberman acknowledged the importance of encouraging think tanks at both ends of the political spectrum to work together. Commenting on the diverse group of think tanks that had assembled for the conference, Lieberman said half jokingly, "To quote from the prophet Isaiah, it is like watching the lambs lying down with the lions."[2]

Lieberman may have been genuinely surprised to observe think tanks with such diverse points of view assembled in the same room, but there have been other occasions where think tanks have been invited to cooperate. According to Leslie Gelb, former president of the Council on Foreign Relations, between 1996 and 1997 an attempt was made to bring together the nation's best foreign policy think tanks to share information about their research plans. The intention was to avoid duplication in research and to ensure that think tanks could meet the needs of their various stakeholders. Chaired by former career ambassador Frank Wisner, who in 1997 joined the American International Group as its vice-chairman for external affairs, representatives from the Council on Foreign Relations, RAND, CSIS, Brookings, Carnegie, Heritage, and the United States Institute for Peace met twice a year for two years. Unfortunately, as Gelb noted with regret, "this undertaking was a flop because people didn't want to share material."[3] Indeed, rather than pooling their resources, think tanks have for the most part continued to pursue their own research plans.

As the table A3.1 in appendix 3 illustrates, since the tragic events of 9/11, several of America's premier foreign policy and defense think tanks have organized conferences, roundtable discussions, policy briefings, and seminars on issues of profound importance to Americans. For example, in 2004 AEI sponsored over a dozen events on issues ranging from the genocide in Sudan and the ongoing conflict in Iraq to the need for serious reform in the intelligence community. The Heritage Foundation, AEI's conservative ally in the war of ideas, was equally committed to addressing these issues. Among the topics discussed in Heritage symposia were the USA Patriot Act, screening for terrorists on passenger planes, and grading the 9/11 Commission report.

In that same year, the Brookings Institution devoted considerable attention to the many issues related to the war on terror, including the growing rift between the United States and Europe and the spread of weapons of mass destruction, a topic discussed by New York senator Hillary Rodham Clinton. Next door at the Carnegie Endowment for International Peace, scholars and policy-makers were involved in timely seminars on such themes as democracy promotion in the Middle East and reducing Russian-American nuclear tensions. Discussions about these and other foreign policy issues were also taking place beyond Dupont Circle. At its Washington office and in its main office at the Harold Pratt House in Manhattan, the Council on Foreign Relations held several meetings to examine threats posed by nuclear terrorism and instability in Iraq. One of the highlights of the year at the CFR was a presentation by Secretary of Defense Donald Rumsfeld on the global war on terror. Think tanks on the West Coast were also preoccupied with confronting this new threat. For example, the Hoover Institution at Stanford University held a two-day conference in May 2002 on how technology could be used to prevent terrorism. In short, in the aftermath of 9/11, policy experts at think tanks were only too willing to share their ideas with policy-makers. As indicated by the number and scope of the conferences that took place, there were few issues that think tanks did not consider.

To reach even larger audiences, think tanks encourage their resident scholars to give lectures at universities, Rotary associations, and other organizations interested in contemporary political affairs. Once again, high-profile speakers from think tanks can serve as ambassadors for their institutes as they travel across the country sharing their thoughts on a host of policy issues. Several think tanks also recognize the importance of conveying ideas to policy-makers and to the public in a more formal manner. Some do so by testifying before various legislative committees or in hearings organized by the House and/or the Senate (see table A3.2 in appendix 3). Providing testimony, particularly to a prominent committee, can attract considerable attention. The oral presentations and written briefs that policy experts provide are included as part of the official record and are often cited by journalists and academics. Agreeing to appear before legislative committees can also promote the credibility of think tanks in the eyes of some policy-makers and help think tank directors to convince potential donors of the widespread influence of their institutes. This consequence may explain why several think tanks prominently display the testimonies given by staff on their Web sites.

There are several other strategies think tanks can draw on to market their message. Many, particularly those with well-established research programs, such as Brookings, Carnegie, Heritage, and AEI, rely on opinion magazines, journals, newsletters, and books to reach their various target audiences. For example, the Heritage Foundation publishes *Policy Review*, an opinion magazine that contains brief articles by many leading conservatives on current policy issues. The *Brookings Review*, published by the Brookings Institution; *The American Enterprise*, produced by AEI; and *American Outlook*, from the Hudson Institute are other examples of opinion magazines distributed by US think tanks. For many think tanks, these types of publications are their most effective product because unlike books, which are often outdated by the time they are released, opinion magazines provide policy-makers with insights into current policy problems. And even more important for policy-makers and their busy staff, they can be read and summarized in a matter of minutes, not hours or days. Often organized around a particular theme, these publications, think tanks hope, will help to frame the parameters of important and relevant policy debates.

Think tanks produce publications for other target groups as well. Several, for example, publish refereed scholarly journals that are intended to be read by university students and faculty members. Among these are *Foreign Affairs*, the flagship journal of the New York-based Council on Foreign Relations; *Foreign Policy*, produced by the Carnegie Endowment for International Peace; the *Washington Quarterly*, a publication of the Center for Strategic and International Studies; and the *Cato Journal*, published by the libertarian Cato Institute. In addition to scholarly journals and opinion magazines, dozens of think tanks produce books and monthly newsletters that are intended to keep readers informed about the most important developments at their institutes.

Think tanks reach potential stakeholders through other forms of communication. For example, the Cato Institute and the Heritage Foundation produce *Cato Audio* and the *Monthly Briefing Tapes* respectively, which include interviews with some of their policy experts as well as lectures given by prominent (mostly conservative) opinion-makers. Among those who have helped Heritage to sell its monthly briefing tapes is former speaker of the House Newt Gingrich. In his endorsement, which appeared in various Heritage publications, Gingrich referred to the tapes as a "monthly dose of conservative common sense. You'll wonder how you ever got along without it."

Those who can get along without listening to audio tapes but still want to be kept apprised of what certain think tanks are doing can access their Web sites. Virtually every think tank in the United States uses a Web site to publicize its work. Although they vary enormously in terms of content and sophistication, most sites provide a wealth of information ranging from an institute's most current publications and staff directory to upcoming conferences and seminars. Several, including the one managed by the Heritage Foundation, allow subscribers to receive e-mail updates on every conceivable policy issue. Through PolicyWire, Heritage can ensure that its analyses and recommendations on a wide range of domestic and foreign policy issues are sent to thousands of policy-makers, journalists, and other opinion leaders as soon as they become available. Heritage and countless other think tanks also allow visitors to download many of their publications, including annual reports, congressional testimony, articles, lectures, and book chapters. This service is extremely useful for consumers, but it also helps think tanks to identify the areas and issues that seem to be attracting the most attention. By keeping track of how often certain publications are downloaded, think tanks can determine if they should devote more resources to examining particular issues. At the very least, sustained interest in specific policy areas may convince think tanks to direct visitors to other sources of information. In fact, many sites provide links to important databases. For instance, the Center for Security Policy provides an extensive national security link to every major organization and agency involved in the defense and security of the United States. Similarly, the Carnegie Endowment has established a link to other valuable resources, including US embassies, international organizations, and think tanks.

Fundraising is yet another way that think tanks attempt to market themselves to the public and to policy-makers, and some have enlisted the support of high-profile policy-makers to attract money. For example, as discussed in chapter 2, in 1982, at the request of Heritage president Edwin Feulner, Edwin Meese III, a special adviser to President Reagan and later US attorney general, wrote a letter to potential Heritage donors encouraging them to join the President's Club, which he suggested would serve as a "vital communications link [between the White House and those who support President Reagan and] this administration will fully cooperate with your efforts."[4]

But of all the public uses of think tank influence, none is more visible than their efforts to secure access to the media. As will be discussed in more detail later in this chapter, since several directors of think tanks often equate media exposure with policy influence, many devote considerable resources to enhancing their public profile. By ensuring that they are regularly quoted in the print and broadcast media, think tanks seek to create the perception that they play a critical role in shaping public policy. However, as we will discover, while it is important for think tanks to communicate their views to the public on television broadcasts or on the op-ed pages of leading American newspapers, media exposure does not necessarily translate into policy influence. Generating media attention may enable some think tanks to plant seeds in the minds of policy-makers and the public, but it does not necessarily guarantee success in the policy-making process.

PRIVATE INFLUENCE

The many channels that think tanks rely on to exercise public influence are relatively easy to observe and document, but it can at times be difficult to monitor how they seek to influence policy-makers privately. The following list provides examples of how think tanks and the scholars affiliated with them seek to exercise private influence. Among the many private forms of influence are the following:

- accepting cabinet, sub-cabinet, or bureaucratic positions in administrations
- serving on policy task forces and transition teams during presidential elections and on presidential advisory boards
- maintaining liaison offices with the House of Representatives and the Senate
- inviting selected policy-makers to participate in closed conferences, seminars, and workshops
- allowing bureaucrats to work at think tanks on a limited-term basis
- offering former policy-makers positions at think tanks
- preparing studies and policy briefs for policy-makers

There are few ways experts from think tanks can get closer to the policy-making process than by becoming policy-makers themselves. As discussed in chapter 1, in several presidential administrations, dozens of personnel from think tanks have been recruited into senior-level positions. Many, including Jeanne Kirkpatrick (AEI) and Zbigniew Brzezinski (CSIS), have served in the president's cabinet, while many others have been appointed to important positions in the bureaucracy (see appendix 2). For think tanks, there are several potential benefits in having staff members appointed to an incoming administration, not the least of which is the publicity surrounding the appointment itself. By assembling a talent pool of scholars for administrations to draw on, think tanks not only enhance their prestige but can foster even stronger ties to those making critical policy decisions. This outcome may explain why some think tanks such as Heritage closely monitor vacancies in the bureaucracy in the hope of placing like-minded colleagues in important positions.

Think tanks can establish and strengthen ties to key decision-makers through other channels. Presidential elections, for example, provide institutes, particularly those that are ideologically in tune with certain candidates, with a tremendous opportunity to help shape the political platform and agenda of aspiring office-holders. As we have examined in some detail earlier, several presidential candidates have turned to experts from think tanks for information and advice on how to address a wide range of domestic and foreign policy issues. In the process, hundreds of policy experts have been invited to serve on policy task forces and/or on transition teams to assist presidential candidates and those elected to office to assume power. Furthermore, during some administrations, think tank scholars have been appointed to important presidential advisory boards, including the President's Foreign Intelligence Advisory Board, the President's Intelligence Oversight Board, and the President's Economic Policy Advisory Board.[5]

Moreover, as discussed in chapter 4, since political power in the United States, unlike in Canada, is not concentrated in the Executive but is largely shared with the legislative branch, American think tanks also develop strategies to strengthen their ties to members of Congress. Several, including Heritage, do so by establishing liaison offices with the House of Representatives and the Senate. Maintaining close contact with the legislature enables think tanks to meet with members regularly to discuss their concerns and policy needs. It also allows think tanks to monitor and track the most important issues on the floor of the House and the Senate, which, in turn, helps them to prepare the type of research policy-makers require to make critical choices. To discuss certain policy issues in more detail, some think tanks regularly invite members of Congress to attend *private* seminars, conferences, and workshops. Once again, this strategy enables policy experts at think tanks to share their insights with those who are in a position to influence legislation. Think tanks such as the Hoover Institution also realize that many newly elected members of Congress, as well as some seasoned policy-makers, could benefit from acquiring additional insight into particular policy issues. As well, they realize the importance of establishing good communications with congressional staff and legislative assistants who frequently advise members of Congress.

Established in 1980, the Hoover Institution's two-day Washington Seminars at its institute in Palo Alto have played an important role in facilitating the exchange of ideas between Hoover scholars and policy-makers. Limited to twelve to fifteen participants, the seminars have been attended by Democratic and Republican members of Congress and congressional staff members from the House and Senate Committees on International Relations/Foreign Relations, Appropriations, Budget, Armed Services, Finance, Ways and Means, and Intelligence and the offices of the Senate majority leader and the House speaker, minority leader, and majority whip. The seminars are usually followed by meetings in Washington to bring together individuals who have participated in the program, Hoover scholars, and other government officials. According to the Hoover Institution, "these meetings and seminars are now playing a critical role in the ongoing dialogue between scholars and policy-makers, which is so important to the effective development and implementation of legislative and executive department policies and programs."[6]

Think tanks can also maintain close contact with bureaucratic departments and agencies through a number of different channels. For instance, through the State Department's Diplomat in Residence program, diplomats can, between assignments, take up residence at think tanks to write, conduct research, and deliver lectures. They have been sent to several think tanks, including the American Enterprise Institute, the Hoover Institution, RAND, the Council on Foreign Relations, the Carnegie Endowment for International Peace, and the Heritage Foundation.

Some policy-makers are so impressed with think tanks that they decide to make them their permanent home after completing public service. However, it is important to point out that many former high-profile policy-makers are not recruited to think tanks because of their potential as researchers but because of their ability to attract funding; this is likely why think tanks often approach former presidents and cabinet secretaries to join their ranks.

Finally, as a matter of course, think tanks hold informal meetings with key policy-makers to discuss studies that their institutes have produced or to simply outline a range of policy options elected officials have at their disposal. Most of these meetings are rarely publicized or talked about, but they nonetheless can have an impact in shaping public policy. Indeed, for many think tanks, working quietly behind closed doors is the most effective channel they have to influence policy-making.

The strategies that think tanks select and the priority they assign to each are influenced not only by the political environment they inhabit but by their mandate and resources. In other words, for advocacy-oriented think tanks such as the Heritage Foundation and AEI, producing opinion magazines, securing access to the media, and holding public forums are profoundly important. On the other hand, for many smaller institutes, including the Project for the New American Century and the Center for

Security Policy, exchanging ideas with policy-makers in meeting rooms instead of with journalists on the air may result in a higher payoff. In short, think tanks develop strategies that allow them to most effectively reach their specific target audiences.

MARKETING THE MESSAGE: THINK TANKS AND THE MEDIA

Testifying before a high-profile congressional committee or publishing a study on a controversial domestic or foreign policy issue may attract attention in some policy-making circles, but it is unlikely to generate the exposure an appearance on *Fox News* or CNN or an op-ed article in the *New York Times* or the *Washington Post* would. The importance of such exposure may explain why some think tanks devote considerable time and resources to gaining access to the print and broadcast media. It may also explain why the competition between think tanks for media exposure is so intense. As Patricia Linden explains, "[for think tanks to compete], their ideas must be communicated; otherwise the oracles of tankdom wind up talking to themselves. The upshot is an endless forest of communiques; reports, journals, newsletters, Op-Ed articles, press releases, books and educational materials. The rivalry for attention is fierce; so much so that the analysts have come out of their think tanks to express opinions on lecture and TV circuits, at seminars and conferences, press briefings and Congressional hearings."[7]

Securing access to the media on a regular basis provides think tanks with a valuable opportunity to shape the parameters of public policy debates. As we will discuss in the case studies on missile defense and the war on terror, although think tanks may not be able to claim responsibility for influencing a particular policy decision, they can take credit for injecting important ideas into the public debate. More important, think tanks understand that media exposure creates the illusion of policy influence, a currency they have a vested interest in accumulating. Few think tanks have devoted more time and resources to targeting the media than the Heritage Foundation. In 2003 it spent over $6.6 million, or 19.3 per cent of its budget, on media and government relations.[8] Heritage's public relations program is based on a simple premise: "provide journalists, opinion leaders and the general public with the positive message of responsible conservatism and conservatism will remain competitive, and even triumph, in the marketplace of ideas." Its goal is even simpler: "Make sure journalists never have a reason for not quoting at least one conservative expert – or for not giving the conservative 'spin' in their stories."[9] The Heritage Foundation has clearly accomplished its goal:

the mainstream media in the United States rely heavily on Heritage and a handful of other conservative think tanks inside the Beltway for their expertise and political commentary.[10]

While this may be so, we should not lose sight of the considerable media exposure generated from more liberal or centrist think tanks such as the Brookings Institution. In 2003 Brookings allocated approximately $1 million, or 3 per cent of its $32 million budget, to communications,[11] an investment that appeared to pay handsome dividends. According to its 2003 annual report, Brookings ranks *first* (italics added) among Washington think tanks for press citations; averages 846 mentions a month in various print, television, radio, wire, and Web outlets; averages 69 mentions each month in the *New York Times*, the *Washington Post*, and the *Los Angeles Times*; had 187 op-ed articles by Brookings scholars appear in print in 2003, including 45 in the *New York Times* and the *Washington Post*; and conducted 845 television and radio interviews in its on-site studio.[12] These data must have stunned the media relations team at AEI, who stated in their 2003 annual report that "AEI's standing in the national media is unmatched by that of any other policy research institute. The work of AEI scholars is cited more frequently and is published more often in the leading U.S. newspapers and public affairs magazines than the work of scholars at other national think tanks. AEI scholars are interviewed more often on television and radio than their peers at rival research institutes."[13] AEI did not provide any figures to support its claims of unmatched media exposure, but colleagues at Heritage did. In its 2003 annual report, Heritage reported that its scholars recorded 1,100 television appearances and 1,418 radio appearances and had their commentaries appear in print and online news outlets 907 times.[14]

Although there is considerable discrepancy among think tanks over which generates the lion's share of media exposure, a problem that we will discuss in the following chapter, they agree that establishing close ties to media outlets is critical. In fact, according to Brian Lee Crowley, president of the Halifax-based Atlantic Institute for Market Studies, securing access to the media might be as important, if not more important, than the ideas being promoted: "[H]aving sound ideas and doing the research to back them up are only one half of your job. The other half is putting a lot of energy into strategic communications, and putting that strategy into effect. The place to start is not with ideas, but with personal relationships. Journalists are moved much more by personal contact than by the best ideas in the world. One way that they economize on scarce time is by having a stable of people, experts in their field, in whom they can have confidence, knowing that if they are told something by these people, they can put a great deal of weight on it without running the risk of looking stupid and foolish."[15] Those in charge of marketing Heritage's message agree that forging arrangements with national media companies, including the *New York Post*, Talk Radio Network, Salem Communications, National Religious Broadcasters, PBS, FOXNews.com, and WND.com, is profoundly important. That is why its Editorial Services department

concentrates on selling Heritage solutions to the nation's editorial and opinion editors – especially the "op-ed" pages where readers can get the "unfiltered" Heritage message. This kind of selling requires face-to-face meetings as well as constant phone calls, letters and notes. Editorial Services staffers visited more than 20 major media markets in 2003, meeting with opinion editors, editorial writers and columnists. Their itineraries included seven of the nation's 10 largest papers and more than half of the top 30. They also searched for new opportunities to secure regular "platforms" for Heritage commentary. The effort paid off handsomely. At year's end, the number of "op-eds" appearing in major print and online news media increased by 35 percent.[16]

The potential benefits of being a guest commentator on a national newscast or radio program or publishing op-ed articles on a regular basis are great. Not only do these activities bode well for think tank scholars looking for a broader audience to which to convey their ideas, but they can also promote the goals of the institutions the scholars represent. As William J. Taylor Jr of the Center for Strategic and International Studies (CSIS) freely admits, he takes advantage of every opportunity to appear on television, not so much for personal reasons, "but for the glory of CSIS and its mission of informing the public. When we're on television, we're up there as individuals, but it says CSIS under our name."[17] Yet as Howard Kurtz, a staff writer with the *Washington Post* and a regular guest on various CNN talk shows, points out, what the viewer fails to learn from the title flashing under Taylor's name – "CSIS Military Analyst" – is that "CSIS is a markedly conservative organization that forms a sort of interlocking directorate with the Washington establishment ... That it has received $50,000 to $250,000 from such defense contractors as Boeing, General Dynamics, Rockwell, Honeywell and Westinghouse. [And that its annual report boasts: 'we network in Washington with the Congress, the executive branch, the scholarly community, the corporate and labor communities and the media.'"[18]

It is not difficult to understand why think tanks covet media attention. After all, as Heritage, AEI, Brookings, and others have discovered, media coverage can and does play a critical role in allowing institutes to effectively market their message. But what makes some think tanks more media friendly than others? This topic will be examined more fully in the next chapter, but a few factors are worth noting here. First, think tanks that have large and diverse research programs supported by dozens of staff are likely better positioned to attract more media exposure than institutes offering only a narrow range of expertise. Think tanks, such as many of those mentioned above, appeal to journalists because they can comment on a range of domestic and foreign policy issues. In a sense, AEI, Heritage, and Brookings function as one-stop policy shops. They also appeal to journalists who are consciously looking for a particular political perspective on an issue. When reporters contact the Heritage Foundation, well known for its commitment to free market principles, they can be assured that any proposal by the president or Congress that will lead to more government intervention will be criticized. Knowing what positions think tanks will generally take may also account for the media's reliance on the same group of think tank scholars. The reliability of policy experts is also a consideration particularly when journalists are under tight deadlines. Sam Donaldson, co-anchor of ABC's *Prime Time Live* and a regular panelist on *This Week*, agrees:

Clearly there are problems with going to the same people ... [But] to sit down while you're facing a deadline and say, "Gee, there must be some other experts we haven't thought of. Let's beat the bushes and launch a search of the city or the country for them." Well, that takes a lot of time and energy because for TV it involves a lot more than flipping a card on the Rolodex. A second reason is that we know [some guys] provide a succinct response. You can't come to me and say, "Sam, I know you're on a deadline, you need to comment on such and such, go out and take a chance on Mr. X. No, I'm sorry folks, I don't have the time to take a chance with Mr. X ... I know Mr. Y ... is going to deliver the goods.[19]

As Donaldson suggests, how effective pundits are at communicating their ideas to the public in a straightforward and meaningful way is also important. Tammy Haddad, formerly of *Larry King Live*, agrees, observing that "there are so many people out there who know so much, but they're lousy guests. They have to be able to explain [issues] in such a way that my mother in Pittsburgh understands what they're talking about."[20] During newscasts, it becomes even more crucial for guests to be brief because they are not given the time to offer long exposés on the state of the world. For those scholars who appreciate what the broadcast media require, their names will continue to find their way on to newsroom Rolodexes.

ACHIEVING POLICY INFLUENCE: WHAT THE
NUMBERS DO NOT TELL US

Though often portrayed as institutes comprised of experts engaged in quiet reflection, think tanks are a hub of activity. On any given day, scholars may be called upon to provide several interviews to the media, participate in seminars, meet with policy-makers, help to launch a new study, or begin working on the next research project. In short, they are expected to pursue multiple channels to market their ideas and the work of their institute. And although some scholars may remain humble despite achieving national prominence, their employers cannot afford to downplay their contribution to policy debates. On the contrary, as if it were considered part of their job description, directors of think tanks often exaggerate or inflate the impact of their organization. For example, a few months after Ronald Reagan entered the Oval Office, Heritage president Edwin Feulner claimed that over 60 per cent of the policy recommendations included in his institute's mammoth study *Mandate for Leadership* had been, or were in the process of being implemented by the Reagan administration. To Feulner's delight, his comments appeared in several newspapers throughout the United States. What most journalists failed to point out, however, was that many of the recommendations he was taking credit for had been proposed by other individuals and institutes years before. The illusion of Heritage's newly acquired policy influence, fostered in part by the media, had become reality.[21] Similarly, in flipping through Brookings's 2003 *Annual Report*, readers can glance at "Brookings by the Numbers," which as the title suggests, tallies its impressive list of achievements.[22] In this one-page summary, we are told that in 2003 the Brookings Institution Press published fifty books and eight scholarly journals. We are also informed that Brookings scholars testified thirty-one times at congressional hearings and that sixty-three public briefings were held at the institute. And that is not all. As noted, several more statistics detail how often Brookings scholars were quoted in the press.

Think tanks are often preoccupied with numbers, and for good reason. In the minds of think tank directors, who are accountable to boards of trustees and directors, numbers translate into policy influence, and policy influence translates into more funding. Although some trustees and donors may want to know more about the nature of the research, they are concerned primarily with the range and volume of products think tanks produce. They are even more interested in how much exposure think tanks generate. After all, think tanks for all intents and purposes are businesses competing in the marketplace of ideas. And as long as numbers relating to books published, testimonies given, and media hits recorded continue to increase, they can claim that their influence is on the rise. Unfortunately, it is what these and other numbers do not tell us that is critical to understanding the complexity of the policy-making process.

Compiling data on media visibility or on how often policy experts testify before congressional committees may tell us how active think tanks are in particular policy debates, but such information provides little insight into how much influence they have had in shaping public policy. To a large extent, evaluating think tank influence is inherently difficult because think tanks, not to mention those who study them, have different perceptions of what constitutes influence and how it can best be measured. As already discussed, for some think tanks, the amount of media exposure their institute attracts or the number of publications they produce is indicative of how much influence they wield. Others rely on different performance indicators, such as how many staff members have been appointed to senior government positions or the size of their budget, to assess their impact. What makes evaluating their influence even more difficult is that the policy-makers, academics, and journalists who subscribe to think tank publications or attend the conferences and workshops they sponsor invariably have different impressions of the relevance and usefulness of their work. As a result, scholars cannot assume that think tanks measure influence in the same way; nor can they assume that policy-makers and other target groups use similar criteria to evaluate their performance.

Even if think tanks adopted the same performance indicators and assigned the same priority to becoming involved at each stage of the policy-making process, numerous methodological obstacles would still have to be overcome to accurately measure their influence in public policy. Since dozens of individuals and organizations seek to influence policy debates, tracing the origin of a policy idea can be problematic. In an increasingly crowded political arena, it is often difficult to isolate the voice or voices that made a difference. Moreover, it can take months, if not years, before an idea proposed by a think tank – or any other non-governmental organization, for that matter – has any discernible impact. Indeed, by the time a policy initiative is introduced, it may no longer resemble the think tank's initial proposal.

As demonstrated, think tanks often provide little more than anecdotal evidence to show how much influence they wield. Unfortunately, claiming to have influence is far simpler than documenting how it was achieved. In the following chapter, we will consider how scholars can use quantitative and qualitative approaches to make more informed judgments about the relevance of think tanks at different stages of policy-making. We will also discuss why it is necessary to re-examine how policy influence is achieved. Rather than assuming that think tanks can be influential only if they produce desirable policy outcomes, we must understand how their influence can be felt at some or all stages of the policy-making process. In short, failure to convince policy-makers to pursue a recommended course of action does not necessarily mean that think tanks lack influence. Indeed, as we will see, there are many ways think tanks can and do leave an indelible mark on the body politic.

CHAPTER SEVEN

Is Anybody Listening? Assessing the Influence of Think Tanks

In the previous chapter, we examined how think tanks rely on various channels to influence public opinion and public policy. The purpose of this chapter is to consider how scholars can better assess the influence or impact of think tanks at different stages of the policy-making process. As noted, although the behaviour of think tanks has been subjected to increased scrutiny in recent years, little progress has been made in evaluating the nature and extent of their contribution to public policy. Indeed, rather than discussing how different methodological approaches can be used to study think tank influence, journalists and scholars have for the most part been content to make sweeping and often unfounded observations about their policy impact. Needless to say, these have done little to advance our knowledge of how think tanks engage with the public and with policy-makers to influence the political agenda.

To address what is clearly a significant shortcoming in the literature, this chapter will discuss the advantages and disadvantages of relying on quantitative and qualitative approaches to evaluating think tank performance. By so doing, we can begin to think more critically about how to overcome some of the many methodological obstacles that limit our ability to make informed observations about the influence of think tanks. Although the concept of influence is ambiguous and difficult to grasp, it is central to any discussion about politics and policy-making. It is also central to any discussion about think tanks and their efforts to become entrenched in the policy-making process. As students in introductory political science courses are reminded, politics is about the struggle for power and the ability of various individuals and organizations to achieve desirable outcomes. But it is also about ideas, the ambition of leaders, and the goals and aspirations of citizens. In short, it is about competing visions of the national interest and the many forces that shape the fate of nations. It is for these reasons that we need to explore more fully how think tanks contribute to policy development.

The American political system, as previously discussed, is the ideal environment for think tanks to inhabit. As organizations competing in the free and open marketplace of ideas, they have innumerable opportunities to share and discuss their ideas with the public, with the media, and with policy-makers. However, as in any business, they must be able to monitor the quality and appeal of their products. Unfortunately, unlike that of Fortune 500 companies and the millions of small businesses across the United States, the success of think tanks cannot be measured in terms of profits and losses. It can only be measured by assessing their ability to influence the views and attitudes of the public and policy-makers. Before delving into the various ways to measure influence, we must first discuss what scholars mean by *influence*. As we will discover, although the process of wielding influence can be easily summarized using lines and arrows, understanding the nature of influence and how it is exercised is far more complicated. Influence is often treated in a linear fashion whereby two parties negotiate policy outcomes, but in reality, a more holistic approach may be required to comprehend how policy influence is achieved.

EASIER SAID THAN DONE: THE ABCs OF INFLUENCE

In one of the more serious treatments of influence in the literature on international relations, K.J. Holsti suggests that influence occurs when A convinces B to do X, convinces B not to do X, or persuades "B to *continue* a course of action or policy that is useful to, or in the interests of, A."[1] A's inability to achieve any of these desired outcomes, which could be the result of a multitude of factors relating to either A or B, would suggest that under these circumstances, A was unable to exercise influence. For Holsti, influence, which he regards as an aspect of power, "is essentially a *means* to an end. Some governments or statesmen may seek influence for its own sake, but for most it is instrumental, just like money. They use it primarily for achieving or defending other goals, which may include prestige, territory, souls, raw materials, security, or alliances."[2]

The easiest way to measure influence, according to Holsti, "is to study the *responses* of those in the influence relationship. If A can get B to do X, but C

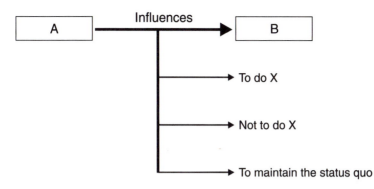

cannot get B to do the same thing, then in that particular issue, A has more influence. If B does X despite the protestations of A, then we can assume that A, in this circumstance, did not enjoy much influence."[3] In other words, influence is perceived to have taken place if B responds to or reacts in a manner acceptable to A. Conversely, influence has not taken place, according to Holsti's model, if B does not abide by A's wishes. In short, influence is tied directly to specific policy outcomes.

In studying the relationship between states in the international system, as Holsti does, it may make sense to employ a linear model of influence. After all, by understanding the power capabilities of two states engaged in conflict and the efforts undertaken by either or both parties to exercise influence, it might be possible to explain what factors may have helped or hindered A's and B's efforts to achieve their goals. Indeed, if scholars are interested in evaluating why some arms control negotiations between the United States and Russia succeeded and others failed, this model could prove to be useful. However, relying on it to evaluate the influence or impact of think tanks and other non-governmental organizations in the policy-making process is problematic.

To begin with, in studying the policy-making process and the various individuals and organizations that participate in it, it is critically important to understand the identities of A and B. In Holsti's model, A and B are sovereign states that have considerable resources at their disposal to exercise influence. Now imagine that A is a resident scholar at a Washington-based think tank with expertise in foreign policy and security studies and B is the chair of the Senate Foreign Relations Committee. A has published a study on national missile defense and is asked to testify before this committee. According to Holsti's model, if A's recommendations are not followed by B and in fact are rejected (in other words, if A's goal is not achieved), A would be perceived as having no influence. Alternatively, if A's recommendations are embraced by B, A would be deemed to have had influence. Yet, as we will discover, both scenarios raise serious methodological problems.

First, we cannot assume that if A's recommendations are dismissed by B, A has had no influence in the policy-making process. Although A may not be able to take credit for influencing a specific policy decision, A could have played an important role in helping the public, policy-makers, and the media to consider other approaches to resolving a potentially difficult policy problem. Indeed, as Peschek and others have argued, think tanks are most effective at framing the parameters of public policy debates. Second, A may be well positioned to share ideas with policy-makers at different levels of government, who in turn could draw further attention to the issues A has flagged. As a result of suggesting that influence is tied directly to policy outcomes, scholars are ignoring the many access points that think tanks and other non-governmental organizations have to the policy-making process. Conversely, by presuming that A has had influence over B because A's preferences are satisfied, Holsti allows himself to fall into a different trap. Even if the recommendations A has proposed closely resemble policies that are introduced, he should not take for granted that A has had influence over B. It is conceivable, as we will discuss, that A has only reinforced what was on B's mind or that other domestic and external forces compelled B to act in a certain way. In reality, despite the perception of having considerable influence over B, A may have exercised very little.

Holsti should also keep in mind that, given the vast number of individuals and organizations that compete in the marketplace of ideas, it is often difficult to identify the source and origin of an idea which could span several generations. As scholars of public policy are well aware, every successful idea has a hundred mothers and fathers. And since many ideas take years before they make their way onto the political agenda, it is also likely that they have grandmothers and grandfathers. Regardless of an idea's gestation period, one thing is certain: every bad policy idea is an orphan.

Think tanks, as noted, have a vested interest in creating the impression that they exercise enormous influence. If this were not a concern, they would not devote so much time and resources to enhancing their profile. However, scholars must resist the temptation of drawing on anecdotal evidence to support or reject these claims. They must also resist the temptation of trying to simplify a process that is anything but simple and straightforward. Influence, like so many other aspects of politics, is far more complicated than the linear model suggests and cannot be reduced to two or three likely outcomes. In fact, contrary to Holsti's model, it is not always possible to confirm when A has or has not had influence. As much as scholars would like to argue with some degree of confidence that A has been able or unable to exercise influence over B, it is increasingly difficult to do so because of the complexity and ad hoc nature of the policy-making process. Rather than concluding that individuals and organizations have or do not have influence, scholars may want to consider the likelihood that participants in policy-making enjoy different degrees or levels of influence at different stages of the policy cycle.

In the following section, we will discuss how scholars can do so by embracing a more holistic approach to the study of policy influence. In addition to offering an alternative to examining influence in a linear fashion – an approach that assumes that two players will rely on various strategies to achieve their desired goals – this model compels scholars to think of the policy-making process as a series of conversations taking place (often simultaneously) between multiple actors in distinct policy environments. In this model, influence is not tied directly to specific policy outcomes but is achieved through the interaction and exchanges between various participants who are directly and indirectly involved in the policy-making process.

A HOLISTIC APPROACH TO POLICY-MAKING

In reflecting on the influence of think tanks on the media, congress and the executive, Leslie Gelb, the former president of the Council on Foreign Relations and Pulitzer Prize–winning correspondent for the *New York Times*, commented that "it is highly episodic, arbitrary, and difficult to predict."[4] His remarks were limited to think tanks, but he could just as easily have been making an observation about the nature of the policy-making process in the United States. It is because policy-making is highly episodic, arbitrary, and difficult to predict that a holistic approach to studying policy influence may prove more useful.

In some respects, this approach builds on the work of scholars who study policy or epistemic communities and issue networks in the United States.[5] Policy communities and issue networks are composed of individuals and organizations that, by virtue of their expertise in a particular policy area, are invited by policy-makers to participate in various stages of the policy-making process. These communities, which are divided into two spheres – the core (sub-government) and the periphery (the attentive public) – seek to influence specific public policies.[6] The approach that we are considering is similar to policy communities in so far as it focuses on different clusters or centres of knowledge and expertise. However, unlike policy communities, which are created in large part to influence one or more government policies

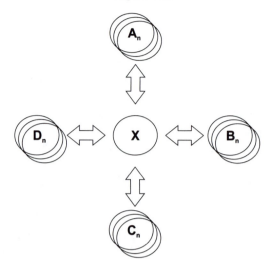

(X), a holistic approach considers how multiple actors (represented by An, Bn, Cn, and Dn) attempt to influence the environment in which policy decisions are made. In other words, a holistic approach to policy-making assumes that while officials in the White House, on Capitol Hill, and in various government departments and agencies attend to the affairs of state, conversations are taking place between policy experts in universities, in think tanks, in interest groups, and in the private sector which, with the assistance of the media and other outlets, can help to enrich policy debates. While elected officials may prefer to insulate themselves from the discussions taking place in or between clusters An, Bn, Cn, and Dn, they cannot ignore how these conversations shape the political agenda.

Among the many benefits of a holistic approach is that it compels scholars to think about policy influence, not in terms of how it is exercised between two players, A and B, but how it can be fostered over time by different individuals and organizations acting alone or working together or in concert with various policy-makers. Such an approach also provides a broader and more sophisticated understanding of policy influence. Recall the example we used of a resident scholar from a Washington-based think tank who was asked to testify on national missile defense to the Senate Foreign Relations Committee. Using Holsti's linear model of influence, we suggested two possible outcomes, given A's preference that the recommendations put forward be adopted: A convinces the chair of the committee (B) to endorse the recommendations, in which case A's influence is achieved, or B rejects A's recommendations, in which case A exercises no influence. The linear model provides an all-or-nothing proposition – A either has or does not have influence.

A holistic model which acknowledges that influence can occur in different ways and at different stages of the policy cycle presents a more realistic picture of how A might achieve influence. Even though A might not be able to convince B to endorse the proposed recommendations, A's testimony may spark a debate in the media, in academic circles, in the Oval Office, at other think tanks, and in countless other places where public policy is discussed and analyzed. The fact that A may not have altered B's position regarding national missile defense does not mean that A lacks influence; nor does it mean that in the medium or long term, A's recommendations will be ignored. Rather, B's unwillingness to fulfill A's wishes suggests simply that in this instance, B is unable and/or unwilling to follow A's advice.

The time frame over which influence occurs is also an important consideration, particularly with respect to matters of war and peace. Although Holsti does not specify what he considers a reasonable time frame for A to influence B, it is clear from the linear model he presents that once B makes a decision, A is no longer in a position to exercise further influence. Unable to convince B to act according to A's preferences, A may seek influence through other channels. This was certainly the case when the Bush administration decided to deploy troops to Iraq after it became clear that the United Nations Security Council would not endorse the invasion. Decisions such as the one leading to the overthrow of Saddam Hussein reinforce why it is important to look beyond the narrowly defined parameters of a linear model of influence; a holistic model encourages scholars to pay attention to what takes place after a decision is made, a period in which *residual influence* may surface. Let me explain. If B does not act according to A's wishes, as the example mentioned above illustrates, it does not necessarily mean that in the short, medium, or long term A will be denied influence. Moreover, if B does act according to A's wishes, it does not mean that A will immediately move on to the next issue. Indeed, B's accommodation of A may provide A with an incentive to influence other decision-makers and stakeholders. In some respects, residual influence can be regarded as goodwill which develops over time between individuals and organizations that have reaped tangible benefits through cooperation. This goodwill in turn could, as early functionalists such as David Mitrany predicted, spill over into more sensitive areas of negotiation.[7]

Unlike a linear model, a holistic approach does not try to reduce influence to an all-or-nothing proposition; as noted, it acknowledges that there are degrees and levels of influence. It also acknowledges that there are individuals and organizations which, by virtue of their expertise and connections to key policy-makers, are well equipped and positioned to influence both the policy-making environment and specific policy decisions. In a holistic approach, it matters if A is a scholar at a think tank, the editor of a newspaper, the head of an interest group, a professor at one of the nation's leading universities, a CEO of a major corporation, or a former cabinet secretary. In the final analysis, it is important to recognize that with any important policy issue, whether it is strategic defense or the war on terror, there are literally hundreds of organizations, including think tanks, that try to convey their ideas to policy-makers. And as scholars interested in how policy agendas are shaped, it is our responsibility to determine the most effective ways to evaluate their contribution to public policy.

A holistic approach to studying policy influence is not neat and tidy, but neither is the process by which public policy is made and implemented. Public policy, as the case studies in the two following chapters demonstrate, cannot be explained by limiting our discussion to two players trying to negotiate favourable outcomes; nor can it be explained through computer-generated flow charts. The process by which think tanks and other non-governmental organizations try to assert influence, like the process of making policy decisions, is, as Gelb reminds us, highly episodic, arbitrary, and difficult to predict. Ironically, this is what makes the study of public policy interesting.

Understanding who exercises influence and under what conditions it is achieved is a constant challenge for scholars in the field. Part of the challenge, in addition to developing an appropriate model to study influence, is determining the most effective ways to measure policy influence. In the following section, we shift our attention to how scholars can use both quantitative and qualitative indicators to assess or evaluate the influence of think tanks. How useful these criteria are for assessing the influence of think tanks on public opinion and public policy is a question that will undoubtedly lead to a lively exchange in academic circles. In the interests of promoting such an exchange, we will begin by focusing on what think tanks seem to value most – making the headlines.

CAN POLICY INFLUENCE BE MEASURED? A QUANTITATIVE APPROACH

The Media

On any given day, you can pick up a newspaper, turn on the radio, watch the news or a current affairs program, or scan the thousands of political Web sites on the Internet to find out what is on the minds of policy experts at

America's leading think tanks. And if that is not enough, you can subscribe to *Think Tank Watch*, a weekly e-mail newsletter prepared and distributed by the Canadian embassy in Washington which summarizes the research activities of Washington-based think tanks. The Canadian high commission in London has recently begun a similar newsletter to monitor the work of British think tanks.

For twenty-four hours a day, seven days a week, the print and electronic media in the United States and around the world look to policy experts to shed light on important and controversial political issues, and think tanks are only too willing to oblige. Often referred to as "talking heads," scholars from think tanks appear with great regularity on the network news and on political talk shows to comment on a wide range of domestic and foreign policy issues. They become particularly visible in the hours and days following historic events such as the terrorist attacks against the World Trade Center and the Pentagon, when journalists and media executives scramble to make sense of what has transpired. When they are not on television or on radio, policy experts from think tanks share their insights on the op-ed pages of major American newspapers. In short, think tanks understand the demands placed on the media and respond by providing them with a steady stream of timely and relevant information.

Think tanks, like corporations involved in the entertainment and advertising industries, appreciate the impact the media have on shaping our perceptions of what and who is important. That is why, as discussed in the previous chapter, they devote so much time and resources to strengthening their ties to various media outlets. Few think tank directors need to be reminded of the potential benefits of generating substantial media exposure; positive exposure not only enhances the credibility of think tanks, but even more importantly, it creates the impression that they wield enormous influence, a valuable currency that can be used to achieve desirable outcomes.

Having influence is something all think tanks covet, but in reality, most settle for the perception of exercising influence. And what better way to create the perception of influence than to capture the attention of the media. As the marketplace of ideas has become increasingly competitive, several think tanks have closely monitored their media exposure relative to their rivals. What is at stake is more than bragging rights; it is the opportunity to translate heightened exposure into additional philanthropic, corporate, and private funding. In the following section, we will examine the amount of media exposure a select group of think tanks with expertise in foreign and defense policy generated in leading American newspapers and on the television net-

Table 7.1
Print media coverage of selected think tanks, January 2001 – January 2005: totals of all media sampled

	Subject							
Think tank	*Iraq*	*Afghan-istan*	*9/11*	*al-Qaeda*	*Terror-ism*	*Missile defense*	*Total*	*Percent-age*
PNAC	60	28	37	20	52	12	209	1.01
Hudson	104	50	97	32	158	30	471	2.27
Center for Security Policy	147	31	81	47	191	66	563	2.71
Hoover	324	125	211	84	354	38	1,136	5.47
Cato Institute	258	121	272	87	437	31	1,206	5.80
Carnegie Endowment	398	187	204	114	409	115	1,427	6.87
AEI	633	181	401	146	629	61	2,051	9.87
Heritage	544	245	386	150	685	119	2,129	10.25
RAND	391	260	528	232	691	63	2,165	10.42
CSIS	742	327	362	231	754	73	2,489	11.98
Council on Foreign Relations	853	358	469	288	846	71	2,885	13.89
Brookings	1,054	495	786	271	1,270	169	4,045	19.47
Total							20,776	

SOURCE: LexisNexis®.
NOTE: Because of similarity of search criteria, there is likely some article overlap in the numbers.

works between 2001 and 2005. The purpose of compiling these data is not to confirm which think tanks do or do not have influence but to demonstrate how this indicator of influence may be used in quantitative evaluations of think tank performance.

Using the database Lexis/Nexis, we recorded the number of times a select group of think tanks – the Project for the New American Century, the Centre for Security Policy, the Hudson Institute, the Carnegie Endowment for International Peace, the Cato Institute, the Heritage Foundation, the Hoover Institution, the Brookings Institution, the Center for Strategic and International Studies, the American Enterprise Institute, the Council on Foreign Relations, and RAND – were mentioned in six major newspapers – the *Wall Street Journal*, the *Christian Science Monitor*, the *Washington Post*, the *Washington Times*, *USA Today*, and the *New York Times* – in relation to six important events or issues – Iraq, Afghanistan, 9/11, al-Qaeda, terrorism, and missile defense – between January 2001 and January 2005 (see table 7.1 and tables A4.1 to A4.6 in appendix 4).[8]

The number of references to each think tank may be inflated since more than one of these terms could appear in a newspaper article, but our purpose here is to simply demonstrate a general pattern in think tank exposure.

Table 7.2
Total television exposure of selected think tanks, January 2001 – January 2005: totals of all media sampled

Think tank	Iraq	Afghan-istan	9/11	al-Qaeda	Terror-ism	Missile defense	Totals	Percent-age
Hudson	0	0	0	0	0	0	0	0.00
PNAC	1	0	0	0	0	0	1	0.14
Hoover	1	1	0	0	1	0	3	0.41
Center for Security Policy	4	1	0	1	4	0	10	1.36
Cato Institute	4	0	0	1	4	0	9	1.22
CSIS	2	3	0	1	6	0	12	1.63
AEI	17	2	0	1	6	0	26	3.53
Heritage	11	3	4	1	10	2	31	4.21
Carnegie Endowment	42	7	4	10	25	8	96	13.04
Council on Foreign Relations	65	8	6	7	36	1	123	16.71
RAND	30	7	7	33	51	1	129	17.53
Brookings	152	31	17	23	68	5	296	40.22
Total							736	

SOURCE: Vanderbilt Television News Archive.

The exact number of citations is not as important as how scholars might use these figures to determine the extent of think tank influence. A think tank receives one media hit for each reference made to the events and issues selected.

Of the twelve think tanks sampled, the Brookings Institution ranked first, receiving over four thousand citations, or 19.48 per cent of all print media references, almost twice the share of exposure generated by AEI, Heritage, and RAND. Other think tanks that attracted considerable exposure included CSIS and the Council on Foreign Relations. The Project for the New American Century, the think tank credited with influencing the Bush doctrine, ranked last, attracting only 1 per cent of media exposure. There was tremendous variation in the exposure think tanks generated across newspapers and issue areas. For example, Brookings's exposure ranged from a low of 10.26 per cent in the more conservative *Washington Times* to a high of 26.17 per cent in the more liberal *Washington Post*. By contrast, the Heritage Foundation, known for its conservative leanings, attracted the most coverage, 21.57 per cent, in the *Washington Times* and the least coverage, 4.49 per cent, in what many would regard as the more liberal *New York Times*. Brookings was quoted most often with respect to Iraq and terrorism, whereas RAND, for instance, was cited most for its views on issues relating to terrorism and 9/11.

The results were similar for the broadcast media (see table 7.2 and tables A4.7 to A4.10 in appendix 4). ABC, NBC, and CNN called on experts from the Brookings Institution or cited one of its studies far more often than from any other think tank: it received 40.22 per cent of all broadcast media citations in this sample, more than twice the share recorded by its closest competitor, the Council on Foreign Relations (16.71 per cent), and almost ten times the exposure generated by the Heritage Foundation (4.21 per cent). The exception was CBS, which relied equally on RAND and Brookings (both received 25.44 per cent of the network's coverage). Once again, PNAC attracted very little attention (0.14 per cent), a step up from the Hudson Institute, which was not the subject of any discussion by the four networks.

In our review of these figures, an obvious question to ask is, Why do some think tanks attract more exposure than others? While there are several factors, including the size of a think tank's budget, size of staff, area of research, ideological orientation, and geographic location, which could help to explain why some think tanks are cited more than others,[9] our concern is less with how and why think tanks attract media coverage and more with what these figures tell us or do not tell us about the extent of their influence.

Scholars interested in using quantitative approaches to studying think tank influence tend to focus on media coverage because it is relatively easy to measure. Although it is time-consuming, scholars can draw on different databases, including the one used in this chapter, to compile information on how much exposure think tanks attract in the print and broadcast media. In so doing, they can record how many times think tanks are quoted, the policy issues they comment on most often, and the period of time over which they appear to enjoy the most visibility. Scholars may also elect to undertake rigorous content analyses of newspaper coverage so that they can measure the number of column inches devoted to think tanks. Moreover, should they be so inclined, they can keep track of whether the ideological leanings of think tanks are identified – liberal, conservative, Marxist, libertarian – and if the institutes are described in a positive or negative manner. All of this information can then make its way into studies evaluating the impact of think tanks.

The major advantage of tracking media exposure is that it enables scholars to identify those institutes that are most active or relevant in framing the parameters of important public policy debates. For those interested in how think tanks become involved at the initial stages of the policy cycle, when ideas from multiple sources are being articulated, assembling a list of organizations making the headlines is critical. By following think tanks that are making the news and the issues that they are addressing, scholars can begin to examine more closely what additional steps they might take to promote their ideas. While some think tanks may be content to have one of their scholars or studies mentioned in a newspaper, others will try to use the media to garner public support for a new policy idea or initiative. As momentum for an idea builds, think tanks can then rely on many of the channels described in the previous chapter to capture the attention of policy-makers. In short, for many think tanks, being in the spotlight is a necessary, though not sufficient, condition for exercising influence.

Unfortunately, other than providing some initial information on which organizations are at the forefront of policy debates, media exposure tells us very little about the nature and extent of think tank influence. Indeed, contrary to what is said in the annual reports issued by various think tanks and their directors to their boards of directors, media visibility should not be equated with policy influence. The fact that a think tank study or report is referred to in the *Washington Post*, for example, does not mean that the public or policy-makers will be swayed by its contents. To suggest otherwise, we would have to be confident that the report was read and understood by a sufficiently large cross-section of Americans. Even if it could be established, through a public opinion survey, that a significant percentage of the American people were aware of a specific think tank report mentioned in the *Washington Post*, it would be difficult to demonstrate, for the reasons stated earlier in the chapter, that the report *influenced* either public attitudes toward a particular issue or the views of policy-makers. Moreover, even if it could be confirmed that public opinion had shifted as a result of this report, we would still have to contend with the many methodological obstacles limiting our ability to trace the origins of an idea to a policy outcome. It is for all these reasons that, as previously discussed, a more holistic approach to studying policy influence could prove more useful. Rather than trying to equate media visibility with policy influence, we should explore how policy issues discussed in the media, in the academic community, in the private sector, and in think tanks eventually make their way to policy-makers.

It is also important to keep in mind that our data on media visibility ignore vital information necessary to make informed observations about think tank influence. What the Lexis/Nexis database search provides is raw numbers on think tank citations. What is left out is the context in which comments by think tank scholars or references to think tank studies are made. Furthermore, the figures included in our charts do not reveal the type and scope of coverage think tanks receive. For instance, we do not know how many of the four thousand citations Brookings recorded in the print media were on the front or back page of newspapers. For obvious reasons, this factor could have a profound impact on the number of potential readers who come across references to this and other institutions. Moreover, we do not know which, if any, articles about the work of think tanks generated the most interest. Using Nielsen ratings, television networks can determine roughly how many viewers watched a particular program, a system that may help scholars study the exposure of think tanks in the broadcast media. However, it would be of little use to those looking at think tanks and the print media. Put simply, tracking the media visibility of think tanks may provide scholars with an important piece of the puzzle, but it is still only a piece. The entire puzzle can only be completed when more information about the involvement of think tanks is known.

Congressional Testimony

In addition to monitoring how much media coverage they receive, think tanks pay close attention to how often their scholars are invited to testify before congressional committees. A list of scholars who have given testimony as well as the full text of their remarks is often available on think tank Web sites. The reason for this practice is obvious. Think tanks want to convey the impression that they are credible and important actors in the policy-making community, and what better way to do this then to advertise their accomplishments? Although there are several factors, according to Andrew Rich and Kent Weaver, that could account for why some think tanks appear before legislative committees more than others,[10] we need to consider how data on congressional testimony can be used to further our understanding of the involvement and impact of think tanks in the policy-making process.

Between 1 January 2001 and 1 January 2005, the same time frame used to track media exposure, policy experts from the think tanks sampled in our study testified 120 times before seven Senate and House committees with responsibility in the areas of foreign and defense policy (see table 7.3 and figs A4.1 to A4.6 in appendix 4).[11] Ranking first in number of appearances made was the Center for Strategic and International Studies, a veritable who's who in the foreign policy-making establishment. Experts from CSIS appeared before legislative committees on 33 separate occasions, or 27.5 per cent of the time, well ahead of its closest competitors, the Brookings Institution (22), AEI (14), and RAND (10). Only a handful of appearances were made by experts at Cato (1), the Hoover Institution (2), PNAC (3), the Hudson Institute (4), the Center for Security Policy (5), and Heritage (8).

According to our data, CSIS was most visible in the Senate, where its scholars appeared 20 times. Most of the testimonies were made before the Senate Foreign Relations Committee where CSIS experts discussed issues

Table 7.3
Combined testimony before US Senate and House of Representatives committees by selected think tanks, January 2001 – January 2005

Think tank	Number of testimonies	Percentage
Cato Institute	1	0.83
Hoover	2	1.67
PNAC	3	2.50
Hudson	4	3.33
Center for Security Policy	5	4.17
Heritage	8	6.67
Carnegie Endowment	9	7.50
Council on Foreign Relations	9	7.50
RAND	10	8.33
AEI	14	11.67
Brookings	22	18.33
CSIS	33	27.50
Total	120	

SOURCE: LexisNexis®.

ranging from bio-terrorism and the threat of infectious diseases to the crisis in Iraq and negotiations with North Korea. In the House of Representatives, CSIS maintained a strong presence (13 appearances), but fell slightly behind the first-ranked Brookings Institution, whose scholars testified 14 times, mostly before the House Committee on International Relations. AEI and Heritage put in strong showings with 10 and 8 appearances respectively.

The data on congressional testimony raise similar methodological problems to that compiled on media exposure. What we are presented with is information that may help us to identify think tanks deemed to be credible (at least in the eyes of some policy-makers) but scarcely any insight into which presentation or presentations given by think tank scholars were considered useful and relevant. Once again, the figures revealed in the charts do not speak to the issue of influence but merely address the frequency with which think tanks are called upon to testify before Congress. And as Rich and Weaver point out, there are several factors that could explain why some think tanks appear more regularly before legislative committees than others.

Without paying close attention to the committee proceedings in which scholars from think tanks testified, it is virtually impossible to predict how much or little influence they exercised. Indeed, in the absence of detailed information about the inner workings of individual committees and the policy preferences and goals of its members, one could reasonably conclude that data on think tank testimony have limited utility. However, if one compares such data to that on media exposure, it becomes clear that this approach to assessing policy influence may prove more promising. In fact, by comparing the visibility of think tanks before Congress and in the media, we can observe that they enjoy different levels of recognition at different stages of the policy cycle. For example, while the Brookings Institution received 40.22 per cent and 19.47 per cent coverage respectively in our sample of the broadcast and print media, its scholars appeared before Congress 18.33 per cent of the time. By contrast, while CSIS enjoyed the strongest presence before Congress (27.50 per cent), its exposure in the broadcast (1.63 per cent) and print (11.98 per cent) media was far less significant. By keeping track of where in the policy cycle some think tanks appear to be most active, we can then explore in more detail the nature of their contributions to specific policy debates. In short, in assessing policy influence, what is important to highlight is not which think tanks ranked first, second, or last in such categories as media exposure and congressional testimony, but which think tanks, relative to other institutes and organizations involved at the same stage of the policy cycle, were best equipped and positioned to influence public policy.

We cannot determine this by focusing solely on quantitative indicators of policy influence. Media exposure, congressional testimony, and other measurements such as number of publications produced and size of staff and budgetary resources can only take scholars so far. Although data on these and other aspects of think tank activity can be useful in documenting patterns and trends in the institutes' behaviour, a more comprehensive understanding of their influence is required to probe more deeply into their involvement in the policy-making process.

THE INVISIBLE CLOAK: THINK TANKS, PUBLIC POLICY, AND QUALITATIVE INDICATORS OF INFLUENCE

Studying public policy and the efforts of non-governmental organizations to shape it would be so much simpler if political scientists could magically transform their academic robes into invisible cloaks. By becoming invisible, they could make their way around the White House, Capitol Hill, and dozens of government departments and agencies as easily as Harry Potter did in the cavernous hallways and staircases of Hogwarts, the fictional school where he and his friends were sent to learn the arts of witchcraft and wizardry. And like the bespectacled wizard whose presence went undetected as long as he remained under his invisible blanket, political scientists could travel effortlessly inside the corridors of power. With their cloaks around them, there is little scholars could not ascertain about who and what was influencing the behaviour of policy-makers. They could observe meetings between high-level officials in the Oval Office, overhear phone conversations between key members of Congress, and gain access to confidential documents. The mysterious and complex world of policy-making would suddenly become open and transparent.

But the world at Hogwarts is very different from the one that policy-makers in Washington inhabit. At Hogwarts it is outsiders such as Harry Potter who can draw on extraordinary powers to uncover what is taking place behind closed doors. By contrast, in Washington, insiders use their authority as elected and appointed leaders to conceal the inner workings of the policy-making process. It is they, not the scholars who study them, who hide behind their invisible cloaks. There are wizards in Washington – the Washington Wizards – but they play in the National Basketball Association; they are not members of ancient societies hoping to uncover the state's most highly guarded secrets.

Since scholars cannot hide behind imaginary cloaks to observe first-hand why certain policy decisions were made, they must find other ways to shed light on the policy-making process. We have already considered some quantitative indicators that may be employed to assess the contribution of think tanks to policy-making. Among other things, we discovered that numbers reflecting the amount of media exposure think tanks generate and/or the frequency with which their experts appear before legislative committees often leave us with more questions than answers. To remedy this problem, we may want to consider how qualitative approaches can be used to provide further insight into how think tanks become involved in policy-making and the nature and extent of their influence.

When scholars refer to qualitative approaches to the study of policy-making, what exactly do they mean? Generally, they are referring to non-statistical methods of analysis, including archival research and interviews, which enable them to reveal the inner workings of the policy-making process. Those employing this approach maintain that while quantitative indicators may be useful in evaluating policy influence, so too are intangibles such as personal contacts with high-level officials who may have a profound impact on shaping policy decisions. For example, in looking at how often experts from think tanks testified before congressional committees, we focused primarily on which institutes logged the most and fewest number of appearances. No consideration was given to the reputation and standing of the experts who testified or to the composition of the congressional committees. Why is this aspect important? It is important because in the policymaking process, it matters who is providing advice and to whom the advice is directed. It makes a difference if testimony is being presented by a former cabinet secretary or a relatively unknown academic from a Washington-based think tank who was called upon at the last minute to fill in for a more seasoned scholar. It also makes a difference whether policy experts are testifying before high-profile or relatively obscure committees, and it makes a difference whether the topic being discussed is a priority for Congress and the administration or is an issue that, like so many others, is forgotten overnight.

As we will discuss in some detail in our case studies, the relationships and contacts that develop between think tanks and policy-makers can often explain why some think tanks are able to enjoy considerable access to various stages of the policy-making process. Heritage president Edwin Feulner's friendship with key members of the Reagan transition team in 1981 certainly played an important role in allowing the foundation to make its *Mandate for Leadership* study known to the incoming administration. The same can be said for PNAC, which relied on several of its more prominent members, including Secretary of Defense Donald Rumsfeld and Vice-President Dick Cheney, to communicate the recommendations outlined in its much publicized report *Rebuilding America's Defenses* to President Bush.

However, while personal contacts and connections to decision-makers may help facilitate access to various levels of government, they do not guarantee that policy experts from think tanks and other organizations will be able to exercise policy influence. As Zbigniew Brzezinski, national security adviser to President Carter, recently acknowledged, different communities of scholars and former policy-makers in Washington attempt to influence public policy. "There are some communities that do not have much influence, except perhaps in shaping public attitudes to some extent through op-eds, television and so forth ... and there are other communities [of policy experts who] have acquired a certain degree of public recognition [and] have some degree of influence, not excessive, but some ... [They have] influence because of their natural access to policy-makers."[12] According to Brzezinski, experts who fall into the latter category can enjoy "a great deal of influence when government policy gets into deep trouble. Take Vietnam, for example, if things are not going well, all of a sudden viewpoints which are divergent from the standard policy gain a great deal of circulation and are listened to much more carefully."[13] Although there may be an incentive for policy-makers to listen to more diverse points of view when their "policy gets into deep trouble," there are several other factors that may explain why some administrations would be more inclined to turn to outside policy experts, a subject that we will explore in the next two chapters.

The importance of qualitative analyses to the study of think tanks cannot be overemphasized. If done properly, archival research and interviews can produce volumes of information that can document in great detail the critical factors which shape public policy. But quantitative methods should not be overlooked or ignored. On the contrary, qualitative approaches can offer scholars something that raw data cannot – the historical and political context in which policy decisions were made. In chapters 8 and 9 we will draw on both qualitative and quantitative approaches in order to evaluate the extent to which a select group of think tanks were able or unable to exercise influence at different stages of the policy cycle. In so doing, we will remain cognizant of the many methodological barriers often encountered in studying policy influence. Assessing policy influence is inherently difficult, but it is necessary if we are to make any progress in studying the involvement of think tanks and other non-governmental organizations in the policy-making process. The alternative – to rely on anecdotal information or data that tell us little about whether policy-makers and the public are listening to the steady stream of information being distributed by think tanks – is not an option.

CHAPTER EIGHT

Think Tanks at Work: The Debate over National Missile Defense

Documenting the activities of think tanks and their connections to policy-makers, philanthropists, and business leaders may help to shed light on their involvement in policy-making. It may also help to paint a more accurate picture of how these organizations contribute to the power structure in America, an argument made recently by John Micklethwait and Adrian Wooldridge in their insightful and thought-provoking study *The Right Nation*.[1] However, in the absence of detailed case studies, scholars can only speculate about how much or little influence think tanks wield. In this chapter and in the one that follows, we will examine how a select group of think tanks with expertise in foreign and defense policy have sought to influence public attitudes and the policy choices of decision-makers in relation to two important, timely, and controversial issues: the development and possible deployment of a national missile defense, or what the Center for Security Policy dubs simply missile defense, and the ongoing war on terror. The latter will take account of the efforts of think tanks to influence public opinion and public policy on issues ranging from the invasion of Iraq to the creation of the Department of Homeland Security.

Both security-related issues have preoccupied President Bush and, in the case of missile defense, his predecessors for many years, and their resolution is critical for the future of American foreign policy and the stability of the international system. How these issues are resolved is also critically important for those think tanks that have invested considerable time and resources to informing public discussions about America's role in the post-9/11 world. If they cannot make their voices heard at a time when America is struggling to redefine itself, when will they do so?

What we will discover in the following case studies is that think tanks have indeed made their presence felt, but not necessarily in the same way or to the same extent. More specifically, while a select group of think tanks were able to advance the cause of missile defense during the Reagan years by becoming deeply embedded in the policy-making process, they have enjoyed far less success in exploring ideas with President Bush and his small and tight-knit group of advisers on how to fight the war on terror. Several think tanks, including Brookings, AEI, Heritage, the Council on Foreign Relations, RAND, Cato, and the Carnegie Endowment, have made a concerted effort to share their insights on this pressing issue with the media, the public, and policy-makers. Yet, with few exceptions, their access to the White House has been severely restricted. These and other think tanks have no doubt played an important role in educating the American people about the implications of the Bush doctrine and continued fighting in the Middle East, but there is little evidence to suggest that their views have penetrated the Oval Office. Unlike other administrations that invited a free and lively exchange between policy-makers and outside policy experts, by most accounts the Bush White House is hermetically sealed. It is for this and other reasons that think tanks have exercised limited influence over Bush's handling of foreign policy.

Although the case studies that have been selected do not even begin to represent the full range of foreign policy issues that have attracted the interest of think tanks in recent years, they nonetheless provide scholars with an outstanding opportunity to observe the many factors responsible for assisting or undermining their efforts to shape public opinion and public policy. By looking into how and why some think tanks were able or unable to become entrenched in the policy-making process, we can begin to lay the foundation for a more informed discussion about the nature and extent of think tank influence. Although the case studies do not reveal any established pattern of think tank behaviour, they offer something even more valuable – a glimpse into the interaction between policy experts operating on the fringes of government and policy-makers entrusted with protecting the national security of the United States.

The chapter begins with an overview of how missile defense, an issue that predates the signing of the Anti-Ballistic Missile (ABM) Treaty in 1972, made its way onto President Reagan's radar screen. We will then examine how a small group of think tanks were able to assist the Reagan administration in its campaign to market what was then referred to as the Strategic Defense Initiative (SDI), or Star Wars, to the American people and the important role that many of these same think tanks continue to play in supporting President Bush's vision of a defensive shield protecting the United States from nuclear missiles. Finally, we will consider how to assess the contribution of think tanks to this important debate and the impact they had at various stages of the policy cycle.

A SHIELD, NOT A SWORD: RONALD REAGAN AND THE BIRTH OF SDI

To Ronald Reagan, the former Hollywood screen actor, governor of California, and fortieth president of the United States, it seemed to make perfect sense: create a multi-layered defense system that was capable of tracking, intercepting, and destroying nuclear missiles. What no longer made sense, according to Reagan, who entered the Oval Office in January 1981, was for the United States and the Soviet Union to invest their mutual security, not to mention the security of the international community, in the Cold War doctrine of mutual assured destruction (MAD), a doctrine based on the belief that the prospect of annihilation would deter the superpowers from launching a nuclear strike. Although the concept of missile defense was not foreign to American military planners and policy-makers, who understood the risks associated with expanding nuclear arsenals, few had considered the possibility of creating a protective shield around the United States, an idea that began to gain momentum shortly after Reagan assumed office. As he points out in his autobiography, *An American Life,*

I came into office with a decided prejudice against our tacit agreement with the Soviet Union regarding nuclear missiles. I'm talking about the MAD policy – "mutual assured destruction" – the idea of deterrence providing safety so long as each of us had the power to destroy the other with nuclear missiles if one of us launched a first strike. Somehow this didn't seem to me to be something that would send you to bed feeling safe. It was like having two westerners standing in a saloon aiming their guns at each other's head – permanently. There had to be a better way.

Early in my first term, I called a meeting of the Joint Chiefs of Staff ... and said to them: Every offensive weapon ever invented by man has resulted in the creation of a defense against it; isn't it possible in this age of technology that we could invent a defensive weapon that could intercept nuclear weapons and destroy them as they emerged from their silos?

They looked at each other, then asked if they could huddle for a few moments. Very shortly, they came out of the huddle and said, "Yes, it's an idea worth exploring." My answer was, "Let's do it." So the SDI was born, and very shortly some in Congress and the press named it "Star Wars."[2]

Reagan may have waited until he got settled in the Oval Office before asking the Joint Chiefs of Staff what they thought about missile defense, but as Martin Anderson, one of Reagan's key advisers on the 1980 campaign, observes, the idea of transforming America's nuclear strategy was on the president's mind well before he assumed the reins of power. As Anderson recounts in his memoir of the Reagan years, it was during a visit to the North American Aerospace Defense Command (NORAD) on 31 July 1979 that Reagan began to internalize how vulnerable America was to a nuclear attack. Accompanied by Anderson and Douglas Morrow, an old Hollywood acquaintance of Reagan's who was able to arrange a special tour of the Cheyenne Mountain facility with General James Hill, then commander of NORAD, Reagan was astounded when he discovered that there was little the military could do to protect the United States once the Soviets launched their missiles. According to Anderson, "A look of disbelief came over Reagan's face. The discussion continued, and we pressed the issue of what would really happen if the Soviets were to fire just one nuclear missile at a U.S. city. 'Well,' the general replied carefully, 'we would pick it up right after it was launched, but by the time the officials of the city could be alerted that a nuclear bomb would hit them, there would be only ten or fifteen minutes left. That's all we can do. We can't stop it.' We didn't ask the general what would happen if the Soviet Union fired hundreds or even thousands of nuclear missiles at us."[3] According to Anderson's detailed account of the daylong tour, Reagan was "deeply concerned about what he learned." If, for whatever reason, nuclear missiles were fired at the United States, "[t]he only options he would have," Reagan said, "would be to press the button or do nothing. They're both bad. We should have some way of defending ourselves against nuclear missiles."[4] Reagan was convinced that the United States had to reconsider developing a comprehensive anti-ballistic missile system, something President Nixon had agreed to abandon when he and Soviet president Brezhnev had signed the ABM Treaty. But for political reasons, Reagan was advised not to propose changes to American nuclear strategy during the 1980 campaign.

Concerned that discussions about missile defense would backfire once the Democrats weighed in, Reagan's advisers convinced him to remain silent on the issue until he was sworn into office.[5] He followed their advice, but within months of his becoming president, a small group of key advisers, including Ed Meese, counsellor to the president, Richard Allen, Reagan's first national security adviser, and Martin Anderson, assistant to the president for policy development, held daily policy meetings in Meese's office to discuss, among other things, how to resurrect the idea of missile defense.[6]

The "policy troika" was soon expanded when George Keyworth, Reagan's science adviser, joined the morning briefings.[7] Keyworth, a scientist who had worked at the Los Almos laboratory in New Mexico, was recommended for the position by his former colleague and friend, the late Edward Teller, father of the hydrogen bomb.[8] Both Teller and Keyworth were staunch supporters of missile defense.

While meetings among top-level officials were taking place in the White House to determine the best way to advance the cause of missile defense in government, support for this initiative was beginning to take hold outside government. Not surprisingly, the most vocal support came from Reagan's so-called kitchen cabinet, a small and influential group of the president's old friends that included Karl Bendetsen, a national security expert who once served as undersecretary of the Army for President Harry Truman, and Joseph Coors, the Colorado beer magnate who had provided seed money to launch the Heritage Foundation. But even more important, missile defense began to attract the interest of a handful of foreign and defense policy experts who were prepared to help Reagan wage this battle in the public arena. The best known and most prominent expert to stake out a position in favour of missile defense was General Daniel Graham, former head of the Defense Intelligence Agency and an adviser to President Reagan. In preparation for the New Hampshire Republican presidential primary in February 1980, Graham briefed Reagan on the concept of a missile shield that, in theory, would help to defend the United States and its allies from incoming ballistic missiles.

In September 1981 Graham founded High Frontier, a Virginia-based think tank[9] with expertise in the areas of missile defense, arms control, nuclear weapons, and strategic systems. A year later, with the assistance of the Heritage Foundation, High Frontier published a report entitled *High Frontier: A New National Strategy*,[10] which set out the organization's vision of a ground-based and spaced-based defense system that could target and, with the use of laser beams, destroy nuclear missiles. The origins of High Frontier and its relationship to Heritage will be discussed in more detail in the next section, but it is important to point out here the extent to which Graham had access to the Reagan White House.

It becomes clear from Anderson's memoir that Graham was involved very early on in discussions about the Strategic Defense Initiative. As he recounts, "The first White House meeting on the missile defense system ... took place in Ed Meese's office ... on September 14, 1981. There were seven people at the meeting [including] Edward Teller, George Keyworth ... General Graham and Karl Bendetsen ... A second meeting with these outside experts took place in the White House four weeks later on October 12, 1981. It was a smaller group ... and Graham and Bendetsen reported ... a growing amount of support and interest from people they had been talking to in Congress, the [National Aeronautics and Space Administration (N A S A),] the C I A, the Air Force and the Department of Defense."[11] Meetings between outside experts and high-level officials in the Reagan administration, including some with the president, took place throughout the remaining months of 1981 and well into 1982. A critically important meeting was held in early 1982 when the "outside advisers" presented their report on the feasibility of missile defense to President Reagan. Encouraged by their findings, the president became fully committed to the Strategic Defense Initiative, a commitment that he shared with America on 23 March 1983.[12]

In his televised address to the nation, Reagan outlined publicly for the first time his vision of an impermeable shield that would protect the United States from nuclear missiles. While the content of the speech sounded familiar to Graham and a handful of other experts who had played such an important role in discussing strategic defense with the president, it baffled some of Reagan's senior officials, including Secretary of State George Shultz and Secretary of Defense Caspar Weinberger, who had had little notice that Reagan would deliver this controversial sermon.[13] After discussing his concerns about the arms race and the many problems associated with maintaining peace through strategies of deterrence, Reagan invited the American people to imagine living in a world where the ominous threat posed by nuclear weapons would be eliminated: "What if free people could live secure in the knowledge that their security did not rest upon the threat of instant U.S. retaliation to deter a Soviet attack, that we could intercept and destroy strategic ballistic missiles before they reached our own soil or that of our allies?"[14] Recognizing that considerable strides would have to be made in research and technology before an effective defense system could be deployed, Reagan "call[ed] upon the scientific community in our country who gave us nuclear weapons, to turn their great talents to the cause of mankind and world peace, to give us the means of rendering these nuclear weapons impotent and obsolete."[15]

The reaction to Reagan's speech was swift. After the initial shock of what the president had proposed set in, critics in Congress,[16] in the scientific community, and in academic circles[17] began to launch their own attacks against an administration that they believed was leading the United States closer to a nuclear war with the Soviet Union, a concern echoed by many of America's European allies.[18] Criticism of SDI generally fell into four categories.

First, concerns were raised about whether a multi-layered anti-ballistic missile system was technically feasible. Several organizations, including the Union of Concerned Scientists (UCS), argued that even if it were possible to construct a defense that could track, intercept, and destroy a handful of missiles (something that has yet to be achieved), such a system could easily be overwhelmed by the sheer size of the Soviet nuclear arsenal. Moreover, there would be little to prevent the Soviet Union or any other country possessing ballistic missiles from launching decoys or countermeasures to severely undermine America's defenses.[19]

Secondly, according to the UCS and other vocal critics of SDI, rather than reducing Cold War tensions, the initiative would surely accelerate the arms race. Just as American military planners had decided to invest more resources into developing more powerful and strategic offensive weapons following the ABM Treaty, so the Soviets would undoubtedly do the same. And more importantly, SDI, contrary to President Reagan's assertions, would in all likelihood violate the terms of the ABM Treaty and lead to the militarization of space. But SDI's critics did not stop there. They expressed concerns about the prohibitive cost of developing and deploying such a sophisticated system, estimated to be in the billions of dollars, and how the proposed initiative would drive a wedge between the United States and many of its Western European allies.[20] However, despite mounting criticism in the United States and from abroad, President Reagan remained committed to strategic defense. Dismissing accusations that he was only using SDI as a bargaining chip to compel the Soviets to make deeper cuts to their nuclear arsenal, he refused to abandon his (and Graham's vision) of a protective shield.

In an attempt to allay the concerns of his critics and to generate more momentum for his proposed initiative, Reagan appointed two panels of experts to study and make recommendations on missile defense: one on the prospects for developing anti-missile defenses and the other on the strategic implications of introducing a new defense and security policy. The findings of the first panel, the Defense Technologies Study Team, became known as the Fletcher report after its chairman, James C. Fletcher, former administrator of NASA and later professor of engineering and technology at the University of Pittsburgh. The findings of the second panel, the Future Security Strategy Study Team, were called the Hoffman report after its chairman, Fred Hoffman of the California defense firm Panheuristics.[21]

Both panels reported to the president in the fall of 1983, and both supported his position on strategic defense.[22] For Reagan, this was all the justification he needed to move forward with an idea that may have had its genesis in the core of the Cheyenne Mountain but required the constant care and nurturing of key decision-makers, lobbyists, think tanks, and interest groups in Washington. They did not disappoint him, nor did he disappoint his supporters. Throughout his two terms in office, Reagan, who was no stranger to political controversy, remained convinced that a defensive shield protecting American lives from a possible nuclear exchange was no longer an option; it was a necessity.

THE TORCH HAS BEEN PASSED: MISSILE DEFENSE FROM BUSH TO BUSH

When Reagan left office in 1989, his vision of a strategic defense had yet to be realized. It was, as his successor and former vice-president George Bush understood, a work in progress. Although Bush distanced himself from many of Reagan's key advisers when he moved into the Oval Office,[23] he did not stray far from the policies that had contributed to much of the success of the Reagan-Bush years. He certainly did not stray far from Reagan's commitment to missile defense. In the *National Security Strategy of the United States: 1991–1992*, a blueprint for US security policy, President Bush reaffirmed his commitment to missile defense. While he remained a strong supporter of SDI, he believed it had to be redirected to respond to the security needs of the United States. According to Bush, "[W]e have redirected SDI to pursue a system providing Global Protection Against Limited Strikes (GPALS). With adequate funding, it will be possible to begin to deploy systems that will better protect our troops in the field from ballistic-missile attack by the mid-1990s and that will protect the United States itself from such attacks by the turn of the century. GPALS is designed to provide protection against a ballistic missile launched from anywhere against a target anywhere in the world. The system will be based on technologies which SDI has pioneered, but would be both smaller and less expensive than the initial deployment originally projected for SDI."[24]

Unlike his predecessor, Bush did not have the luxury of a second term in office to make further decisions about missile defense. Despite his enormous approval ratings during the height of the Gulf War in 1991, he could not generate sufficient support among the American people to secure his reelection bid.[25] Following his humiliating defeat in the 1992 presidential campaign, Bush could only hope that his successor, Arkansas governor Bill Clinton, would agree that the various programs being pursued under the auspices of SDI were vitally important for the future of America's national security. On the campaign trail, Clinton promised Americans that he would "focus like a laser beam on the economy."[26] Fortunately for supporters of missile defense, he did not lose sight of the other potential use for lasers or, more likely, interceptors: to defend the United States against ballistic missiles. After a difficult first term in office, when it became clear that he had to devote far more attention to foreign policy,[27] Clinton began to consider the potential advantages of missile defense.

During the Clinton years, research and development on what had become known as national missile defense (NMD) continued, but as the president acknowledged during a speech at Georgetown University in September 2000, "We need more tests against more challenging targets, and more simulations before we can responsibly commit our nation's resources to deployment."[28] At the time of Clinton's address, only "three of the 19 planned intercept tests"[29] had been held, and the results were mixed. Given that the purpose of NMD is to "track enemy warheads [and destroy them with] highly accurate, high speed, ground-based interceptors,"[30] Clinton had good reason to be cautious. "One test proved that it is, in fact, possible to hit a bullet with a bullet. Still, though the technology for NMD is promising, the system as a whole is not yet proven. After the initial test succeeded, our two most recent tests failed, for different reasons, to achieve an intercept."[31]

In the end, Clinton decided not to deploy NMD, preferring instead to leave this very important matter to the incoming president. He did express confidence that NMD could be operational by 2006 or 2007, but he was not prepared, given the number of kinks that still had to be ironed out, to authorize deployment. But Clinton also appeared to be concerned about the political fallout from the issue. Indeed, on several occasions during his speech, he emphasized the importance of cooperating with America's European allies and with Russia to ensure that NMD would not generate further conflict but would be used to address common security threats. He also acknowledged that, if deployed, it would violate the ABM Treaty, and he therefore encouraged the United States to work closely with Russia to amend or abolish this historic and controversial agreement.[32]

Had Al Gore succeeded Bill Clinton, as most political commentators and pundits anticipated, it is likely that Clinton's strategy for dealing with NMD, the ABM Treaty, and other issues related to missile defense would have remained largely intact. But because of a series of bizarre twists and turns that eventually led to the controversial outcome of the 2000 presidential election, Gore did not become president.[33] George W. Bush, the eldest son of America's forty-first president, did, and his approach to missile defense, not to mention American foreign policy generally, took on a very different tenor.

During the campaign that propelled him to the nation's highest office, it became painfully obvious to Bush and to those whom he granted interviews that foreign policy was not his strong suit. His father's wide-ranging knowledge of and interest in international affairs apparently had not rubbed off on the younger Bush, who often found it difficult to understand the world beyond America's shores. In the Texas state legislature in Austin, where Governor Bush became embroiled in policy debates about crime prevention, health care, and education, he had little reason to pick up a copy of *Foreign Affairs, Foreign Policy*, or the *Economist*. However, if he aspired to be president, he realized that he could no longer afford to ignore the world in which the United States was the remaining superpower.

As discussed in chapter 1, Bush sought to enhance his limited knowledge of international relations by relying on the advice of a small but prominent group of seasoned foreign policy experts, including Brent Scowcroft and Condoleezza Rice, former advisers to Bush's father. By the fall of 1999 it became clear that their lessons were beginning to pay off. In a speech at the Citadel in Charleston, South Carolina, on 23 September 1999, Bush rolled out his blueprint for American foreign policy, which, among other things, stressed the importance of deploying an anti-ballistic missile defense. He stated:

At the earliest possible date, my administration will deploy anti-ballistic missile systems, both theater and national, to guard against attack and blackmail. To make this possible, we will offer Russia the necessary amendments to the anti-ballistic missile treaty – an artifact of Cold War confrontation. Both sides know that we live in a different world from 1972, when the treaty was signed. If Russia refuses the changes we propose, we will give prompt notice, under the provisions of the treaty, that we can no longer be party to it. I will have a solemn obligation to protect the American people and our allies, not to protect arms control agreements signed almost 30 years ago.[34]

Bush did not change his position on or his plans for missile defense when he became president. On 1 May 2001, less than six months after he was sworn into office, he proclaimed at Washington's National Defense University: "We need a new framework that allows us to build missile defenses to counter the different threats of today's world. To do so, we must move beyond the constraints of the 30 year old ABM Treaty. This treaty does not recognize the present, or point us to the future. It enshrines the past. No treaty that prevents us from addressing today's threats, that prohibits us from pursuing promising technology to defend ourselves, our friends and our allies is in our interests or in the interests of world peace."[35] Despite the horrific terrorist attacks on American soil on September 11, 2001, which in all likelihood could not have been prevented, even if an anti-ballistic missile defense system were in place, Bush remained committed to NMD. On 13 December 2001, he notified Russian president Vladimir Putin of his intention to withdraw from the ABM Treaty,[36] and six months later, with Secretary of Defense Donald Rumsfeld leading the applause,[37] Bush announced that the United States had pulled out of the 1972 accord.[38] Following this historic declaration, Representative Dennis Kucinich and thirty-one other House Democrats filed a lawsuit against the president claiming that he did "not have the authority to unilaterally withdraw from a treaty without seeking congressional consent first."[39] On 30 December 2002 Judge John Bates of the US District Court for the District of Columbia ruled in a thirty-one-page written opinion that the plaintiffs "have no standing to challenge President Bush's withdrawal from the ABM Treaty without congressional approval ... and that the case presents a 'political question' not suitable for resolution by the courts."[40] He did "not rule on the merits of whether the Constitution requires a president to obtain congressional approval of termination of a treaty, holding that 'there is no claim that Congress, as an institution, has asserted its role in the treaty termination process.'"

For Bush, the greatest obstacle to deploying NMD is no longer the restrictions imposed on it by the ABM Treaty. Rather, it is developing and fine-tuning the technology that is required to make the system operational. After two more failed tests, military officials announced that "flight tests of the nation's missile defense system will not resume until fall [2005] at the earliest." Although the Bush administration indicated that the system would be working in 2004, it "has not had a successful intercept of a target since October 2002."[41] Notwithstanding these setbacks and perhaps because of them, the prospect of missile defense remains a topic of intense discussion and debate in the White House, on Capitol Hill, and in many of the country's premier think tanks. In the following section, we will take a closer look at how a select group of think tanks have shaped policy discussions about missile defense over the past two decades and how they have been able to advance and market this initiative. We will then turn our attention to evaluating their contributions at different stages of the policy cycle.

AT WORK AND IN PLAY: THINK TANKS AND MISSILE DEFENSE

General Daniel Graham was one of America's strongest advocates of missile defense. He was also a pioneer and a visionary who had the good fortune to find a loyal patron in the Heritage Foundation and high-powered support-ers in the Reagan White House to endorse his concept of a protective shield against ballistic missiles. Building on the success of its massive volume, *Mandate for Leadership*, widely considered a blueprint for the incoming Reagan administration, Heritage turned its attention to several important foreign and security policy issues, including missile defense. According to Baker Spring, a research fellow in national security policy at Heritage, in the early 1980s the foundation "brought under its wing if you will, a group of individuals who were interested in missile defense issues in particular, and space policy issues more generally ... The group, chaired by Dan Graham, was looking for a place that would essentially sponsor them, give them the infrastructure to do the research and to produce the report they wanted to produce. The report they produced was called *High Frontier*."[42]

What Heritage was able to offer Daniel Graham and other members of his group was far more than modest financial assistance and a place to con-duct research. It was able to provide them with an association, however brief, with a think tank whose star was clearly on the rise in the early 1980s. Graham had advised Reagan during the 1980 campaign, but having the support of the Heritage Foundation and its extensive ties to key members of his administration and kitchen cabinet would have only enhanced his access to the White House. At the very least, Heritage's support would have pro-vided Graham with even greater credibility.

Following the completion of the initial *High Frontier* study at Heritage, "Graham founded his own organization, called High Frontier, and pro-duced and printed a glossier edition of the original study about a year later. This is how it [High Frontier] became a key advocate for pursuing missile defense capabilities."[43] As discussed earlier this chapter, Graham was one of a handful of outside experts who were invited to participate in early discus-sions about missile defense with President Reagan and his top advisers. In the weeks and months leading up to the president's speech on 23 March 1983, Graham had numerous opportunities to explain his plan for a multi-layered defense. Clearly, his efforts to provide a range of options for protecting the United States from ballistic missiles did not fall on deaf ears. As President Reagan acknowledged in a letter to Graham on 25 November 1985, "I appreciate the important work that you and your colleagues have done to prepare the way for a more secure America ... You, and all those [who] made the High Frontier project a reality, have rendered our country an invaluable service for which all future generations will be grateful. I value greatly your continuing efforts to help us build a national consensus and to find the difficult answers for the profound strategic problems that face all of us in this nuclear age. We have a great opportunity and challenge before us in making nuclear weapons obsolete and I truly appreciate your special efforts in attaining that goal."[44]

In 1991, on the occasion of High Frontier's tenth anniversary, President Reagan again recognized the important contribution Graham and his colleagues had made to the cause of missile defense:

As you know, Dan, you and I were talking missile defense before you set up High Frontier in September of [19]81. Remember that famous debate in February 1980 in Nashua, New Hampshire? I remember just before that debate, you briefed me on your concept of a missile shield to protect our nation. It was exceedingly important. Dick Allen [Reagan's key foreign policy adviser during the 1980 campaign and later national security adviser] was there – he said, "We've just seen history made."
The following spring at the White House when we discussed your ideas again I remember telling Jim Baker [then chief of staff] to make sure Cap Weinberger [secretary of defense] heard your presentation. You and a small group of dedicated, determined people helped us move the SDI concept over all the roadblocks put up by people of less vision and belief in American capacity. It wasn't easy. But we did it. You and all those supporting and making it happen in High Frontier have my thanks and the thanks of the nation.[45]

There is little doubt that Daniel Graham and High Frontier played a critical role in helping the Reagan administration advance the cause of SDI. Reagan's testimonials and Anderson's memoir acknowledge the extent of their contributions. However, as noted, by the time Reagan left office, there was much that had to be done both technically and politically before an effective missile defense could be deployed. Graham's vision of a protective shield paved the way for Reagan to embark on this bold initiative, but several roadblocks remained, not the least of which was the ABM Treaty. Rarely shy about rolling up its sleeves to become involved in highly contentious political disputes, the Heritage Foundation devoted considerable time and resources to removing this formidable obstacle. As Baker Spring points out, "basically our purpose in life at the Heritage Foundation was to debunk the national security value that was perceived with the policy of mutually assured destruction and, most specifically, to do things to get us out from under ABM Treaty restrictions."[46]

"What we did," according to Spring, who joined Heritage in 1989 after serving as a foreign and defense policy expert with two US senators, "was to work with both the House and Senate to put down legislative markers."[47] These markers were intended to instruct policy-makers about America's legal obligations under the ABM Treaty. There were many issues related to the 1972 treaty that Heritage flagged for members of Congress, including whether the collapse of the Soviet Union in 1991 prevented that country from fulfilling its obligations under the treaty and "whether the Senate was required to provide advice and consent on any changes made to the ABM Treaty."[48]

"Our [efforts] in Congress [were] a good example of how the Heritage Foundation does work in the foreign policy, national security field," Spring added. "Congress has always been our strong suit and was clearly the institution of government used here in terms of how we advanced this agenda. Now let me say too that we did it totally consistent with the Heritage Foundation's view. We didn't lobby; we educated."[49] Although he acknowledged that the "Heritage Foundation had no sway with the Clinton people in national security,"[50] it was not discouraged from "educating" the Republican-controlled Congress about the importance of withdrawing from the ABM Treaty. The Bush administration did not require the same lesson plan. As we have seen, Bush was a strong advocate of missile defense and welcomed the day when the United States would no longer be subjected to restrictions imposed by a treaty that, in his mind, no longer served the national interest.

Thus far we have observed how a select group of think tanks were able to share their ideas on missile defense with officials in the White House and with members of Congress. It is also important to consider, particularly if we employ a holistic approach to policy-making, how think tanks interact with each other, with academics, with the media, and with the defense industry to advance their cause. This perspective is imperative for scholars interested in how the so-called military-industrial complex shapes foreign and defense policy, a subject that we will discuss briefly in the concluding section. In her study *The New Nuclear Danger*,[51] Helen Caldicott argues that the relationship between think tanks and the government departments and corporations with whom they associate is critical to understanding how policy institutes perpetuate the military-industrial complex. She writes: "The think tanks exert a huge amount of influence on behalf of the military-industrial complex. The Heritage Foundation is still very much involved in promoting the nuclear arms race in all arenas, and actively lobbying for Star Wars. Other powerful right-wing think tanks that involve themselves in American 'nuclear strategy' include the American Enterprise Institute and the Cato Institute. Yet another think tank, the Center for Security Policy (CSP), serves as the nerve center of the Star Wars lobby."[52] Frank Gaffney Jr, the president of the CSP, whom Caldicott refers to as "a high priest of missile defense,"[53] would likely be flattered by her description of his organization (which he is reluctant to call a think tank) as the nerve centre of the Star Wars lobby. If the CSP has indeed become the nerve centre of the Star Wars or missile defense lobby, he would have accomplished what he set out to do in 1988 when he established the institute. As Gaffney remarked recently, "rather than creating another place that would do the sort of research and symposia that are the stock and trade of most think tanks ... the raison d'être of the [CSP] was to constitute a network of security policy practitioners ... We [try] to build coalitions and expand that network to develop a better awareness of the sorts of problems we're concerned with and get people who might not otherwise engage."[54]

Having served as an undersecretary of defense during the Reagan administration, Gaffney understands all too well the benefits of establishing a network that facilitates communication between policy-makers in government and policy experts residing in universities and think tanks: "Based on my own experience in the government, it was vitally important that people who held the sorts of jobs that I held have access to such a network in a convenient and timely way ... So the idea of the network was to disseminate information that was of interest coming out of the government and to inject back into it or into the body politic or, for that matter, the general public's consciousness, the sort of thinking and philosophy and principles that guided us during our time in office. That's what we've tried to do ever since."[55] At any given time, the small staff at the CSP manage a wide range of projects relating to missile defense and other security policy issues. The publications they distribute within their network are typically short, mostly taking the form of decision briefs, press releases, or national security alerts. Although the CSP keeps track of how often its staff and publications are cited in the media, Gaffney claims that "it's not a preoccupation."[56] What is more important for him is to know that the work of CSP is being recognized by the president, his senior advisers, and members of his growing network: "Although I've never had a meeting with President Bush, I like to think that his enthusiasm for the issue [missile defense] and his commitment to it, is a product of work we've been doing over many years ... Partly because I think it was, in all modesty, seminal work and partly because I think people who wound up being very central to his national security campaign team were friends and colleagues of mine [including Secretary of Defense Donald Rumsfeld] who felt as we did. I think we enforced the point and nurtured in him [Bush] an appreciation of its importance."[57]

Even so, Gaffney acknowledges that it is difficult to determine how much or how little influence CSP wields inside the missile defense lobby: "Sometimes [influence is about] preventing bad things from happening, and you can't always be sure that's simply because of what you did. For that matter, you can't always be sure that what comes out that's good is just because of what you're doing. I like to think that in both cases, we can at least take some satisfaction, if not formal credit. I think in part it's an intangible thing that people who are in the field recognize that what you do or what you say or what you've written or what you've agitated for has helped them make a difference. That's really, as I said, going back to the roots of the organization. That's what we're all about."[58] For the Heritage Foundation, the CSP, and other conservative and libertarian think tanks that believe passionately in missile defense, Bush's 2004 election victory over Senator John Kerry was seen as a victory for the future of American national security. But not surprisingly, for scholars at the Brookings Institution, the Carnegie Endowment, the Union of Concerned Scientists, and other organizations that have expressed serious reservations about missile defense, the president's re-election generated further cause for concern.

Think tanks on both the left and the right of the political spectrum continue to engage in lively exchanges about missile defense and, like battle-hardened warriors, show no sign of giving up; they have staked out their positions, from which they are unlikely to waiver. In large part, think tanks involved in the missile defense debate are unwilling to concede ground because they continue to satisfy the needs of their stakeholders. Just as the Heritage Foundation, High Frontier, the CSP, and other think tanks speak to the interests of policy-makers, defense contractors, and donors who believe strongly, for political and economic reasons, in NMD, so Brookings, Carnegie, and other more liberal think tanks have struck a responsive chord with those critical of this initiative. The challenge for scholars, as discussed in the previous chapter, is to assess the nature of their contributions and the various factors that may be responsible for facilitating or frustrating their efforts to influence public policy. It is to this discussion that we now turn.

WIN, LOSE, OR DRAW? THE DEBATE OVER MISSILE DEFENSE

It is a fair question and one that deserves a candid and honest response. But as we discussed in chapter 7, determining which think tanks won and which lost the debate over missile defense ultimately depends on our perception and understanding of how influence is achieved in the policy-making process. If we maintain that both the policy-making process – that is, the different stages at which policy issues are addressed (issue articulation, policy formulation, and policy implementation) – and the process by which influence is exercised within each of these stages is linear, then it would be reasonable to reach the following conclusion: based on their involvement with high-level officials in the White House, in Congress, and in the broader defense policy community, the most active and hence influential think tanks were High Frontier, the Heritage Foundation, and the CSP.

But if we accept that influence may be achieved in a non-linear fashion (even if we assume that the policy-making process moves directly from point A to point B), our conclusions would likely be very different. Consider the case of High Frontier. We have already established that its founder, General Graham, briefed Ronald Reagan on the concept of a missile shield during the Republican presidential primaries in 1980 and that he was a key member of a small group of outside experts who were invited to participate in regular policy briefings with the president and his advisers shortly after Reagan assumed office. We also know, based on Reagan's testimonials, that High Frontier played an important role in advancing the cause of missile defense. Although the organization may not be able to take credit for planting the idea of missile defense in Reagan's mind, an idea that apparently came to him during his visit to NORAD headquarters in 1979, High Frontier's contribution was vitally important in reinforcing, refining, and marketing this initiative. It can certainly take credit for presenting a comprehensive plan to Reagan and his staff on how such a system might function.

But there were experts besides Graham who discussed missile defense in the White House. In the same meetings that he attended, Bendetsen, Coors, Keyworth, Teller, and others also participated. Moreover, during the same time frame, there were meetings in the State Department, in the Defense Department, in the National Security Council, and in other departments and agencies of the US government where missile defense was on the table. Recognizing this wider picture, can we reasonably conclude that only Graham and High Frontier had influence in moving missile defense along? Or is more likely that several participants made their presence felt? Indeed, is it conceivable that, compared to the charismatic Teller and the well-heeled Coors, Graham's influence was modest?

Few other think tanks had as much input into the missile defense debate during Reagan's first term in office as High Frontier. Still, we cannot ignore the contributions made by other individuals and think tanks to this ongoing initiative. We certainly cannot afford to ignore the efforts of the Heritage Foundation to educate members of Congress about the ABM Treaty; nor can we overlook the important role that the CSP continues to play in expanding its network of security policy practitioners. And in line with the holistic approach to policy-making, we cannot dismiss the conversations taking place between think tanks, academics, journalists, and policy-makers who support or oppose the deployment of NMD. These are particularly important when we examine how this debate has played out in the media. Interestingly enough, despite the endorsement by several Republican and Democratic administrations of missile defense, think tanks such as the Brookings Institution, which tends to be critical of deployment, have attracted more television and print media exposure than pro-NMD think tanks, including the CSP and the Heritage Foundation. For example, according to our media tables in chapter 7, between January 2001 and January 2005 Brookings recorded 169 print and 5 television references in relation to missile defense. By contrast, Heritage attracted 119 print and 2 television citations, considerably more than the media exposure enjoyed by the CSP (66 print and 0 television).

As discussed in chapter 5, how much or little media exposure think tanks generate can be attributed to several factors. However, in the conclusion to this chapter, some consideration should be given to why think tanks such as High Frontier and Heritage enjoyed, relative to other think tanks, unparalleled access to the Reagan White House. In addition to sharing Reagan's philosophy, conservative think tanks benefited greatly from the president's management style. Unlike Jimmy Carter and Bill Clinton, who preferred to oversee virtually every detail surrounding policy initiatives,[59] Reagan was comfortable delegating important matters to his subordinates. Some criticized him for delegating too much authority, a criticism that appeared warranted in light of the Iran-Contra scandal,[60] but his willingness to trust his advisers and the experts they endorsed created valuable opportunities for think tanks to establish a strong foothold in his administration. This management style in large part explains the success of Heritage and High Frontier in advocating missile defense. They backed the right issue at the right time and had the expertise and the political know-how to nurture it through the policy-making process. But even more importantly, they had the support of the president, whose growing popularity in his first term allowed him to secure a landslide victory in 1984. In short, in their efforts to promote and market missile defense, everything that could go right for conservative think tanks during the Reagan years did. But think tanks critical of missile defense did not have their voices stifled. On the contrary, as evidenced through their publications, congressional testimony, and media appearances, think tanks on the other side of the missile defense debate helped to enrich and foster informed and educated discussions about how to protect the United States

in the nuclear age. Although Brookings, Carnegie, the Union of Concerned
Scientists, and other opponents of SDI and NMD may not have been able to
dissuade Reagan and his successors from pursuing missile defense, they
nonetheless identified key issues of concern to both policy-makers and the
public. To suggest, then, that they were ineffective or lacked influence
would be shortsighted. As we will discuss in the following chapter, regardless of the actions policy-makers take in the name of the national interest,
the public interest cannot be served if think tanks remain silent; nor can it be
served if they allow their ideological agenda to cloud their judgment.

CHAPTER NINE

A Hard-Fought Battle: 9/11, the Bush Doctrine, and the War of Ideas

Under normal circumstances, the Brookings Institution would have had cause for celebration: one of its publications was attracting considerable exposure throughout the United States and had, within months of its release in 2001, sold thousands of copies. Written by Paul Pillar, a former official in the CIA and the National Intelligence Council, the book dealt with terrorism and counter-terrorism, topics that would soon preoccupy the Bush administration and Americans. "Intended as a guide to constructing and executing counterterrorist policy,"[1] *Terrorism and U.S. Foreign Policy* could not have been more timely, relevant, or prescient. As Michael Armacost, the former president of the Brookings Institution, stated in the foreword to Pillar's illuminating and path-breaking study, "Few events can sear the national consciousness as deeply as a terrorist attack. The upsurges of concern that follow such incidents tend to lead to new laws, new commissions, fresh commitments of resources, and calls for something more – or effective – to be done to combat terrorism. As the twenty-first century dawns, however, there is little basis to expect that terrorism will become less of a concern in the years ahead or that the United States will become a less desirable target."[2] Unfortunately, Armacost was right.

Policy-makers in Washington barely had time to digest Pillar's recommendations for designing a more comprehensive counter-terrorism strategy before three hijacked commercial airliners, flown by suicide bombers, reduced the twin towers of the World Trade Center and parts of the Pentagon to rubble.[3] Whatever progress the United States thought it had made in minimizing the threat of terrorism in the 1990s quickly vanished as the death toll in New York and Washington mounted. Indeed, the tragic events of September 11, 2001, a day that will forever be etched on America's soul, served as a wake-up call, both to the United States and to its allies, that terrorist organizations could and would use whatever means necessary to bring the West to its knees. In the days and weeks following the unprecedented terrorist attacks on American soil, policy-makers in the White House, in Congress, and in the bureaucracy devoted considerable attention to how best to address what had clearly become America's most pressing security concern. Americans, for good reason, had plenty of questions about who had orchestrated these heinous acts and how President Bush intended to respond to the September 11th attacks. Not surprisingly, policy experts in universities and in think tanks were anxiously waiting to provide answers.

As President Bush and his inner circle of advisers began to map out a strategy for striking back at the terrorists responsible for 9/11, battle plans for a different war were being drawn in the media, in academic circles, and in the offices and boardrooms of the nation's premier defense and foreign policy think tanks. Even before the clouds of debris above ground zero had dissipated, policy experts began staking out positions on what President Bush had to do at home and abroad to defeat terrorism. In countless articles, books, op-eds, and interviews with different media outlets, think tank scholars immersed themselves in a policy debate that quickly consumed America and the world. The war of ideas was clearly underway.

The purpose of this chapter is to examine the extent to which think tanks have become involved in policy debates surrounding the war on terror and how effective they have been in conveying their ideas to the media, to members of Congress, and to the Bush White House. Unlike the previous chapter, which focused on a single issue, national missile defense, this case study deals with a policy matter that is far more elusive – the Bush administration's campaign to defeat terrorists and the states that grant them refuge. President Bush's war on terror has been waged on multiple fronts: it has been fought in the mountainous terrain of Afghanistan, in the streets of Baghdad, on Capitol Hill, and in the United Nations. It has also been fought in the media and on the campaign trail in 2004, where the president and several of his current and former advisers, including Condoleezza Rice, Donald Rumsfeld, Paul Wolfowitz, Dick Cheney, and Colin Powell, have repeatedly defended the government's right and moral obligation to protect its citizens against those intent on destroying the American way of life.

But our concern in this chapter is not about whether the president is justified in fighting a war that may never be won; nor is it about recounting in intimate detail the events that led the United States to deploy troops to

Afghanistan and to Iraq. Bob Woodward, the award-winning journalist with the *Washington Post,* has written two books that provide useful overviews of the decisions that resulted in US military intervention in both countries, and several other authors have since followed suit.[4] Rather, our interest here is to explore how think tanks have sought to become part of a debate that has galvanized the nation.

As in the case of missile defense, think tank scholars have communicated their ideas about various aspects of the war on terror through a range of channels. They have written dozens of books, articles, and newsletters; held conferences, workshops, and seminars; granted hundreds of interviews to the media; and testified before key congressional committees. However, while many of these strategies have enhanced their exposure in the public arena, few think tanks have been able to make their presence felt in the Bush White House. The exception, according to some pundits, is the Project for the New American Century, a small Washington-based think tank with strong ties to members of Bush's inner circle. How much influence PNAC has had on shaping Bush's foreign policy is debatable. What is certain is that Bush refuses to hang a welcome sign for think tank scholars outside the Oval Office. Apparently, he would much prefer to have it displayed at the Reagan Library in Simi Valley, California, where former experts from some of America's leading conservative think tanks occasionally make a pilgrimage to pay homage to their fallen leader.

Bush's reluctance to create a more open foreign policy-making environment in the White House and the elusive nature of the war on terror have created formidable obstacles for think tanks looking to influence policy at the highest levels of government. While several think tanks have been able to contribute to public discussions about terrorism and national security, for the most part they have been unable to leave their mark on Bush's foreign policy. Even think tanks with whom President Bush has much in common have had little impact in convincing the president to alter his behaviour. As Ivo Daalder and James Lindsay observe in their study *America Unbound*, once Bush makes a decision, he rarely returns to the blackboard. The contrast between the involvement of think tanks in the debate over missile defense and the debate over the war on terror provides further evidence that the ability of think tanks to influence both policy-making and actual policy decisions depends on a multitude of factors, many of which are beyond their control.

The chapter begins by examining the response of foreign and defense policy think tanks to the disturbing events of September 11, 2001. In addition to discussing the various ways think tanks attempted to shape the parameters of public discussions about terrorism and US foreign policy, we will identify some of the many issues they highlighted in an effort to educate both policy-makers and the public about this emerging threat in the international community. We will also consider how think tanks have responded to concerns about the domestic and global implications of America's war on terrorism. We will then turn our attention to PNAC, the think tank thought to be responsible for laying the groundwork for the Bush doctrine, a doctrine that justifies pre-emptive strikes against adversaries who pose an imminent threat to US security.

In virtually every category, including budget, staff size, media exposure, publications, conferences, and congressional testimony, PNAC pales in comparison to Washington's more established think tanks. But despite its low visibility and limited resources, it has been singled out by several domestic and foreign journalists and scholars as the think tank most responsible for influencing the content and direction of Bush's foreign policy. The evidence these and other pundits offer is far from compelling. Nonetheless, the information they uncover will serve as a useful backdrop for our analysis of this institute and its ties to members of the Bush administration.

In the second section, we will explain why it is important to consider the decision-making styles of presidents in any assessment of think tank influence. Just as President Reagan's willingness to trust the advice of policy experts helped think tank scholars to establish a strong foothold in his administration, so President Bush's reluctance to expand his small circle of advisers has had the opposite effect. Rather than inviting input from a larger and more diverse group of experts, something Zbigniew Brzezinski suggested administrations do when their policies go awry, Bush has refused to stray from the path that he and his advisers have followed since 9/11. Despite the countless mistakes the president has made in waging the war on terror, he has remained steadfast in his commitment to defeat terrorism. This position has left little room for outside policy experts to communicate their views on how to advance American interests in a world that has been turned upside down.

Finally, we will evaluate the contribution of think tanks to the ongoing debate over the war on terror and the threat terrorism poses to American national security. By acknowledging that influence need not be tied directly to a specific policy outcome but can occur at different stages of the policy-making process, we can identify how think tanks have helped to shape and mould this critical policy issue. In the process, we will provide a more accurate picture of how and under what circumstances they can make a difference in the political arena. We begin by examining the reaction of the think tank community to the horrific events of September 11, 2001, which, as Michael Armacost predicted, have been seared into the national consciousness.

AND THEY ARE OFF: THINK TANKS AND 9/11

On 30 October 1938, the day before Halloween, Orson Welles directed a radio adaptation of the science fiction novel *The War of the Worlds*. Under his direction, the presentation, which was heard by millions of Americans, "was written and performed so it would sound like a news broadcast about an invasion from Mars, a technique that, presumably, was intended to heighten the dramatic effect."[5] It worked. As Dorothy Thompson observed in the *New York Tribune*, "They have proved that a few effective voices, accompanied by sound effects, can convince masses of people of a totally unreasonable, completely fantastic proposition as to create a nation-wide panic."[6] On September 11, 2001, millions of Americans driving to work listened to radio broadcasts about a different invasion. But this time the events that unfolded on the air were not based on a science fiction novel or a Hollywood screenplay. And this time the director of 9/11 was not Orson Welles or Steven Spielberg; it was Osama bin Laden, the mastermind behind al-Qaeda, whose hatred of the West inspired nineteen Islamic extremists to meticulously plan and execute the attacks against the World Trade Center and the Pentagon.

For days and weeks following the terrorist attacks of 9/11, viewers across the United States and the world could not escape the frightening images of dozens of innocent people falling to their deaths from the burning towers of a complex that had once dominated New York's skyline. But the shock, horror, and immense grief of Americans soon turned to anger. They wanted answers to how a relatively small group of terrorists could carry out these vicious and hateful acts and what had to be done to prevent another 9/11. While President Bush assured the American people that, under his leadership, the United States would ultimately win the war on terror, policy experts at think tanks throughout the United States began to provide a more detailed assessment of why the attacks had occurred and what measures could be taken to protect the nation.

Given the magnitude of what had transpired, it is not surprising that the print and broadcast media in the United States became preoccupied with America's war on terror; nor is it surprising that journalists regularly turned to policy experts for their insights. Just as scholars from America's leading think tanks were called upon to inform the American public about what was at stake in the Gulf War in 1991, so the media relied on them to provide extensive commentary on Washington's latest war. Think tanks were more than prepared to offer assistance, and within days of 9/11, several think tank scholars became regular fixtures on the major television networks and in the op-ed pages of America's most prominent newspapers.

However, gaining access to the media is only one of the strategies think tanks have employed in the war of ideas. They have also organized conferences, seminars, and workshops; testified before congressional committees and subcommittees; and published a steady stream of books, articles, and newsletters. In short, since 9/11, think tanks have made their presence felt on multiple fronts; they have spoken loud and clearly on a range of issues and have made a series of recommendations to policy-makers. But before we evaluate their impact both on the policy-making environment and on actual policy decisions, it is important to review briefly how they have sought to convey their ideas.

TALKING SHOP AND TALKING HEADS: THINK TANKS AND THE WAR OF IDEAS

As discussed in chapter 6, for many think tank scholars, the most effective way to communicate their ideas to the public and to policy-makers is through the media. They do so by appearing as guests on the network news and on political talk shows, by providing commentary on various radio programs, and by submitting op-ed pieces to dozens of domestic and international newspapers. Although it is difficult to determine the extent to which heightened media exposure translates into policy influence, think tanks continue to assign a high priority to enhancing their visibility.

If the war of ideas (not to be confused with the war on terror) were decided solely on the basis of which think tank generated the most exposure on television and in print, the Brookings Institution could easily claim victory. According to the data on media exposure presented in chapter 7, Brookings leads its closest competitors (the Council on Foreign Relations, CSIS, RAND, Heritage, AEI, Carnegie Endowment, and Cato) with close to 20 per cent of all print media references to various aspects of the war on terror. Brookings's lead over its rivals exposure is considerably greater in televison, where it has obtained more than 40 per cent of all references. On virtually every issue ranging from the events of 9/11 to the wars in Afghanistan and Iraq, Brookings scholars are cited more often than their colleagues from any other think tank. But the war of ideas is not limited to the battles that take place between think tank scholars on television and in the op-ed pages. Other important battles are taking place in conferences and seminars organized by think tanks and in legislative hearings where policy experts from America's leading institutes are summoned to advise policy-makers. They are also being waged in the dozens of books and articles that think tanks have generated since 9/11.

THE SECOND FRONT: CONFERENCES, WORKSHOPS, AND SEMINARS

President Bush's war on terror is tailor-made for think tanks looking to find timely, relevant, and interesting subjects for conferences, workshops, and seminars. Indeed, given the multiple dimensions of terrorism and America's efforts to come to grips with this new and elusive enemy, there is no limit to the range of topics that could be explored. From all accounts, think tanks have made a concerted effort to identify several worthy subjects for discussion. Since 9/11, those specializing in foreign and defense policy have arranged hundreds of conferences and workshops. For example, in 2004 AEI held close to two dozen workshops that focused on the Bush doctrine, "An End to Evil: How to Win the War on Terror," Operation Iraqi Freedom, and intelligence reform. At the Carnegie Endowment the workshops and seminars focused on slightly different themes. In that year, Carnegie scholars looked at Strategic Asia and the War on Terrorism, WMD in Iraq: Evidence and Implications, and Integrating Democracy Promotion into US Middle East Policy. Other think tanks inside and beyond the Beltway also offered an interesting array of seminars.[7]

By organizing conferences, seminars, and workshops, not only are think tanks able to discuss timely and relevant policy issues, but, more importantly, they can provide a forum for scholars, journalists, and policy-makers to meet and interact. Rather than staring into a television camera in the hope of reaching millions of viewers or waiting for feedback on a newspaper article they may have published, policy experts attending conferences are able to exchange ideas directly with interested participants. The result may be additional meetings, conversations, and other opportunities to explore policy options. At the very least, conferences and seminars in which policy-makers and their staff participate can help think tanks to establish closer ties to those in positions of power. And in the process, they may bring them one step closer to achieving policy influence.

FOR THE CONGRESSIONAL RECORD: THINK TANKS ON CAPITOL HILL

As noted, in the aftermath of 9/11, policy experts from several of America's leading think tanks were more than prepared to share their insights on the war on terror with the media and with their colleagues and invited guests at a host of sponsored events. Moreover, as the Bush administration's blueprint for confronting terrorists and the states that sponsored them began to take shape, think tank scholars seemed equally willing to advise members of Congress on the potential costs and benefits of Washington's plan of attack.

Experts from CSIS, RAND, AEI, Heritage, Brookings, and other think tanks have testified before Senate and House committees on several important issues related to national security in the post-9/11 world. Among other things, they have discussed the relationship between civil liberties and national security; reconstruction and rehabilitation in Iraq; combating weapons of mass destruction; the Middle East view of terrorism; terrorism, extremism, and regional stability in Central Asia; and the terrorist attacks in Madrid.[8] The frequency with which think tanks scholars have testified before congressional committees since Osama bin Laden left his calling card in New York and in Washington does not only reflect their willingness to rely on Congress to inject their ideas into the policy-making process. It also reflects the importance that members of Congress assign to the work and scholarship being undertaken at the nation's foreign and defense policy think tanks.

Much of this work has been revealed in the testimonies presented by think tank scholars, but it is also discussed, in considerably more detail, in the books and articles they have published. In the following section, we will provide an overview of some of the major works produced by think tank scholars that deal with critical stages in the war on terrorism. Although far from comprehensive, the review will highlight some of the many issues that think tank scholars believe are critically important for policy-makers and the public to consider as the government continues to wage war on its adversaries.

PUBLISH AND PERISH: COMBATING GLOBAL TERROR

The terrorist attacks of 9/11 served as a wake-up call for millions of Americans, but the United States could hardly ignore the various acts of terrorism carried out against its citizens over the past two decades, including the murder of 220 marines and 21 service members in Beirut in 1983. While they were asleep in their barracks, a large delivery truck carrying 12,000 pounds of explosives drove through a barbed-wire fence and a gate and into the lobby of their building. In the ensuing years, the United States was the target of other terrorist attacks. These included the bombings of the World Trade

Center in 1993, the US embassies in Nairobi and Dar es Salaam in 1998, and the uss *Cole* on 12 October 2000 in the port of Aden, Yemen. Many of these attacks were also organized by Osama bin Laden.[9]

Yet, despite the increase in terrorist activity during the 1990s, little was being done in the intelligence community to protect the United States against future attacks, a concern expressed by Stephen Flynn of the Council on Foreign Relations. In an article published in his think tank's flagship journal, *Foreign Affairs*, in 2000, Flynn outlined a scenario whereby bin Laden "might exploit our perilously exposed transportation system to smuggle and detonate a weapon of mass destruction on our soil."[10] To Flynn's delight, the article sparked interest in the policy-making community and eventually led to briefings about the vulnerability of America's transportation system. Unfortunately, his fears about terrorism were not widely shared, and policy-makers were unwilling to take the necessary precautions to protect the American homeland. As he points out, "The common refrain I heard was, 'Americans need a crisis to act. Nothing will change until we have a serious act of terrorism on U.S. soil.'"[11] His frustration as an outsider must have paled in comparison to that experienced by Richard Clarke, the first national coordinator for security, infrastructure protection, and terrorism, whose best-selling book *Against All Enemies* confirmed what others had told Flynn – nothing will happen until terrorists strike the United States.

When terrorists did strike the United States, policy-makers had no alternative – at least no viable alternative – but to react. But how they reacted and the effectiveness of their response have spawned an intense debate in the academic and think tank communities in the United States and abroad. As the initial shock and horror of what occurred on 9/11 began to wear off, scholars in the nation's think tanks and universities took time to reflect on why the attacks took place and what the United States had to do to protect its citizens. For policy experts on the left, the storyline was clear: Islamic terrorists had made their way to the United States to punish America's leaders for their foreign policy in the Middle East and in particular their steadfast support for Israel. Once the United States adopted a more even-handed approach to resolving the Israeli-Palestinian conflict and abandoned its imperialist goals, the threat of terrorism would be significantly reduced.[12] If it did this, it would no longer have to worry about the bin Ladens of the world. Order, rather than chaos and fear, would come to reflect the state of the international community. As an added bonus, America's strained relations with the United Nations and with much of Western Europe would improve dramatically, and the rising tide of anti-Americanism sweeping across the globe would gradually subside.[13]

But for those on the right who believed that this solution could only work in fairy tales, America's response to dealing with terrorism had to convey a very different message. Rather than coddling terrorists and the states that either directly or indirectly support them, what was needed, according to many conservative policy experts, was a clear and forceful demonstration of American resolve. As David Frum and Richard Perle of AEI state in their book *An End to Evil*; "The war on terror is not over. In many ways, it has barely begun. Al-Qaeda, Hezbollah, and Hamas still plot murder, and money still flows from donors worldwide to finance them. Mullahs preach jihad from the pulpits of mosques from Bengal to Brooklyn. Iran and North Korea are working frantically to develop nuclear weapons. While our enemies plot, our allies dither and carp, and much of our own government remains ominously unready for the fight. We have much to do and scant time in which to do it."[14] For Frum and for Perle, nicknamed the Prince of Darkness for his hardline anti-Soviet policies when he served as an assistant secretary of defense under President Reagan,[15] the invasion of Afghanistan in October 2001 was a good start. Among other things, it enabled the United States and its coalition partners to topple the Taliban regime and destroy bin Laden's terrorist training camps. Although bin Laden was not killed or captured during the invasion, the Bush administration and its supporters claimed victory in Afghanistan. But the victory came at an extremely high price: thousands of innocent lives were lost, and the United States and its allies had just begun to fight the war on terror. To quote the great American poet Robert Frost, "The woods are lovely, dark and deep. / But I have promises to keep. / And miles to go before I sleep."[16] Bush had miles to go before he could put the threat of terrorism to rest, but he took comfort in what had been accomplished in Kandahar and Kabul. The Taliban were forced from power, and Washington could now turn its attention to preventing Afghanistan from becoming a haven for terrorists, a long-term goal to which President Bush remains committed. While the continuing conflict among different political and ethnic factions in this war-torn country will likely result in a resurgence in terrorist activity, there is little doubt in Frum's and Perle's mind that the Bush administration did the right thing. An even better idea, according to the two AEI residents, was invading Iraq in 2003, a much overdue intervention that allowed the United States to remove another dictator from its roster of enemies. However, they insist that for America to win the war on terror, much more has to be done, including removing terrorist mullahs in Iran, ending the terrorist regime in Syria, and adopting tighter security measures at home.[17]

Frum and Perle's recipe for defeating terrorism has found strong support among several conservative members of Congress and think tank scholars, including Brooking's Ken Pollack, whose book *The Threatening Storm* made a strong case for the invasion of Iraq.[18] But, not surprisingly, their recommendations for future interventions have generated considerable controversy in more liberal policy-making circles. The absence of an exit strategy in Iraq,[19] combined with an escalating body count, has produced little tolerance for additional conflicts. Regardless of how well or poorly Frum and Perle's grand plan for winning the war on terror has been received, their insights help to shed light on the complexity of waging a war that must be fought but may never be won. Although they are reluctant to admit it, President Bush and his advisers realize that this war cannot be won by relying solely on force. As Stephen Flynn reminds us, defeating terrorism requires a significant overhaul of the US and international intelligence communities and more cooperation between local, state, and federal law-enforcement officials.[20] Most importantly, it requires the willingness of leaders in the Muslim community to condemn those who use the teachings of Islam to justify murder.[21] Until they do so, the war on terror and the war of ideas will continue to be waged.

Despite President Bush's assurance that America is winning the war in Iraq, there is little evidence that this bloody conflict will soon come to an end. Should the fighting continue into the next presidential election, there is no doubt that the sins of the Bush administration will be visited upon the 2008 Republican presidential nominee. And there is no doubt that academics and policy experts critical of the Bush administration's handling of Iraq will use their privileged positions in the policy-making community to once again raise some or all of the following questions about why the United States invaded Iraq. Was President Bush truly concerned about weapons of mass destruction,[22] or did he use this issue as a pretext to seek revenge against a leader who had tried to assassinate his father? Was the United States more interested in securing access to Iraqi oil[23] than in fighting one of the most significant sponsors of terrorism, Saudi Arabia?[24] What was the extent of the Bush administration's deception,[25] and did it not play on the public's fears of another terrorist attack to justify introducing stronger and discriminatory security measures at home.[26] Was it necessary for Congress to adopt the USA PATRIOT (Uniting and Strengthening America by Providing Appropriate Tools Required to Intercept and Obstruct Terrorism) Act in 2001 and to create the Department of Homeland Security in 2002?[27] And was the Bush doctrine worth risking America's relationship with most of its allies and driving an even wider wedge between the United States and the United Nations?

If the past is any indication, scholars at think tanks and at universities will not wait for the results of the 2008 election to ask and answer these and other questions. In their ongoing efforts to dissect the Bush administration's handling of the war on terror, they will continue to offer different explanations for what motivates American foreign policy. They may also comment on the think tanks that are best positioned and equipped to influence the policies of the incoming administration and may again succumb to the temptation of assuming that proximity to those in power guarantees policy influence. This was the mistake that several journalists, scholars, and pundits made in claiming that the blueprint for the Bush administration's foreign policy was drawn entirely by the Project for the New American Century. But as we will discuss below, while PNAC can take credit for advancing the president's political agenda, several influences were brought to bear on Bush's foreign policy.

PSST! IT'S PNAC

By the time George W. Bush was sworn in as the forty-third president of the United States, it had become Washington's worst kept secret: a small think tank with modest resources but powerful connections to key members of the Bush team was rumoured to have developed a comprehensive foreign policy for the incoming administration. The think tank that had become a favourite topic of discussion for journalists covering Washington politics and for pundits searching for any clues that would help them predict Bush's behaviour in his first hundred days in office was not the Heritage Foundation or AEI, the darlings of the conservative movement. The heir apparent was PNAC, a neo-conservative think tank whose foray into the policy-making community in 1997 sparked considerable interest among and support from several high-level policy-makers, including Dick Cheney, Donald Rumsfeld, Paul Wolfowitz, Scooter Libby, and Jeb Bush, the governor of Florida and the president's younger brother.

If there were any doubts about which sources of information would help the president manage American foreign policy in the post-9/11 world, they were put to rest when the decision was made to invade Iraq. When journalists and scholars skimmed through PNAC's September 2000 study *Rebuilding America's Defenses*, they thought they had discovered the Holy Grail. In its study, PNAC made several policy recommendations that closely resembled initiatives being pursued by the Bush administration. Indeed, the recommendations it made four months before President Bush entered the Oval

Office, such as "defending the homeland and fight[ing] and win[ning] multiple, simultaneous major theater wars,"[28] may as well have been taken directly from his playbook.

Could this have been just a coincidence? Not according to several journalists and scholars who made the connection between PNAC, members of Bush's inner circle, and the foreign policy the United States had embraced. Writing in the *Guardian* in the fall of 2003, Michael Meacher, a British Labour member of Parliament, stated:

We now know that a blueprint for the creation of a global Pax Americana was drawn up for Dick Cheney, Donald Rumsfeld, Paul Wolfowitz, Jeb Bush, and Lewis Libby. The document, entitled *Rebuilding America's Defences* [italics added], was written in September 2000 by the neoconservative think tank, Project for the New American Century (PNAC).

The plan shows Bush's cabinet intended to take military control of the Gulf region whether or not Saddam Hussein was in power. It says, "while the unresolved conflict with Iraq provides the immediate justification, the need for a substantial American force presence in the Gulf transcends the issue of the regime of Saddam Hussein." The PNAC blueprint supports an earlier document attributed to Wolfowitz and Libby which said the US must "discourage advanced industrial nations from challenging our leadership or even aspiring to a larger regional or global role."[29]

Meacher's assessment of PNAC is similar in tone to the one presented by Andrew Austin, who writes: "Not content with waiting for the next Republican administration, Wolfowitz and several other intellectuals formed PNAC, a think tank 'to make the case and rally support for American global leadership.' Top corporate, military, and political figures aligned themselves with PNAC ... Powerful economic interests [also] threw their support behind PNAC.[30]

Similar comments about PNAC's origins and its strong ties to the policy-making establishment and to the business community continue to make their way into the academic literature on the neo-conservative network in the United States.[31] However, other than portraying PNAC as an elite organization with unparalleled access to the White House, we know very little about the inner workings of this think tank and whether it has lived up to its billing as the architect of Bush's foreign policy. As we will discuss below, evaluating the extent of PNAC's influence is not as straightforward as Meacher and others maintain.

PEELING AWAY THE RHETORIC: PNAC'S MANDATE, MOTIVES, AND PRINCIPLES

Gary Schmitt, the president of PNAC, spent years in the academic community and in government before running a think tank. He understood the world of Washington politics and how decisions were made in Congress, in the White House, and in the bureaucracy. And he understood and appreciated that the right ideas presented at the right time could make a profound difference. That is why Schmitt, like many conservatives, relished the opportunity to present new and challenging ideas to a Republican administration. They did not have to wait long. When Al Gore failed to defeat George W. Bush in the 2000 election, Schmitt and his colleagues were given their chance.

Founded in 1997 to promote American global leadership, PNAC spent its early years developing a new conservative approach to foreign policy. This strategy was based on the belief that the United States could and should become a "benevolent global hegemon." As William Kristol and Robert Kagan stated in their 1996 essay "Toward a Neo-Reaganite Foreign Policy;"

Having defeated the "evil empire," the United States enjoys strategic and ideological predominance. The first objective of U.S. foreign policy should be to preserve and enhance that predominance by strengthening America's security, supporting its friends, advancing its interests, and standing up for principles around the world ... In a world in which peace and American security depend on American power and the will to use it, the main threat the United States faces now and in the future is its own weakness. American hegemony is the only reliable defense against a breakdown of peace and international order. The appropriate goal of American foreign policy, therefore, is to preserve that hegemony as far into the future as possible. To achieve this goal, the United States needs a neo-Reaganite foreign policy of military supremacy and moral confidence.[32]

Kristol and Kagan's article struck a responsive chord with several conservative policy-makers and policy experts, who encouraged the authors to create an organization that would promote their vision of American foreign policy. As Schmitt points out, "we got approached by a lot of people saying, 'Why don't you try to institutionalize this?'"[33] After Kristol and Kagan convinced Schmitt to become PNAC's president, they secured sufficient funding to launch the new institute.

Building on the success of their 1996 article, Kagan and Kristol, both project directors at PNAC,[34] published an edited collection in 2000 entitled *Present Dangers*, which further explored the options and opportunities available to the United States as it set out to redefine its role in the international community. Among the many topics addressed by the long and impressive list of contributors were regime change in Iraq, Israel and the peace process, and missile defense, all of which became hot-button issues for President Bush. But it was the release in September 2000 of *Rebuilding America's Defenses*, a seventy-six-page document endorsed by several people who would come to occupy senior positions in the Bush administration, that propelled PNAC into the national spotlight.[35]

The report, written by Thomas Donnelly, Donald Kagan (Robert Kagan's brother), and Gary Schmitt, was intended to encourage debate among policy-makers and the public about America's military strength and how it could be harnessed to achieve the country's foreign policy goals. Based on a series of seminars in which participants with specialized areas of expertise were encouraged to exchange ideas about a wide range of defense and foreign policy issues, the document left few stones unturned. But did this document or blueprint, as it is often described, amount to an "extreme makeover" of US foreign policy, or did it simply propose some minor modifications? Moreover, were PNAC's ideas for advancing American national security interests in a world in which the United States could market itself as a "benevolent global hegemon" the product of original thinking, something think tanks are encouraged to do, or were they recycled from other sources?

The PNAC document, as Schmitt acknowledged recently, was intended to provide a more coherent conservative vision of American foreign policy. "We weren't satisfied with what the isolationists and realists were saying about foreign policy [and felt] that they were very much drawing the United States back from the world at large ... We thought that even though the Cold War had ended, the principles of conservative foreign policy enunciated during the Reagan years were still applicable to the world today."[36] What was needed, according to Schmitt and his colleagues, was a new way of looking at an old problem – how to advance American political, economic, and security interests without becoming the world's policeman. To do so, policy-makers had to work closely with the Pentagon to ensure that the military had the resources in place to allow the United States to achieve its political objectives. Was PNAC proposing a radically different approach to US foreign policy? Not necessarily. Many of the ideas it put forward, including moving ahead on missile defense and confronting the world's remaining dictators, had been discussed for years. Nevertheless, what it recommended required policy-makers to think outside the box. In this sense, the PNAC study offered new and innovative ways of promoting American interests in the post-Cold War era. Ironically, when the study came out, "its real impact was on the Clinton folks, not on the Bush people." As Schmitt recalls,

We briefed it to a lot of the joint chiefs and military commands, and there was a team that the Clinton administration had of civilians within the Pentagon. We briefed it to them and here's how it had an impact on them; their view was "Look, we recognize we haven't spent enough on the military, so there is a gap between strategy and the indispensable nation sort of rhetoric and what the military can do." Their view, which was sensible enough was "We've got to bring the strategy back down to something manageable with this kind of military." Our response was that it was not an unreasonable way of proceeding, but that the country's interests would be better served by saying that rather than tailoring our strategy to fit our resources, why not increase our resources to fit our strategy? To their credit, I think that if they had won, there is every indication that they would have said, "Yeah, that's fair." So ironically, the big impact of the defense study was on the team leaving. The Clinton people were not dumb, and the Pentagon people were beginning to realize ... they were going to have a huge military train wreck if resources didn't turn around or the strategy wasn't changed dramatically.[37]

Unfortunately for Schmitt and for PNAC, *Rebuilding America's Defenses* attracted "very little response from Republicans [and] even less response from the Bush campaign." Reflecting on the inner workings of the 2000 Bush campaign, Schmitt notes:

One of the things about the Bush campaign was that unlike other campaigns I've known, either Democrat or Republican, when people run for president, what they tend to do is have a circle of close advisers and then they have a whole slew of people from think tanks and universities writing position papers. This is designed to keep the team together. The Bush people didn't do that. They had their little group of close advisers ... and they didn't give a shit about anybody else. What they did in the campaign is exactly what they did in office. I'm trying to make an even larger point, which is Bush [and] the eight or so other people who make decisions have very little tolerance or interest in the larger process of developing policy. Some of them are my friends, so it's a little harsh for me to say this, but basically, they think they can handle everything on their own, and of course, now it's perfectly clear they can't.[38]

Although Schmitt is critical of how the Bush administration makes policy, he acknowledges the important contributions that key members of Bush's team have made to developing a stronger and more coherent foreign policy, a goal reflected in the controversial Bush doctrine. While the origins of the

Bush doctrine have been linked to PNAC, Schmitt admits that it would be unfair for his organization to take credit. "We would love to take credit for the Bush doctrine, but in all honesty we can't."[39] The credit belongs to Cheney, Rumsfeld,[40] and Wolfowitz, who years ago identified key threats to the United States. "If you look at what they had to say about the dangers posed by undemocratic states, weapons of mass destruction, and how vulnerable we are to terrorist attacks ... and how these three concerns come together, you have the basis of the Bush doctrine."[41]

But when it comes to evaluating the work of his institute, Schmitt, like any responsible policy entrepreneur, can ill afford to be modest. "I think we do a good job of getting our vision on the table because I think we're very good at what we do ... We get a lot of feedback from editorialists, and you can tell they read the stuff. If you make a poignant argument and present a case that's well reasoned and brief, you have a lot of impact, or you can at least have some impact. "[42] This was certainly Schmitt's hope when he and Kristol appeared on ABC's *Nightline* on 5 March 2003 to discuss their institute's role and its efforts to inject new ideas into the policy-making process. As Ted Koppel introduced the lead story to millions of viewers, the stage was set for Schmitt and Kristol to leave a lasting impact.

Koppel's introduction was so flattering to PNAC that it likely made Schmitt and Krisol blush:

Take away the somewhat hyperbolic references to conspiracy, however, and you're left with a story that has the additional advantage of being true. Back in 1997, a group of Washington heavyweights, almost all of them neo-conservatives, formed an organization called the Project for the New American Century. They did what former government officials do when they're out of power, they began formulating a strategy ... that might bring influence to bear on the Administration then in power. Or failing that, on a new Administration that might someday come to power. They were pushing for the elimination of Saddam Hussein and proposing the establishment of a strong US military presence in the Persian Gulf. All of that might be of purely academic interest were it not for the fact that among the men behind that campaign were such names, as Dick Cheney, Donald Rumsfeld, and Paul Wolfowitz. What was, back in 1997, merely a theory, is now, in 2003, US policy. Hardly a conspiracy, the proposal was out there for anyone to see. But certainly an interesting case of how columnists, commentators, and think-tank intellectuals can, with time and the election of a sympathetic president, change the course of American foreign policy.[43]

Following Koppel's lengthy introduction, Schmitt and Kristol were given an opportunity to explain how and why their organization had become a major player in the policy-making process. "I think we've had a lot of influence," Schmitt remarked, "because I think we've set the terms ... [about] how to think about the world that ... have been picked up in some measure by this Administration." Reflecting on why the principles enshrined by PNAC have had widespread appeal in some policy-making circles, Kristol added, "I think the principles are those of Ronald Reagan. A strong America. A morally-grounded foreign policy. As well as a foreign policy that defended American security and American interests. And understanding that American leadership was key to, not only world stability, but any hope for spreading democracy and freedom around the world."[44]

Interestingly enough, the most insightful comment about why PNAC had become a rising star in the policy-making community was not made by Schmitt or Kristol but by another *Nightline* guest, Ian Lustick of the University of Pennsylvania. He stated, "Before 9/11, this group was in the position it is in but could not win over the President to this extravagant image of what foreign policy required. After 9/11, it was able to benefit from the gigantic eruption of political capital, combined with the supply of military preponderance in the hands of the President. And this small group, therefore, was able to gain direct contact and even control, now of the White House."[45] Although Schmitt would take issue with Lustick's comment that PNAC was able to gain control of the White House, he would certainly agree that the events of 9/11 made his organization's founding principles and policy recommendations more palatable. Prior to 9/11, "I'd say there was a limitation to what we could do because the reality is, the argument we were making was that there was a remarkable opportunity in front of us if we acted strategically. [But] the truth is, there was no evident threat and so by and large it's very hard to move people, politicians and certainly a nation without a threat. I think that was a real limitation on what we could do."[46]

Scholars studying PNAC's ascendancy in the political arena cannot possibly overlook the fact that several of the original signatories to its statement of principles received high-level positions in the Bush administration. As Koppel pointed out, you do not have to be a conspiracy theorist to acknowledge the intimate ties between some of Bush's closest advisers and PNAC. However, acknowledging these important connections is a far cry from making the claim that the institute was the architect of Bush's foreign policy. The president did not appoint Rumsfeld, Wolfowitz, and other foreign policy experts to serve in his administration because they were card-carrying members of PNAC or of any other think tank; they were recruited because they were people he could trust. Although Bush appeared to be sympathetic to many of the ideas presented by PNAC, we should not assume that this or any other organization dictated his foreign policy. As Daalder and Lindsay point out, it is reasonable to conclude that the greatest influence on George W. Bush was George W. Bush.[47] In the following section, we will discuss President Bush's management of foreign policy and why, according to some scholars, it has impeded the efforts of think tanks and other non-governmental organizations to leave their mark in the White House.

KNOCK, KNOCK ... WHO'S THERE?

Fifty years from now, historians looking back on the presidency of George W. Bush will, in all likelihood, conclude that his demeanour and leadership style changed dramatically after the terrorist attacks of 9/11. The president who entered the Oval Office under a cloud of controversy on 20 January 2001 was very different from the president who surfaced amidst the ruins of the World Trade Center. Ridiculed on the campaign trail as a politician who had gone very far on very little, Bush himself and few others could have predicted that his bid for the presidency would result in a nationwide scandal. But it did, and he assumed his responsibilities as president with the full understanding that the Supreme Court, not the American people, had propelled him into office.

Given the circumstances surrounding Bush's election victory, it is not surprising that he appeared to lack confidence during his first months in office. Bombarded with accusations that he had stolen the presidency, he could hardly be expected to exude confidence. What made matters worse was being embarrassed and humiliated by journalists who questioned his competency to govern. Few will ever forget Bush's performance on a pop quiz administered during the 2000 campaign by Andy Hiller, a political correspondent with WHDH-TV in Boston; Bush was barely able to come up with one correct answer.[48]

To limit the potential fallout from his dismal performance, Karen Hughes, Bush's campaign spokeswoman and later counsellor to the president, and Karl Rove, Bush's chief strategist,[49] encouraged the Texas governor to meet regularly with a group of experienced foreign policy experts to get up to speed on foreign policy. As previously discussed, many of these advisers, including Brent Scowcroft and Condoleezza Rice, had worked in the first Bush administration. If anyone needed a crash course in international relations, it was George W. Bush. The eldest son of the forty-first president of the United States shared his father's love of baseball but showed little interest in world affairs. This disinterest was reflected in the limited number of trips Bush took abroad. By the time he became president in 2001,

"Bush's foreign travels [had] been limited to three visits to Mexico, two trips to Israel, a three-day Thanksgiving visit in Rome with one of his daughters in 1998 and a six-week excursion to China with his parents in 1975 when his father was the U.S. envoy to Beijing."[50]

What Bush did not learn about foreign policy on his travels or from his advisers, he learned on the job. When terrorists struck the United States on September 11, 2001, millions of Americans prayed that he was a quick study. To the surprise of many political pundits, including AEI's David Frum, a former speech writer for Bush, the president was up to the challenge.[51] Like many world leaders, the younger Bush found his voice in a time of crisis; he had come of age. The inexperienced and untested leader who, months earlier, could not answer some basic questions about foreign affairs had become America's war president, a position that in time he would come to relish. According to Daalder and Lindsay, "As Air Force One flew over Iraq, Bush could say that he had become an extraordinarily effective foreign policy president. He had dominated the American political scene like few others. He had been the unquestioned master of his own administration. He had gained the confidence of the American people and persuaded them to follow his lead."[52]

Shortly after Bush's campaign against terrorism went into full swing, his leadership style had clearly begun to change. The insecurity and sense of vulnerability that accompanied him to the Oval Office was replaced by a growing confidence and bravado that other commanders-in-chief, including Ronald Reagan, John F. Kennedy, Franklin Roosevelt, and Theodore Roosevelt, had exhibited.[53] No longer content with assuming the role of student listening diligently to his teachers, Bush began to assert his leadership. Although he continued to rely on the advice of Rice, Rumsfeld, and the other "Vulcans," it became clear to those outside the inner sanctum that the president had little interest in expanding his circle of advisers. To put it bluntly, to policy experts residing in think tanks and at universities, the foreign policy-making process at the highest levels of government was, for all intents and purposes, closed. As Daalder observed,

This is a very, very, very closed system. I think the president does rely on a small group of people, [but] I don't think he's listening to the arguments. I think the arguments in and of themselves are being muted more and more. When [Bush] became president, he was always in receiving mode. He'd just sit there and listen. Now he's in broadcasting mode. He spends all his time telling other people what he thinks. Foreign leaders who met with him in his first year thought he was interested in listening to them, and now it's all about telling them what he thinks needs to be done. He still listens, but he already knows what he wants. I think he's becoming more confident that he knows what he's doing and he doesn't need anybody's advice. So for these reasons, it is true that the process is not particularly open to outside influence.[54]

The relatively closed policy-making environment that has come to character-ize the Bush White House may have impeded the access of policy experts from outside government, but it does not appear to have undermined the presi-dent's ability to make policy decisions. Rather, limiting the number of partici-pants involved in high-level policy matters has allowed him to wage the war on terror more effectively. According to Daalder and Lindsay, the president has a clear vision of what he wants to accomplish and will not allow even his closest and most trusted advisers to interfere with his agenda. Moreover, con-trary to the assertions of countless journalists and scholars that a small band of neo-conservatives have hijacked the Oval Office, they claim that the presi-dent has remained the master of his destiny. As the two think tank scholars point out, "The man from Midland [Texas] was not a figurehead in someone else's revolution. He may have entered the Oval Office not knowing which general ran Pakistan, but during his first thirty months in office he was the puppeteer, not the puppet. He governed as he said he would on the campaign trail. He actively solicited the counsel of seasoned advisers, and he tolerated if not encouraged vigorous disagreement among them. When necessary, he overruled them. George W. Bush led his own revolution."[55]

Daalder and Lindsay's assessment of President Bush and the way in which he has managed the war on terror is consistent with the statist paradigm advanced by Stephen Krasner in *Defending the National Interest*. As dis-cussed in chapter 3, proponents of that paradigm maintain that foreign pol-icy is determined by the state, not by powerful interest groups or an entrenched elite. If President Bush has indeed exercised as much control over foreign policy as the two authors claim, it stands to reason that think tanks and other NGOs have had difficulty gaining access to the highest levels of government. But what about PNAC and its ties to the Bush White House? What accommodation does the statist paradigm make for think tanks that appear to have enormous clout in the Oval Office? In this case, very little. After all, it is not PNAC that has clout; it is several members of the Bush administration who just happen to have had an affiliation with this group. Since members of Bush's cabinet and White House staff are considered part of the state and not representatives of a think tank or interest group, the assumptions underlying the statist paradigm appear to remain intact.

While that paradigm may help to explain why the efforts of think tanks to exercise policy influence in the executive branch have been thwarted, those employing it cannot ignore the success think tanks have had in conveying their ideas about the war on terror to the media and to policy-makers on Capitol Hill and throughout the bureaucracy. Again, a holistic approach to policy-making would be more useful in this regard. If we assume that influence can be exercised at different times and during different stages of the policy-making process, then the statist paradigm may have limited utility. It certainly has limited utility in explaining why think tanks were able to play such a critical role in promoting missile defense in the Reagan White House, a subject that we will return to in the conclusion of this study. In the final section of this chapter, we will consider what think tanks have been able to accomplish in this ongoing policy debate and what conclusions can be drawn regarding the extent and nature of their influence. As in the previous case study, it is important to keep in mind that influence is rarely an all-or-nothing proposition.

WINNING BATTLES AND WAGING WARS: THINK TANKS AFTER 9/11

Think tanks prepared for the debates over the war on terror much as armies prepare for battle. The took stock of their resources, assessed their capabilities, designed a strategy, and determined the most effective ways in which it could be executed. Although their efforts may not always have paid off, think tanks have and continue to stake out and defend their positions in the war of ideas. Through their publications, conferences, and seminars, congressional testimony, and ongoing interaction with the media, America's leading defense and foreign policy think tanks have made a significant contribution to shaping the national conversation.

But how much of an impact they have had in influencing the substance and direction of the Bush administration's campaign to eradicate terrorism is a question that has yet to produce any definitive answers. In evaluating the extent to which think tanks have made a difference, scholars must, like any competent detective, review what they know and what they do not know about the involvement of these organizations in this controversial policy debate. What scholars who have monitored the debates over various aspects of the war on terror know is that several think tanks, including RAND, CSIS, AEI, Brookings, Heritage, PNAC, the Council on Foreign Relations, the Carnegie Endowment, and the CSP, have relied on multiple channels to convey their ideas to the public and to policy-makers on a wide range of issues. Among other things, think tanks have discussed the problems and prospects of homeland security, the need to overhaul intelligence agencies both at home and abroad, and the importance of mending the growing rift between the United States and many of its European allies. In short, scholars acknowledge that when it comes to ideas about how to fight a successful war against terrorists, think tanks have spoken loudly and clearly.

Several scholars and journalists have also acknowledged that some think tanks have been better positioned than others to capture the attention of policy-makers. Indeed, the consensus is that no think tank has been more effective at communicating its ideas to the Bush White House than PNAC. In the press and in much of the academic literature that has surfaced since President Bush assumed office, a lot has been made of the strong ties between PNAC and key members of his administration. Even more has been made of how closely the policy recommendations outlined in several of its publications and letters to policy-makers resemble the policies Bush has pursued since 9/11. But we also know that President Bush, unlike President Reagan, has been reluctant to solicit the advice of non-governmental policy experts, preferring instead to surround himself with a small circle of advisers whom he trusts to execute his foreign policy.

By probing more deeply into the relationship between PNAC and the Bush administration, we were able to uncover further information. For instance, we learned that the ideological underpinnings of the Bush doctrine, which, among other things, helped to justify the war in Iraq, did not originate at PNAC but were closely linked to recommendations made by several members of his cabinet. As Gary Schmitt acknowledged, "It's perfectly obvious that Bush's war on terror was not something we articulated before 9/11 ... Bush pulled together a strategic vision based on the advice he received from Cheney, Wolfowitz, and Rumsfeld."[56]

Although PNAC has been effective in articulating a vision of how the United States can better advance its goals in the international community and would dearly like to take credit for being the architect of Bush's foreign policy, it has resisted the temptation. Still, this position has not prevented the media and some members of the academic community from claiming that Bush's battle plans for the war on terror originated with a small Washington think tank. Had journalists and scholars been more diligent in analyzing the many sources of influence in the Bush administration, they would have discovered a much longer list. In addition to identifying other think tanks with whom President Bush and his key advisers have had close contact, including AEI, the Council on Foreign Relations, and the CSP,[57] they would have considered the potential impact Bush's father[58] and other individuals close to the president could have had on his thinking.

To suggest that before he assumed the reins of power, President Bush had given little thought to missile defense, weapons of mass destruction, and the potential danger of Iraq and other rogue states to the United States is completely without foundation. His many campaign speeches on foreign policy highlight his thinking on these and other important issues. It is also unreasonable to conclude that it was because of PNAC that issues relating to the war on terror made their way onto Bush's agenda. If Richard Clarke was unable to convince Condoleezza Rice of the imminent threat that Osama bin Laden and al-Qaeda posed to the United States, why would we expect PNAC to have been able to attract attention in the Bush White House? It was not PNAC that made a difference in the White House; it was a tight-knit group of seasoned foreign policy experts with previous ties to this think tank who left an indelible mark on the president's foreign policy agenda. But despite the presence of several outside influences, in the final analysis, as Daalder and Lindsay remind us, it was the president and the president alone who spearheaded a new revolution in American foreign policy.

Conclusion: Think Tanks, Foreign Policy, and the Public Interest

Until a few years ago, it was unusual for courses on American foreign policy to devote more than a passing reference to think tanks and their involvement in the policy-making process. While interest groups, corporations, trade unions, and the media figured prominently in discussions about the domestic sources of foreign policy, the subject of think tanks rarely made its way into lectures and seminars. However, as think tanks have become more visible on the political landscape over the past several decades, scholars and journalists have begun to pay closer attention to how and to what extent they participate in the national conversation. This increased interest has led to several recent studies which, among other things, have traced the origins of think tanks in the United States and their efforts to establish and solidify ties to key stakeholders.

Although the academic literature on these organizations continues to grow, for the most part, scholars have been reluctant to address a fundamental question: how much influence do think tanks wield in the policy-making process? Indeed, rather than trying to develop an appropriate analytical framework within which to evaluate their influence in shaping public opinion and public policy, those studying these organizations have, almost without exception, relied on anecdotal evidence to support their claims about think tank influence. The result is that we are left with an inventory of thousands of newspaper clippings, dozens of academic articles, and a smattering of books that tell us virtually everything we need to know about think tanks but how to measure or assess their impact.

After delving into the mysterious and complex world of think tanks, scholars have understandably shied away from a methodological problem that in all likelihood will never be resolved. But as with many other difficult questions that emerge in political science and in related disciplines, it is essential that we begin to address an issue that is critically important to our understanding of both think tanks and the study of policy-making. In this book, I have tried to do just that. In studying the rise of think tanks in the United States and the various features of the political system that have enabled them to flourish, I have sought to explain why it is often difficult to evaluate the nature and extent of their influence. Part of the problem is that directors of think tanks and the scholars who study these institutions have different notions of what constitutes influence and how it is achieved.

Think tanks, much like other organizations that inhabit the policy research community, try to convey their ideas to various target audiences. And like corporations vying for a larger market share, they make strategic decisions about how and where to channel their efforts. Although think tanks are often portrayed as scholarly institutions detached from the political process and the world around them, in reality they are acutely aware of the need to establish a strong foothold in the policy research community. To do so, they have learned to be entrepreneurial; they seize opportunities to make their views known and raise the funds necessary to enhance their visibility. In the United States, a country that has become a breeding ground for think tanks, this entrepreneurial spirit is encouraged and supported by individual donors, corporations, and philanthropic foundations that recognize the importance of competing in the marketplace of ideas. To compete successfully, many think tanks devote considerable resources to attracting media exposure, a critical strategy for capturing the attention of policymakers. In addition, they hold conferences, encourage their staff to testify before congressional committees, and share their research findings with members of Congress, the Executive, and the bureaucracy, all with a view to influencing public policy.

In the final analysis, the responsibility of evaluating their ability or inability to influence public opinion and public policy falls on the shoulders of scholars, who are both fascinated with think tanks and enormously frustrated by the obstacles they need to overcome to measure the performance of these organizations. To better assess the behaviour of think tanks, I have suggested adopting an alternative approach to studying policy influence. Rather than employing a linear model to evaluate influence, I have proposed a holistic approach, one that recognizes that influence is an ongoing process which takes place at different stages of policy-making when participants exchange ideas about various aspects of public policy. It is the conversations that take place among and between policy-makers, policy experts, academics, journalists, activists, and members of the attentive public that ultimately help to shape the political agenda. That is why it is imperative for scholars interested in studying the role of think tanks and the nature of policy-making to closely monitor these conversations.

Influence need not, as Holsti and others have argued, be tied directly to policy outcomes. Think tanks and other active participants in the ideas industry clearly understand this and attempt to make their presence felt, to varying degrees, throughout the policy-making process. While some think tanks may be more effective at defining the parameters of policy debates, as evidenced through their heightened exposure in the media, others may be more inclined to focus their efforts on working closely with policy-makers to advance particular initiatives. But regardless of where think tanks elect to concentrate their efforts, we cannot overlook the fact that policy-making is a process that can take months, if not years, to unfold. As a result, to conclude that influence can be achieved only if an individual or an organization manages to convince a policy-maker or a group of policy-makers to adopt its preferences ignores the reality of the policy-making process.

By embracing a holistic approach, scholars are implicitly acknowledging that the process of making policy decisions is, as Leslie Gelb points out, highly episodic, arbitrary, and difficult to predict. This is another reason why it is futile to treat policy influence in a linear fashion. The process by which policy-makers arrive at decisions cannot be explained by looking at a flow chart, but can only be understood by examining the goals, motives, and priorities of policy-makers. Recognizing this complexity, I presented two case studies in the book. In chapter 8 I examined the efforts of a select group of think tanks to influence the debate over national missile defense, an initiative that grew out of President Reagan's controversial Star Wars project, and in chapter 9 I explored how think tanks have become involved in the ongoing debate over the war on terror. The findings of the two case studies helped to shed light on the role of think tanks in the foreign policy-making process and the various factors that may facilitate or undermine their efforts to exercise policy influence. Before we proceed to a broader discussion about think tanks and foreign policy, it is worthwhile reviewing our findings.

The case study on the origins of SDI and the pursuit of NMD provides several interesting insights about the involvement of think tanks in the foreign policy-making process. Among other things, this case illustrates that in some instances, think tanks do not require multi-million-dollar budgets or several dozen researchers to gain access to the highest levels of government. As Daniel Graham of High Frontier discovered, presenting the right idea at the right time to the right people can create innumerable opportunities for think tanks to inject their ideas into the policy-making process. Lacking adequate funds to prepare his study on strategic missile defense, Graham sought refuge at the Heritage Foundation, a conservative think tank whose study *Mandate for Leadership* had transformed the nascent organization into one of Washington's premier policy research institutes. Graham's affiliation with Heritage may have given his organization more cachet with senior members of the Reagan administration, but it was his commitment to strategic defense and his vision for a defensive shield protecting the United States from incoming ballistic missiles that enabled him to gain access to the president and to the president's principal advisers.

What also helped to explain Graham's success in advancing the cause of missile defense was President Reagan's steadfast commitment to finding an alternative to the Cold War doctrine of mutual assured destruction. Reagan's willingness to listen to a range of ideas on how best to safeguard the territorial integrity of the United States played a key role in allowing organizations such as High Frontier and the Heritage Foundation to present their ideas to policy-makers. When Reagan left office in 1989, research and development on missile defense was in full swing, but an operational system had yet to be deployed. Interestingly enough, close to two decades after Reagan announced his desire to render nuclear weapons impotent and obsolete, scientists are still trying to discover how to make his dream a reality. So are think tanks such as Heritage and the Center for Security Policy, which continue to stress the benefits of missile defense to policy-makers on Capitol Hill and throughout the bureaucracy.

The second case study also reveals some interesting insights about think tanks and foreign policy. As in the case of missile defense, the think tank most often cited for having exercised considerable influence over President Bush's war on terror, PNAC, is an organization with extremely modest resources. Although there is some question as to how much of a role it has played in shaping Bush's foreign policy, its close ties to members of the president's inner circle once again demonstrates that think tanks need not have deep pockets to become active participants in foreign policy debates. Indeed, the two case studies confirm that for some think tanks, securing access to policy-makers who are sympathetic to their views may on occasion be an even more valuable currency. But what both cases also show is that think tanks would be unwise to place all of their eggs in one basket. Even if an administration that appears to endorse the policy recommendations made by particular think tanks comes to power, directors of think tanks realize that in politics, as in war, there are no friends, only interests. This factor may in part explain why think tanks often wage battles on multiple fronts and why having a sizable budget may be critical for their long-term success.

Establishing close ties to high-level policy-makers, as High Frontier, PNAC, and other think tanks have done, is important. But equally, if not more, important is developing an extensive network of contacts in the media, on Capitol Hill, and in various government departments and agencies. Doing so helps think tanks to develop the infrastructure they require to ensure that their voices are heard. As the marketplace of ideas becomes increasingly congested, they cannot afford to be ignored.

THINK TANKS AND FOREIGN POLICY

It was not long ago that discussions about foreign policy focused almost exclusively on issues of power, diplomacy, war, and peace. And it was not long ago that matters of foreign policy were reserved for the president and his senior advisers and for diplomats, ambassadors, and foreign envoys. Foreign policy was something that leaders debated behind closed doors in boardrooms where the pursuit of the national interest was the only item on the agenda. But the world in which many seasoned foreign policy experts, including George Kennan, Dean Acheson, and Henry Kissinger, honed their skills[1] is very different from the world in which US foreign policy is now being developed.

The dismal outcome of the Vietnam War not only gave rise to the Vietnam syndrome – a general reluctance on the part of policy-makers to become involved in military conflicts – but it created a different environment in which policy-makers were expected to make foreign policy decisions. Under public pressure to make the foreign policy-making process more transparent, the president and those who advise him on matters of national security now feel compelled to bring their case before the American people. But the president and his advisers no longer monopolize discussions about foreign policy. Joining them are countless think tanks, interest groups, and other non-governmental organizations that are committed to directing America's performance on the world stage.

While think tanks represent but one set of actors competing for influence in the political arena, they possess a distinctive voice that deserves to be recognized. At times, their tactics and strategies mirror those pursued by interest groups. But think tanks, particularly those that specialize in foreign and defense policy, have a long and rich history in the United States. The list of prestigious foreign-affairs think tanks in America is impressive, as is the number of policy experts from these institutions who make their way into government. In the world of think tanks, the United States is at the top of the food chain.

Given the complexity of the foreign policy-making process and the vast number of individuals and organizations that seek to shape it, how can scholars properly examine the role and function of think tanks? They attempt to do so by introducing competing theoretical approaches. Pluralists, elite theorists, institutionalists, and those claiming that foreign policy is a product of the state and not external forces have all claimed to understand what motivates think tanks and how they manage to navigate their way through the policy-making process. In some respects, each of these approaches can provide a piece of the puzzle. Unfortunately, there is no single approach that can offer a comprehensive explanation. The results of the two case studies confirm that scholars must draw on more than one theoretical model or paradigm to reveal why think tanks have or have not been able to achieve their objectives.

Explaining why some think tanks succeed and others fail to exercise influence is not as simple as predicting the outcome of presidential elections. Some think tanks are able to successfully convey their ideas to stakeholders because they have the resources in place to reach those in positions of power. Still, in some instances, the amount of money and size of staff on which think tanks can draw bear no relation to how effective they are in swaying public opinion and public policy. As noted, think tanks with modest resources can at times achieve impressive results. Think tanks, like world-class athletes, play to their strengths. In doing so, they make decisions about how and where in the policy-making process to establish themselves and enhance their profile. Scholars who study think tanks need to recognize that as much as they would like to provide a definitive conclusion about how much or how little influence these organizations wield, they may not be able to put this matter to rest. Rather, since it is virtually impossible to measure influence accurately, they may have no alternative but to assess think tanks and the policy issues in which they are engaged on a case-by-case basis. As Aaron Steelman noted in his review of my earlier book *Do Think Tanks Matter?* "such a cautious conclusion may be the best that we can expect."[2]

Being cautious in making observations about the nature of think tank influence does not in any way suggest that scholars are avoiding this important research question. On the contrary, it means that they recognize the limitations of their discipline and the subject that they are exploring. Scholars criticized for being overcautious, a euphemism for being non-committal, appreciate that the process by which leaders make foreign policy choices rarely proceeds in a logical fashion. They should therefore resist the temptation to simplify the policy-making process. Scholars need to acknowledge that foreign policy-making is indeed complicated and is often made more complex by those who allow their emotions to interfere with their judgment. This phenomenon in part explains why it is so difficult to isolate the many factors that may play a role in influencing a leader's behaviour.

THINK TANKS AND THE PUBLIC INTEREST

Despite some of the many challenges think tanks confront in their daily operations,[3] it is unlikely that their numbers will diminish. In an environment that encourages individuals and organizations to participate in the political life of the nation, there is little reason to expect the think tank population to decline. Indeed, so long as there are policy entrepreneurs willing to promote their views and donors prepared to lend their support, think tanks will continue to make their presence felt. However, as the marketplace of ideas becomes increasingly crowded, think tanks will have to make more strategic choices in attracting the attention of policy-makers and the public. But in the process of determining the most effective ways to convey their ideas, they should not lose sight of their primary mission.

At the beginning of the twentieth century, some of America's most prominent foreign affairs think tanks were created to help advance the national interests of the United States. Unfortunately, in recent decades many think tanks have lost sight of what they can do to serve the public interest. Americans and the people they elect to represent them deserve research institutions comprised of scholars who are committed to promoting the well-being of the nation.

In foreign policy, as in domestic policy, what is desperately needed is the wise counsel and judgment of experts operating at arm's length from government who can present a range of options to political leaders. If policy experts from think tanks can do so without framing their recommendations to suit their political preferences, they will make an invaluable contribution to the policy-making process. On the other hand, if the political and ideological beliefs of think tank scholars taint their recommendations, there is little to be gained.

Policy-making is often portrayed as a game that inevitably results in winners and losers. Yet, as the events that have unfolded since 9/11 have illustrated, policy-making is much more than a game; it is a long-term investment made on behalf of the nation that must show positive returns. In the United States both the public and the private sectors have made important investments in the country's think tanks. We can only hope that this investment pays handsome dividends and that think tanks, and the stakeholders they serve, capitalize on their ideas.

Appendices

Profiles and Annual Budgets of Selected American Think Tanks

Table A1.1
Profiles of selected American think tanks, 2004, in order of founding date

Institution	Founded	Location	Staff	Budget	Web site
Carnegie Endowment for International Peace	1910	Washington, DC	35 FTR, 62 staff	$19,410,569	www.ceip.org
Brookings Institution	1916	Washington, DC	43 FTR, 200 staff	$47,694,000	www.brook.edu
Hoover Institution on War, Revolution and Peace	1919	Stanford, CA	201 staff	$25,000,000	www.hoover.stanford.edu
Century Foundation	1919	New York, NY	7 FTR, 24 staff	$3,600,000 (2003)	www.tcf.org
Council on Foreign Relations	1921	New York, NY	200 staff	$29,295,100	www.cfr.org
Battelle Memorial Institute	1929	Columbus, OH	16,000 staff	$1,316,800,000 (2003)	www.battelle.org
American Enterprise Institute for Public Policy Research	1943	Washington, DC	50 FTR	$24,410,000	www.aei.org
RAND	1946	Santa Monica, CA	1,600 FTR and PTR	$227,199,000 (2003)	www.rand.org
Foreign Policy Research Institute	1955	Philadelphia, PA	30 PTR, 10 staff	$1,500,000	www.fpri.org
American Security Council Foundation	1956	Culpeper, VA	n/a	n/a	www.ascfusa.org
ANSER (formed with assistance from RAND)	1958	Arlington, VA	n/a	n/a	www.anser.org
East-West Center	1960	Honolulu, HA	35 FTR, 165 staff	$37,600,000	www.eastwestcenter.org
Atlantic Council of the United States	1961	Washington, DC	9 FTR, 16 PTR, 22 staff	n/a	www.acus.org
Hudson Institute	1961	Washington, DC	23 FTR, 4 PTR, 11 staff	$8,500,000	www.hudsondc.org

Table A1.1 (continued)

Institution	Founded	Location	Staff	Budget	Web site
Center for Strategic and International Studies	1962	Washington, DC	220 staff, 100 interns	$25,000,000	www.csis.org
Institute for Policy Studies	1963	Washington, DC	30 staff	$1,400,000 (2003)	www.ips-dc.org
Arms Control Association	1971	Washington, DC	3 FTR, 5 staff	$650,000	www.armscontrol.org
Center for Defense Information	1972	Washington, DC	25 staff	$2,100,000 (2003)	www.cdi.org
Institute for Contemporary Studies	1972	Oakland, CA	10 staff	n/a	www.icspress.com
Heritage Foundation	1973	Washington, DC	58 FTR, 152 staff	$34,600,000 (2003)	www.heritage.org
Worldwatch Institute	1974	Washington, DC	7 FTR, 2 PTR, 12 staff	$3,000,000	www.worldwatch.org
Cato Institute	1977	Washington, DC	43 FTR, 90 PTR, 33 staff	$14,000,000	www.cato.org
American Foreign Policy Council	1982	Washington, DC	11 staff	n/a	www.afpc.org
Bildner Center for Western Hemisphere Studies	1982	New York, NY	n/a	n/a	
Carter Center	1982	Atlanta, GA	20 FTR, 150 staff	$81,981,850 (2002)	www.cartercenter.org
American Defense Institute	1983	Alexandria, VA	5 staff	$900,000 (2003)	ojo.org/adi/
American Institute for Contemporary German Studies	1983	Washington, DC	4 FTR, 10 staff, 3 interns	$1,561,605 (2003)	www.aicgs.org
Economic Policy Institute	1986	Washington, DC	10 FTR, 50 staff	$3,796,875 (2002)	www.epinet.org
British American Security Information Council (USA)	1987	Washington, DC	13 staff	$206,327	www.basicint.org
Institute for International Studies (Stanford)	1987	Stanford, CA	150 staff	$20,000,000 (2003)	iis.stanford.edu
Alexis de Tocqueville Institution	1988	Washington, DC	n/a	n/a	www.adti.net
Center for Security Policy	1988	Washington, DC	5 FTR, 9 staff	$850,000 (2003)	www.centerforsecuritypolicy.org
Middle East Forum	1990	Philadelphia, PA	10 staff	$1,100,000	www.meforum.org
Watson Institute for International Studies	1991	Providence, RI	25 FTR, 20 staff	$4,700,000	www.watsoninstitute.org
Boston Research for the 21st Century	1993	Cambridge, MA	n/a	n/a	www.brc21.org

Table A1.1 (continued)

Institution	Founded	Location	Staff	Budget	Web site
Empower America (Citizens for a Sound America)	1993	Washington, DC	n/a	n/a	www.empoweramerica.org
Nixon Center for Peace and Freedom	1994	Washington, DC	10 staff	$1,600,000 (2003)	www.nixoncenter.org
Project for the New American Century	1997	Washington, DC	n/a	n/a	www.newamericancentury.org
Center for American Progress	2003	Washington, DC	89 staff	n/a	www.americanprogress.org

Table A1.2
Annual budgets of selected American think tanks in descending order

Institution	Budget
RAND	$227,199,000.00
Carter Center	$81,981,850.00
Brookings Institution	$47,694,000.00
East-West Center	$37,600,000.00
Heritage Foundation	$34,600,000.00
Council on Foreign Relations	$29,295,100.00
Hoover Institution on War, Revolution and Peace	$25,000,000.00
Center for Strategic and International Studies	$25,000,000.00
American Enterprise Institute for Public Policy Reseach	$24,410,000.00
Institute for International Studies (Stanford)	$20,000,000.00
Carnegie Endowment for International Peace	$19,410,569.00
United States Institute of Peace	$16,256,000.00
Cato Institute	$14,000,000.00
Hudson Institute	$8,500,000.00
Watson Institute for International Studies	$4,700,000.00
Economic Policy Institute	$3,796,875.00
Century Foundation (formerly Twentieth Century Fund)	$3,600,000.00
Worldwatch Institute	$3,000,000.00
Center for Defense Information	$2,100,000.00
Nixon Center for Peace and Freedom	$1,600,000.00
American Institute for Contemporary German Studies	$1,561,605.00
Foreign Policy Research Institute	$1,500,000.00
Institute for Policy Studies	$1,400,000.00
Middle East Forum	$1,100,000.00
American Defense Institute	$900,000.00
Center for Security Policy	$850,000.00
Arms Control Association	$650,000.00
British American Security Information Council (USA)	$206,327.00

Government Positions Held by Staff
at Selected Think Tanks

Name	Title	Government positions
AMERICAN ENTERPRISE INSTITUTE		
Claude E. Barfield	Resident scholar and director of science and technology policy studies	Professional staff member, Senate Governmental Affairs Committee, Senate, 1977–79; co-staff director, President's Commission for a National Agenda for the Eighties, 1979–81; consultant, Office of the US Trade Representative, 1982–85
Walter Berns	Resident scholar, political philosophy, constitutional law, and legal issues	Consultant, State Dept, 1983–87
John Bolton	Former senior vice-president	Assistant attorney general, Dept of Justice, 1985–89; assistant secretary for international organizational affairs, State Dept, 1989–93; undersecretary, arms control and international security, 2001–05; current US ambassador to the UN
Lynne V. Cheney	Senior fellow, culture and education	Served on Texas governor George W. Bush's education team; married to Vice-President Dick Cheney
Christopher DeMuth	President	Staff assistant to the president, White House, 1969–70; executive director, Presidential Task Force on Regulatory Relief, White House, 1981–83; administrator, Office of Information and Regulatory Affairs, Office of Management and Budget, 1981–84
Thomas Donnely	Resident fellow, defense and national security	Professional staff member, Committee on National Security, House of Reps, 1995; director, Policy Group, Committee on National Security (now Committee on Armed Services), House of Reps, 1996–99
Mark Falcoff	Resident scholar emeritus, Latin America	Professional staff member, Senate Foreign Relations Committee, 1986–88; member of the US delegation to the UN Human Rights Commission, 2003
David Frum	Resident scholar	Former special assistant to President Bush for economic speech writing, 2001–02
Reuel Marc Gerecht	Resident fellow, Afghanistan, Iran, intelligence, Middle East, terrorism, Central Asia, former Soviet Union	Political and consular officer, State Dept, 1985–94; Middle Eastern specialist, CIA, 1985–94

Name	Title	Government positions
Newt Gingrich (also at Hoover)	Senior fellow, health-care policy, information technology, military, US politics	Member, House of Reps, 1979–99; speaker, House, 1995–99
Robert A. Goldwin	Resident scholar, constitutional studies, education, human rights and democracy	Special adviser to the US ambassador to NATO, 1973–74; special consultant to President Ford, 1974–76; adviser to secretary of defence, 1976
R. Glenn Hubbard	Visiting scholar, tax policy and health care	Deputy assistant secretary, Dept of the Treasury, 1991–93; President's Council of Economic Advisers, 2001–03
Jeane J. Kirkpatrick	Senior fellow, defense, Latin America, Europe, United Nations, Middle East, national security, Russian region	US permanent representative to the UN, 1981–85; member, Presidential Commission on Space, 1985–87; member, President's Foreign Intelligence Advisory Board, 1985–90; member, Defense Policy Review Board, 1985–93; chair, Commission on Fail Safe and Risk Reduction, Dept of Defense, 1990–92; Chair, US Delegation to the UN Human Rights Commission, 2003
Michael A. Ledeen	Freedom scholar, state sponsors of terrorism, Iran, the Middle East, Europe (Italy, US – China relations, intelligence, and Africa (Mozambique, South Africa, and Zimbabwe)	Special adviser to the secretary of state, 1981–82; consultant, National Security Council and State and Defense Depts, 1982–86; commissioner, US-China Commission, 2001–03
James R. Lilley	Senior fellow, Korea, China, Taiwan	National intelligence officer for China, 1975–78; deputy assistant secretary of state for East Asian affairs, 1985–86; US ambassador to the People's Republic of China, 1989–91, and to the Republic of Korea, 1986–89; assistant secretary of defense for international affairs, 1991–93
Lawrence B. Lindsay	Visiting scholar, tax policy, fiscal policy, international economic development, monetary policy	Senior staff economist for tax policy, President's Council of Economic Advisers, 1981–84; special assistant to the president for domestic economic policy, White House, 1989–91; governor, Federal Reserve System, 1991–97; chief economic adviser, George W. Bush campaign, 1999–2000; assistant to the president for economic policy and director of the National Economic Council, 2001–02
Richard Perle	Resident fellow, defense, Europe, intelligence, Middle East, national security, Russian region	Senate staff, 1969–80; assistant secretary of defense for international security policy, 1981–87; member, Defense Policy Board, Dept of Defense, 1987–2004; chairman, 2001–03

Name	Title	Government positions
Danielle Pletka	Vice-president, foreign and defense policy studies – Middle East, terrorism, South Asia (India Pakistan, and Afghanistan), weapons proliferation	Senior professional staff member for Near East and South Asia, Senate Committee on Foreign Relations, 1992–2002
Michael Rubin	Resident scholar, Arab democracy; domestic politics in Iraq, Iran, and Turkey; Kurdish society	Staff assistant, Iran and Iraq, Office of the Secretary of Defense, 2002–04; political adviser, Coalition Provisional Authority (Baghdad, 2003–04)
Radek Sikorski	Resident fellow and executive director of the New Atlantic Initiative – NATO; Eastern Europe, alliance politics, missile defense, Afghanistan, Angola	Deputy minister of defense, Poland, 1992; deputy minister of foreign affairs, Poland, 1998–2001; secretary of foreign affairs of the Polish Solidarity party, 1999–2002
Fred Thompson	Visiting fellow, national security and intelligence (China, North Korea, and Russia)	Minority counsel, Senate Select Committee on Presidential Campaign Activities ("Watergate Committee"), 1973–74; special counsel to Lamar Alexander, governor of Tennessee, 1980; special counsel, Senate Committee on Foreign Relations, 1980–81; special counsel, Senate Committee on Intelligence, 1982; senator from Tennessee, 1994–2003; chair, Senate Committee on Governmental Affairs, 1997–2001
Peter J. Wallison	Resident fellow, banking and financial services, financial markets, GSEs (Fannie Mae and Freddie Mac)	Special assistant to Governor Nelson A. Rockefeller and counsel during his vice-presidency, 1972–76; general counsel of Treasury Dept, 1981–85; counsel to President Ronald Reagan, 1986–87
Ben J. Wattenberg	Senior fellow, demographics, politics, and US culture and public opinion	Aide and speech writer, President Lyndon Johnson, 1966-68; campaign adviser, Senator Hubert Humphrey, 1970, and Henry M. Jackson, 1972 and 1976; member and vice-chair, Board for International Broadcasting, 1981–91; member, Task Force on US Government International Broadcasting, 1991; member, Commission on Broadcasting to the People's Republic of China, 1992

BROOKINGS INSTITUTION

Lael Brainard	Senior fellow, economic studies, foreign policy studies	Deputy national economic adviser and deputy assistant to the president for international economics, Clinton administration; personal representative, sherpa to the president at the G7/8

Name	Title	Government positions
Richard C. Bush III	Director, Centre for Northeast Asian Policy Studies, and senior fellow, foreign policy studies	Director for committee liaison, Committee of Foreign Affairs, House of Reps, 1994; director for Minority Liaison, Committee on International Relations, House of Reps, 1995; national intelligence officer for East Asia, National Intelligence Council, 1995–97
Daniel L. Byman	Non-resident senior fellow, Saban Center for Middle East Policy; foreign policy studies	Political analyst, CIA, 1990–93 professional staff member, Joint 9/11 Inquiry, House and Senate Intelligence Committees, 2001–02
Stephen P. Cohen	Senior fellow, foreign policy studies	Member, Policy Planning Staff, State Dept, 1985–87
Ivo H. Daalder	Senior fellow, foreign policy studies; Sydney Stein Jr Chair	Director for European affairs, National Security Council, 1995–96
Kenneth Dam	Senior fellow, economic studies	Deputy secretary, Dept of Treasury; deputy secretary, State Dept
Francis M. Deng	Non-resident senior fellow, foreign policy studies; co-director, Brookings-SAIS Project on Internal Displacement	Representative of the UN secretary-general on internally displaced persons; minister of state for foreign affairs, the Sudan, 1976–80; Sudanese ambassador to the United States, to Scandinavia, and to Canada
Joshua M. Epstein	Senior fellow, economic studies	Member, State Dept and Senate Armed Services Committee
Rafael Fernandez de Castro	Non-resident senior fellow, foreign policy studies	North American desk, Mexican Foreign Affairs Ministry
Christopher H. Foreman Jr	Non-resident senior fellow, governance studies	Staff member, President's Commission for a National Agenda for the Eighties, Carter administration
Raymond L. Garthoff	Guest scholar, foreign policy studies	US ambassador to Bulgaria; deputy director, Bureau of Politico-Military Affairs, State Dept; executive officer and senior adviser to the State Dept delegation to the SALT I and ABM Treaty negotiations, 1969–73
James E. Goodby	Non-resident senior fellow, Center for Northeast Asian Policy Studies; foreign policy studies	US foreign service officer, rank of career minister, retired; US ambassador to Finland; ambassador, principal negotiator, and special representative of President Clinton for nuclear security and dismantlement; chief negotiator for cooperative threat reduction agreements, Nunn-Lugar program; vice-chair, US delegation to US-Russian strategic arms reduction talks; head, US delegation to conference on disarmament in Europe; member, secretary of state's Policy Planning Staff; deputy assistant secretary of state for European affairs and for political-military affairs

Name	Title	Government positions
Lincoln Gordon	Guest scholar, foreign policy studies	Director, Marshall Plan Mission, and minister for economic affairs, US embassy, London, 1952–55; US ambassador to Brazil, 1961–66; assistant secretary of state for inter-American affairs, 1966–68
Martin S. Indyk	Senior fellow, foreign policy studies; director, Saban Center for Middle East Policy	Special assistant to the president and senior director for Near East and South Asian affairs, National Security Council, 1993–95; US ambassador to Israel, 1995–97, 2000–01; assistant secretary of state for Near East affairs, State Dept, 1997–2000
Flynt L. Leverett	Senior fellow, Saban Center for Middle East Policy; foreign policy studies	CIA senior analyst, 1992–2001; Middle East/counterterrorism expert, State Dept Policy Planning Staff, 2001–02; senior director for the Middle East Initiative, National Security Council, 2002–03
Michael E. O'Hanlon	Senior fellow, foreign policy studies; Sydney Stein Jr Chair	Defense and foreign policy analyst, National Security Division, Congressional Budget Office, 1989–94
Kenneth M. Pollack	Senior fellow, foreign policy studies; director of research, Saban Centre for Middle East Policy	Iran-Iraq military analyst, CIA, 1988–95; director for Near East and South Asian affairs, National Security Council, 1995–96; director for Persian Gulf affairs, National Security Council, 1999–2001
Charles L. Pritchard	Visiting fellow, foreign policy studies	Ambassador and special envoy for negotiations with North Korea and US representative to the Korean Peninsula Energy Development Organization, State Dept; special assistant to the president and senior director for Asian affairs, National Security Council; director for Asian affairs, National Security Council; deputy chief negotiator for Korean peace talks, State Dept; United States Army attaché, American embassy, Tokyo, Japan; country directory for Japan, Office of the Secretary of Defense
Susan E. Rice	Senior fellow, foreign policy studies	Director for international organizations and peacekeeping, National Security Council, 1993–95; special assistant to the president and senior director for African affairs, National Security Council, 1995–97; assistant secretary of state for African affairs, 1997–2001
David Shambaugh	Non-resident senior fellow, Center for Northeast Asian Policy Studies; foreign policy studies	Intern and analyst on Chinese and Indochina affairs, Bureau of Intelligence and Research, Office of East Asia and the Pacific, State Dept, 1977; staff assistant, East Asia Bureau, National Security Council, 1977–78
Peter W. Singer	Senior fellow, foreign policy studies; director, Project on US Policy towards the Islamic World	Action officer, Balkans Task Force, Office of the Secretary of Defense

Name	Title	Government positions
Helmut Sonnenfeldt	Guest scholar, foreign policy studies	Director, Office of Research on the Soviet Union and Eastern Europe, State Dept, 1952–69; senior staff member, National Security Council, 1969–74; counsellor, State Dept, 1974–77
James B. Steinberg	Vice-president and director, foreign policy studies	Deputy national security adviser to President Clinton; director, Policy Planning Staff, State Dept; deputy assistant secretary for regional analysis, Bureau of Intelligence and Research, State Dept; national security counsel to Senator Edward M. Kennedy from Massachusetts
Strobe Talbott	President	Ambassador-at-large and special adviser to the secretary of state on the new independent states, 1993–94; deputy secretary of state, 1994–2001
Shibley Telhami	Non-resident senior fellow, Center for Middle East Policy; foreign policy studies	US mission to the UN; adviser, Congressman Lee H. Hamilton from Indiana
Justin Vaisse	Affiliated scholar, Center on the United States and Europe; foreign policy studies	Special assistant, Policy Planning Staff, French Ministry of Foreign Affairs; speech writer for Alain Richard, French minister of defense, 1998–99

CARNEGIE ENDOWMENT FOR INTERNATIONAL PEACE

Joseph Cirincione	Senior associate and director for non-proliferation	Professional staff, Committee on Armed Services and Committee on Government Operations, House of Reps; staff director, Military Reform Caucus under Congressmen Tom Ridge and Charles Bennett
Michele Dunne	Editor, *Arab Reform Bulletin*	Middle East specialist, National Security Council, US embassy in Cairo, Policy Planning Staff of State Dept, and the US consulate in Jerusalem
Rose Gottemoeller	Senior associate	Director of the Office of Non-proliferation and National Security, Dept of Energy, from 1997; assistant secretary for non-proliferation and national Security, with responsibility for all non-proliferation cooperation with Russia and the newly independent states; deputy undersecretary for defense nuclear non-proliferation, Dept of Energy
Husain Haqqani	Visiting scholar, South Asia Project	Adviser to Pakistani prime ministers Ghulam Mustafa Jatoi, Nawaz Sharif, and Benazir Bhutto; Pakistani ambassador to Sri Lanka, 1992–93
Robert Kagan	Senior associate	In State Dept, 1984–88, as member of the Policy Planning Staff, principal speech writer for Secretary of State George P. Shultz, and deputy for policy, Bureau of Inter-American Affairs

Name	Title	Government positions
Jessica Tuchman Mathews	President	Director of the Office of Global Issues, National Security Council, covering nuclear proliferation, conventional arms sales policy, chemical and biological warfare, and human rights, 1977–79; deputy to the undersecretary of state for global affairs from 1993
Martha Brill Olcott	Senior associate	Special consultant to former secretary of state Lawrence Eagleburger
George Perkovich	Vice-president for studies	Speech writer and foreign policy adviser to Senator Joe Biden, 1989–90
Sandra Polaski	Senior associate and director, Trade, Equity and Development Project	Secretary of state's special representative for international labour affairs to 2002
Ashley Tellis	Senior associate	Senior adviser to the US ambassador to India; member, National Security Council staff as special assistant to the president and senior director for strategic planning and Southwest Asia
Jon Wolfsthal	Associate and deputy director for non-proliferation	Special policy adviser on non-proliferation, Dept of Energy; special assistant to the assistant secretary for non-proliferation and national security

CENTER FOR STRATEGIC AND INTERNATIONAL STUDIES

David M. Abshire	Vice-chair, Board of Trustees; president, Centre for the Study of the Presidency	Congressional staff, 1958–60; assistant secretary of state for congressional relations, 1970–73; US ambassador to NATO, 1983–87; special counsellor to President Reagan, 1987; also chair, Board for International Broadcasting, 1975–77; member, Murphy Commission, 1974–75, President's Foreign Intelligence Advisory Board, 1981–82, and the President's Task Force on US Government International Broadcasting, 1991
Frank Almaguer	Senior associate, Americas Program	US ambassador to the Republic of Honduras, 1999–2002; completed 30 years as member of the US foreign service; member, Senior Seminar at the Foreign Service Institute, State Dept
Jon B. Alterman	Director, Middle East Program	Member, Policy Planning Staff, State Dept, and special assistant to the assistant secretary of state for Near Eastern affairs; legislative aide to Senator Daniel P. Moynihan, responsible for foreign policy and defense
Daniel Benjamin	Senior fellow, International Security Program	Special assistant to the president and National Security Council director for speech writing, 1994–97; member, National Security Council staff, 1994–99; director for Transnational Threats, 1998–99, with principal responsibility for counter-terrorism and coordinating US counter-terrorism policy, programs, and budgets within the federal government

Name	Title	Government positions
William T. Breer	Japan chair	Senior adviser, Policy Planning Staff, State Dept, 1993–96; political officer, political counsellor, and deputy chief of mission, US embassy in Japan with Ambassadors Michael Armacost and Walter Mondale; country director for Japan in Washington
Greg Broaddus	Chief financial officer and senior vice-president for operations	Military asistant to the deputy secretary of defense
Zbigniew Brzezinski	Trustee and counsellor	Member, Policy Planning Council, State Dept, 1966–68; chair, Humphrey Foreign Policy Task Force in 1968 presidential campaign; director, Tri-lateral Commission, 1973–76; principal foreign policy adviser to Jimmy Carter in 1976 presidential campaign; national security adviser to President Carter, 1977–81; member, President's Chemical Warfare Commission, 1985; member, NSC-Defense Dept Commission on Integrated Long-Term Strategy, 1987–88; member, President's Foreign Intelligence Advisery Board, 1987-89; co-chair, Bush National Security Advisery Task Force, 1988
Janusz Bugajski	Director, Eastern Europe Project	Consultant on East European affairs, US Agency for International Development, Dept of Defense; chair, South Central Europe, Balkans Area Studies program for US foreign service officers, Foreign Service Institute, State Dept; testified before various congressional committees, including Helsinki Commission, Senate Foreign Relations Committee, and House Defense Appropriations Committee
Richard Burt	Senior adviser	Ambassador and chief negotiator, Strategic Arms Reduction Talks with former Soviet Union; assistant secretary of state for European and Canadian affairs, 1983–85; US ambassador to the Federal Republic of Germany, 1985–89
Kurt Campbell	Senior vice-president; director, International Security Program; Henry A. Kissinger Chair in National Security	Reserve officer in the US Navy serving on the Joint Chiefs of Staff and the Special Advisory Group to the Chief of Naval Operations; White House fellow, Dept of the Treasury, 1992–93; director on National Security Staff, 1994; deputy special counsellor to the president for NAFTA; deputy assistant secretary of defense, 1995–2000
Pierre Chao	Senior fellow and director of defense industrial initiatives	Expert analyst for the defense and aerospace industry for Senate Armed Services Committee, House Science Committee, Office of the Secretary of Defense, Dept of Defense Science Board, Army Science Board, NASA, DGA (France), NATO, and Aerospace Industries Association Board of Governors

Name	Title	Government positions
William Clark Jr	Senior adviser	Deputy chief of mission in Tokyo, 1981–85; deputy chief of mission and chargé d'affaires in Cairo, 1985–86; principal deputy assistant secretary of state for East Asian and Pacific affairs, 1986–89; US ambassador to India, 1989–92; assistant secretary of state for East Asia and Pacific affairs, 1992–93
Jennifer G. Cooke	Deputy director, Africa Program	Staff assistant, House Foreign Affairs Subcommittee on Africa and for Office of News and Public Information and Committee on Human Rights, National Academy of Sciences
Anthony H. Cordesman	Arleigh A. Burke Chair in Strategy	National security assistant to Senator John McCain of the Senate Armed Services Committee; director of intelligence assessment, Office of the Secretary of Defense; civilian assistant to the deputy secretary of defense; also served in the State Dept and on the NATO international staff; director, policy and planning for resource applications, Dept of Energy; numerous foreign assignments, including posts in Lebanon, Egypt, and Iran and work in Saudi Arabia and the Persian Gulf
Ralph A. Cossa	President, Pacific Forum	US Air Force, 1966–93, reaching rank of colonel and last serving as special assistant to the commander-in-chief, US Pacific Command
Bathsheba N. Crocker	Fellow and co-director, Post-Conflict Reconstruction Project International Security Program	Attorney-adviser, Legal Adviser's Office, State Dept; focused on foreign assistance, appropriations law, and economic sanctions issues; executive assistant to the deputy national security adviser, White House; member of CSIS-led reconstruction assessment in Iraq in 2003 requested by the Dept of Defense
Mary DeRosa	Senior fellow, Technology and Public Policy Program	Attorney for the Advisory Board on the Investigative Capability of the Dept of Defense, 1994; special counsel to the General Counsel, Dept of Defense, 1995–97; deputy legal adviser and then special assistant to the president and legal adviser, National Security Council, 1997–2001
Amanda J. Dory	International affairs fellow, International Security Program	Permanent affiliation with Office of the Secretary of Defense; OSD country director for Southern Africa and for West Africa; worked in OSD on strategy development, force assessment, and policy planning issues
Robert E. Ebel	Chair, Energy Program	With the CIA for 11 years; with Office of Oil and Gas, Dept of the Interior, for over 7 years

Name	Title	Government positions
Robert J. Einhorn	Senior adviser, International Security Program	US Arms Control and Disarmament Agency, 1972–84; represented ACDA in START talks, 1982–86; senior adviser, Policy Planning Staff, State Dept, 1986–92; deputy assistant secretary for non-proliferation, Political-Military Bureau, State Dept, 1992–99; assistant secretary for non-proliferation, State Dept, 1999–2001
Gerald L. Epstein	Senior fellow, Homeland Security Program	Congressional Office of Technology Assessment, 1983–89 and 1991–95; worked on international security topics; with White House Office of Science and Technology Policy, most recently as assistant director for national security; a joint appointment as senior director for science and technology, National Security Council
Richard Fairbanks	Counsellor and trustee	Ambassador-at-large under President Reagan; chief US negotiator for the Middle East peace process; assistant secretary of state for congressional relations
Jay C. Farrar	Senior vice-president for external affairs	Deputy assistant secretary for legislative affairs, Dept of Defense; director of legislative affairs, National Security Council; legislative assistant to the chair of the Joint Chiefs of Staff
Lowell R. Fleischer	Senior associate, Americas Program	In US embassy in Belgrade, Yugoslavia; on various arms control delegations in Geneva
Michèle A. Flournoy	Senior adviser, International Security Program	Principal deputy assistant secretary of defense for strategy and threat reduction; deputy assistant secretary of defense for strategy
Bonnie S. Glaser	Senior associate, International Security Program	Consultant on Asian affairs, Dept of Defense, State Dept, Sandia National Laboratories, and other agencies of US government since 1982
Gerrit W. Gong	Senior associate, Asia Program	In US embassy in Beijing; Office of Senior Career Officer, State Dept; undersecretary for political affairs, State Dept
John J. Hamre	President and CEO	In Congressional Budget Office, 1978–84; became its deputy assistant director for national security and international affairs; professional staff member, Senate Armed Services Committee; undersecretary of defense, comptroller, 1993–97; deputy secretary of defense, 1997–99
Alan S. Hegburg	Senior fellow, Energy Program	Career diplomat, State Dept, with assignments in Washington, DC, and Europe; senior official in the Dept of Energy
Charles M. Herzfeld	Senior associate	Director, defense research and engineering, Dept of Defense, and senior consultant to the science adviser of the president; member, Chief of Naval Operations Executive Panel, since 1970; served on the Defense Science Board and the Defense Policy Board

Name	Title	Government positions
David Heyman	Director, Homeland Security Program	In National Security and International Affairs Division, Science and Technology Policy, White House, 1995–98; senior adviser to the secretary of energy, 1998–2001
Fred C. Ikle	Distinguished scholar	Undersecretary of defense for policy, 1973–77; director of US Arms Control and Disarmament Agency
Tiiu Kera	Adjunct senior fellow, Russia/Eurasia Program	In US Air Force for 28 years, retiring as a major general; director of intelligence at headquarters, US Strategic Command; deputy chief, Central Security Service, National Security Agency; first US defense attaché resident in Lithuania; represented the US defense leadership to the Lithuanian Ministry of Defense and Armed Forces; advised the US ambassador on defense matters; managed US security assistance programs
Jeff Kojac	International affairs fellow, International Security Program	Speech writer for the commandant of the Marine Corps and the Marine Corps' service chief, and member of the Joint Chiefs of Staff; director for current operations, Defense Policy and Arms Control Directorate, National Security Council
Robert H. Kupperman	Co-director, Global Organized Crime Project	Chief scientist at the US Arms Control and Disarmament Agency; served in the Executive Office of the President and the Office of Emergency Preparedness, and as director of the transition team, Federal Emergency Management Agency; consultant to government agencies, foreign governments, and multinational corporations
Vinca LaFleur	Visiting fellow, International Security Program	Speech writer for the secretary of state; political and human rights analyst, US Commission on Security and Cooperation in Europe, for 4 years; director for speech writing and special assistant to the president, National Security Council, 1995–98; authored more than 100 speeches and statements on foreign policy, defense, terrorism, trade, and other national security issues
Brian Latell	Senior associate and director, Central America and Caribbean Project Americas Program	Served in the US Air Force; foreign intelligence officer and Latin America specialist, CIA and National Intelligence Council
James L. LeBlanc	Senior associate, Americas Program	Chief of staff to secretary of state for external affairs and international trade and minister of science and technology in the Canadian government; executive assistant to the Canadian ambassador for international security and arms control; other experience at senior levels in the Canadian government

Name	Title	Government positions
Dong-bok (D.B.) Lee	Senior associate, International Security Affairs	Member, Korean National Assembly; served on the Unification and Foreign Affairs Committee and the National Defense Committee; member, Executive Council, United Liberal Democrats; special assistant to the director, National Intelligence Service, and to the prime minister
Alexander T. J. Lennon	Editor-in-chief, *Washington Quarterly*	Political-military officer, State Dept; principally responsible for bilateral security relations with Israel
James Andrew Lewis	Senior fellow and director, technology policy	Member of the foreign service and the senior executive service; worked on a range of security, technology, and intelligence issues, including Asian basing and access negotiations, the Cambodia Peace Talks, the Five Power Talks on Arms Transfer Restraint, the Wassenaar Arrangement, policies for communications and remote sensing satellites, encryption, and technology transfer issues with China; other assignments related to Central America, the National Security Council, and the Persian Gulf
Edward N. Luttwak	Senior fellow, preventive diplomacy	Consultant to the Office of the Secretary of Defense, National Security Council, and State Dept; member, National Security Study Group, Dept of Defense
Jenifer Mackby	Fellow, International Security Program	Senior political affairs officer, Conference on Disarmament in Geneva, serving as secretary of the committee that negotiated the Nuclear Test Ban; also secretary, Group of Seismic Experts, and secretary, Committee on Transparency in Armaments; worked for the Comprehensive Nuclear Test Ban Treaty Organization Preparatory Commission in Vienna, serving as secretary of the Group on Verification; previously worked as political affairs officer for outer space and disarmament issues at the UN; secretary, Group of Experts on Nuclear Weapons of the Special Commission on Iraq; secretary, government experts study on nuclear weapons; secretary, Drafting Committee of the Treaty on the Non-Proliferation of Nuclear Weapons fourth review conference; secretary, Disarmament Commission Subcommittees on Nuclear Weapons and South Africa's Nuclear Capability; deputy secretary, international conference on outer space
Dwight N. Mason	Senior associate, Canada Project, Americas Program	Foreign service officer, 1962–91; served in Morocco, Colombia, and Ecuador, at the US Arms Control and Disarmament Agency, at the US State Dept, and at the US embassy in Ottawa; deputy chief of mission and minister in Ottawa; chair, US section, Permanent Joint Board on Defense, Canada-United States, 1994–2002

Name	Title	Government positions
Mary O. McCarthy	Visiting fellow, international security	Analyst and then manager, Directorate of Intelligence, CIA, holding positions in both African and Latin American analysis; senior policy adviser to the deputy director for science and technology, CIA; member, National Intelligence Council, from 1991; special assistant to the president and senior director for intelligence programs, National Security Council, to 2001
J. Kevin McLaughlin	National defence fellow, Technology and Public Policy Program	Special assistant to the deputy secretary of defense for space commission implementation
Phillip McLean	Senior associate, Americas Program	In the US embassy in Panama; led Office of Andean Affairs, State Dept, at time of intensified US counter-narcotics activities in the area in 1980s; in the US embassy in Bogotá, Colombia; deputy assistant secretary with responsibility for South America; assistant secretary for management at the Organization of American States; served as adviser to OAS secretary Cesar Gaviria until 1997
Derek J. Mitchell	Senior fellow, International Security Program	Assistant to the senior foreign policy adviser to Senator Edward M. Kennedy, 1986–88; special assistant for Asian and Pacific affairs, Office of the Secretary of Defense, 1997–2001; country director for Japan, 1997–98; senior country director for the Philippines, Indonesia, Malaysia, Brunei, and Singapore, 1998–99; director for regional security affairs, 1998–2000; senior country director for China, Taiwan, Mongolia, and Hong Kong, 2000–01
Joseph Montville	Senior associate	Diplomat for 23 years with posts in the Middle East and North Africa; chief of the Near East Division and director of the Office of Global Issues, Bureaus of Near Eastern and South Asian Affairs and Intelligence and Research, State Dept
J. Stephen Morrison	Executive director, HIV/AIDS Task Force; director, Africa Program	Senior staff member, House Foreign Affairs Subcommittee on Africa, 1987–91; democracy and governance adviser to the US embassies and USAID missions in Ethiopia and Eritrea, 1992–93; first deputy director, Office of Transition Initiatives, USAID; conceptualized and launched the office and created post-conflict programs in Angola and Bosnia, 1993–95; served on the Policy Planning Staff, Secretary of State, 1996–2000; responsible for African affairs and global foreign assistance issues; led the State Dept's initiative on illicit diamonds and chaired an inter-agency review of the US government's crisis humanitarian programs

Name	Title	Government positions
Clark A. Murdock	Senior adviser, international security	Worked on European nuclear issues in the office of the secretary of defense; employed at CIA; senior policy adviser to House Armed Services Committee chair Les Aspin, 1987–93; headed Policy Planning Staff, Office of the Undersecretary of Defense for Policy; deputy director, US Air Force's Headquarters Planning Function, 1995–2000
Richard W. Murphy	Senior associate	Legislative assistant and principal policy adviser to Senator Hugh Scott, 1964–69
William Perry	Senior associate, Americas Program	Chief staff member for Latin American matters, Senate Foreign Relations Committee; director of Latin American affairs, National Security Council; in charge of hemispheric issues for both the Bush-Quayle campaigns
Linnea P. Raine	Senior fellow, Transnational Threats Initiative	Coordinated foreign terrorism intelligence program, Dept of Energy; played a lead role in developing intelligence community inter-agency counter-terrorism initiatives; managed headquarters policy-development activities for protecting DOE's nuclear weapons complex from sub-national adversaries, 1979–85; coordinator, Washington-based planning staff, Sinai peacekeeping multinational force and observers
Joseph W. Ralston	Distinguished senior adviser	Entered the US Air Force in 1965; commander of Air Combat Command, Langley Air Force Base; deputy chief of staff for plans and operations, US Air Force; commander, Alaskan Command; director of operational requirements, Office of the Deputy Chief of Staff for Plans and Operations, US Air Force; vice-chair, Joint Chiefs of Staff, 1996–2000; supreme allied commander Europe, 2000–03; responsible for all US military activities in 89 countries and territories in Europe, Africa, and the Middle East, involving the activities of all US Army, Navy, Air Force, and Marine Corps forces
Mitchell B. Reiss	Senior associate, International Security Program	Special assistant to the national security adviser, White House, and consultant to the US Arms Control and Disarmament Agency, the State Dept, the Congressional Research Service, and the Los Alamos National Laboratory
Ben Rowswell	Pritzker International Fellow, Americas Program	Member of the Canadian foreign service; assignments included UN, Cairo, and Ottawa; adviser to the deputy prime minister of Canada; currently serving in Baghdad, Iraq
Theodore E. Russell	Adjunct fellow, Eastern Europe Project	First US ambassador to Slovakia, 1993–96; deputy director for European regional political and economic affairs, State Dept; deputy assistant administrator for international activities, Environmental Protection Agency

Name	Title	Government positions
Thomas M. Sanderson	Deputy director and fellow, Transnational Threats Initiative	Conducted extensive studies of terrorist groups and terrorism policy for the Defense Intelligence Agency
Teresita C. Schaffer	Director, South Asia Program	Deputy assistant secretary of state for South Asia, the senior South Asia position in the State Dept, 1989–92; US ambassador to Sri Lanka, 1992–95; director, Foreign Service Institute, 1995–97
Keith C. Smith	Senior associate, Europe Program	US ambassador to Lithuania, 1997–2000; in addition to other State Dept assignments, has served as director of policy for Europe, senior adviser to the deputy secretary of state for support of East European democracy (the SEED Program) and director of area studies at the Foreign Service Institute; retired from the State Dept in 2000
Yuki Tatsumi	Adjunct fellow, International Security Program	Special assistant for political affairs, Japanese embassy in Washington, DC, 1996–99
Lloyd R. Vasey	Founder and senior adviser for policy; vice-chair, Board of Governors Pacific Forum	Chief of strategic plans and policies, US Pacific Command Headquarters; secretary to the Joint Chiefs of Staff; deputy director, National Military Command Centre, Pentagon; chief of staff for commander, US 7th Fleet
Howard J. Wiarda	Senior associate, Americas Program	Adviser to four presidents and consultant to State Dept, Dept of Defense, and other government agencies
Joel S. Wit	Senior fellow, International Security Program	In the State Dept for 15 years in positions related to Northeast Asia, nuclear arms control, and weapons proliferation; senior adviser to Robert L. Gallucci, ambassador-at-large, in charge of policy toward North Korea, 1993–95
Anne A. Witkowsky	Senior fellow, Technology and Public Policy Program	In the Office of the Secretary of Defense, 1988–93; policy analyst in OSD's office of Russian, Ukrainian, and Eurasian affairs,1992–93; director for defense policy and arms control, National Security Council, from 1993
Lee S. Wolosky	Adjunct fellow, Russia/Eurasia Program	Director for transnational threats and director of the International Crime Group, National Security Council; coordinated aspects of the Bush administration's Russia policy review
Mona Yacoubian	Adjunct fellow, Middle East studies	North Africa analyst, Bureau of Intelligence and Research, State Dept, 1990–97

COUNCIL ON FOREIGN RELATIONS

Richard K. Betts	Adjunct senior fellow, national security studies	Staff member, Senate Select Committee on Intelligence, 1975–76; staff member, National Security Council, 1977
Jagdish N. Bhagwati	Senior fellow, international economics	Special adviser to the UN and the World Trade Organization

Name	Title	Government positions
Lee Feinstein	Senior fellow, US foreign policy; deputy director of studies	Official, Dept of Defense and State Dept; principal deputy director, Policy Planning Staff, State Dept; special assistant senior adviser for peacekeeping policy, Office of the Secretary of Defense
Stephen E. Flynn	Jeane J. Kirkpatrick Senior Fellow for National Security Studies	Director, Office of Global Issues, National Security Council, 1997; consultant on homeland security, US Commission on National Security (Hart-Rudman Commission), 2000–01
Alton Frye	Presidential senior fellow emeritus	Senate staff director, 1968–71; frequent consultant to both legislative and executive branches of government
Leslie H. Gelb	President emeritus	Executive assistant to Senator Jacob K. Javits, 1966–67; director of policy planning and arms control for international security affairs, Dept of Defense, 1967–69; assistant secretary of state for political-military affairs, 1977–79
James M. Goldgeier	Adjunct senior fellow	State Dept and National Security Council, 1995–96
Richard N. Haass	President	Various posts in Dept of Defense, 1979–80, and State Dept, 1981–85; special assistant to President George Bush, 1989–93; director for European affairs, National Security Council, 1993–94; US coordinator for policy toward the future of Afghanistan and lead US government official in support of the Northern Ireland peace process; director of policy planning, State Dept, and a principal adviser to Secretary of State Colin Powell to 2003
Charles A. Kupchan	Senior fellow and director of Europe studies	Director for European affairs, National Security Council, 1993–94
James M. Lindsay	Vice-president; Maurice R. Greenberg Chair; director of studies	Director, global issues and multilateral affairs, National Security Council, 1996–97
Princeton N. Lyman	Ralph Bunche Senior Fellow in Africa Policy Studies	In the State Dept and the Agency for International Development for over 30 years; US ambassador to South Africa and to Nigeria; director of the US Aid Mission to Ethiopia at USAID; assistant secretary of state for international organization affairs
David L. Phillips	Senior fellow and deputy director, Centre for Preventive Action	Senior adviser to the Bureau for European and Canadian Affairs, State Dept; foreign affairs expert to the Bureau for Near Eastern Affairs, State Dept, to 2003
Nancy E. Roman	Vice-president and director, Washington Program	Press secretary and legislative assistant for foreign affairs, office of Representative Clay Shaw, 1988–91
Gideon Rose	Managing editor, *Foreign Affairs*	Associate director for Near East and South Asian affairs, National Security Council, 1994–95

Name	Title	Government positions
Stephen R. Sestanovich	George F. Kennan Senior Fellow for Russian and Eurasian Studies	Senior legislative assistant for foreign policy, office of Senator Daniel Patrick Moynihan, 1980–81; member, Policy Planning Staff, State Dept, 1981–84; director of political-military affairs, National Security Council, 1984–85; senior director for policy development, NSC, 1985–87; ambassador-at-large and special adviser to the secretary for the newly independent states, State Dept, 1997–2001
Elizabeth D. Sherwood-Randall	Adjunct senior fellow, alliance relations	Deputy assistant secretary of defense for Russia, Ukraine, and Eurasia, 1994–96; chief foreign affairs and defense policy adviser to Senator Joe Biden
Gene B. Sperling	Director, Center for Universal Education	National economic adviser to President Clinton and head of the National Economic Council, 1996–2000

HERITAGE FOUNDATION

Name	Title	Government positions
Donald Abenheim	Research fellow	Associate director since 1993 of a State Dept program that provides international military education and training to officials serving in Central and Eastern Europe
Spencer Abraham	Distinguished visiting fellow	Co-chair, National Republican Congressional Committee, 1991–93, and deputy chief of staff to Vice-President Dan Quayle, 1990–91; senator for Michigan, 1995–2001; secretary of energy from 2001
Richard V. Allen	Senior fellow	Foreign policy coordinator to President Nixon, 1968; chief foreign policy adviser to Ronald Reagan, 1977–80; President Reagan's first national security adviser, 1981–82; currently member, Defense Policy Board Advisory Committee
Martin Anderson	Keith and Jan Hurlbut Senior Fellow	Special assistant to the US president, 1969–70; special consultant to the president for systems analysis, 1970–71; assistant to the president for policy development, 1981–82; member, Defense Manpower Commission; member, Committee on the Present Danger, 1977–91; member, President's Foreign Intelligence Advisory Board, 1982–85; member, President's Economic Policy Advisory Board, 1982–89; member, President's General Advisory Committee on Arms Control; member California governor's Council of Economic Advisers, 1993–98; chair, Congressional Policy Advisory Board, 1998–2001; member, Defense Policy Board, 2001; member, Defense Advisory Committee on Military Compensation, 2005
Bruce Berkowitz	Research fellow	Began career at the CIA; served as a professional staff member for the Senate Select Committee on Intelligence

Name	Title	Government positions
Peter Brookes	Senior fellow for national security affairs; director, Asian Studies Centre	Deputy assistant secretary of defense, Asian and Pacific affairs, office of Defense Secretary Donald Rumsfeld; professional staff member with the Republican staff of the Committee on International Relations in the House of Reps, focusing on East and South Asian affairs; intelligence officer with the Directorate of Operations, CIA, focusing on global political affairs, arms control, and weapons proliferation
Richard Burress	Senior fellow	Counsel to the House Republican leadership, 1965–69; deputy counsel to President Richard Nixon, 1969–71; assistant to President Gerald Ford, 1973–74
Dana Robert Dillon	Senior policy analyst, Asian Studies Center	In US Army for 20 years, 8 years as an infantry officer, 12 as a foreign area officer, specializing in Southeast Asia political and military events, and the last 6 at the Pentagon, where he specialized in army intelligence
Sidney Drell	Senior fellow	Member, President's Foreign Intelligence Advisory Board, 1993–2001; member, Commission on Maintaining US Nuclear Weapons Expertise and the President's Science Advisory Committee; consultant for the National Security Council, the US Arms Control and Disarmament Agency, and the Congressional Office of Technology Assessment
Harvey Feldman	Senior fellow in China policy, Asian Studies Centre	Served in Hong Kong for 8 years, Taiwan for 6, and Japan for 4; as member of the Policy Planning Staff, State Dept, helped to plan President Richard Nixon's first visit to China; continued involvement in relations with China as director of the Office of Republic of China Affairs
Edwin J. Feulner	President	Counsellor to vice-presidential candidate Jack Kemp, 1996; consultant for domestic policy to President Reagan; adviser to several government depts and agencies; member, President's Commission on White House Fellows, 1981–83; member, secretary of state's UNESCO Review Observation Panel, 1985–89; member, Carlucci Commission on Foreign Aid, 1983
Nile Gardiner	Fellow in Anglo-American security policy, Kathryn and Shelby Cullom Davis Institute for International Studies	Foreign policy researcher for British prime minister Margaret Thatcher; has advised executive branch of the US government on a range of key issues, from the role of international allies in post-war Iraq to US-British leadership in the war on terror

Name	Title	Government positions
James S. Gilmore III	Distinguished fellow	Virginia attorney general from 1993 and governor from 1997; chairs Congressional Advisory Panel to Assess Domestic Response Capabilities for Terrorism Involving Weapons of Mass Destruction, established by Congress in 1999
Charles Hill	Research fellow	Deputy assistant secretary for the Middle East; involved in the 1974 Panama Canal negotiations; member of the Policy Planning Staff as a speech writer for Secretary of State Henry Kissinger in 1975; appointed chief of staff of the State Dept in 1983; aide to Secretary of State George P. Shultz, 1985–89; special consultant on policy to the UN secretary-general, 1992–96
Stephen Johnson	Senior policy analyst, Kathryn and Shelby Cullom Davis Institute for International Studies	Former State Dept officer; worked at the Bureaux of Inter-American Affairs and Public Affairs
Edwin Meese III	Ronald Reagan Distinguished Fellow in Public Policy	Executive assistant and chief of staff to California governor Ronald Reagan, 1969–74; chief of staff and senior issues adviser for the Reagan-Bush Committee; council to the president, 1981–85; attorney general, 1985–88; member, National Security Council, Domestic Policy Council, and National Drug Policy Board
James Noyes	Research fellow	Deputy assistant secretary of defense for Near Eastern, African, and South Asian affairs (international security affairs), 1970–76
William Perry	Senior fellow	Undersecretary of defense for research and engineering, 1977–81; deputy secretary of defense, 1993–94; secretary of defense, 1994–97
Condoleezza Rice	Thomas and Barbara Stephenson Senior Fellow; on leave	Director of Soviet and East European affairs, National Security Council, 1989; special assistant to President George Bush for national security affairs and senior director for Soviet affairs, National Security Council; assistant to the President George W. Bush for national security affairs from 2000; secretary of state from 2005
Peter M. Robinson	Research fellow	Chief speech writer to Vice-President George Bush, 1982–83; special assistant and speech writer to President Ronald Reagan, 1983–88; wrote the historic Berlin Wall address in which Reagan called on Mikhail Gorbachev to "tear down this wall!"
Henry Rowen	Senior fellow	Deputy assistant secretary of defense for international security affairs, 1961–64; responsible for European policy issues; assistant secretary of defense for international security affairs, 1989–91
Ken Sheffer	Counsellor to the president	Member, National Security Council staff, 1981–82

Name	Title	Government positions
George Shultz	Thomas W. and Susan B. Ford Distinguished Fellow	Chair of President Ronald Reagan's Economic Policy Advisory Board; secretary of state, 1982–89
Kiron K. Skinner	W. Glenn Campbell Research Fellow	Member, Defense Secretary Donald Rumsfeld's Defense Policy Board
Baker Spring	F.M. Kirby Research Fellow in National Security Policy	Defense and foreign policy expert in the offices of two US senators
Richard Staar	Senior fellow	US Ambassador to the Mutual and Balanced Force Reduction negotiations in Vienna, Austria; a consultant to the Dept of Defense, US Arms Control and Disarmament Agency, 1983–87, and Sandia National Laboratories, Albuquerque, NM, 1991–92
John J. Tkacik Jr	Research fellow in China policy	In the State Dept from 1971; served in Taiwan and Hong Kong; directed junior officer training at the dept's Foreign Service Institute, 1986–89; deputy US consul general in Guangzhou, China, 1989–92; chief of China analysis, State Dept, from 1992
Malcolm Wallop	Chung Yu-Jung Fellow for Policy Studies	Senator, 1976–94
Pete Wilson	Senior research fellow	Mayor, San Diego, 1971–83; senator, 1983–91; governor of California, 1991–99
Charles Wolf Jr	Senior research fellow	With the State Dept, the Economic Cooperation Administration, and the Foreign Operations Administration
Larry M. Wortzel	Visiting fellow, Kathryn and Shelby Cullom Davis Institute for International Studies	Collected communications intelligence in the Army Security Agency; counter-intelligence officer and foreign intelligence collector for the Army Intelligence and Security Command; military attaché at the US embassy in China for the Defense Intelligence Agency; currently commissioner on the congressional US-China economic and security review commission, appointed by Speaker Hastert

Conferences, Workshops, Seminars, and Congressional Testimony on Missile Defence and the War on Terror Provided by Selected Think Tanks

Table A3.1
Conferences, workshops, and seminars on missile defence
and the war on terror held by selected think tanks

Year	Topic

AMERICAN ENTERPRISE INSTITUTE
2004
- Operation Iraqi Freedom: A Strategic Assessment (September)
- Sudan: Genocide, Terrorism, and America's National Interest (August)
- What's Next? Iraqis Take Control (June)
- Educating Iraq: New Schools and New Lessons for a New Nation (June)
- The Hand-off: Toward Iraqi Sovereignty (June)
- Naming Names: The Torturers of Saddam's Abu Ghraib and Their Place in the New Iraq (June)
- The Connection: How al-Qaeda's Collaboration with Saddam Hussein Has Endangered America (June)
- The Good, the Bad, and the Ugly: The Transfer of Sovereignty, the Future Iraqi Leadership, and the Real Meaning of Re-Baathification (May)
- The Bush Doctrine: Exceptions to the Rule? (May)
- Selling America: How Well Does US Government Broadcasting Work in the Middle East? (May)
- Winning Iraq: A Briefing on the Anniversary of the End of Major Combat Operations. With keynote address by Douglas Feith, undersecretary of defense for policy (May)
- United We Stand? Evaluating Sectarian Divides in Iraq (April)
- Address by Senator Fred Thompson: The War in Iraq, Terrorism, and the 2004 Presidential Election (April)
- Leave No Continent Behind: US National Security Interests in Africa (April)
- One Year Later: An Update on Iraq. Preceded by briefing with Spanish ambassador Javier Ruperez (March)
- Serious Intelligence Reform (March)
- Toward Democracy: A Briefing by Ahmad Chalabai, Member of the Iraqi Governing Council Delegation to the United Nations and United States (January)
- Trying Saddam Hussein: International Law, NGOs, and the Death Penalty (January)
- Saving Iraqi History: The Iraqi Memory Project (January)
- An End to Evil: How to Win the War on Terror (January)

2003
- Justice for Saddam, Justice for Iraq: War Crimes, Pursuing Justice, and Sovereignty. Special black coffee briefing on the Future of Iraq (December)
- The Future of Iraq. Black coffee briefing (December)
- Breaking the Axis of Evil, How to Finish the Job? (October)
- The Patriot Act and Civil Liberties: Too Far or Not Far Enough? (October)
- The Road Ahead: Aid to Iraq and Afghanistan (October)

Table A3.1 (continued)

Year	Topic
	• The Future of Iraq. Black coffee briefing (October) • New Information on Iraq. An AEI briefing (September) • Securing America in a Post-9/11 World (September) • Securing Our Liberty: How America Is Winning the War on Terror (August) • Prosecuting Terrorists: Civil or Military Courts? (August) • The Continuing War on Terror: An Address by the Vice-President (July) • Progress and Peril in Postwar Iraq: Rebuilding Post-Saddam Iraq (June) • Iraq: Lessons Learned (June) • Picking Up the Pieces: US-Russian Relations after Iraq (May) • America's Plan to Dispose of Weapons-Grade Plutonium: Atoms for Peace or a Gift to Terrorists? (April) • Iraq: What Lies Ahead? Black coffee briefings on the war in Iraq (April) • The Ripple Effects of the War against Iraq: Economy Watch (March) • The Road to War ... and Beyond. Special Friday briefing (March) • The Middle East in 2003: Towards a New Strategic Environment? (March) • Constitutional Issues and Federalism: Ethnicity and Justice in Post-Saddam Iraq (March) • The Road to War: Colin Powell before the UN (February) • Post-Saddam Iraq: Territorial Integrity, External Security, and Internal Security, Challenges for the Future (February)
2002	• Fighting Terror and Winning (November) • Demobilizing, Reforming, and Rebuilding the Iraqi Armed Forces and Dismantling and Transforming Iraq's Military Industries (November) • Reagan's War and the War on Terrorism: Applying the Lessons of the Cold War Victory (November) • The Day After: Planning for a Post-Saddam Iraq (October) • The War against the Terror Masters: How We Got There, Where We Are Now, How We'll Win (September) • Winning the War against Terror (April) • American Jihad: The Terrorists Living among Us (February) • What Should the United States Do about Iraq? (January)
2001	• Winning the War against Terrorism: Next Steps (November) • Bioterrorism and Pharmaceuticals: Looking Ahead (November) • The Battle for Ideas in the US War on Terrorism (October) • What If Congress Were Obliterated? (October) • Press Briefing on Terrorist Attacks (September) • Prospects for Prosperity and Freedom in the Middle East (February)
2000	• Study of Revenge: Saddam Hussein's Unfinished War against America (October) • Saddam's Iraq and the Next Administration: A Briefing by Ambassador Richard Butler (September) • Cyber Attacks and Critical Infrastructure: Where National Security and Business Converge (June)

Table A3.1 (continued)

Year	Topic

BROOKINGS INSTITUTION

2004
- Rebuilding Iraq's National Security Infrastructure (October)
- Iraq Update: The Prospects for Peace, Reconstruction, and the January Elections (October)
- A View from Jordan: Iraq, the Peace Process, and Arab Reform (September)
- Intelligence Reform in the Wake of the 9/11 Commission Report (September)
- Are We At a Turning Point in Iraq? (September)
- June 30 and Beyond: What Happens after the US Transfers Power to Iraq? (May)
- Winning the War in Iraq: A Strategy for Success on the Battlefront and the Home front. With Senator Joseph I. Lieberman (D-Conn) (April)
- The United States and Europe: One Year after the War in Iraq (April)
- Instability in Iraq: Initiatives in the Middle East Heartland: A Look at the Latest Iraqi Developments and a Preview of Upcoming Visits by Mubarak and Sharon (April)
- A New Partnership for the Greater Middle East: Combating Terrorism, Building Peace. With Senator Richard G. Lugar (March)
- Fighting Terror and the Spread of Weapons of Mass Destruction. With Senator Hillary Rodham Clinton (February)

2003
- First-Hand Views from Iraq (December)
- Iraq: The Road Ahead. A luncheon discussion with Hoshyar Zebari (October)
- The Future of American Operations in Iraq. With Senator John Kerry (September)
- The Israeli-Palestinian Crisis in the Shadow of Iraq. A luncheon discussion with Shimon Peres (September)
- The Media and the War on Terrorism (September)
- The Road Map and the Reconstruction of Iraq: Where Does the United States Go from Here? (September)
- Dealing With Iraq: Is U.S. Policy Working? With Senator Joseph R. Biden Jr (July)
- Assessing Media Coverage of the War in Iraq: Press Reports, Pentagon Rules, and Lessons for the Future (June)
- G-8 Preview: Bush and Allies to Discuss Repairing Their Rift and Rebuilding Iraq (May)
- Phase III in the War on Terrorism? Challenges and Opportunities (May)
- The United States and France after the War in Iraq (May)
- The Iraqi Marshlands: Can They Be Saved? Assessing the Human and Ecological Damage (May)
- The Quest for Stability in Iraq and the Middle East (April)
- Endgame in Iraq: Ending the War, Keeping the Peace, and Creating Regional Stability (April)
- The Bumpy Road to Baghdad: The Hard Fighting Leads to Political Reverberations at Home and Abroad (April)
- Repairing the Rift: The United Stated and Europe after Iraq (April)

Table A3.1 (continued)

Year	Topic
	• Mounting Concerns in Iraq: Street-to-Street Fighting, Humanitarian Diseases, More Military and Civilian Casualties (March)
	• On to Baghdad: What Will Coalition Forces Face Next? (March)
	• Brookings Experts Assess Early Phase of the War (March)
	• The Power and Peril of High Speed Warfare: Will an Attack on Iraq Be Clean and Quick or a Series of Nasty Surprises? (March)
	• The Iraq Crisis: What Does the World Think about the Diplomatic Wrangling at the UN? Release of New Study on Arab Attitudes toward War (March)
	• Iraq: Debating War, Preparing for Reconstruction (March)
	• Preparing for a War with Iraq: Coalition Building and Homeland Defense (February)
	• Brookings Experts Hold Conference Call with Reporters on Blix Report to UN Security Council (February)
	• Iraq Confrontation Splits Allies (February)
	• Preparing for War in Iraq: Protecting the Civilian Population (February)
	• Showdown with Iraq: Inauguration of Weekly Brookings Iraq Briefing (February)
	• UN Weapons Inspectors' Report (January)
	• Protecting the American Homeland: A Second Look at How We're Meeting the Challenge (January)
	• Jordan First? Internal Politics and the Approaching Iraq War (January)
2002	• Senator John Edwards to Outline His Agenda for Homeland Security (December)
	• Iraq's Declaration on Weapons of Mass Destruction (December)
	• The UN's Iraq Resolution (November)
	• Impact of US Foreign Policy on East Asia Since September 11 (October)
	• September 11, One Year Later: What's Ahead for an Altered Homeland (September)
	• Homeland Security: The White House Plan Explained and Examined (September)
	• Brookings Report Urges Congress to Revise President Bush's Homeland Security Proposal (July)
	• The War in Afghanistan: Is It Over? Did the United States Win? What's Next? (June)
	• Homeland Security: New Brookings Study Analyzes Bush Administration's Proposals, Recommends Additional Steps (April)
2001	• Stabilizing Afghanistan (December)
	• Countering Terrorism: The Fall of Kabul and Its Aftermath (November)
	• Coverage of the War on Terrorism: The Conflicting Needs of the Media and the Department of Defense (November)
	• Countering Terrorism: Developments at Home and Abroad (October)
	• The Campaign against Terrorism; Month Two: Three Fronts? Military, Diplomatic, Humanitarian (October)
	• America Strikes Back: What Comes Next? (October)
	• Countering Terrorism: Political and Economic Strategies (October)

Table A3.1 (continued)

Year	Topic

- America's Response to Terrorism: Reaction at Home and Abroad (September)
- The Response to Terror: America Mobilizes (September)
- President Bush's National Missile Defense Plan. Too Much, Too Little, or Just Right? (May)
- Terrorism and US Foreign Policy (April)
- Iraq and America: Ten Years after Desert Storm: What We Have Learned and What We Should Do Next (February)

CARNEGIE ENDOWMENT FOR INTERNATIONAL PEACE

2004
- Do Governments Have an Incentive to Fight Corruption? (October)
- Integrating Democracy Promotion into US Middle East Policy: A Discussion of Michele Dunne's Carnegie Paper on Promoting Reform in the Middle East (September)
- What War in the Philippines Should Have Taught George Bush (September)
- Political Reform in the GCC States. A two-day workshop held in Dubai with experts, researchers, and political activists from the GCC states, the US, and Europe (September)
- Strategic Asia and the War on Terrorism (September)
- The Problems and Prospects of the New Alaska Missile Interceptor Site (September)
- Beyond Mutual Assured Destruction: Reducing Russian-American Nuclear Tensions (May)
- WMD in Iraq: Evidence and Implications (February)

2003
- Iraq briefing with Jessica Mathews (November)
- Second Moscow International Non-proliferation Conference (September)
- Tactical Nuclear Weapons: Emergent Threats in an Evolving Security Environment (September)
- Beyond the Nuclear Shadow: A Phased Approach for Improving Nuclear Security (June)
- Hearing: WMD Threat Reduction: How Far Have We Come – Where Are We Heading? (May)

2002
- Assessing the Threats: 2002 Carnegie International Non-proliferation Conference (December)
- Iraq: A New Approach (September)
- The Sum of All Fears (June)
- Racing for the Bomb (May)
- US Nuclear Policy (February)

2001
- Missile Technology Control Regime: How Effective Is It? (June)
- Human Factor in Proliferation Official Release (May)
- Biological Weapons in the Twentieth Century (May)
- New Nuclear Posture for the United States (April)
- Plutonium Disposition Roundtable (March)

Table A3.1 (continued)

Year	Topic

2000
- Saddam's Bomb Maker (November)
- International Perspectives on National Missile Defense (September)
- National Missile Defense Debate (June)
- The Case against the National Missile Defense System: The Interactions (May)
- Non-proliferation Trust: An Update (February)

CENTER FOR STRATEGIC AND INTERNATIONAL STUDIES

2004
- Iraqi Prime Minister's Visit: A Preview. Experts to Analyze Prospects for Uniting, Stabilizing Iraq (September)
- Iraq's Journey toward Sovereignty: Former Interior Minister to Discuss Transition Challenges (June)
- Managing Expectations for NATO's Istanbul Summit (June)
- Afghanistan Moves Forward: President Hamid Karzai to Discuss US-Afghan Partnership (June)
- Afghanistan: The Security Outlook. Lt Gen. David W. Barno (May)
- DOD's Role in Pre-war Iraq Intelligence: Setting the Record Straight. Remarks by US Senator Jon Kyl (May)
- Winning the War on Terror. Jim Turner, ranking member of the House Select Committee on Homeland Security, released a plan on 27 April to eliminate the threat of al-Qaeda to the United States (April)
- Getting It Right in Iraq. United States Senator Joseph Biden (April)
- Afghanistan. Zalmay Khalilzad (April)

2003
- On Iraq: Fighting the Battle for Hearts and Minds: US Army Corps of Engineers and Iraqi Electrical Power (December)
- Retired Admiral Dennis Blair, former Pacific commander-in-chief, delivered the luncheon keynote address on US force restructuring at a conference on the impact of the war in Iraq on Asian security issues (July)
- Remarks on Iraq. Douglas J. Feith, undersecretary of defense for policy (July)
- Iraq: Still Failing to Disarm. Secretary of State Colin L. Powell (March)

2002
- Security and Defense: From Enduring Freedom to a New National Agenda (September)
- Forum on Emergency Management and First Responders. Bruce Baughman, director of FEMA's Office of National Preparedness (August)
- The Challenges of Maritime Security. Admiral Thomas H. Collins, commandant of the US Coast Guard (July)
- US Space-Based Military Capabilities. General Lance Lord, commander of the US Air Force Space Command (June)
- The United States, Europe, and the Muslim World: Revitalizing Relations after September 11th (May)

2001
- Strategy for Success: Fighting the War on Terrorism. John Hamre (November)
- Canada-US Security and Terrorism. Christopher Sands (November)
- Revitalizing US Nuclear Deterrence. Michele Flournoy (November)

Table A3.1 (continued)

Year	Topic

- US Biowarfare Defense: A Cost-Effective Strategy to Create Highly Efficacious Strategic Reserves of Therapeutics and Vaccines. Anne G. K. Solomon (October)
- Military Response to Terrorism. Jay Farrar (October)
- Pakistan and Afghanistan: What's Next? Teresita Schaffer (October)
- Terrorism Task Force Meeting. Kurt Campbell (October)
- Middle East Policy Forum. Robin Niblett (October)
- Nuclear Modernization Meeting. Michele Flournoy (October)
- Military Strategy Forum. Steve Cambone and Michele Flournoy (October)
- Campaign against Terrorism: Brzezinski, Scowcroft, Hamre Analyze Impact on Foreign Policy (September)
- Military Strategy Forum. Ike Skelton and Kurt Campbell (September)
- Congressional Fellows Security Policy Dialogue. John Hamre (July)
- Military Strategy Forum. Kurt Campbell (June)
- Technology and Security in a Networked World. Jim Lewis (March)

COUNCIL ON FOREIGN RELATIONS
2004
- An Update on the Global War on Terror with Donald Rumsfeld (October)
- Nuclear Terrorism: The Ultimate Preventable Catastrophe (September)
- A Meeting with Iraqi Interim Prime Minister Ayad Allawi (September)
- Securing America in an Age of Terrorism (September)
- America the Vulnerable: How Our Government is Failing to Protect us from Terrorism (July)
- The War on Terrorism (May)
- Iraq: The Test of a Generation (April)
- Power, Terror, Peace, and War: American's Grand Strategy in a World at Risk (April)
- Iraq: One Year After (March)
- Iraq: Intelligence, Facts, and Fantasies (March)
- After Iraq: New Direction for U.S. Intelligence and Foreign Policy (March)
- The Future of Iraq: A Debate (February)

HERITAGE FOUNDATION
2004
- The War on Terrorism and Beyond: Principles and Issues for the Quadrennial Defense Review (December)
- What's in a Name? The Debate over Words in the War on Terrorism (December)
- Global Energy Security in the Time of World Terror (November)
- Profiles in Terror: The Guide to Middle East Terrorist Organizations (October)
- Secure Flight: Screening for Terrorists on Passenger Planes (October)
- Regional and State Homeland Security Management: Is There a Need for a Regional Homeland Security Organization? (October)
- A Missile Defense for the US: How We Got Here and Where We Should Go (September)
- Following the Method of Mohammad: Jihadist Strategies in the War on Terror (August)
- Foreign Students and Homeland Security: Issues and Answers (August)

Table A3.1 (continued)

Year	Topic

- Grading the 9/11 Commission Report (July)
- Unearthing the Legacy of a Dictator: Iraq's Reign of Terror (July)
- Toward a Maritime Security Strategy for the 21st Century: Options and Solutions for Homeland Security (July)
- Building a Democratic Iraq: A Situation Report (June)
- The Connection: How al-Qaeda's Collaboration with Saddam Hussein Has Endangered America (June)
- Revitalizing the Iraqi Oil Industry: Implications for the World Oil Market (June)
- Remembering Saddam (May)
- Rumsfeld's War: The Untold Story of America's Anti-Terrorist Commander (May)
- Strategic Intelligence and Terrorism From the 1970s to Today: How We Got Here from There (May)
- A War of a Different Kind: Military Force and America's Search for Homeland Security (May)
- Protecting Civil Liberties and Fighting Terrorism: The USA Patriot Act (May)
- Al-Qaeda and Europe (April)
- International Cooperation and Its Role in Securing Our Homeland (March)
- Iraq: One Year Later (March)
- Defense Transformation: Efforts and Opportunities (February)
- Terrorist Hunter: An Undercover Look at Radical Islamic Groups Operating in America (January)

2003
- A Critique of the Markle Report on Trusted Information Networks for Homeland Security (December)
- Funding Evil: How Terror Is Financed and How to Stop it (December)
- Toward a National Strategy: Preparing for Catastrophic Bioterrorism (November)
- The Iraq War: A Military History (November)
- Airpower in Small Wars: Fighting Insurgents and Terrorists (October)
- Grading Progress in Homeland Security: Before and After 9/11 (October)
- Losing bin Laden (October)
- Reports from the Front Lines of Freedom: Iraq (October)
- Defense Transformation: The End of Term Report Card (October)
- Preparation and Response: Ensuring America's Recovery (September)
- Setting the Record Straight on Iraq (September)
- After 9/11 and the Iraq War: Oil Security in the Middle East (September)
- Securing America's Borders while Safeguarding Commerce (September)
- Leading the Department of Homeland Security: Progress and Challenges of Transition during the War on Terrorism (August)
- The Road to the Department of Homeland Security (July)
- Perspectives on President Bush's Missile Defense Directive (July)
- European Opposition to American Just War (April)
- The Role of State and Local Governments in Protecting Our Homeland (January)
- Harnessing Information Technology to Improve Homeland Security (January)

Table A3.1 (continued)

Year	Topic
2002	• The Future of a Post-Saddam Iraq: A Blueprint for American Involvement (September)
	• Consolidation in the Department of Homeland Security: Making the Case for First Responders (September)
	• The National Guard in Homeland Security: A View from Local, State, and Federal Leaders (September)
	• Pilots with Guns: The Last Line of Defense against Terrorists? (July)
	• Building Missile Defense in a Post-ABM Treaty World (June)
	• Bioterrorism 101: The Truth behind the Risk (June)
	• Breaking the Stovepipes: Improving Intelligence Sharing for Homeland Security (May)
	• Narco-Terror: The International Connection between Drugs and Terror (April)
	• America's Priority at the UN: Taking on Terror (February)
	• What Next in Afghanistan? (January)
	• A Homeland Security Agenda for 2002: Priorities from the State of the Union Address (January)
	• Defending the American Homeland: The Heritage Foundation Task Force on Homeland Security (January)
2001	• Victory: What Will It Take to Win? (December)
	• The American Family and the War on Terrorism (December)
	• The Diplomatic Front of the War on Terrorism: Can Promoting Democracy and Human Rights Tip the Scales? (November)
	• The Next Frontier: Combating Biological Warfare (November)
	• Securing the Skies? The Promise and Perils of the Aviation Security Act (October)
	• The War in Afghanistan (October)
	• Freedom and Security: Preserving Constitutional Liberties in Times of War (October)
	• The Road Ahead: Securing the Home Front in the 21st Century (October)
	• Defending America: A Homeland Defense Strategy for the 21st Century (October)
	• Global Terrorism: America Faces a New Reality (September)
	• The Price of Security: The Bush Administration's Case for Increasing Defense Spending (September)
	• A New Agenda for America: What We Must Do (September)
	• Osama bin Laden and the International Terrorist Threat (September)
	• Best of Intentions: America's Campaign against Strategic Weapons Proliferation (June)
	• Missile Defense and America's Allies (June)
	• Working Together: How the US and the UK Can Cooperate on Ballistic Missile Defense (February)

HIGH FRONTIER

2001	• Global Defense: Return from Indifference to Rational Assessment. Ambassador Henry F. Cooper (March)

Table A3.1 (continued)

Year	Topic

HOOVER INSTITUTION

2002
- Beyond the Color Line: New Perspectives on Race and Ethnicity in America (June)
- Our Brave New World: The Impact of September 11th (March)
- Conference on Technology for Preventing Terrorism (March)
- Managing American Power in a Dangerous World (February)

Table A3.2

Topics on missile defence and the war on terror presented to Congress by selected think tanks, January 2001 – January 2005

Think tank	Date	Topic discussed
SENATE COMMITTEE ON THE ARMED SERVICES		
AEI	Apr-04	Law of the Sea Treaty
Cato Institute	Apr-04	The Law of the Sea Treaty: Inconsistent with American Interests
CSIS	Aug-04	Implications for the Department of Defense and Military Operations of Proposals to Reorganize the United States Intelligence Community
	Feb-02	Iraq and the Risk Posed by Weapons of Mass Destruction
	Feb-02	Weapons of Mass Destruction Programs in Iraq
Heritage		none
Brookings		none
RAND	Nov-01	Terrorism: Current and Long-Term Threats
Hoover		none
Hudson		none
Center for Security Policy		none
CFR		none
PNAC		none
Carnegie Endowment		none
SENATE COMMITTEE ON FOREIGN RELATIONS		
AEI	July-03	Corruption in North Korea's Economy
	Mar-03	Testimony on North Korea
	Feb-02	How Do We Promote Democratization, Poverty Alleviation, and Human Rights to Build a More Secure World?
Cato Institute		none
CSIS	July-04	US Strategy in Pakistan: High Stakes, Heavy Agenda
	June-04	The Greater Middle East Initiative – Sea Island and Beyond
	May-04	The Crisis in Iraq – Oral Testimony
	May-04	The "Post-Conflict" Lessons of Iraq and Afghanistan
	Mar-04	The Terrorist Attacks in Madrid: Implications for Transatlantic Relations and Cooperation in the War on Terrorism
	Mar-04	Civilian Post-Conflict Reconstruction Capabilities
	Oct-03	Iranian Threats and US Policy: Finding the Proper Response

Table A3.2 (continued)

Think tank	Date	Topic discussed
	Oct-03	The Iran Nuclear Issue
	Sept-03	Iraq: Next Steps
	July-03	Iraq's Post-Conflict Reconstruction
	Mar-03	Regional Implications of the Changing Nuclear Equation on the Korean Peninsula
	Mar-03	Negotiations with North Korea
	Feb-03	Security and WMD Issues in a Post-Saddam Iraq
	May-01	The Threat of Bioterrorism and the Spread of Infectious Diseases
	Mar-01	Iraq and America's Foreign Policy Crisis in the Middle East
	Feb-01	NATO: Facing the Challenges Ahead
Brookings	July-04	North Korea: The Energy Component of a Theoretical Resolution
	Apr-04	Finding the Right Media for the Message in the Middle East
	Apr-04	Securing Iraq
	Apr-04	The Iraq Mission
	Mar-04	The Madrid Bombings and US Policy
	Feb-04	Getting the Arab-Israeli Peace Process Back on Track
	June-03	Political Classification and Social Structure in North Korea
	Oct-01	Contributions by Central Asian Nations to the Campaign against Terrorism
RAND	Mar-04	The Effect of the Terrorist Attacks in Spain on Transatlantic Cooperation in the War on Terror
	Sept-03	Next Steps in Iraq and Beyond
Hoover	May-04	Iraq: The Way Ahead
Hudson	July-03	Corruption in Economy of North Korea
	Apr-02	Non-proliferation Efforts in the Former Soviet Union
CFR	Mar-02	Reconstruction of Iraq
	July-02	Military Involvment in Iraq
	Mar-01	US Policy towards Iraq
	Feb-01	State of the NATO Alliance
Center for Security Policy	July-02	Nuclear Treaty with Russia
PNAC	Feb-02	Next Phase in the War on Terrorism
Carnegie Endowment	Apr-03	US Energy Security: Russia and the Caspian
	Apr-03	Global Energy Security
	Nov-02	The Treaty on Strategic Offensive Reductions
	May-02	Nuclear Posture Review
SENATE SELECT COMMITTEE ON INTELLIGENCE		
AEI		none
Cato Institute		none
CSIS	July-04	Reform and Reorganization of the US Intelligence Community
Brookings		none
RAND	Mar-02	The Lessons of 9/11

Table A3.2 (continued)

Think tank	Date	Topic discussed
Hoover		none
Hudson	Oct-02	Investigation of September 11
Center for Security Policy		none
CFR		none
PNAC		none
Carnegie Endowment		none
HOUSE COMMITTEE ON ARMED SERVICES		
AEI	Apr-04	Military Implications of the UN Conventions on the Law of the Sea
	Nov-03	US National Security Strategy
	Oct-03	Encouraging Developments among Iraq's Rising Majority
	Sept-02	The Need for UN Weapons Inspections in Iraq
	Sept-02	Testimony before the House International Relations Committee
	May-02	United States in the War on Terrorism
	Mar-01	US National Security
Cato Institute		none
CSIS	Aug-04	Implications of the Recommendations of the 9/11 Commission on the Department of Defense
	Oct-03	Reconstruction and Rehabilitation in Iraq
	June-01	Re-evaluating the Two Major Theater War Strategy
	Mar-01	A National Security Strategy for the New Century
Heritage	June-04	no title
	Mar-04	Combatting Weapons of Mass Destruction
	June-02	Yasser Arafat and the Palestinian Authority: Credible Partners for Peace
Brookings	June-04	Why the US Forces/Korea Plan Makes Sense
	Oct-03	A Relatively Promising Counter-insurgency War
	Oct-02	War against Saddam's Regime: Winnable but No Cakewalk
RAND	Mar-04	Towards an Expeditionary Army
Hoover		none
Hudson		none
CFR	May-02	Middle East View of Terrorism
	May-02	Support That Friendly Middle East Countries Are Providing to the US
Center for Security Policy	May-02	Middle East View of Terrorism
	May-02	Support That Friendly Middle East Countries Are Providing to the US
PNAC	Mar-01	US National Security Strategy
Carnegie Endowment	Oct-03	Reconstruction and Stability in Iraq
HOUSE SELECT COMMITTEE ON INTELLIGENCE		
AEI		Securing Freedom and the Nation: Collecting Intelligence under the Law

Table A3.2 (continued)

Think tank	Date	Topic discussed
Cato Institute		none
CSIS	Aug-04	9/11 Commission Recommendations: Counter-terrorism Analysis and Collection: The Requirement for Imagination and Creativity
Heritage	Sep-04	Statement
	Apr-03	Securing Freedom and the Nation: Collection Intelligence under the Law
Brookings	Aug-04	The 9/11 Commission's Findings: Sufficiency of Time, Attention, and Legal Authority
	Aug-04	The 9/11 Commission Report: Limitations of Imagination
RAND	Mar-02	The Lessons of 9/11
	Sept-01	Rethinking Terrorism in Light of a War on Terrorism
Hoover		none
Hudson		none
Center for Security Policy		none
CFR		none
PNAC		none
Carnegie Endowment		none

HOUSE COMMITTEE ON INTERNATIONAL RELATIONS

AEI	Mar-04	Domestic Determinants of Russia's Policy toward the United States
	Mar-04	US Russian Relations
Cato Institute		none
CSIS	July-04	Transatlantic Relations: A Post-Summit Assessment
	Feb-02	Russian Foreign Policy: Implications of Pragmatism for US Foreign Policy
	Nov-01	Russia's Foreign Policy Objectives and Opportunities
	Nov-01	Africa and the War on Global Terrorism
	Oct-01	Caucasus and Caspian Region: Understanding US Policy
	Oct-01	Iraq Policy Considerations after September 11
	Mar-01	America's Sudan Policy: A New Direction?
Heritage	May-04	The United Nations Convention on the Law of the Sea
	Feb-04	US Foreign Assistance after September 11
	Oct-03	Radical Islam and US Interests in Central Asia
Brookings	July-04	Transatlantic Relations: A Post-Summit Assessment
	Feb-04	US Foreign Assistance After September 11
	July-03	Central Asia: Terrorism, Religious Extremism, and Regional Instability
	June-03	The Future of Transatlantic Relations: A View from Europe
	June-03	Separatism and Terrorism in the Phillipines
	June-02	Oil Diplomacy
	Nov-01	The Future of Afghanistan
	Sept-01	The War on Terror and the Palestinian Intifada
	July-01	Silencing Central Asia: The Voice of Dissidents
RAND	June-04	Hong Kong at the Crossroads

Table A3.2 (continued)

Think tank	Date	Topic discussed
	Apr-02	The Future of NATO and Enlargement
	Dec-01	Southeast Asia after 9/11
Hoover	Sept-03	Russia's Transition to Democracy
Hudson	Apr-02	Future of NATO
CFR	Mar-04	US-Russia Relations
	May-02	The Future of US-Saudi Relations
	Apr-01	US-European Relations
Center for Security Policy	May-04	UN Law of the Sea
PNAC	May-02	The Future of US-Saudi Relations
Carnegie Endowment	July-04	US Economic Aid to Egypt
	Oct-03	Terrorism, Extremism, and Regional Stability in Central Asia
	June-03	US Non-proliferation Policy after Iraq
	Feb-02	US Russian Relations after September 11, 2001

SOURCE: LexisNexis®.

Print Media Coverage, Television Exposure, and Congressional Testimony, January 2001 – January 2005

Table A4.1
Print media coverage of selected think tanks: *Christian Science Monitor*

Subject

Think tank	Iraq	Afghani-stan	9/11	al-Qaeda	Terrorism	Missile defense	Total	Percent-age
PNAC	5	2	3	1	3	0	14	0.59
Center for Security Policy	6	2	1	1	4	2	16	0.68
Hoover	16	3	9	3	14	4	49	2.07
Hudson	12	3	19	5	18	6	63	2.66
AEI	49	11	30	12	42	8	152	6.42
Cato Institute	42	20	32	16	48	2	160	6.76
Heritage	57	23	38	16	23	12	169	7.14
Carnegie Endowment	75	32	30	26	70	16	249	10.52
CSIS	102	37	51	37	87	5	319	13.47
Council on Foreign Relations	108	50	57	41	92	3	351	14.82
RAND	59	50	75	68	96	6	354	14.95
Brookings	143	47	79	33	145	25	472	19.93
Total							2,368	

SOURCE: LexisNexis®.
NOTE: Because of similarity of search criteria, there is likely some article overlap in the numbers.

Table A4.2
Print media coverage of selected think tanks: *New York Times*

Think tank	Iraq	Afghani-stan	9/11	al-Qaeda	Terrorism	Missile defense	Total	Percent-age
Center for Security Policy	3	0	0	0	1	4	8	0.21
Hudson	8	1	7	2	10	2	30	0.77
PNAC	17	6	9	4	10	4	50	1.28
Cato Institute	24	12	41	10	44	5	136	3.49
Hoover	42	11	28	11	41	6	139	3.57
Heritage	53	17	35	6	60	4	175	4.49
Carnegie Endowment	60	22	39	17	68	26	232	5.95
RAND	104	64	137	45	179	26	555	14.23
AEI	119	34	76	29	120	8	386	9.90
CSIS	124	60	58	29	136	18	425	10.90
Council on Foreign Relations	246	102	140	72	262	24	846	21.70
Brookings	247	106	164	66	291	43	917	23.52
Total							3,899	

SOURCE: LexisNexis®.

NOTE: Because of similarity of search criteria, there is likely some article overlap in the numbers.

Table A4.3
Print media coverage of selected think tanks: *USA Today*

Think tank	Iraq	Afghani-stan	9/11	al-Qaeda	Terrorism	Missile defense	Total	Percent-age
PNAC	1	2	2	0	3	1	9	0.41
Center for Security Policy	5	1	1	0	3	2	12	0.54
Hudson	9	6	7	3	10	4	39	1.76
Hoover	16	11	14	5	28	2	76	3.43
Carnegie Endowment	37	17	22	13	34	12	135	6.09
RAND	25	20	37	15	57	1	155	6.99
Cato Institute	34	27	29	16	50	6	162	7.30
AEI	71	20	44	14	63	10	222	10.01
Heritage	48	29	45	20	72	16	230	10.37
CSIS	104	46	39	26	89	10	314	14.16
Council on Foreign Relations	104	49	50	37	93	5	338	15.24
Brookings	138	75	106	28	161	18	526	23.72
Total							2,218	

SOURCE: LexisNexis®.

NOTE: Because of similarity of search criteria, there is likely some article overlap in the numbers.

Table A4.4
Print media coverage of selected think tanks: *Wall Street Journal*

Think tank	Iraq	Afghani-stan	9/11	al-Qaeda	Terrorism	Missile defense	Total	Percent-age
PNAC	2	0	1	1	1	0	5	0.34
Center for Security Policy	5	0	2	1	6	2	16	1.09
Hudson	12	4	9	2	14	0	41	2.79
Carnegie Endowment	12	12	10	7	18	10	69	4.70
Cato Institute	25	6	21	3	26	0	81	5.52
Heritage	25	12	22	6	34	1	100	6.82
Hoover	38	18	25	13	32	1	127	8.66
Brookings	51	15	37	12	40	9	164	11.18
CSIS	60	25	33	12	59	4	193	13.16
AEI	62	18	43	18	60	7	208	14.18
Council on Foreign Relations	64	16	42	25	63	2	212	14.45
RAND	41	23	98	13	73	3	251	17.11
Total							1,467	

SOURCE: LexisNexis®.
NOTE: Because of similarity of search criteria, there is likely some article overlap in the numbers.

Table A4.5
Print media coverage of selected think tanks: *Washington Post*

Think tank	Iraq	Afghani-stan	9/11	al-Qaeda	Terrorism	Missile defense	Total	Percent-age
Center for Security Policy	6	3	8	3	10	3	33	0.61
Hudson	21	10	19	4	30	6	90	1.67
PNAC	26	11	14	11	25	6	93	1.73
Hoover	33	10	21	8	33	5	110	2.05
Cato Institute	43	21	50	14	81	6	215	4.00
Heritage	66	28	60	10	96	20	280	5.21
Carnegie Endowment	167	77	80	38	157	39	558	10.38
AEI	190	44	111	40	161	17	563	10.47
RAND	107	75	132	68	201	15	598	11.12
CSIS	188	90	104	79	206	21	688	12.80
Council on Foreign Relations	213	92	124	76	214	23	742	13.80
Brookings	342	188	298	94	445	40	1,407	26.17
Total							5,377	

SOURCE: LexisNexis®.
NOTE: Because of similarity of search criteria, there is likely some article overlap in the numbers.

Table A4.6
Print media coverage of selected think tanks: *Washington Times*

Think tank	Iraq	Afghani-stan	9/11	al-Qaeda	Terrorism	Missile defense	Total	Percent-age
PNAC	9	7	8	3	10	1	38	0.70
Carnegie Endowment	47	27	23	13	62	12	184	3.38
Hudson	42	26	36	16	76	12	208	3.82
RAND	55	28	49	23	85	12	252	4.63
Council on Foreign Relations	118	49	56	37	122	14	396	7.27
Cato Institute	90	35	99	28	188	12	452	8.30
Center for Security Policy	122	25	69	42	167	53	478	8.78
AEI	142	54	97	33	183	11	520	9.55
CSIS	164	69	77	48	177	15	550	10.10
Brookings	133	64	102	38	188	34	559	10.26
Hoover	179	72	114	44	206	20	635	11.66
Heritage	295	136	186	92	400	66	1,175	21.57
Total							5,447	

SOURCE: LexisNexis®.
NOTE: Because of similarity of search criteria, there is likely some article overlap in the numbers.

Table A4.7
Television exposure of selected think tanks: ABC

Think tank	Iraq	Afghani-stan	9/11	al-Qaeda	Terrorism	Missile defense	Total	Percent-age
CSIS	0	0	0	0	0	0	0	0.00
Hudson	0	0	0	0	0	0	0	0.00
Hoover	0	0	0	0	0	0	0	0.00
Cato Institute	1	0	0	0	0	0	1	0.41
PNAC	1	0	0	0	0	0	1	0.41
Heritage	1	0	0	0	0	1	2	0.82
Center for Security Policy	2	0	0	0	0	0	2	0.82
AEI	9	1	0	0	3	0	13	5.31
Carnegie Endowment	17	0	0	1	5	2	25	10.20
RAND	15	2	1	4	13	0	35	14.29
Council on Foreign Relations	33	4	1	3	15	1	57	23.27
Brookings	57	15	7	6	21	3	109	44.49
Total							245	

SOURCE: Vanderbilt Television News Archive.

Table A4.8
Television exposure of selected think tanks: CBS

Think tank	Iraq	Afghani-stan	9/11	al-Qaeda	Terrorism	Missile defense	Total	Percent-age
						Subject		
CSIS	0	0	0	0	0	0	0	0.00
PNAC	0	0	0	0	0	0	0	0.00
Hudson	0	0	0	0	0	0	0	0.00
Hoover	0	0	0	0	0	0	0	0.00
AEI	1	0	0	0	0	0	1	0.88
Cato Institute	1	0	0	0	1	0	2	1.75
Center for Security Policy	1	1	0	0	2	0	4	3.51
Heritage	4	1	2	1	2	0	10	8.77
Council on Foreign Relations	6	1	1	2	5	0	15	13.16
Carnegie Endowment	9	0	3	2	8	2	24	21.05
Brookings	16	3	1	2	6	1	29	25.44
RAND	5	1	2	9	11	1	29	25.44
Total							114	

SOURCE: Vanderbilt Television News Archive.

Table A4.9
Television exposure of selected think tanks: CNN

Think tank	Iraq	Afghani-stan	9/11	al-Qaeda	Terrorism	Missile defense	Total	Percent-age
						Subject		
PNAC	0	0	0	0	0	0	0	0.00
Hudson	0	0	0	0	0	0	0	0.00
Hoover	0	1	0	0	0	0	1	0.49
AEI	3	0	0	0	0	0	3	1.48
Cato Institute	1	0	0	0	2	0	3	1.48
Center for Security Policy	1	0	0	1	2	0	4	1.97
CSIS	2	3	0	1	6	0	12	5.91
Heritage	5	2	2	0	6	1	16	7.88
Council on Foreign Relations	11	1	2	1	4	0	19	9.36
Carnegie Endowment	12	7	1	4	0	3	37	18.23
RAND	5	3	1	14	17	0	40	19.70
Brookings	38	6	4	6	13	1	68	33.50
Total							203	

SOURCE: Vanderbilt Television News Archive.

Table A4.10
Television exposure of selected think tanks: NBC

Think tank	Iraq	Afghanistan	9/11	al-Qaeda	Terrorism	Missile defense	Total	Percentage
Center for Security Policy	0	0	0	0	0	0	0	0.00
CSIS	0	0	0	0	0	0	0	0.00
PNAC	0	0	0	0	0	0	0	0.00
Hudson	0	0	0	0	0	0	0	0.00
Hoover	1	0	0	0	1	0	2	1.16
Heritage	1	0	0	0	2	0	3	1.74
Cato Institute	1	0	0	1	1	0	3	1.74
AEI	4	1	0	1	1	0	7	4.07
Carnegie Endowment	4	0	0	3	2	1	10	5.81
RAND	5	1	3	6	10	0	25	14.53
Council on Foreign Relations	15	2	2	1	12	0	32	18.60
Brookings	41	7	5	9	28	0	90	52.33
Total							172	

SOURCE: Vanderbilt Television News Archive.

Fig. A4.1
Testimony before the Senate Committee on Armed Services
by selected think tanks (percentages)

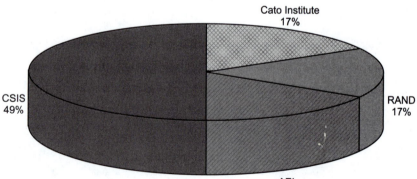

Fig. A4.2
Testimony before the Senate Committee on Foreign Relations
by selected think tanks (percentages)

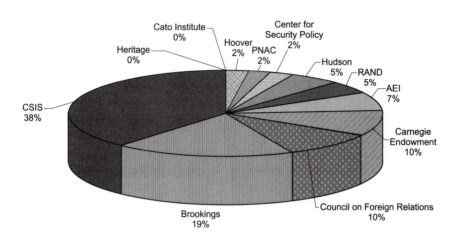

Fig. A4.3
Testimony before the Senate Select Committee on Intelligence
by selected think tanks (percentages)

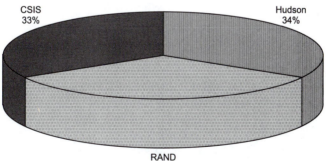

Fig. A4.4
Testimony before the House Committee on Armed Services
by selected think tanks (percentages)

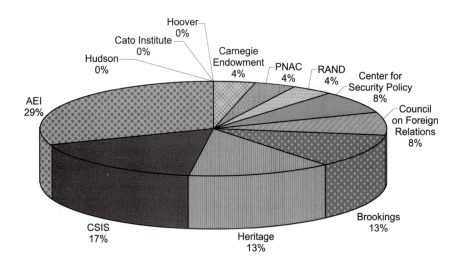

Fig. A4.5
Testimony before the House Committee on Intelligence
by selected think tanks (percentages)

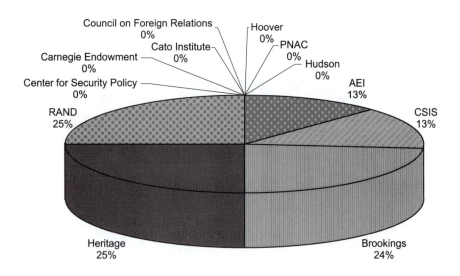

Fig. A4.6
Testimony before the House Committee on International Relations
by selected think tanks (percentages)

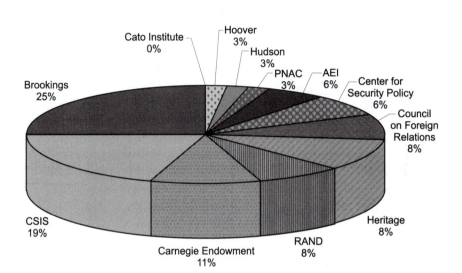

Selected Publications on Missile Defence and the War on Terror from American Think Tanks

Journal articles not available from the institute's Web site may be accessible online from a local library.

AMERICAN ENTERPRISE INSTITUTE
Missile Defense

Kirkpatrick, Jeane J. "Target America: The Need for a Missile Defense System." American Enterprise Institute, 1 January 2000. Available at: http://www.aei.org/publications/pubID.10058,filter.all/pub_detail.asp.

Perle, Richard. "A Better Way to Build a Missile Defense." American Enterprise Institute, 13 July 2000. Available at: http://www.aei.org/publications/pubID.11754,filter.all/pub_detail.asp.

War on Terror

DeMuth, Christopher. "Guns, Butter, and the War on Terror." American Enterprise Institute, 29 April 2004. Available at: http://www.aei.org/publications/pubID.20391,filter.all/pub_detail.asp.

Donnelly, Thomas. "Iraq Is the Central Front." American Enterprise Institute, 24 September 2003. Available at: http://www.aei.org/publications/pubID.19234,filter.all/pub_detail.asp.

– "Mind the Gap." American Enterprise Institute, 10 June 2004. Available at: http://www.aei.org/publications/pubID.20685,filter.all/pub_detail.asp.

– "Naming the Enemy." American Enterprise Institute, 5 August 2004. Available at: http://www.aei.org/publications/pubID.21022,filter.all/pub_detail.asp.

– "The Top Ten Questions for the Post-9/11 World." American Enterprise Institute, 23 July 2004. Available at: http://www.aei.org/publications/pubID.20965,filter.all/pub_detail.asp.

– "What's Next? Preserving American Primacy, Institutionalizing Unipolarity." American Enterprise Institute, 22 April 2003.

Donnelly, Thomas, and Vance Serchuk. "Fighting a Global Counterinsurgency." American Enterprise Institute, 4 December 2003. Available at: http://www.aei.org/publications/pubID.19546,filter.all/pub_detail.asp.

Frum, David, and Richard Perle. "Beware the Soft-Line Ideologues." American Enterprise Institute, 8 January 2004. Available at: http://www.aei.org/publications/pubID.19702,filter.all/pub_detail.asp.

Gingrich, Newt. "Principles for Victory." American Enterprise Institute, 1 November 2001. Available at: http://www.aei.org/publications/pubID.13273,filter.all/pub_detail.asp.

Ledeen, Michael A. *The War against the Terror Masters: Why It Happened, Where We Are Now, How We'll Win.* New York: St. Martin's Press, 2002.

Zinsmeister, Karl. "The Election's Over–Now Fight the War." *The American Enterprise (Online)*, December 2004. Available at: http://www.taemag.com/issues/articleid.18290/article_detail.asp.

BROOKINGS INSTITUTION

Missile Defense

Lindsay, James M., and Michael E. O'Hanlon. "Defending America: A Plan for a Limited National Missile Defense." *Brookings Policy Brief*, no. 70 (February 2001). Available at: http://www.brookings.edu/comm/policybriefs/pb70.htm.

O'Hanlon, Michael E. "Beyond Missile Defense: Countering Terrorism and Weapons of Mass Destruction." *Brookings Policy Brief*, no. 86 (August 2001). Available at: http://www.brookings.edu/comm/policybriefs/pb86.htm.

War on Terror

Gordon, Philip H., and Michael E. O'Hanlon. "Should the War on Terrorism Target Iraq? Implementing a Bush Doctrine on Deterrence." *Brookings Policy Brief*, no. 93 (January 2002). Available at: http://www.brookings.edu/comm/policybriefs/pb93.htm.

Nayak, Polly. "Reducing Collateral Damage to Indo-Pakistani Relations from the War on Terrorism." *Brookings Policy Brief*, no. 107 (September 2002). Available at: http://www.brookings.edu/comm/policybriefs/pb107.htm.

Rice, Susan E. "The New National Security Strategy: Focus on Failed States." *Brookings Policy Brief*, no. 107 (February 2003). Available at: http://www.brookings.edu/comm/policybriefs/pb116.htm.

CARNEGIE ENDOWMENT FOR INTERNATIONAL PEACE

Missile Defense

Lewis, George, et al. "National Missile Defense: An Indefensible System." *Foreign Policy*, no. 117 (winter 1999/2000): 120.

War on Terror

Abramowitz, Morton. "Dear Dubya." *Foreign Policy*, no. 130 (May/June 2002): 78.

Burke, Jason. "Al Qaeda." *Foreign Policy*, no. 142 (May/June 2004): 18–26.

Cannistraro, Vincent. "Terror's Undiminished Threat." *Foreign Policy*, no. 137 (July/August 2003): 69.

Deutch, John, and Jeffrey H Smith. "Smarter Intelligence." *Foreign Policy*, no. 128 (January/February 2002): 64.

Homer-Dixon, Thomas. "The Rise of Complex Terrorism." *Foreign Policy*, no. 128 (January/February 2002): 52.

Hutchings, Robert L. "X + 9/11." *Foreign Policy*, no. 143 (July/August 2004): 70.

Krasner, Stephen D. "The Day After." *Foreign Policy*, no. 146 (January/February 2005): 68.

Lieven, Anatol. "Fighting Terrorism: Lessons from the Cold War." *Carnegie Policy Brief*, no. 7 (October 2001). Available at: http://www.ceip.org/files/pdf/Lieven-7.pdf.

Naim, Moises. "Collateral Damage." *Foreign Policy*, no. 127, (November/December 2001): 108.

– "Devour and Conquer." *Foreign Policy*, no. 145 (November/December 2004): 96.

Naim, Moises, and Michael O'Hanlon. "Reinventing War." *Foreign Policy*, no. 127 (November/December 2001): 30.

Nye, Joseph S., Jr. "The Velvet Hegemon." *Foreign Policy*, no. 136 (May/June 2003): 74.

Obaid, Nawaf E. "In Al-Saud We Trust." *Foreign Policy*, no. 128 (January/February 2002): 72.

Ottaway, Marina, and Thomas Carothers. "Middle East Democracy." *Foreign Policy*, no. 145 (November/December 2004): 22.

Rogoff, Kenneth. "The Cost of Living Dangerously." *Foreign Policy*, no. 145 (November/December 2004): 70.

Rothkopf, David J. "Business versus Terror." *Foreign Policy*, no. 130 (May/June 2002): 56.

Sprinzak, Ehud. "The Lone Gunmen." *Foreign Policy*, no. 127 (November/December 2001): 72.

Takeyh, Ray. "Two Cheers from the Islamic World." *Foreign Policy*, no. 12 (January/February 2002): 70.

Talbott, Strobe. "The Other Evil." *Foreign Policy* no. 127 (November/December 2001): 75.

Tellis, Ashley J. *Assessing America's War on Terror: Confronting Insurgency, Cementing Primacy.* Seattle, WA: The National Bureau of Asian Research in cooperation with the Carnegie Endowment for International Peace, 2004. Available at: http://www.carnegieendowment.org/files/ NBRAnalysis-Tellis_December2004.pdf.

CATO INSTITUTE

Missile Defense

Eland, Ivan. "Let's Make National Missile Defense Truly 'National.'" *Cato Foreign Policy Briefing Paper*, no. 58 (16 March 1999). Available at: http://www.cato.org/pubs/fpbriefs/fpb58.pdf.

Eland, Ivan, and Daniel Lee. "The Rogue State Doctrine and National Missile Defense." *Cato Foreign Policy Briefing Paper*, no. 65 (29 March 2001). Available at: http://www.cato.org/pubs/fpbriefs/fpb65.pdf.

Forden, Geoffrey. "Reducing a Common Danger: Improving Russia's Early-Warning System." *Cato Policy Analysis*, no. 399 (3 May 2001). Available at: http://www.cato.org/pubs/pas/pa399.pdf.

Peña, Charles V. "Arms Control and Missile Defense: Not Mutually Exclusive." *Cato Policy Analysis*, no. 376 (26 July 2000). Available at: http://www.cato.org/pubs/pas/pa376.pdf.

– "From the Sea: National Missile Defense Is Neither Cheap Nor Easy." *Cato Foreign Policy Briefing Paper*, no. 60 (6 September 2000). Available at:http://www.cato.org/pubs/fpbriefs/fpb60.pdf.

– "Missile Defense: Defending America or Building Empire?" *Cato Foreign Policy Briefing Paper*, no. 77 (28 May 2003). Available at: http://www.cato.org/pubs/fpbriefs/fpb77.pdf.

– "Theater Missile Defense: A Limited Capability Is Needed." *Cato Policy Analysis*, no. 309 (22 June 1998). Available at: http://www.cato.org/pubs/pas/pa-309.html.

Peña, Charles V., and Barbara Conry. "National Missile Defense: Examining the Options." *Cato Policy Analysis*, no. 337 (16 March 1999). Available at: http://www.cato.org/pubs/pas/pa337.pdf.

Peña, Charles V., and Edward L. Hudgins. "Should the United States 'Weaponize' Space? Military and Commercial Implicatons." *Cato Policy Analysis*, no. 427 (18 March 2002). Available at: http://www.cato.org /pubs/pas/pa427.pdf.

War on Terror

Atal, Subodh. "Extremist, Nuclear Pakistan: An Emerging Threat?" *Cato Policy Analysis*, no. 472 (5 March 2003). Available at: http://www.cato.org/pubs/pas/pa472.pdf.

Bandow, Doug. "Befriending Saudi Princes a High Price for a Dubious Alliance." *Cato Policy Analysis*, no. 428 (20 March 2002). Available at: http://www.cato.org/pubs/pas/pa428.pdf.

– "Fighting the War against Terrorism: Elite Forces, Yes; Conscripts, No." *Cato Institute Policy Analysis*, no. 430 (10 April 2002). Available at: http://www.cato.org/pubs/pas/pa430.pdf.

Dempsey, Gary T. "Old Folly in a New Disguise: Nation Building to Combat Terrorism." *Cato Policy Analysis*, no. 429 (21 March 2002). Available at: http://www.cato.org/pubs/pas/pa429.pdf.

Eland, Ivan. "Robust Response to 9/11 Is Needed but Poking the Hornets' Nest Is Ill-Advised." *Cato Foreign Policy Briefing Paper*, no. 69 (18 December 2001). Available at: http://www.cato.org/pubs/fpbriefs/fpb69.pdf.

– "War against Terror Expands Excessively." *A Cato Daily Commentary*, 30 January 2002. Available at: http://www.cato.org/current/terrorism/pubs/eland-020130.html.

Hadar, Leon T. "Pakistan in America's War against Terrorism: Strategic Ally or Unreliable Client?" *Cato Policy Analysis*, no. 436 (8 May 2002). Available at: http://www.cato.org/pubs/pas/pa436.pdf.

Harris, James W. "Building Leverage in the Long War: Ensuring Intelligence Community Creativity in the Fight against Terrorism." *Cato Policy Analysis*, no. 439 (16 May 2002). Available at: http://www.cato.org/pubs/pas/pa439.pdf.

Healy, Gene. "Deployed in the U.S.A.: The Creeping Militarization of the Home Front." *Cato Policy Analysis*, no. 503 (17 December 2003). Available at: http://www.cato.org/pubs/pas/pa503.pdf.

Peña, Charles V. "The Anti-Terrorism Coalition: Don't Pay an Excessive Price." *Cato Foreign Policy Briefing Paper*, no. 68 (11 December 2001). Available at: http://www.cato.org/pubs/fpbriefs/fpb68.pdf.

– "Bush's National Security Strategy Is a Misnomer." *Cato Policy Analysis*, no. 496 (30 October 2003). Available at: http://www.cato.org/pubs/pas/pa496.pdf.

Salhani, Claude. "The Syria Accountability Act: Taking the Wrong Road to Damascus." *Cato Policy Analysis*, no. 512 (18 March 2004). Available at: http://www.cato.org/pubs/pas/pa512.pdf.

CENTER FOR SECURITY POLICY

Missile Defense

Center for Security Policy. "Anti-anti-missile Defense." 5 April 2004. Available at: http://www.centerforsecuritypolicy.org/ index.jsp?section=papers&code=04-D_15.

– "The Bush Nuclear Posture Review: Adults at Work on Restoring the Credibility of America's Deterrent." 11 March 2002. Available at: http://www.centerforsecuritypolicy.org/ index.jsp?section=papers&code=02-D_14.

– "Decision to Cancel Navy Missile Defense Program Should Be Reversed and New Management, Willing to Deploy Sea-Based Systems, Hired." 17 December 2001. Available at: http://www.centerforsecuritypolicy.org/index.jsp?section=papers&code=01-D_ 80.

– "Empty Words?" 14 June 2004. Available at: http://www.centerforsecuritypolicy.org/index.jsp?section=papers&code=04-D_ 27.

– "Exiting the A.B.M. Treaty –A Model for Dealing with Iraq." 9 September 2002. Available at: http://www.centerforsecuritypolicy.org /index.jsp?section=papers&code=02-D_45.

– "Get On with It: Time to Deploy Sea-Based Missile Defenses." 27 November 2002. Available at: http://www.centerforsecuritypolicy.org/ index.jsp?section=papers&code=02-F_43.

– "Go Navy Missile Defense!" 28 February 2005. Available at: http:// www.centerforsecuritypolicy.org/index.jsp?section=papers&code=05-D_10.

– "Hail to the Chief! Bush Withdraws from the ABM Treaty and Commitment to Deploy Defenses ASAP: Second Successful Navy Intercept Shows the Way Ahead." 14 June 2002. Available at: http://www.centerforsecuritypolicy.org/ index.jsp?section=papers&code=02-D_29.

– "Hail to the Chief: George W. Bush Demonstrates Couragerous, Visionary Leadership –Again –by Jettisoning A.B.M. Treaty." 13 December 2001. Available at: http://www.centerforsecuritypolicy.org/ index.jsp?section=papers&code=01-F_84.

– "In Memoriam of an Unsung Hero of the Cold War: William T. Lee." 4 November 2002. Available at: http://www.centerforsecuritypolicy.org/ index.jsp?section=papers&code=02-D_57.

- "It's Over: The A.B.M. Treaty Is History; Now Let's Get On with Deploying Missile Defenses!" 13 June 2002. Available at: http://www.centerforsecuritypolicy.org/ index.jsp?section=papers&code=02-F_22.
- "It's Time to 'Move Beyond' the A.B.M. Treaty." 4 December 2001. Available at: http://www.centerforsecuritypolicy.org/ index.jsp?topic=missile&section=center.
- "Make Missile Defense Happen." 11 June 2002. Available at: http:// www.centerforsecuritypolicy.org/index.jsp?section=papers&code=02-D_27.
- "National Security Alert for the Week of December 17, 2001." 17 December 2001. Available at: http://www.centerforsecuritypolicy.org/ index.jsp?section=papers&code=01-A_37.
- "National Security Alert for the Week of January 28, 2002." 28 January 2002. Available at: http://www.centerforsecuritypolicy.org/ index.jsp?section=papers&code=02-A_02.
- "Navy Missile Defense Success Offers Bush a Chance to Issue a Challenge for the History Books." 28 January 2002. Available at: http://www.centerforsecuritypolicy.org/ index.jsp?section=papers&code=02-D_05.
- "The New Gender Gap: American Women Even More Supportive than Men of Need for Missile Defense." Online. 28 November 2001. Available at: http:// www.centerforsecuritypolicy.org/index.jsp?section=papers&code=01-F_82.
- "The 'Next War': Will Carl Levin Be Allowed to Leave America Vulnerable to Missile Attack?" 20 May 2002. Available at: http:// www.centerforsecuritypolicy.org/index.jsp?section=papers&code=02-D_24.
- "President Bush Applauded for Ending the A.B.M. Treaty, Urged to Move to Deploy Missile Defenses A.S.A.P." 21 December 2001. Available at: http:// www.centerforsecuritypolicy.org/index.jsp?section=papers&code=01-F_87.
- "Reagan's Vision." 21 March 2003. Available at: http:// www.centerforsecuritypolicy.org/index.jsp?section=papers&code=03-D_11.
- "Restructure, Don't Cut, the Missile Defense Program; Focus Should Be on Deployment of Near-Term Anti-Missile Systems." 28 April 2004. Available at: http://www.centerforsecuritypolicy.org/ index.jsp?section=papers&code=04-D_19.
- "The Senate Democrats' True Colors on Defense." 24 June 2002. Available at: http://www.centerforsecuritypolicy.org/ index.jsp?section=papers&code=02-D_31.
- "Serious about Defending America." 16 December 2002. Available at: http://www.centerforsecuritypolicy.org/index.jsp?section=papers&code=02-D_ 63.

- "Veto Bait: Levin Efforts to Replace Treaty-Based Impediments to Missile Defense with Legislative Ones Must Be Thwarted." 6 May 2002. Available at: http://www.centerforsecuritypolicy.org/ index.jsp?section=papers&code=02-D_22.

War on Terror

Center for Security Policy. "Balancing Security and Privacy during Wartime." 2 April 2004. Available at: http://www.centerforsecuritypolicy.org /index.jsp?section=papers&code=04-F_08.
- "Beware of the Gaza Trap." 14 April 2004. Available at: http:// www.centerforsecuritypolicy.org/index.jsp?section=papers&code=04-F_10.
- "The Choice." 1 November 2004. Available at: http:// www.centerforsecuritypolicy.org/index.jsp?section=papers&code=04-D_48.
- "A Fateful Choice." 9 February 2004. Available at: http://www.centerforsecuritypolicy.org/index.jsp?section=papers&code=04-D_ 06.
- "Happy Birthday, Patriot Act!" 26 October 2004. Available at: http:// www.centerforsecuritypolicy.org/index.jsp?section=papers&code=04-F_17.
- "Hatchet Job." 25 October 2004. Available at: http:// www.centerforsecuritypolicy.org/index.jsp?section=papers&code=04-D_47.
- "It Is a Global War on Terror." 11 March 2004. Available at: http:// www.centerforsecuritypolicy.org/index.jsp?section=papers&code=04-F_06.
- "Kill (the) Bill." 6 December 2004. Available at: http:// www.centerforsecuritypolicy.org/index.jsp?section=papers&code=04-D_54.
- "Know Thy Enemy." 9 August 2004. Available at: http:// www.centerforsecuritypolicy.org/index.jsp?section=papers&code=04-D_36.
- "October Surprise: Latest bin Laden Tape Confirms Effectiveness of Bush War on Terror." 1 November 2004. Available at: http:// www.centerforsecuritypolicy.org/index.jsp?section=papers&code=04-D_49.
- "Privatizing Counterproliferation." 26 January 2004. Available at: http:// www.centerforsecuritypolicy.org/index.jsp?section=papers&code=04-D_04.
- "The Right Questions." 2 February 2004. Available at: http:// www.centerforsecuritypolicy.org/index.jsp?section=papers&code=04-D_05.
- "Taking Down Bush." 22 March 2004. Available at: http:// www.centerforsecuritypolicy.org/index.jsp?section=papers&code=04-D_12.
- "Unactionable." 12 April 2004. Available at: http:// www.centerforsecuritypolicy.org/index.jsp?section=papers&code=04-D_16.
- "U.S. Strategy for the War on Terrorism." 14 April 2004. Available at: http:// www.centerforsecuritypolicy.org/index.jsp?section=papers&code=052.

- "The War on Terror Can't Be Won by Losing Iraq." 20 September 2004.
  Available at: http://
  www.centerforsecuritypolicy.org/index.jsp?section=papers&code=04-D_42.
- "A Win for Terror." 15 March 2004. Available at: http://
  www.centerforsecuritypolicy.org/index.jsp?section=papers&code=04-D_11.
- "A World Without Israel." 12 January 2005. Available at: http://
  www.centerforsecuritypolicy.org/index.jsp?section=papers&code=05-F_01.

CENTER FOR STRATEGIC AND INTERNATIONAL STUDIES

Missile Defense

Binnendijk, Hans, and George Stewart. "Toward Missile Defenses from the Sea."
  Washington Quarterly 25, no. 3 (2002): 193–206.
Lindsay, James M., and Michael E. O'Hanlon. "Missile Defense after the ABM
  Treaty." *Washington Quarterly* 25, no. 3 (2002): 163–76.
McLaughlin, Kevin. "Would Space-Based Defenses Improve Security?"
  Washington Quarterly 25, no. 3 (2002): 177–91.

War on Terror

Al Sayyid, Mustafa. "Mixed Message: The Arab and Muslim Response to
  'Terrorism.'" *Washington Quarterly* 25, no. 2 (March 2002): 177–90.
Arend, Anthony Clark. "International Law and the Preemptive Use of Military
  Force." *Washington Quarterly* 26, no. 2 (2003): 89–103.
Blinken, Antony J. "Winning the War of Ideas." *Washington Quarterly* 25, no. 2
  (March 2002): 101–14.
Campbell, Kurt M. "Globalization's First War?" *Washington Quarterly* 25, no. 1
  (January 2001): 7–14.
Delpech, Therese. "The Imbalance of Terror." *Washington Quarterly* 25, no. 1
  (January 2002): 31–40.
Desker, Barry, and Kumar Ramakrishna. "Forging an Indirect Strategy in
  Southeast Asia." *Washington Quarterly* 25, no. 2 (March 2002): 161–76.
Dibb, Paul. "The Future of International Coalitions: How Useful? How
  Manageable?" *Washington Quarterly* 25, no. 2 (March 2002): 131–44.
Dory, Amanda J. "American Civil Security: The U.S. Public and Homeland
  Security." *Washington Quarterly* 27, no. 1 (2003): 37–52.
Freedman, Lawrence. "Prevention, Not Preemption." *Washington Quarterly* 26,
  no. 2 (2003): 105–14.

Gunaratna, Rohan. "The Post-Madrid Face of Al Qaeda." *Washington Quarterly* 27, no. 3 (2004): 91–100.

Guoliang, Gu. "Redefine Cooperative Security, Not Preemption." *Washington Quarterly* 26, no. 2 (2003): 135–45.

Heisbourg, François. "A Work in Progress: The Bush Doctrine and Its Consequences." *Washington Quarterly* 26, no. 2 (2003): 75–88.

Isherwood, Michael W. "U.S. Strategic Options for Iraq: Easier Said than Done." *Washington Quarterly* 25, no. 2 (March 2002): 145–59.

Layne, Christopher. "Offshore Balancing Revisited." *Washington Quarterly* 25, no. 2 (2002): 233–48.

Lennon, Alexander T. "Editor's Note." *Washington Quarterly* 27, no. 4 (2004): 111–14.

Lugar, Richard G. "Redefining NATO's Mission: WMD Terrorism." *Washington Quarterly* 25, no. 3 (2002): 7–13.

Mazarr, Michael J. "Saved from Ourselves?" *Washington Quarterly* 25, no. 2 (March 2002): 221–32.

Miller, Steven E. "The End of Unilateralism or Unilateralism Redux?" *Washington Quarterly* 25, no. 1 (January 2002): 15–29.

Mills, Greg. "Africa's New Strategic Significance." *Washington Quarterly* 27, no. 4 (2004): 157–69.

Mohan, C. Raja. "A Paradigm Shift toward South Asia?" *Washington Quarterly* 26, no. 1 (2002–03): 141–55.

Morrison, J. Stephen. "Somalia's and Sudan's Race to the Fore in Africa." *Washington Quarterly* 25, no. 2 (March 2002): 191–205.

Parachini, John. "Putting WMD Terrorism into Perspective." *Washington Quarterly* 26, no. 4 (2003): 37–50.

Pillar, Paul R. "Counterterrorism after Al Qaeda." *Washington Quarterly* 27, no. 3 (2004): 101–13.

Raghavan, V.R. "The Double-Edged Effect in South Asia." *Washington Quarterly* 27, no. 4 (2004): 147–55.

Rosa, Mary De. "Privacy in the Age of Terror." *Washington Quarterly* 26, no. 3 (2003): 27–41.

Serfaty, Simon. "The New Normalcy." *Washington Quarterly* 25, no. 2 (March 2002): 209–19.

Simon, Steven, and Jeff Martini. "Terrorism: Denying Al Qaeda Its Popular Support." *Washington Quarterly* 28, no. 1 (2004–05): 131–45.

Stepanova, Ekaterina. "War and Peace Building." *Washington Quarterly* 27, no. 4 (2004): 127–36.

Takeyh, Ray, and Nikolas Gvosdev. "Do Terrorist Networks Need a Home?" *Washington Quarterly* 25, no. 3 (2002): 97–108.

Watanabe, Akio. "A Continuum of Change." *Washington Quarterly* 27, no. 4 (2004): 137–46.

Weidenbaum, Murray L. "Economic Warriors against Terrorism." *Washington Quarterly* 25, no. 1 (January 2002): 43–52.

Windsor, Jennifer L. "Promoting Democratization Can Combat Terrorism." *Washington Quarterly* 26, no. 3 (2003): 43–58.

Wu, Xinbo. "The Promise and Limitations of a Sino-U.S. Partnership." *Washington Quarterly* 27, no. 4 (2004): 115–26.

COUNCIL ON FOREIGN RELATIONS

Missile Defense

Butler, Richard. *Fatal Choice: Nuclear Weapons and the Illusion of Missile Defense*. New York: Council on Foreign Relations, 2002.

Ivanov, Igor. "The Missile-Defense Mistake." *Foreign Affairs* 79, no. 5 (September/October 2000): 15–21.

Newhouse, John. "The Missile Defense Debate." *Foreign Affairs* 80, no. 4 (July/August 2001): 97.

Perry, William J. "Preparing for the Next Attack." *Foreign Affairs* 80, no. 6 (November/December 2001): 31.

Schell, Jonathan. "The Folly of Arms Control." *Foreign Affairs* 79, no. 5 (September/October 2000): 22–45.

War on Terror

Albright, Madeline K. "Bridges, Bombs, or Bluster?" *Foreign Affairs* 82, no. 5 (September/October 2003): 2–20.

Betts, Richard K. "The New Politics of Intelligence: Will Reforms Work This Time?" *Foreign Affairs* 83, no. 3 (May/June 2004): 2.

Byford, Grenville. "The Wrong War." *Foreign Affairs* 81, no. 4 (July/August 2002): 34.

Byman, Daniel. "Should Hezbollah Be Next?" *Foreign Affairs* 82, no. 6 (November/December 2003): 54.

Crocker, Chester A. "Engaging Failing States." *Foreign Affairs* 82, no. 5 (September/October 2003): 32–44.

Dobriansky, Paula J., and Thomas Carothers. "Democracy Promotion." *Foreign Affairs* 82, no. 3 (May/June 2003): 141.

Flynn, Stephen E. "America the Vulnerable." *Foreign Affairs* (January/February 2002): 60.

Flynn, Stephen E., Gary Hart, and Warren B. Rudman. *America –Still Unprepared, Still in Danger*. Council on Foreign Relations Press, October 2002. Available at: http://www.cfr.org/pdf/Homeland_TF.pdf.

Fuller, Graham E. "The Future of Political Islam." *Foreign Affairs* 81, no. 2 (March/April 2002): 48.

Greenberg, Maurice R., William F. Wechsler, and Lee S. Wolosky. *Terrorist Financing*. Council on Foreign Relations, October 2002. Available at: http://www.cfr.org/pdf/Terrorist_Financing_TF.pdf.

Greenberg, Maurice R., Mallory Factor, William F. Wechsler, and Lee S. Wolosky. *Update on the Global Campaign against Terrorist Financing*. Council on Foreign Relations, June 2004. Available at: http://www.cfr.org/pdf/Revised_Terrorist_Financing.pdf.

Hills, Carla A., Richard C. Holbrooke and Charles G. Boyd. *Improving the U.S. Public Diplomacy Campaign in the War against Terrorism*." Council on Foreign Relations, November 2001. Available at: http://www.cfr.org/pub4215/richard_c_holbrooke_charles_g_boyd_carla_a_hills/improving_the_us_public_diplomacy_campaign_in_the_war_against_terrorism.php.

Hoffman, David. "Beyond Public Diplomacy." *Foreign Affairs* 81, no. 2 (March/April 2002): 83.

Hoffmann, Stanley. "Clash of Globalizations." *Foreign Affairs* 81, no. 4 (July/August 2002): 104.

Independent Task Force on America's Response to Terrorism. *Strengthening the U.S. Saudi Relationship*. Council on Foreign Relations Paper, 30 May 2002. Available at: http://www.cfr.org/pub4604/special_report/strengthening_the_ussaudi_relationship.php.

Luft, Gal, and Anne Korin. "Terrorism Goes to Sea." *Foreign Affairs* 83, no. 6 (November/December 2004): 61.

Lyman, Princeton N., and J. Stephen Morrison. "The Terrorist Threat in Africa." *Foreign Affairs* 83, no. 1 (January/February 2004): 75.

Mallaby, Sebastian. "The Reluctant Imperialist." *Foreign Affairs* 81, no.2 (March/April 2002): 2.

Mead, Walter Russell. *Power, Terror, Peace, and War*. New York: Council on Foreign Relations, 2004.

Mosi, Dominique. "Reinventing the West." *Foreign Affairs* 82, no. 6 (November/December 2003): 67.

Nossel, Suzanne. "Smart Power." *Foreign Affairs* 83, no. 2 (March/April 2004): 131.

O'Hanlon, Michael E. "A Flawed Masterpiece." *Foreign Affairs* 81, no. 3 (May/June 2002): 47.

Rogers, Steven. "Beyond the Abu Sayef." *Foreign Affairs* 83, no. 1 (January/February 2004): 15.

Rotberg, Robert I. "Failed States in a World of Terror." *Foreign Affairs* 81, no. 4 (July/August 2002): 127.

Roth, Kenneth. "The Law of War in the War on Terror." *Foreign Affairs* 83, no. 1 (January/February 2004): 2.

Rumsfeld, Donald H. "Transforming the Military." *Foreign Affairs* 81, no. 3 (May/June 2002): 20.

Telhami, Shibley. "The Ties That Bind: Americans, Arabs, and Israelis after September 11." *Foreign Affairs* 83, no. 2 (March/April 2004): 8.

Wedgwood, Ruth, and Kenneth Roth. "Combatants or Criminals? How Washington Should Handle Terrorists." *Foreign Affairs* 83, no. 3 (May/June 2004): 126.

HERITAGE FOUNDATION

Missile Defense

Sokolski, Henry. "Missile Nonproliferation and Missile Defense." *Heritage Lecture*, no. 761 (6 September 2002). Available at: http://www.heritage.org/Research/NationalSecurity/hl761.cfm.

Spencer, Jack. "Bush and Kerry: Stark Contrasts on National Security." *Executive Memorandum*, no. 947 (20 October 2004). Available at: http://www.heritage.org/Research/NationalSecurity/em947.cfm.

Spring, Baker. "Congress Should Commend Britain on Missile Defense Radar Upgrade." *Executive Memorandum*, no. 861 (21 February 2003). Available at: http://www.heritage.org/Research/NationalSecurity/em861.cfm.

– "Keeping Missile Defense at the Heart of Defense Transformation." *Executive Memorandum*, no. 874 (7 May 2003). Available at: http://www.heritage.org/Research/NationalSecurity/em874.cfm.

– "No Defense for Criticism on Missile Defense Testing." *WebMemo*, no. 215 (28 February 2003). Available at: http://www.heritage.org/Research/NationalSecurity/wm215.cfm.

– "Use New Acquisition Procedures for Missile Defense." *WebMemo*, no. 414 (4 February 2004). Available at: http://www.heritage.org/Research/NationalSecurity/wm414.cfm.

War on Terror

Arcos, Cresencio. "The Role of the Department of Homeland Security Overseas." *Heritage Lecture*, no. 840 (7 June 2004). Available at: http://www.heritage.org/Research/HomelandDefense/hl840.cfm.

Billingslea, Marshall. "Waging War on Terrorism." *WebMemo*, no. 256 (11 April 2003). Available at: http://www.heritage.org/Research/ NationalSecurity/wm256.cfm.

Bolton, John R. "Beyond the Axis of Evil: Additional Threats from Weapons of Mass Destruction." *Heritage Lecture*, no. 743 (6 May 2002). Available at: http://www.heritage.org/Research/NationalSecurity/HL743.cfm.

Bush, George W. "Turning Back the Terrorist Threat: America's Unbreakable Commitment." *Heritage Lecture*, no. 809 (19 November 2003). Available at: http://www.heritage.org/Research/MiddleEast/HL809.cfm.

Carafano, James Jay. "The Army Goes Rolling Along: New Service Transformation Agenda Suggests Promise and Problems." *Backgrounder*, no. 1729 (23 February 2004). Available at: http://www.heritage.org/Research/ HomelandDefense/bg1729.cfm.

– "Missions, Responsibilities, and Geography: Rethinking How the Pentagon Commands the World." *Backgrounder*, no. 1792 (26 August 2004). Available at: http://www.heritage.org/Research/NationalSecurity/bg1792.cfm.

– "Strategy and Security in the Information Age: Grading Progress in America's War on Terrorism." *Heritage Lecture*, no. 824 (17 March 2004). Available at: http://www.heritage.org/Research/HomelandDefense/hl824.cfm.

Carafano, James Jay, and Stephen Johnson. "Strengthening America's Southern Flank Requires a Better Effort." *Backgrounder*, no. 1727 (20 February 2004). Available at: http://www.heritage.org/Research/NationalSecurity/bg1727.cfm.

Dillon, Dana R. "The War on Terrorism in Southeast Asia: Developing Law Enforcement." *Backgrounder*, no. 1720 (22 January 2004). Available at: http://www.heritage.org/Research/AsiaandthePacific/BG1720.cfm.

Gardiner, Nile. "The Myth of U.S. Isolation: Why America Is Not Alone in the War on Terror." *WebMemo*, no. 558 (7 September 2004). Available at: http://www.heritage.org/Research/Europe/wm558.cfm.

Gardiner, Nile, and John Hulsman. "After Madrid: Preserving the Alliance against Terrorism." *Backgrounder*, no. 1743 (9 April 2004). Available at: http://www.heritage.org/Research/NationalSecurity/1743.cfm.

Habeck, Mary R. "Jihadist Strategies in the War on Terrorism." *Heritage Lecture*, no. 855 (8 November 2004). Available at: http://www.heritage.org/Research/NationalSecurity/hl855.cfm.

Harmon, Christopher C. "How al-Qaeda May End." *Backgrounder*, no. 1760 (19 May 2004). Available at: http://www.heritage.org/Research/ NationalSecurity/bg1760.cfm.

Holmes, Kim R. "Threats and Opportunities in the World." *Heritage Lecture*, no. 833 (4 May 2004). Available at: http://www.heritage.org /Research/NationalSecurity/hl833.cfm.

Pasicolan, Paolo, and Balbina Y. Hwang. "The Vital Role of Alliances in the Global War on Terrorism." *Backgrounder*, no. 1607 (24 October 2002). Available at: http://www.heritage.org/Research/NationalSecurity/bg1607.cfm.

Phillips, James A. "Bin Laden's October Surmise." *WebMemo*, no. 602 (4 November 2004). Available at: http://www.heritage.org/Research/MiddleEast/wm602.cfm.

– "National Security Isn't Just about Terrorism." *WebMemo*, no. 472 (9 April 2004). Available at: http://www.heritage.org/Research/NationalSecurity/wm472.cfm.

– "Somalia and al-Qaeda: Implications for the War on Terrorism." *Backgrounder*, no. 1526 (5 April 2002). Available at: http://www.heritage.org/Research/HomelandDefense/BG1526.cfm.

– "Undue Criticism for September 11." *WebMemo*, no. 100 (20 May 2002). Available at: http://www.heritage.org/Research/HomelandDefense/WM100.cfm.

Rosenzweig, Paul, and James Jay Carafano. "Preventive Detention and Actionable Intelligence." *Legal Memorandum*, no. 13 (16 September 2004). Available at: http://www.heritage.org/Research/HomelandDefense/lm13.cfm.

Spencer, Jack. "Before the Overseas Basing Commission." Testimony, 1 September 2004. Available at: http://www.heritage.org/Research/NationalSecurity/tst090104a.cfm.

– "Focusing Defense Resources to Meet National Security Requirements." *Backgrounder*, no. 1638 (21 March 2003). Available at: http://www.heritage.org/Research/NationalSecurity/bg1638.cfm.

– "The New National Security Strategy: An Effective Blueprint for the War on Terror." *WebMemo*, no. 149 (25 September 2002). Available at: http://www.heritage.org/Research/HomelandDefense/WM149.cfm.

– "Presidential Authority in the War on Terrorism: Iraq and Beyond." *Backgrounder*, no. 1600 (2 October 2002). Available at: http://www.heritage.org/Research/MiddleEast/bg1600.cfm.

– "The War on Terrorism and Beyond: Principles and Issues for the Quadrennial Defense Review." *WebMemo*, no. 619 (10 December 2004). Available at: http://www.heritage.org/Research/NationalSecurity/wm619.cfm.

Spencer, Jack, and Ha Nguyen. "Are We Safer Today than before 9/11?" *WebMemo*, no. 335 (10 September 2003). Available at: http://www.heritage.org/Research/HomelandDefense/wm335.cfm.

Spring, Baker, and Jack Spencer. "In Post-War Iraq, Use Military Forces to Secure Vital U.S. Interests, Not for Nation-Building." *Backgrounder*, no. 1589 (25 September 2002). Available at: http://www.heritage.org/Research/MiddleEast/bg1589.cfm.

Thawley, Michael. "Australia's Continuing Role in the War on Terrorism." *Heritage Lecture*, no. 830 (31 March 2004). Available at: http://www.heritage.org/Research/NationalSecurity/hl830.cfm.

Wortzel, Larry M. "Conservative Principles, Political Reality, and the War on Terrorism." *Heritage Lecture*, no. 847 (2 August 2004). Available at: http://www.heritage.org/Research/NationalSecurity/HL-847.cfm.

INSTITUTE FOR INTERNATIONAL POLICY STUDIES

War on Terror

Borgu, Aldo. "Combating Terrorism in East Asia –a Framework for Regional Cooperation." *Asia Pacific Review* 11, no. 2 (November 2004): 48–59.

Campbell, Kurt M., and Yuki Tatsumi. "In the Aftermath of the Storm: US Foreign Policy in the Wake of 9/11 and Its Implications for the Asia-Pacific region." *Asia Pacific Review* 9, no. 2 (1 November 2002): 31–44.

Desker, Barry, and Arabinda Acharya. "Targeting Islamist Terrorism in Asia Pacific: An Unending War." *Asia Pacific Review* 11, no. 2 (November 2004): 60–80.

Imai, Ryukichi. "Weapons of Mass Destruction: Major Wars, Regional Conflicts, and Terrorism." *Asia Pacific Review* 9, no. 1 (1 May 2002): 88–99.

RAND

Missile Defence

Larson, Eric V., and Glenn A. Kent. *A New Methodology for Assessing Multilayer Missile Defense Options*. Santa Monica, CA: RAND, 1994.

Lussier, Frances M., et al. *Army Air and Missile Defense: Future Challenges*. Santa Monica, CA: RAND, 2002.

Mosher, David E., and Lowell H. Schwartz. "Excessive Force: Why Russian and U.S. Nuclear Postures Perpetuate Cold War Risks." *RAND Review* 27, no. 3 (fall 2003). Available at: http://www.rand.org/publications/randreview/issues/fall2003/force.html.

Preston, Bob, et al. *Space Weapons: Earth Wars*. Santa Monica, CA: RAND, 2002.

Swaine, Michael D., Rachael M. Swanger, and Takashi Kawakami. *Japan and Ballistic Missile Defense: The Case of Japan*. Santa Monica, CA: RAND, 2001.

War on Terror

Benard, Cheryl. *Civil Democratic Islam: Partners, Resources, and Strategies.* Santa Monica, CA: RAND, 2003. Available at: http://www.rand.org/publications/MR/MR1716/MR1716.pdf.

– "Five Pillars of Democracy: How the West Can Promote an Islamic Reformation." *RAND Review* 28, no. 1 (spring 2004). Available at: http:// www.rand.org/publications/randreview/issues/spring2004/ pillars.html.

Dobbins, James. "Nation-Building: The Inescapable Responsibility of the World's Only Superpower." *RAND Review* 27, no. 2 (summer 2003). Available at: http://www.rand.org/publications/randreview/issues/summer2003/.

Fair, C. Christine. *The Counterterror Coalitions: Cooperation with Pakistan and India.* Santa Monica, CA: RAND, 2004. Available at: http://www.rand.org/pubs/monographs/2004/RAND_MG141.pdf.

Hoffman, Bruce. *Insurgency and Counterinsurgency in Iraq.* Santa Monica, CA: RAND, 2004. Available at: http://www.rand.org/publications/ OP/OP127/OP127.pdf.

– "Redefining Counterterrorism: The Terrorist Leader as CEO." *RAND Review* 28, no. 1 (spring 2004). Available at: http://www.rand.org/publications/ randreview/issues/spring2004/ceo.html.

Jenkins, Brian Michael. "Redefining the Enemy: The World Has Changed, but Our Mindset Has Not." *RAND Review* 28, no. 1 (spring 2004). Available at: http://www.rand.org/publications/randreview/issues/spring2004 /enemy.html.

Khalizad, ZalMay, and Daniel Byman. "Afghanistan: The Consolidation of a Rogue State." *Washington Quarterly* 23, no. 1 (winter 2000): 65–78. Available at: http://www.twq.com/winter00/231Byman.pdf.

Larrabee, F. Stephen. *The Middle East in the Shadow of Afghanistan and Iraq.* Santa Monica, CA: RAND, 2003. Available at: http://www.rand.org/publications/CF/CF191/.

Quinlivan, James T. "Selective Service: Bring Back the Draft in Iraq, Not Here." *RAND Review* 28, no. 2 (summer 2004). Available at: http://www.rand.org/ publications/randreview/issues/summer2004/ service.html.

Rabasa, Angel, et al. *The Muslim World after 9/11.* Santa Monica, CA: RAND, 2004. Available at: http://www.rand.org/pubs/monographs/2004/ RAND_MG246.pdf.

FURTHER READINGS ON MISSILE DEFENSE AND THE WAR ON TERROR

Missile Defense

Baucom, Donald. *The Origins of SDI, 1944–1983.* Lawerence: University of Kansas Press, 1992.

Brennan, D.G. "The Case for Missile Defense." *Foreign Affairs* 47 (April 1969): 433–48.

Brown, Harold, ed. *The Strategic Defense Initiative: Shield or Snare?* Boulder: Westview Press, 1987.

Brzezinski, Zbigniew, ed. *Promise or Peril, the Strategic Defense Initiative: Thirty-Five Essays by Statesman, Scholars, and Strategic Analysts.* Washington, DC: Ethics and Public Policy Center, 1986.

Cirinione, Joseph. "Why the Right Lost the Missile Defense Debate." *Foreign Policy,* no. 106 (spring 1997): 38–55.

Coffey, J.I. "The Anti-Ballistic Missile Debate." *Foreign Affairs* 45 (April 1967): 403–13.

Cordesman, Anthony H. *Strategic Threats and National Missile Defenses: Defending the U.S. Homeland.* Westport, CT: Praeger, 2002.

FitzGerald, Francis. *Way Out There in the Blue: Reagan, Star Wars, and the End of the Cold War.* New York: Simon & Schuster, 2000.

Gormley, Dennis M. "Enriching Expectations: 11 September's Lessons for Missile Defense." *Survival* 44, no. 2 (summer 2002): 19–45.

– "Missile Defense Myopia: Lessons from the Iraq War." *Survival* 45, no. 4 (winter 2003): 61–86.

Lewis, George, and Lisbeth Gronlund. "An Assessment of the Missile Defense 'Endgame Success' Argument." *Union of Concerned Scientists Working Paper,* 2 December 2002. Available at: www.ucsusa.org/global_security/missile_defense/page.cfm?pageID=1066.

Lindsay, James M. *Defending America: The Case for Limited National Missile Defense.* Washington, DC: Brookings Institution Press, 2001.

Lord, Carnes. "A Strategic Defense Initiative: Building a Better Shield." *National Interest,* no. 76 (summer 2004): 84–92.

Matlock, Jack F., Jr. *Reagan and Gorbachev: How the Cold War Ended.* New York: Random House, 2004.

Payne, Keith B. "The Case for National Missile Defense." *Orbis* 44, no. 2 (spring, 2000): 187–96.

Sessler, Andrew, et al. "Countermeasures: A Technical Evaluation of the Operational Effectiveness of the Planned US National Missile Defense System." *Union of Concerned Scientists Working Paper*, April 2000. Available at: www.ucsusa.org/publications/report.cfm?publicationID=132.

Teller, Edward. *Better a Shield than a Sword: Perspectives on Defense Technology*. New York: Free Press, 1987.

Wirtz, James J., and Jeffery A. Larsen, eds. *Rockets' Red Glare: Missile Defenses and the Future of World Politics*. Boulder, CO: Westview Press, 2001.

Yanarella, Ernest J. *The Missile Defense Controversy: Strategy, Technology, and Politics, 1955–1972*. Lexington: University Press of Kentucky, 1977.

War on Terror

Allison, Graham. "How to Stop Nuclear Terror." *Foreign Affairs* 83, no. 1 (January/February 2004): 64.

Andreas, Peter. "Redrawing the Line: Borders and Security in the Twenty-First Century." *International Security* 28, no. 2 (2003): 78–111.

Anonymous. *Imperial Hubris: Why the West Is Losing the War on Terror*. Washington, DC: Brassey's, 2004.

Baker, Nancy V. "National Security versus Civil Liberties." *Presidential Studies Quarterly* 33, no. 3 (September 2003): 547–67.

Barton, Frederick D., and Bathsheba Crocker. "Winning the Peace in Iraq." *Washington Quarterly* 26, no. 2 (15 September 2003): 7–22.

Bowden, Mark. "The Dark Art of Interrogation." *Atlantic Monthly* 292, no. 3 (October 2003): 51–76.

Cirincione, Joseph. "Can Preventive War Cure Proliferation?" *Foreign Policy*, no. 137 (July/August 2003): 66–9.

Clarke, Richard. "Ten Years Later." *Atlantic Monthly* 295, no. 1 (January/February 2005): 61–77.

Coll, Steve. *Ghost Wars: The Secret History of the CIA, Afghanistan, and Bin Laden, from the Soviet Invasion to September 10, 2001*. New York: The Penguin Press, 2004.

Dawisha, Adeed, and Karen Dawisha. "How to Build a Democratic Iraq." *Foreign Affairs* 82, no. 3 (May/June 2003): 36.

Debat, Alexis. "Vivisecting Jihad." *National Interest*, no. 76, (summer 2004): 18–23.

Delong, Mike. *Inside CENTCOM: The Unvarnished Truth about the War in Afghanistan and Iraq*. Washington, DC: Regnery Publishing, 2004.

Diamond, Larry. "What Went Wrong in Iraq." *Foreign Affairs* 83, no. 5 (September/October 2004): 34.

Dobbins, James. "Iraq: Winning the Unwinnable War." *Foreign Affairs* 84, no. 1 (January/February 2005): 16–25.

Falkenrath, Richard A. "Problems of Preparedness: U.S. Readiness for a Domestic Terrorist Attack." *International Security* 25, no. 4 (March 2001): 147–86.

Fallows, James. "The Fifty-First State?" *Atlantic Monthly* 290, no. 4 (November 2002): 53–64.

Feinstein, Lee, and Anne-Marie Slaughter. "A Duty to Prevent." *Foreign Affairs* 83, no. 1 (January/February 2004): 136.

Gannon, Kathy. "Afghanistan Unbound." *Foreign Affairs* 83, no. 3 (May/June 2004): 35.

Glennon, Michael J. "Why the Security Council Failed." *Foreign Affairs* 82, no. 3 (May/June 2003): 16.

Ignatieff, Michael. *Empire Lite: Nation Building in Bosnia, Kosovo, and Afghanistan.* Toronto: Penguin Canada, 2003.

– *The Lesser Evil: Political Ethics in an Age of Terror.* Toronto: Penguin Books, 2004.

– "Why Are We in Iraq? (and Liberia? and Afghanistan?)" *New York Times Magazine,* 7 September 2003, 38.

Kaplan, Robert D. *Soldiers of God: With Islamic Warriors in Afghanistan and Pakistan.* New York: Vintage Books, 2001.

– "Supremacy by Stealth: Ten Rules for Managing the World." *Atlantic Monthly* 292, no. 1 (July/August 2003): 61–83. .

Keegan, John. *The Iraq War.* New York: A.A. Knopf, 2004.

Leiken, Robert S. "Europe's Angry Muslims." *Foreign Affairs* 84, no. 4 (July/August 2005): 120–135.

Lewis, Bernard. "Freedom and Justice in the Middle East." *Foreign Affairs* 84, no. 3 (May/June 2005): 36–51.

Lindsay, James M. "Deference and Defiance: The Shifting Rhythms of Executive-Legislative Relations in Foreign Policy." *Presidential Studies Quarterly* 33, no. 3 (September 2003): 530–46.

Margolis, Eric. *War at the Top of the World: The Struggle for Afghanistan, Kashmir and Tibet.* New York: Routledge, 2002.

Metz, Steven. "Insurgency and Counterinsurgency in Iraq." *Washington Quarterly* 27, no. 1 (25 November 2003): 25–36.

O'Toole, Tara, and Donald A. Henderson. "A Clearly Present Danger." *Harvard International Review* 23, no. 3 (fall 2001): 49–53.

Ottaway, Marina, and Anatol Lieven. "Rebuilding Afghanistan." *Current History* 101, no. 653 (March 2002): 133–8.

Relyea, Harold C. "Organizing for Homeland Security." *Presidential Studies Quarterly* 33, no. 3 (September 2003): 602–24.

Ross, Dennis. "The Middle East Predicament." *Foreign Affairs* 84, no. 1 (January/February 2005): 61–74.

Rubin, Barnett R. "Afghanistan under the Taliban." *Current History* 98, no. 625 (February 1999): 79–91.

Schlesinger, Arthur, Jr. *War and the American Presidency*. New York: W.W. Norton, 2004.

Snyder, Robert S. "The Myth of Preemption: More than a War against Iraq." *Orbis* 47, no. 4 (autumn 2003): 653–60.

Starr, Frederick S. "Silk Road to Success." *National Interest*, no. 78 (winter 2004/2005): 65–72.

Taft, William H., IV, and Todd F. Buchwals. "Preemption, Iraq, and International Law." *American Journal of International Law* 97, no. 3 (July 2003): 557–63.

Notes

PREFACE

1 Smith, *The Idea Brokers*.
2 See Abelson, *Do Think Tanks Matter?* and Rich, *Think Tanks, Public Policy and the Politics of Expertise*.
3 Ricci, *The Transformation of American Politics*.
4 Interview with David Frum, 20 May 2004.
5 American Enterprise Institute, *Annual Report, 2003*, 5; italics added.
6 Ibid, 35.
7 Bentley, *The Process of Government*; Truman, *The Governmental Process*; and Lowi, *The End of Liberalism*.
8 Hellebust, *Think Tank Directory*.
9 McGann, *The Competition for Dollars, Scholars and Influence* 9.

INTRODUCTION

1 For more on the relationship between presidential candidates and think tanks, see Abelson and Carberry, "Policy Experts in Presidential Campaigns."
2 Smith, *The Idea Brokers*.
3 McGann and Weaver, *Think Tanks and Civil Societies*.
4 Stone and Denham, *Think Tank Traditions*.
5 Struyk, *Reconstructive Critics*.
6 McGann, *Think Tanks: Catalysts for Ideas*.

7　Observation made by several officials in the Canadian embassy in Washington, DC, during a roundtable discussion on think tanks, 17 May 2004.

8　Interview with Ivo Daalder, 20 May 2004.

9　On think tanks in parliamentary democracies, see Abelson, *Do Think Tanks Matter?* 58–73.

10　On the role of German think tanks, see Thunert, "Think Tanks in Germany."

11　Interview with Michael O'Hanlon, 19 May 2004.

12　Information obtained from their 2004 annual reports.

13　Figures provided by Gary Schmitt, executive director of PNAC, in interview, 19 May 2004.

14　Brookings Institution, *Annual Report 2003*, 42.

15　Heritage Foundation, *Annual Report 2002.*

16　Weaver, "The Changing World of Think Tanks."

17　McGann, "Academics to Ideologues."

18　McGann and Weaver, *Think Tanks and Civil Societies.*

19　Peschek, *Policy Planning Organizations.*

20　Ibid., 6.

21　Although this study draws primarily on the work of scholars in the United States and in Canada who have examined the role of American think tanks, it is important to note that several scholars throughout Europe have become interested in how and to what extent these organizations become entrenched in the policy-making process. Moreover, there are now several studies that offer comparative analyses between American think tanks and those found in other industrial and developing countries. Among the many studies edited or authored by non–North American scholars are Stone et al., *Think Tanks across Nations*; Stone and Denham, *Think Tank Traditions*; Denham, *Think-Tanks of the New Right*; Struyk, *Reconstructive Critics*; Telgarsky and Ueno, *Think Tanks in a Democratic Society*; Thunert, "Think Tanks in Germany"; Faupin, "How Thought Serves Action"; Braml, *U.S. and German Policy Research Institutes*; Beland and Waddan, "From Thatcher (and Pinochet) to Clinton?"; and Boston, "American Right-Wing Libertarians."

22　Project for the New American Century, *Rebuilding America's Defenses*, iv–v.

23　Woodward, *Plan of Attack*, 10.

24　See, for instance, Meacher, "This War on Terrorism Is Bogus."

25　See Abelson and Carberry, "Policy Experts in Presidential Campaigns."

26　See Governor Bush's speech, "A Period of Consequences." For more on Bush's politics before he assumed the presidency, see Mitchell, *W: Revenge of the Bush Dynasty.*

27　Bush, "A Period of Consequences."

28 For Bush's behaviour as governor of Texas, see Mitchell, *W: Revenge of the Bush Dynasty*; Ivins and Dubose, *Shrub*; and Minutaglio, *First Son*; and Lind, *Made in Texas*.
29 Van Slambrouck, "California Think Tank."
30 Swanson, "Brain Power."
31 Judis, "Taking Care of Business."
32 Interview with Martin Anderson, 19 March 1990.

CHAPTER ONE

1 While presidential candidates must raise their own funds during the primaries, the nominees selected by each party can, should they elect to, draw on public funds for the general election. If presidential nominees accept public funding, they cannot draw on any private sources of money.
2 Abelson and Carberry suggest that two characteristics of presidential candidates – their status as a Washington insider or outsider and the strength of their ideological views as approximated by voter election studies – can help to explain the recruitment patterns of think tanks by candidates. See their article "Policy Experts in Presidential Campaigns."
3 Swanson, "Brain Power." Think tanks have different policies for members of staff who advise presidential candidates. Some, such as the Cato Institute, actively discourage staff members from becoming too closely associated with particular candidates, preferring them to make their advice available to any candidate who wants it. Others, such as the Center for National Policy, which are more concerned about keeping the Internal Revenue Service (IRS) at bay, insist that scholars take a leave of absence if they decide to work on a campaign. The IRS expressly forbids non-profit organizations from participating in political campaigns. For more on this subject, see Morin and Deane, "The Ideas Industry."
4 Shoup, *The Carter Presidency and Beyond*, 39.
5 Ibid., 43.
6 For a detailed examination of the Trilateral Commission, see Gill, *American Hegemony and the Trilateral Commission*, and Sklar, *Trilateralism*. For more information on how Carter was selected to become a member of the Trilateral Commission, see "Memorandum from George Franklin to Gerard Smith on the circumstances of Carter coming with the Commission," box 4, 1/1/76–6/3/77, Gerard Smith's Personal Files, Jimmy Carter Library.
7 Quoted in Perloff, *The Shadows of Power*, 156.
8 Ibid.
9 Rockefeller, *Memoirs*, 417.

10 Ibid.

11 Shoup, *The Carter Presidency and Beyond*, 50.

12 Perloff, *The Shadows of Power,*157.

13 Shoup, *The Carter Presidency and Beyond*, 51.

14 Carter, *Why Not the Best?* 164. Although Carter acknowledges the benefits from participating on the Trilateral Commission in his autobiography, he does not even mention the commission in his memoirs, *Keeping Faith*.

15 Contrary to Brzezinski's assertions that the Trilateral Commission did not advise Carter, Brzezinski did discuss several foreign policy issues with Carter in his capacity as director of the commission. See, for instance, box 8, 7/1/75–8/31/75, and box 5, 1/1/75–1/31/75, Brzezinski's Personal Files on the Trilateral Commission, Jimmy Carter Library.

16 Interview with Zbigniew Brzezinski, 30 May 1991.

17 Quoted in Perloff, *The Shadows of Power*, 158.

18 Rockefeller, *Memoirs*, 417.

19 Robert Pastor, Carter's Latin American specialist on the National Security Council, claims that the president's foreign policy toward Latin America was significantly influenced by two reports issued by the Commission on US-Latin American Relations: *The Americas in a Changing World* and *The US and Latin America*. The commission, chaired by Ambassador Sol Linowitz, was a bipartisan group of approximately twenty-five leaders from universities, think tanks, and corporations. Pastor, who served as executive director of the commission before joining the National Security Council, states, "The reports helped the administration define a new relationship with Latin America, and twenty-seven of the twenty-eight specific recommendations in the second report became US policy." For additional information on the background of the Linowitz commission and its contribution to US foreign policy in Latin America, see Pastor, "The Carter Administration and Latin America," 62–5 .

20 Ronald Reagan was governor of California from 1967 to 1975.

21 Anderson, *Revolution*, 47.

22 The various factors influencing Reagan's decision to leave the Democratic Party are discussed in his autobiography, *An American Life*, 132–6.

23 The slogan "ideas move nations" was coined by Easterbrook and is used as the title of his article on the rise of conservative think tanks, which appears in the *Atlantic Monthly* in January 1986.

24 Anderson, *Revolution*, 8. Anderson has apparently changed his mind about universities serving as reservoirs for policy ideas. In his book *Impostors in the Temple*, he claims that many universities have become inundated by academic frauds unable to maintain acceptable scholarly standards.

25 Anderson, *Revolution*, 165.
26 It is not uncommon for policy task forces to be created during presidential campaigns to provide candidates with information and advice. Several presidents, including John F. Kennedy, relied on policy task forces for advice. For more on this topic, see Campbell, *Managing the Presidency*, and Hess, *Organizing the Presidency*.
27 Anderson, *Revolution*, 166.
28 Seventy-four economists participated on the economic policy task forces. Six chaired issue task forces in various areas of economic policy: Arthur F. Burns (task force on international monetary policy), Alan Greenspan (task force on budget policy), Paul McCracken, former chairman of the Council of Economic Advisers (task force on inflation), Charles E. Walker, former deputy secretary of the treasury (task force on tax policy), Murray L. Weidenbaum (task force on regulatory reform), and Caspar Weinberger (task force on spending control). The other members of the coordinating committee were Milton Friedman; Michel T. Halbouty, former president of the American Association of Petroleum Geologists and chairman of the task force on energy policy; Jack Kemp; James T. Lynn, former director of the Office of Management and Budget; William E. Simon, former secretary of the Treasury, and Walter Wriston, chairman of Citi-bank/Citicorp.
29 Interview with Richard V. Allen, 29 May 1991. For a more detailed discussion of the role and function of policy task forces during the 1980 campaign, see Wood, *Whatever Possessed the President?* 140–3.
30 Interview with Jeane Kirkpatrick, 20 May 2004.
31 Quoted in Anderson, *Revolution*, 167.
32 Meese, *With Reagan*, 59.
33 Anderson, *Revolution*, 167.
34 Meese, *The Transition to a New Administration*, 11.
35 Anderson, *Revolution*, 170.
36 The Institute for Contemporary Studies (ICS) in San Francisco was established by Caspar Weinberger and Edwin Meese III as a non-profit organization in 1972. It and its affiliated institutes publish studies on economic, social, and foreign policy issues. For an interesting analysis on the founding of the ICS, see Beers, "Buttoned-Down Bohemians."
37 Background information on these and other members of the Reagan administration can be found in Brownstein and Easton, *Reagan's Ruling Class*.
38 Since some scholars belonged to one or more think tanks before joining the Reagan administration, I have provided an approximate figure only.
39 A list of members from the Committee on the Present Danger who served in the Reagan administration can be found in Sanders, *Peddlers of Crisis*, 287–8.

According to Eric Alterman, the Committee on the Present Danger eventually furnished fifty-nine members to the Reagan national security team. See his book *Sound and Fury*, 80. For additional information on the Committee on the Present Danger, see Dalby, *Creating the Second Cold War*.

40 Figures for the AEI, CSIS, and the Heritage Foundation are cited in Blumenthal, *The Rise of the Counter-Establishment*, 35–8.

41 Quoted in Weinraub, "Conservative Group's Blueprint for Reagan."

42 Omang, "The Heritage Report."

43 Heatherly, *Mandate for Leadership*. In preparation for the 1984 and 1988 presidential campaigns, the Heritage Foundation produced similar volumes, which examined a wide range of domestic and foreign policy issues. See Butler et al., *Mandate for Leadership II*, and Heatherly, *Mandate for Leadership III*. The Heritage Foundation also issued an interim report during the first term of the Reagan administration; see Holwill, *Agenda '83*. Heritage was not the first think tank to produce detailed "blueprints" for the Executive and Congress. Since 1971, the Brookings Institution has published an annual series entitled *Setting National Priorities*, which provides policy-makers and scholars with in-depth analyses of domestic and foreign policy issues. Moreover, following the 1992 campaign, Will Marshall and Martin Schram of the Progressive Policy Institute produced a blueprint for the Clinton administration entitled *Mandate for Change*, a title apparently borrowed from the Heritage Foundation's series *Mandate for Leadership*.

44 In an interview with the author on 29 May 1991, Richard Allen, President Reagan's first national security adviser, confirmed that Feulner presented Meese and Allen with a copy of *Mandate for Leadership* in mid-November. Allen added that the study "was immediately reproduced and distributed to our entire transition team." It is not surprising that he was willing to accept and reproduce Feulner's study; the two had established close ties as early as 1965 through the Intercollegiate Studies Institute, the first national conservative student organization in the United States. Eventually, through Allen, Feulner became a Hoover Institution fellow. For a discussion on the relationship between Feulner and Allen, see Blumenthal, *The Rise of the Counter- Establishment*, 46–8.

45 Omang, "The Heritage Report."

46 Knickerbocker, "Heritage Foundation's Ideas." Meese also acknowledged receiving studies from the National Academy of Public Administration and from the Kennedy School of Government at Harvard. When asked if he had received a study from the Hoover Institution, he remarked, "I don't think so. There's nobody left there; they're all here in Washington working with us, helping out." See Meese, *The Transition to a New Administration*, 7.

47 Meese, *With Reagan*, 60.

48 Ibid. On two occasions Edwin Feulner took leave from the Heritage Foundation to serve as a special consultant in the White House on specific strategic planning projects, and throughout the two terms he was an informal adviser to President Reagan and members of his cabinet.

49 Ibid. For a discussion about which policy recommendations in the Heritage study were adopted by the Reagan administration during the early 1980s, see Horwill, *Agenda '83*.

50 Duignan and Rabushka, *The US in the 1980s*. Interview with Glenn Campbell, 2 May 1990. Campbell added that when Edwin Feulner was a public affairs fellow at the Hoover Institution, he admitted to Campbell that he was "a retailer not a wholesaler of ideas." Campbell remarked jokingly that he would "buy a used idea from Feulner anytime."

51 Richard Allen resigned as national security adviser in early 1981 amidst allegations of wrongdoing and was replaced by Judge William Clark. Clark left the National Security Council (NSC) in October 1983 to become secretary of the interior. He was replaced by the deputy national security adviser, Robert "Bud" McFarlane. For background information on the transfer of power in the NSC, see Menges, *Inside the National Security Council*.

52 Anderson, *Revolution*, 3.

53 Weinraub, "Conservative Group's Blueprint for Reagan."

54 Quoted in Knickerbocker, "Heritage Foundation's Ideas."

55 Quoted in Wheeler, "Heritage Chiefs Recall Decade of Growth."

56 Interview with Annelise Anderson, 19 August 1996. Richard Allen agrees that President Bush went to great lengths to distance himself from the Reaganites. By doing so, Allen stated, Bush cut himself off from some of America's most important and influential policy experts. Interview with Richard Allen, 6 September 1996.

57 For an interesting analysis of President Bush's reaction to public opinion polls during the Gulf War, see Brace and Hinckley, *Follow the Leader*.

58 Interview with Martin Anderson, Hoover Institution, 19 March 1990.

59 Heatherly, *Mandate for Leadership*.

60 The Carnegie Endowment for International Peace, the Citizens Transition Project, and the American Enterprise Institute were among the many organizations that outlined a series of domestic and foreign policy recommendations. See Rosenbaum, "Torrent of Free Advice."

61 David Osborne, a fellow at the PPI and co-author of *Reinventing Government*, helped to introduce Clinton to the think tank set. See Fineman, "Clinton's Team."

62 Several books have been written on the 1992 presidential election. These
   include Allen and Portis, *The Comeback Kid*; Brummett, *High Wire*;
   Germond and Witcover, *Mad as Hell*; Goldman et al., *Quest for the Presidency 1992*; Hohenberg, *The Bill Clinton Story*; and Moore and Ihde,
   Clinton.

63 Clinton resigned as chair of the DLC shortly before announcing his candi-
   dacy for the presidency. The DLC is currently chaired by Tom Vilsack, governor of Iowa. Al From is the organization's president and executive director.
   The DLC currently has a staff of over twenty people and an annual budget of
   approximately $2.5 million, which is raised from private philanthropists,
   corporate donors, and grassroots organizations.

64 The DLC has approximately 3,000 members, including about 750 elected
   officials nationwide, with 32 US senators and 142 current and former House
   members. It also has chapters in twenty-eight states in every region of the
   country. For more on the DLC's membership, see Barnes, "Will DLC Be a
   Lobbying Heavyweight?"; Grove, "Steering His Party toward the Center";
   and Towell, "DLC Moves into Driver's Seat."

65 Achenbach, "Wonk if You Love Clinton."

66 Although Clinton appeared to draw heavily on the PPI's study *Mandate for
   Change*, only a few members from the PPI and the DLC received appointments in the Clinton administration. Bruce Reed and Bill Galston were given
   positions in the domestic policy office. Reed was issues director in the campaign and deputy director of the transition for domestic policy. He was later
   appointed as White House domestic policy adviser. Will Marshall, Al From,
   and Robert Shapiro, the PPI's vice-president (who later resigned over the
   Whitewater scandal), were Clinton campaign advisers. From also served in
   the transition. For more on Clinton's inner circle of policy advisers, see
   Fineman, "Clinton's Team"; Weisberg, "Clincest"; and Bandow, "New
   Democrats Lose Think-Tank War."

67 Marshall and Schram, *Mandate for Change*. In addition to providing
   Clinton with several policy ideas to consider during the campaign, the DLC
   engaged in an active lobbying effort to support a number of the president's
   policies. For instance, it devoted considerable resources to convince members of Congress to ratify the North American Free Trade Agreement. For
   more on this, see Barnes, "Will DLC Be a Lobbying Heavyweight?"

68 For a complete text of the Clinton-Gore Economic Conference, including the
   list of presenters, see Clinton and Gore, *President Clinton's New Beginning*.

69 Philip Lader, a South Carolina businessman, was the founding father of the
   annual Renaissance Weekends, which began in 1980. Their purpose is to
   provide leaders from various careers with an opportunity to share ideas in

an informal setting. Seminars are held during the retreat, and journalists are prohibited from commenting on the proceedings. Bill and Hillary Clinton have attended the Renaissance Weekends since the mid-1980s. For more on Clinton's involvement, see two articles by Maraniss: "Letter from Never-Never Land" and "A Weekend with Bill & Friends." Also see Jehl, "Clinton, Others Begin 5-Day 'Thinking Party,'" and Baer, "A Network for the Nineties."

70 For more on George W. Bush's career as Texas governor, see Ivins and Dubose, *Shrub*; Mitchell, *W: Revenge of the Bush Dynasty*; and Minutaglio, *First Son*.

71 Russo, "Bush Battling Questions of Brain Power." Also see Daalder and Lindsay, "Bush: Still Needs Work."

72 For more on the relationship between George W. Bush and the Hoover Institution, see Hager, "Bush Shops for Advice"; and Healy and Hebel, "Academics Start to Line Up."

73 Lindsey had also served as an adviser to President George Bush. For more on his background, see Kessler, "Economic Adviser Has Knack."

74 Maggs, "Tax Cuts, Big and Small."

75 Gorman, "Bush's Lesson Plan."

76 Kitfield, "Periphery Is Out." Also see Kitfield, *War and Destiny*.

77 For more on Rice's background, see Mufson, "For Rice, a Daunting Challenge."

78 For more on Zoellick's appointment, see Babington, "Bush Names Zoellick as Trade Representative."

79 Mann, *Rise of the Vulcans*.

80 Interview with Ivo Daalder, 20 May 2004.

81 Quoted in Kitfield, "Periphery Is Out."

82 Ibid.

CHAPTER TWO

1 McGann, "Why Political Science?" In addition, see McGann and Johnson, *Comparative Think Tanks, Politics and Public Policy*.

2 Weaver, "The Changing World of Think Tanks," and McGann, *The Competition for Dollars, Scholars and Influence*. McGann and Weaver have recently collaborated on a study that provides additional insight into how to classify think tanks. See their edited book *Think Tanks and Civil Societies*, especially the Introduction. Also see Wallace, "Between Two Worlds."

3 Interview with Jeane Kirkpatrick, 20 May 2004. A similar observation is made by Micklethwait and Wooldridge in *The Right Nation*, 72–3.

4 Weaver, "The Changing World of Think Tanks," 564.
5 Despite portraying themselves as scholarly institutions, both the Brookings Institution and the Hoover Institution have been criticized for their partisan leanings. In part, this criticism stems from the contributions that individuals at these institutions have made in support of particular presidential candidates. For more on this subject, see Abelson and Carberry, "Policy Experts in Presidential Campaigns."
6 Weaver, "The Changing World of Think Tanks," 567.
7 Dickson, *Think Tanks*.
8 Ibid., 9. For more on government consultants, see Guttman and Willner, *The Shadow Government*.
9 Smith, *The Idea Brokers*, 24.
10 Ibid., 26.
11 Ibid., 30.
12 For background information on the AEA and the AHA, see Domhoff, *The Higher Circles*, 158–60, and Smith, *The Idea Brokers*, 24–37. Two other professional organizations that grew out of the ASSA were the American Political Science Association in 1903 and the American Sociological Association in 1905.
13 See Domhoff, *Who Rules America? Who Rules America Now? The Higher Circles, The Powers That Be*, and *The Bohemian Grove and Other Retreats*.
14 Domhoff, *The Higher Circles*, 164.
15 Ibid., 165.
16 In addition to lending his support to the NCF, Edward A. Filene endowed a public policy research organization in 1911 called the Twentieth Century Fund. A brief description of the organization is included in Smith, *The Idea Brokers*, 290–1.
17 Ibid., 35.
18 Ibid., 169.
19 Ibid.
20 Ibid., 36.
21 Ibid.
22 Ibid.
23 Ibid.
24 Ibid.
25 Ibid.
26 For an examination of the relationship between philanthropic organizations and research institutions, see Berman, *The Influence of the Carnegie, Ford, and Rockefeller Foundations*.
27 Several American think tanks are the beneficiaries of large endowments. The Russell Sage Foundation was created with an initial endowment of $10 mil-

lion, as was the Carnegie Endowment for International Peace. The Brookings Institution and the Hoover Institution were also the recipients of endowments.

28 For instance, during the mid-1980s several philanthropic foundations, including the John M. Olin Foundation and the Smith Richardson Foundation, decided not to renew grants to the American Enterprise Institute, which, unlike other policy-planning organizations such as the Brookings Institution and the Hoover Institution, is not the recipient of a several-million-dollar endowment.

29 According to McGann, the growth of think tanks can be divided into four periods that were marked by a major domestic or international upheaval: World War I, World War II, the War on Poverty, and the War of Ideas. See his article "Academics to Ideologues."

30 The Institute for Government Research merged with the Institute of Economics and the Robert Brookings Graduate School of Economics and Government in 1927 to form the Brookings Institution.

31 For more on the history of the foundation, see Glenn, Brandt, and Andrews, *The Russell Sage Foundation, 1907–1946*.

32 Smith, *The Idea Brokers*, 39.

33 Ibid., 40.

34 Ibid., 44.

35 Quoted ibid., 43.

36 Ibid.

37 Elihu Root served as secretary of state in the Roosevelt administration between 1905 and 1909. He had held the post of secretary of war between 1901 and 1904.

38 The objectives of the Carnegie Endowment for International Peace were proposed in a letter written by Mead, Dutton, and Holt to Carnegie in 1908. See Wall, *Andrew Carnegie*, 898.

39 Ibid.

40 Ibid.

41 Ibid., 899.

42 Ibid.

43 Ibid., 897.

44 Ibid.

45 According to Wall, John Bigelow was one of Carnegie's oldest acquaintances. However, no mention is made of him in Carnegie's autobiography, written in 1920. Moreover, it is interesting to note that with the exception of an editorial note provided by John C. Van Dyke, there is no other reference to the Carnegie Endowment for International Peace in Carnegie's autobiography. See Carnegie, *Autobiography*, 286.

46 Quoted in Wall, *Andrew Carnegie*, 900.

47 According to Poultney Bigelow, the son of John Bigelow, Carnegie "never gave a cent that wasn't returned to him tenfold in public adulation." In his autobiography, Bigelow states, "Never before in the history of plutocratic America had any one man purchased by mere money so much social advertising and flattery. No wonder that he felt himself infallible, when Lords temporal and spiritual courted him and hung upon his words. They wanted his money, and flattery alone could wring it from him. Ask him for aid in a small deserving case or to assist a struggling scientific explorer – that would be wasted time. He had no ears for any charity unless labelled with his name ... He would have given millions to Greece had she labelled the Parthenon Carnegopolis." Quoted in Wall, *Andrew Carnegie*, 822.

48 Carnegie Endowment Web site: www.carnegieendowment.org.

49 Critchlow, *The Brookings Institution*, 9. For more on the Institute for Government Research and the early years of the Brookings Institution, see Smith, *Brookings at Seventy-Five*.

50 Critchlow, *The Brookings Institution*, 32.

51 Ibid.

52 Ibid., 36. For a discussion on the specific details of the proposed national budget, see ibid., 36–40.

53 Ibid., 32.

54 Ibid., 38.

55 Ibid.

56 Ibid., 40.

57 The War Industries Board was the principal economic coordinating agency during World War I.

58 Critchlow, *The Brookings Institution*, 42.

59 Ibid., 62.

60 For background information on the creation of the Graduate School, see Saunders, *The Brookings Institution*.

61 In its publications, the Brookings Institution states that it "maintains its position of neutrality on issues of public policy in order to safeguard the intellectual freedom of the staff."

62 Saunders, *The Brookings Institution*.

63 Brookings Institution, *Annual Report 2003*, 5.

64 McPherson, *To The Best of My Ability*, 218.

65 Nash, *Herbert Hoover and Stanford University*, 49.

66 Ibid.

67 Ibid., 49.

68 Quoted in Feinsilber, "The Hoover-Reagan Campaign Resource."

69 Nash, *Herbert Hoover and Stanford University*, 79.

70 Duignan, *The Hoover Institution on War, Revolution and Peace*, 8.

71 Ibid. Among the more important foreign affairs think tanks created during the 1920s were the New York–based Foreign Policy Association, founded in 1921, and the Institute of Pacific Relations, established in Honolulu in 1925. For background information on these organizations, see Thomas, *The Institute of Pacific Relations*, and Raucher, "The First Foreign Affairs Think Tanks."

72 McPherson, *To the Best of My Ability*, 220.

73 Ibid., 219.

74 Duignan, *The Hoover Institution on War, Revolution and Peace*, 13.

75 Ibid.

76 At the request of the US ambassador to Germany, Hoover reluctantly agreed to accept an invitation to meet Hitler while visiting Berlin in March 1938. From all accounts, it was a stormy encounter.

77 Nash, *Herbert Hoover and Stanford University*, 109.

78 Ibid., 20.

79 Ibid., 136.

80 Ibid., 141.

81 Ibid., 124.

82 Duignan, *The Hoover Institution on War, Revolution and Peace*, 29. For additional information on the Hoover Institution's relationship with Stanford University, see Anderson, *Stanford and Hoover and Academic Freedom*.

83 For an interesting analysis of Ronald Reagan's ties to the Hoover Institution, see Seifert and Tuthill, "Scholarship and Public Policy."

84 The tensions between the Hoover Institution and Stanford University became particularly pronounced when President Reagan contemplated depositing his presidential papers at the Hoover Institution. Although the controversy over the creation of the Ronald Reagan Presidential Library eventually convinced Reagan to build his library in Simi Valley, California, the relationship between Hoover and Stanford has remained tense. Several other issues, including the early retirement of Glenn Campbell, have led to suggestions that ties between the Hoover Institution and Stanford be severed. For more on the Hoover-Stanford controversy, see Abouzeid, "Hoover Institute"; Bethell, "Liberalism, Stanford Style"; Bishop, "Stanford and Hoover Institute at Odds"; Harris, "Stanford-Hoover 'Divorce' Suggested"; Irving, "Stanford Faculty to Challenge Hoover Institution"; Otten, "On Stanford's Campus"; Otten, "Ronald Reagan's Presidential Papers May Come to the Hoover Institution"; Otten, "Campbell Comments on Hoover-Stanford Ties"; Otten, "Faculty Senate Postpones New Study of Stanford-Hoover Ties"; Turner, "Liberals at

Stanford Protest Ties to Hoover Institute"; and Workman, "Stanford Faculty Wants Review of Hoover Institute."

85 Shoup and Minter, *Imperial Brain Trust*, 15.

86 For the early history of the Council on Foreign Relations, see Council on Foreign Relations, *A Record of Fifteen Years*, and *A Record of Twenty-Five Years*.

87 Council on Foreign Relations, *1989 Annual Report*, 6.

88 In 1917 Edward M. House, a personal confidant to President Wilson, recruited approximately one hundred well-educated and affluent individuals possessing some knowledge of foreign affairs to draw up plans for the peace settlement. This elite group became known as The Inquiry; it began working in secret at the American Geographical Society headquarters in New York. Background information on the role of this organization is included in Schulzinger, *The Wise Men of Foreign Affairs*, 2.

89 Ibid., 3.

90 Quoted ibid., 4.

91 To a large extent, growing anti-British sentiments in the United States during the early 1920s can be attributed to the outcome of the 1919 Paris Peace Conference. In short, many observers believed that British leaders had used their influence at the end of the war to deceive Wilson into expanding the British Empire. See Schulzinger. *The Wise Men of Foreign Affairs*, 5.

92 Ibid., 6.

93 Shoup and Minter, *Imperial Brain Trust*, 16.

94 A membership roster of the Council on Foreign Relations is available in its annual reports.

95 Kraft, "School for Statesmen."

96 Through its national program, the Council on Foreign Relations supports programs in several US cities, including Chicago, Boston, Dallas, and Los Angeles.

97 The Council on Foreign Relations, *1989 Annual Report*, 6.

98 For a list of CFR publications from 1929 to 1983, see Schulzinger, *The Wise Men of Foreign Affairs*, 294–303. CFR studies published since 1983 can be found in its annual reports and on its Web site: www.cfr.org.

99 A discussion of the origins of the War and Peace Studies project can be found in Schulzinger, *The Wise Men of Foreign Affairs*, 59–79, and in Santoro, *Diffidence and Ambition*.

100 Council on Foreign Relations, *1989 Annual Report*, 175.

101 For an interesting discussion of whether think tanks have violated the spirit or the letter of the law, see Chisolm, "Sinking the Think Tanks Upstream." Also see Linden, "Powerhouses of Policy," 99–106, 170, and 174–9.

102 Schulzinger, *The Wise Men of Foreign Affairs*, ix.
103 Council on Foreign Relations, *1989 Annual Report*, 8.
104 The Rand Corporation also has a branch office in Washington, DC.
105 Nelson, *The First Heroes*, 104.
106 Orlans, *The Nonprofit Research Institute*, 19.
107 A thorough account of the removal of Project Rand from the Douglas Aircraft Company is provided in B.L.R. Smith, *The Rand Corporation*, 51–74.
108 Orlans, *The Nonprofit Research Institute*, 21.
109 In addition to its expertise in defense and national security issues, RAND conducts research on a wide range of domestic policy concerns, including civil and criminal justice, health, education, economic development, women's issues, and immigration. To train future researchers, the institute offers a PhD in public policy analysis through its own graduate school (in cooperation with the University of California, Los Angeles) and graduate degrees in health policy analysis and Soviet international behaviour.
110 RAND also receives funding from the Department of Health and Human Services/National Institutes of Health, other federal and government agencies, private firms, associations, and international agencies, foundations, and individuals. As well, it draws on its sizable endowment to support its research. See RAND, *An Introduction to RAND*.
111 Dickson, *Think Tanks*, 222–3.
112 Urban Institute, 30: *The Urban Institute, 1968–1998*, 7.
113 Ibid., 9.
114 Ibid, 7.
115 Ibid., 3.
116 See McGann, *The Competition for Dollars, Scholars and Influence*.
117 McGann, "Academics to Ideologues," 736.
118 For a more detailed analysis of the various factors contributing to the rise of think tanks in the United States, see Ricci, *The Transformation of American Politics*.
119 Interview with Dennis Bark, 19 March 1990.
120 Several of these scholars, including Henry Kissinger and Zbigniew Brzezinski, are employed by prestigious think tanks; however, they rose to national prominence as foreign policy experts while they were teaching at Ivy League universities in the United States.
121 For a brief profile of the Institute for Policy Studies, see Muravchik, "The Think Tank of the Left."
122 Interview with Thomas Henriksen, 5 July 1989.
123 Senator Gary Hart, Senator Robert Dole, Reverend Jesse Jackson, Pat Robertson, former secretary of the interior Bruce Babbitt, Jack Kemp, and Pat

Buchanan are among the many former office-holders who have created their own think tanks. For an interesting discussion of whether these individuals have violated the spirit and/or the letter of the law by circumventing campaign finance reform legislation, see Chisolm, "Sinking the Think Tanks Upstream."

124 There are several examples of high-profile political leaders who have endorsed the fundraising campaigns of think tanks. During the 1980s Newt Gingrich, Jack Kemp, and Edwin Meese III, among others, wrote letters on behalf of the Heritage Foundation to help the organization raise money.

125 For a discussion on the techniques think tanks use to exercise influence, see chapter 6.

126 Weaver, "The Changing World of Think Tanks," 567. In Canada and Britain, where the parliamentary principle of strong party unity is enforced, there has not been a proliferation of think tanks comparable to that occurring in the United States. However, strong party unity alone does not appear to explain why so few think tanks exist in these countries. The strength of individual ministries and their ability to rely on the civil service may account for the basic difference. See Savoie, *Thatcher, Reagan, Mulroney* and *Breaking the Bargain*, 103–1.

127 Peschek, *Policy-Planning Organizations*, 28. Also see Peschek's study "Free the Fortune 500!" For additional information on the history of AEI, see Ford, "American Enterprise Institute for Public Policy Research," 29–33.

128 Blumenthal, *The Rise of the Counter-Establishment*, 39.

129 Ibid., 38.

130 Ibid., 39.

131 Ibid.

132 Linden, "Powerhouses of Policy," 102.

133 Ibid.

134 Melvin Laird was secretary of defense in the Nixon administration from 1969 to 1973.

135 Quoted in Blumenthal, *The Rise of the Counter-Establishment*, 43–4.

136 For additional information on the mismanagement of the AEI under William Baroody Jr, see the following: Blumenthal, "Think Tank Adrift in the Centre"; Emery, "New Troubles for an Old Think Tank"; and Goode and Hallow, "Struggling Institute Fights to Survive."

137 Linden, "Powerhouse of Policy," 102.

138 On the firing of William Baroody Jr and the appointment of Christopher C. DeMuth, see Balzano, "The Sacking of a Centrist"; DeMuth, "President's Report," 2; Seabrook, "Capital Gain"; and Sussman, "Conservative Think Tank Comes Back from Brink."

139 Linden, "Powerhouse of Policy," 102.

140 Quoted in Matlack, "Marketing Ideas," 1553.

141 AEI, *Annual Report, 2003*, 2.

142 Based on 2004 figures.

143 Remarks made by Jeffrey Gedmin at the conference "Think Tanks in the USA and Germany: Democracy at Work: How and Where Do Public Decision-Makers Obtain Their Knowledge?" University of Pennsylvania, Philadelphia, 18–20 November 1993.

144 Blumenthal, *The Rise of the Counter-Establishment*, 45. Pines resigned his position at the Heritage Foundation on 13 April 1992. See Hallow, "Pines Quits as Heritage Senior vp."

145 Heritage Foundation, *2003 Annual Report*, 2.

146 Ibid., 22.

147 Tyman, "A Decade-Long Heritage of Conservative Thought."

148 Feulner, "Ideas, Think-Tanks and Governments."

149 Ibid., 5.

150 McCombs, "Building a Heritage in the War of Ideas."

151 Heritage Foundation, *2003 Annual Report*.

152 Edwin Feulner and his associates at Heritage frequently recommended staff and other individuals with close ties to the institution for vacant positions in the Reagan administration. Most letters of recommendation were sent to Edwin Meese III, counsellor to President Reagan and later attorney general. A handful of other think tanks, including the Hoover Institution, also submitted letters of recommendation for their staff to Meese.

153 According to Heritage Foundation, *2003 Annual Report*, there are 1,729 President's Club members, whose donations of $1,000 or more raised $2.1 million for Heritage in 2003. There are also 453 members of the President's Club Executive Committee, donors of at least $2,500 or more but less than $10,000, who provided Heritage with nearly $1.7 million.

154 Kurtz, "Meese Helps Group to Raise Funds."

155 Ibid.

156 Ibid.

157 Ibid.

158 Heritage Foundation, *2003 Annual Report*.

159 According to its *2003 Annual Report* (24), Heritage scholars made 1,100 television appearances and 1,418 radio appearances and had their commentaries appear in major print and online news outlets 907 times. In addition, Heritage claims that its Web site, www.heritage.org, was visited 3.6 million times.

160 *Oakland Tribune*, "Reagan Team Consults Heritage Foundation."

161 The Heritage Foundation's contribution to these and other initiatives is discussed by Peschek in *Policy Planning Organizations*.

162 Heritage Foundation, *1990 Annual Report*, 4–5.

163 Quoted in Fischer, "Country Report: American Think Tanks."

164 Micklethwait and Wooldridge, "For Conservatives, Mission Accomplished."

165 See the Carter Center's Web site at www.cartercenter.org.

166 Ibid.

167 Ibid.

168 Hayward, *The Real Jimmy Carter*.

169 See the Nixon Center Web site at www.nixoncenter.org.

170 Center for Responsive Politics Web site at www.opensecrets.org.

171 Ibid. For more on the relationship between politicians and think tanks, see Chisolm, "Sinking the Think Tanks Upstream."

172 Ibid.

173 Ibid.

174 CSIS mission statement. For a detailed history of the organization, see Smith, *Strategic Calling*.

175 Information obtained from the Center for Security Policy's Web site at www.centerforsecuritypolicy.org.

176 Interview with Frank Gaffney Jr, 18 May 2004.

177 Ibid.

178 Ibid.

179 Other recipients of this award include former speaker of the House Newt Gingrich and President Ronald Reagan. See Caldicott, *The New Nuclear Danger*, 27.

180 Quotation obtained from CSP Web site.

181 Interview with Gary Schmitt, 19 May 2004.

182 See Kristol and Kagan, "Toward a Neo-Reaganite Foreign Policy." In addition to being affiliated with PNAC, Kagan is senior associate at the Carnegie Endowment for International Peace.

183 See PNAC's Web site at www.newamericancentury.org.

184 Ibid.

185 Abelson, *American Think Tanks and Their Role in US Foreign Policy*, 93.

186 Several articles have been written on IPS. For example, see Muravchik, "The Think Tank of the Left"; and Yoffe, "IPS Faces Life." Also see Powell, *Covert Cadre*.

187 See www.ips-dc.org.

188 Institute for Policy Studies, *Annual Report 2002*, 11.

CHAPTER THREE

1 See, for instance, Peschek, *Policy Planning Organizations*; Dye, *Who's Running America?*; Domhoff and Dye, *Power Elites and Organizations*; and Saloma, *Ominous Politics*.

2 While Marxists and elite theorists are concerned with the economic relationship between think tanks and the state, the assumptions underlying their approaches are very different. Indeed, there are tremendous variations within Marxism, Gramscian, and other theoretical approaches that form part of this research tradition. For a Gramscian approach to the study of think tanks, see Gill, *American Hegemony and the Trilateral Commission*. On Gramsci more generally, see Golding, *Gramsci's Democratic Theory*. And on the main streams of Marxism, see Kolakowski, *Main Currents of Marxism*.

3 Domhoff, *The Power Elite and the State*.

4 See Newsom, *The Public Dimension of Foreign Policy*, 141–62.

5 The American pluralist tradition is strongly based in the belief that society is composed of individual groups that compete for power and status in the policy-making community. Two studies in particular have had a major impact on shaping this perspective: Truman, *The Governmental Process*, and Bentley, *The Process of Government*.

6 See Pal and Weaver, *The Government Taketh Away*.

7 See Evans, Reuschemeyer, and Skocpol, *Bringing the State Back In*.

8 Krasner, *Defending the National Interest*.

9 Steelman, Review of *Do Think Tanks Matter?* 165.

10 Krasner, *Defending the National Interest*, 11.

11 Steelman, Review of *Do Think Tanks Matter?* 165.

12 For more on the relationship between Richard Nixon and the US Congress, see Schlessinger, *The Imperial Presidency*.

13 See Smith, *George Bush's War*.

14 On the relationship between the Executive and Congress in US foreign policy, see Hinckley, *Less than Meets the Eye*.

15 On the different management styles of presidents, see Campbell, *Managing the Presidency*.

16 See Critchlow, The Brookings Institution; Schulzinger, *The Wise Men of Foreign Affairs*; Edwards, *The Power of Ideas*; and Smith, *The Rand Corporation*.

17 For instance, see Dickson, *Think Tanks*; Smith, *The Idea Brokers*; Ricci, *The Transformation of American Politics*; Lindquist, "A Quarter-Century of

Think Tanks in Canada"; McGann and Weaver, *Think Tanks and Civil Societies*; and Stone, *Capturing the Political Imagination.*

18 For a more detailed discussion of epistemic and policy communities, see Haas, *Knowledge, Power, and International Policy Coordination*; Pross, *Group Politics and Public Policy*, esp. chapter 5; and Coleman and Skogstad, *Public Policy and Policy Communities.*

19 See Heclo, "Issue Networks"; Lindquist, "Think Tanks or Policy Clubs?"; and Stone, *Capturing the Political Imagination.*

20 See Kingdon, *Agendas, Alternatives, and Public Policies*, and Stairs, "Public Opinion and External Affairs."

21 See Mills, *The Power and Elite*, and Smith, *The Power Game.*

22 For an example of how not to construct a grand theory of international politics, see Waltz, *Theory of International Politics.*

CHAPTER FOUR

1 Madison, "Federalist No. 10."
2 Ibid.
3 Ibid.
4 This expression is taken from the title of Stone's book, *Capturing the Political Imagination.*
5 Rich, *Think Tanks, Public Policy, and the Politics of Expertise*, 210.
6 For a useful analysis of German think tanks, see Thunert, "Think Tanks in Germany."
7 For more on de Tocqueville and his views of America, see Ledeen, *Tocqueville on American Character*, and Wolin, *Tocqueville between two worlds.*
8 In recent years, Robert Putnam has argued that Americans have been less inclined to join associations, a development he believes can have profound consequences for American civic culture. See his study *Bowling Alone.*
9 The French political philosopher Bernard Henri-Levy has written a fascinating study based on his efforts to retrace de Tocqueville's travels in America. See his article "In the Footsteps of Tocqueville."
10 McGann, "Academics to Ideologues," 733.
11 Remarks made by McGann at the University of Passau, 3 December 2003.
12 Simon and Stevenson, "Thinking outside the Tank," 90.
13 A similar argument is advanced by Kramer in *Ivory Towers on Sand.*
14 On the Executive Office of the President and other agencies and departments that support the White House, see Hart, *The Presidential Branch*, and Weko, *The Politicizing Presidency.*

15 Rich, *Think Tanks, Public Policy, and the Politics of Expertise,* 75.

16 Although policy-makers in Canada have traditionally been distrustful of the external policy research community, they appear more willing to strengthen their ties to some think tanks and other NGOs. For more on this subject, see Savoie, *Breaking the Bargain,* 103–31.

17 See Orlans, *The Nonprofit Research Institute.*

18 For example, in Canada and in other parliamentary democracies with strong political parties, it is very difficult for non-governmental organizations to influence the policy preferences and choices of members of Parliament. This is why many NGOs focus their attention on the cabinet and on the bureaucracy. A useful discussion of this subject appears in Young and Everitt, *Advocacy Groups.*

19 Abelson, *American Think Tanks and Their Role in US Foreign Policy,* 56.

20 For more on the process of nominating and confirming presidential appointments, see Twentieth Century Fund, *Obstacle Course.*

21 Ibid.

22 Interview with David Frum, 20 May 2004.

23 Ibid.

24 The role and function of public think tanks is the focus of Robinson's study "Public Think Tanks in the United States."

25 For more on the Congressional Policy Advisory Board, see House Policy Committee, "Congressional Policy Advisory Board Meets with House Leadership," at House Policy Committee Web page: policy.house.gov/news/releases/1998.

26 Information obtained by congressional aide to former California Republican representative Christopher Cox.

27 Ibid.

28 On the role of policy experts in presidential administrations, see Pfiffner, *The Strategic Presidency,* and Brauer, *Presidential Transitions.*

29 See Goldwin and Licht, *Foreign Policy and the Constitution.*

30 Quoted in Abelson, *American Think Tanks and Their Role in US Foreign Policy,* 73.

31 Abelson and Carberry, "Following Suit or Falling Behind?" 546–7.

32 Kingdon, *Agendas, Alternatives, and Public Policies,* 129.

33 Ibid., 130.

34 Harrison and Hoberg, "Setting the Environmental Agenda in Canada and the United States."

35 Ibid. For more on theories of entrepreneurship, see Schneider and Teske, "Toward a Theory of the Political Entrepreneur." On the role of institu-

tional structures in influencing policy entrepreneurship, see Checkel, *Ideas and International Political Change.*

36 Abelson and Carberry, "Following Suit or Falling Behind?" 548.

37 For more on the origins of the Fraser Institute, see Lindquist, *Behind the Myth of Think Tanks,* esp. 377–80.

38 Drawing on their extensive service in the public sector, Kirby and Pitfield played an important role in recognizing the need for policy-makers to draw on policy expertise both inside and outside government. Pitfield served as deputy secretary to the cabinet (plans) and deputy clerk of the Privy Council (1969–73). He also served as clerk of the Privy Council and secretary to cabinet (1975–79). Kirby was assistant secretary to the prime minister (1974–76), secretary to the cabinet for federal-provincial relations (1980–82), and deputy clerk of the Privy Council Office (1981–82). On the contribution of senior civil servants to think tank development, see Lindquist, *Behind the Myth of Think Tanks.*

39 Abelson and Carberry, "Following Suit or Falling Behind?" 548.

40 Ibid.

41 For more, see Bremner, *American Philanthropy;* Whitaker, *The Foundations;* and O'Connell, *America's Voluntary Spirit.*

42 Lipset, *Continental Divide,* 142–9.

43 Abelson and Carberry, "Following Suit or Falling Behind?" 549.

44 For more on the role of foundations in the United States, see Berman, *The Influence of the Carnegie, Ford and Rockefeller Foundations on American Foreign Policy;* and Sealander, *Private Wealth and Public Life.*

45 AEI's financial crisis during the mid-1980s was also a result of poor management. See Abelson, *American Think Tanks and Their Role in US Foreign Policy,* 53–4.

46 Morgan, "Think Tank or Hired Gun?" For more on the relationship between think tanks and corporate donors, see Stefancic and Delgado, *No Mercy.*

CHAPTER FIVE

1 Peschek, *Policy Planning Organizations,* 19.

2 There is long-standing debate in the literature about the extent to which interest groups and other non-governmental organizations act independently of government departments and agencies. Although some scholars, including Arthur Bentley and David Truman, argue that public policy reflects the outcome of interest-group competition, where the state plays little more than a mediating role, others, such as Hugh Heclo and Evert Lindquist, maintain

that many public policies are the product of the ongoing interaction between governmental and non-governmental organizations in specific policy communities. See, for example, Heclo, "Issue Networks and the Executive Establishment," and Lindquist, "Public Managers and Policy Communities." In short, the so-called split between public and private uses of power is debatable.

3 See Smith, *The Idea Brokers*.

4 For example, see Brock, *The Republican Noise Machine*, and Lieberman, *Slanting the Story*.

5 For example, see Rosenau, *The Scientific Study of Foreign Policy*.

6 Diane Stone has used a similar analogy to describe the work of think tanks; see "Recycling Bins, Garbage Cans or Think Tanks?

7 Nossal, "Opening Up the Black Box," 533.

8 For a useful summary of the rational actor paradigm, see Allison, *The Essence of Decision*, 32–5.

9 On the reluctance of the Supreme Court to become involved in disputes between the Executive and Congress over foreign policy, see Uhlmann, "Reflections on the Role of the Judiciary in Foreign Policy."

10 Allison, *The Essence of Decision*.

11 By leaking confidential information to the media and to Congress, reducing the flow of information to a snail's pace, and creating loyalty networks throughout the bureaucracy, individual departments and agencies can undermine the ability of political leaders to pursue particular policies. The extent to which public servants can frustrate the efforts of policy-makers is examined in Albert Breton and Ronald Wintrobe's study "An Economic Analysis of Bureaucratic Efficiency."

12 Herbert Simon has written extensively on theories of individual and organizational behaviour. See his *Administrative Behaviour, Models of Man*, and, with James March, *Organizations*.

13 Allison, *The Essence of Decision*, 71.

14 Ibid. For an analysis of Herbert Simon's theory of satisficing, see his study *Administrative Behaviour*, 38–41, 80–1 and 240–4. For more on his contributions to organizational theory, see his autobiography *Models of My Life*.

15 Charles E. Lindblom agrees that contrary to the assumptions underlying the rational actor model, policy-makers do not consider all possible options before selecting a course of action. Rather, they look to previous policy decisions to determine how to respond to a particular problem. Lindblom argues that, through a process of incrementalism, policy-makers simply modify existing policies to deal with newly emerging issues. Since decision-makers

are familiar with policies that have failed and those that have succeeded in satisfying their objectives, they have no incentive to develop new policy positions. However, while Lindblom's theory is useful in explaining why some governmental policies appear consistent over time, it cannot explain major changes in the direction of foreign and domestic policy. See his study "The Science of Muddling Through."

16 Allison, *The Essence of Decision*, 72.

17 Hundreds of books have been written on virtually every aspect of the Reagan presidency. For a comprehensive analysis of his time in office, see Cannon, *President Reagan*; Brownlee and Graham, *The Reagan Presidency*; and Wallison, *Ronald Reagan*.

18 On Kennedy's vision of America, see Dallek, *An Unfinished Life*. For Clinton's views of America and the world, see Clinton, *My Life*.

19 While Allison made an important contribution to the bureaucratic theory of decision-making, he was not the first scholar to adopt this approach. Richard Neustadt's *Presidential Power* portrayed the president as being constrained by a permanent bureaucracy. Other scholars, including Morton Halperin, in *Bureaucratic Politics and Foreign Policy*, and Roger Hilsman, in *The Politics of Policy Making in Defense and Foreign Affairs*, have also examined the decision-making process from a bureaucratic politics perspective.

20 ExCom refers to the Executive Committee of the National Security Council. During the Cuban Missile Crisis, ExCom included President Kennedy; Attorney-General Robert Kennedy; Secretary of State Dean Rusk; Secretary of Defense Robert McNamara; Director of the CIA John McCone; Secretary of the Treasury Douglas Dillon; President Kennedy's adviser on national security affairs, McGeorge Bundy; presidential counsel Ted Sorenson; Undersecretary of State George Ball; Deputy Undersecretary of State U. Alexis Johnson; General Maxwell Taylor, chairman of the Joint Chiefs of Staff; Edwin Martin, assistant secretary of state for Latin America; Llewellyn Thompson, State Department Soviet expert (replaced Chip Bohlen, who became ambassador to France); Roswell Gilpatric, deputy secretary of defense; Paul Nitze, assistant secretary of defense (international security affairs); Vice-President Lyndon B. Johnson; Adlai Stevenson, ambassador to the United Nations; Ken O'Donnell, special assistant to the president, Don Wilson, deputy secretary of the United States Information Agency; former secretary of state Dean Acheson; and former secretary of defense Robert Lovett.

21 See Krasner, "Are Bureaucracies Important?" and *Defending the National Interest*.

22 Allison, *the Essence of Decision*, 144.

23 Ibid., 169.

24 Dozens of books and hundreds of articles have been written on the Cuban Missile Crisis. For a useful overview of this critical foreign policy confrontation, see Stern, *Averting "the Final Failure."*

25 For an interesting analysis of the many constraints confronting decision-makers during the 1967 Arab-Israeli war, see Stein and Tanter, *Rational Decision-Making.*

26 Steinbruner, *The Cybernetic Theory of Decision*, 47.

27 Ibid., 66.

28 Ibid., 67.

29 For example, see Cigler and Loomis, *Interest Group Politics.*

30 The symbiotic relationship between government officials, the military, and defence contractors has also been referred to as the "Iron Triangle." According to Hedrick Smith, the Iron Triangle has considerable influence on the formulation of national security policy. See his *The Power Game*, 173–215.

31 See Abelson, *American Think Tanks and Their Role in US Foreign Policy*; Caldicott, *The New Nuclear Danger*; and Mann, *Rise of the Vulcans.*

32 These arguments are advanced by Domhoff and Dye in their study *Power Elites and Organizations.* Domhoff has written several studies on elites in the United States in which he comments on the role of think tanks. Two of them should be referred to: *The Higher Circles* and *The Powers That Be.* Dye has also written extensively on elite behaviour in the United States. His research on the role of think tanks in the United States is examined in "Oligarchic Tendencies in National Policy Making." For an interesting critique of Domhoff and Dye's views of think tanks, see Fischer, "Country Report."

33 For example, see Hodgson, "The Establishment," and Parmar, *Think Tanks and Power in Foreign Policy.*

CHAPTER SIX

1 For more on the increased competition among think tanks, see McGann, *The Competition for Dollars, Scholars and Influence.*

2 Remarks recorded by author, who attended the conference entitled "Restoring Fiscal Sanity – While We Still Can," Washington, DC, 18 May 2004.

3 Interview with Leslie Gelb, 22 February 2005.

4 Ibid.

5 Some presidents have relied far more heavily on scholars from think tanks to serve on presidential advisory boards than others. For instance, President Reagan invited several from the Hoover Institution to sit on the President's

Foreign Intelligence Advisory Board. Conversely, of the eleven members of the PFIAB appointed by President Clinton and chaired by Warren Rudman, none had a permanent position at a think tank. In a break with the past, President Bush has kept the names of the sixteen members of his PFIAB secret, only revealing that Brent Scowcroft serves as chair. For more on this subject, see Corn, "Who's on PFIAB?" On the role of these boards, see Abelson, *American Think Tanks and Their Role in US Foreign Policy*, 75-9.

6 Ibid., 68.

7 Linden, "Powerhouses of Policy," 100.

8 Heritage Foundation, *2003 Annual Report*, 34. Heritage's operating revenue for 2003 was $34,660, 679.

9 Heritage Foundation, *1998 Annual Report*.

10 See Rich and Weaver, "Think Tanks, the Media and the Policy Process." Also see Dolny, "What's in a Label?"

11 Brookings Institution, *Annual Report 2003*, 41-2.

12 Ibid, 44.

13 American Enterprise Institute, *Annual Report*, 2003, 35.

14 Heritage Foundation, *2003 Annual Report*, 24.

15 Crowley, "How Can Think Tanks Win Friends?"

16 Heritage Foundation, *2003 Annual Report*, 24.

17 Quoted in Abelson, *American Think Tanks and Their Role in US Foreign Policy*, 88.

18 Quoted ibid.

19 Quoted ibid, 86.

20 Quoted ibid.

21 Abelson, "Policy Experts and Political Pundits."

22 Brookings Institution, *Annual Report 2003*, 44.

CHAPTER SEVEN

1 Holsti, *International Politics*, 142.

2 Ibid., 141.

3 Ibid., 150.

4 Interview with Leslie Gelb, 22 February 2005.

5 See, for instance, Heclo, "Issue Networks and the Executive Establishment."

6 A detailed discussion of policy communities is provided by Lindquist in "Public Managers and Policy Communities."

7 On theories of functionalism and integration and how they can be used to explain the success of interstate cooperation, see Mitrany, *A Working Peace System*.

8 These think tanks were selected because of their interest and expertise in foreign and defense policy. I also selected six major newspapers that cover American politics inside the Beltway very closely. The issues and events that were chosen represent some of the most important challenges confronting American decision-makers in the last four years. In the area of domestic politics, other critical issues, such as health care, energy, and education, could have been identified. As noted, the purpose in compiling these data was to demonstrate a pattern in think tank exposure and to identify one indicator that could be used by scholars interested in using quantitative approaches to study think tank influence.

9 See Abelson, *Do Think Tanks Matter?* 90–106.

10 Rich and Weaver argue that think tanks located inside the Beltway and those that are ideologically compatible with the majority party in Congress are more likely to be called upon to testify before legislative committees. See their study "Think Tanks, the Media and the Policy Process," and Rich, "Think Tanks as Sources of Expertise for Congress."

11 The study looked at the total number of appearances by scholars from twelve think tanks before the following committees: Senate Foreign Relations Committee, Senate Intelligence Committee, Senate Armed Services Committee, House Permanent Select Committee on Intelligence, House Committee on Armed Services, House Committee on International Relations, and House Committee on Homeland Security.

12 Interview with Zbigniew Brzezinski, 20 May 2004.

13 Ibid.

CHAPTER EIGHT

1 Micklethwait and Wooldridge, *The Right Nation*. Several others have made the argument that think tanks form an integral part of the power elite in the United States. See, for example, Domhoff and Dye, *Power Elites and Organizations*; Domhoff, *The Power Elite and the State*; Perloff, *The Shadows of Power*; and Shoup and Minter, *Imperial Brain Trust*.

2 Reagan, *An American Life*, 547–8.

3 Anderson, *Revolution*, 82–3

4 Ibid., 83.

5 Ibid., 86.

6 Ibid., 90.

7 Ibid.

8 For a fascinating look at Edward Teller and his involvement in SDI, see Broad, *Teller's War*.

9 High Frontier was originally located in Washington, DC.

10 For more on the report, go to www.highfrontier.org. Also see Graham, *We Must Defend America and Save the World from Madness*.

11 Anderson, *Revolution*, 94–5.

12 Ibid., 96.

13 The content of Reagan's speech was known by only a handful of his closest advisers, including Deputy National Security Adviser Robert McFarlane. His secretaries of state and defense and the Joint Chiefs of Staff were notified only two days before Reagan addressed the nation. For more on the secrecy surrounding the SDI speech and the reaction of some senior officials, see McFarlane and Smardz, *Special Trust*, 227–35 and 301–20; Shultz, *Turmoil and Triumph*, 249–69; and Weinberger, *Fighting for Peace*, 291–329.

14 Reagan, "Address to the Nation on Defense and National Security."

15 Ibid.

16 On the reaction in Congress to Star Wars, see Pressler, *Star Wars*.

17 For more on debates within the academic community over Star Wars, see Miller and Van Evera, *The Star Wars' Controversy*, and Bundy, *The Nuclear Controversy*.

18 For more on the reaction to Reagan's Star Wars speech, see two books by Peter Schweizer: *Victory* and *Reagan's War*.

19 See Union of Concerned Scientists, *Empty Promise* and *The Fallacy of Star Wars*. Also see Bowman, *Star Wars*, and Brown, "Is SDI Technically Feasible?"

20 Union of Concerned Scientists, *Empty Promise* and *The Fallacy of Star Wars*.

21 Pressler, *Star Wars*, 127.

22 Ibid., 115.

23 As discussed in chapter 1, President Bush, in what some conservative Republicans considered an act of treason, fired many of Reagan's advisers when he assumed office. As Annelise Anderson, a former advisor to Bush, observed, this was done in part to allow the new president to step out of Reagan's shadow.

24 Bush, *National Security Strategy of the United States: 1991–1992*, 105-6.

25 On George Bush's presidency, see Greene, *The Presidency of George Bush*; Parmet, *George Bush*; and Bush and Scowcroft, *A World Transformed*.

26 Balz, "Change Doesn't Come Cheap."

27 Campbell and Rockman, *The Clinton Presidency*.

28 Clinton, "Remarks by the President on National Missile Defense."

29 Ibid.

30 Ibid.

31 Ibid.

32 Ibid.

33 For interesting accounts of the 2000 presidential election, see Kaplan, *The Accidental President*, and Tapper, *Down & Dirty*.

34 Bush, "A Period of Consequences."

35 Bush, Speech at the National Defense University, Washington, DC, 1 May 2001.

36 See "America Withdraws from ABM Treaty" and "Bush to Withdraw from ABM treaty."

37 From the beginning of the Bush administration, Donald Rumsfeld has been seen as the point man on missile defense. For more on his role in trying to sell this initiative at home and abroad, see Hartung and Ciarrocca, "Star Wars: The Next Generation."

38 For reactions to Bush's announcement, see "Bush Marks End of ABM Treaty."

39 "US House Democrats Sue Bush over ABM Treaty Withdrawal." A similar lawsuit was filed by Senator Barry Goldwater in 1979 against President Jimmy Carter for his decision to abrogate the US mutual defense treaty with Taiwan. The case eventually made its way to the US Supreme Court, where the justices "dismissed Goldwater's suit without ruling whether the president could independently terminate a treaty." See Boese, "U.S. Withdraws from ABM Treaty."

40 Lawyers' Committee on Nuclear Policy and Western States Legal Foundation, "Judge Allows Bush's Withdrawal from ABM Treaty to Stand."

41 Lumpkin, "Tests Put Off on Missile Defense Plan."

42 Interview with Baker Spring, 18 May 2004.

43 Ibid.

44 Letter from President Reagan to General Daniel Graham, 25 November 1985. Available on High Frontier Web site: www.highfrontier.org.

45 President Reagan's telephoned remarks on High Frontier's tenth anniversary, September 1991. Available on High Frontier Web site: www.highfrontier.org.

46 Interview with Baker Spring, 18 May 2004.

47 Ibid.

48 Ibid.

49 Ibid.

50 Ibid.

51 Caldicott, *The New Nuclear Danger*, 24–9.

52 Ibid., 26. There are other think tanks, such as the Committee on the Present Danger, that have been associated with the Star Wars lobby. See Abelson, *American Think Tanks and Their Role in U.S. Foreign Policy*, 62–4.

53 Ibid., 26–7.
54 Interview with Frank Gaffney, 18 May 2004.
55 Ibid.
56 Ibid.
57 Ibid.
58 Ibid.
59 For more on Carter's and Clinton's management of foreign policy, see Brown, *The Faces of Power*.
60 On Reagan and the Iran-Contra scandal, see Cohen and Mitchell, *Men of Zeal*, and Draper, *A Very Thin Line*.

CHAPTER NINE

1 Pillar, *Terrorism and U.S. Foreign Policy*, 10.
2 Ibid., vii.
3 For detailed coverage of the events of 9/11, see Bernstein, *Out of the Blue*.
4 See Woodward, *Bush at War* and *Plan of Attack*. Also see Bovard, *The Bush Betrayal*; Johnson, *Overconfidence and War*; and Sammon, *Fighting Back*.
5 Transparency, "War of the Worlds, Orson Welles, and the Invasion from Mars."
6 Ibid.
7 For a complete list of conferences, seminars, and workshops, see appendix 3.
8 A list of think tank testimonies before the House and Senate is included in appendix 3.
9 See Pillar, *Terrorism and U.S. Foreign Policy*, 2–11.
10 Flynn, *America the Vulnerable*, xi.
11 Ibid., xii.
12 For this perspective, see Callinicos, *The New Mandarins of American Power*; Gardner and Young, *The New American Empire*; Hamm, *Devastating Society*; Hollander, *Understanding Anti-Americanism*; Ross and Ross, *Anti-Americanism*; and Sarder and Davies, *Why Do People Hate America?*
13 On the relationship between the United States and Western Europe since 9/11, see Gordon and Shapiro, *Allies at War*; Kagan, *Of Paradise and Power*; and Nye, *The Paradox of American Power*.
14 Frum and Perle, *An End to Evil*, 4.
15 Perle has been affiliated with several conservative think tanks throughout the United States, including AEI, the Committee on the Present Danger, the Hudson Institute, and the Center for Security Policy. For more on Perle, see

Friedman, *The Neoconservative Revolution*; Halper and Clarke, *America Alone;* Hamm, *Devastating Society*; and Micklethwait and Wooldridge, *The Right Nation.*

16 Frost, Robert, "Stopping by Woods on a Snowy Evening," in *New Hampshire.*

17 Frum and Perle, *An End to Evil*, especially chapters 3, 5, and 8.

18 For another study supportive of the Iraq war, see Kaplan and Kristol, *The War over Iraq.*

19 On the importance of finding an exit strategy in Iraq, see Preble, *Exiting Iraq.* Also see Eisenstadt and Mathewson, *U.S. Policy in Post-Saddam Iraq*, and Feldman, *What We Owe Iraq.*

20 Flynn, *America the Vulnerable.*

21 See Century Foundation, *Defeating the Jihadists*, and Satloff, *The Battle of Ideas in the War on Terror.*

22 On the debate over weapons of mass destruction, see Rampton and Stauber, *Weapons of Mass Deception*, and Blix, *Disarming Iraq.*

23 America's interest in oil has long been thought to be a motivating factor behind its foreign policy in the Middle East. See Everest, *Oil, Power and Empire.*

24 America's incestuous relationship with Saudi Arabia is thoughtfully explored in Unger's book *House of Bush, House of Saud.*

25 This subject was the focus of the National Commission on Terrorist Attacks upon the United States; see *The 9/11 Commission Report.* Also see Alterman and Green, *The Book on Bush*; Bovard, *The Bush Betrayal*; Corn, *The Lies of George W. Bush*; Jackson, *Writing the War on Terrorism*; and Prados, *Hoodwinked.*

26 See Piven, *The War at Home.*

27 For a thorough discussion on the PATRIOT Act and the Department of Homeland Security, see Crotty, *The Politics of Terror*; Brookings Institution, *Protecting the American Homeland: A Preliminary Analysis* and *Protecting the American Homeland: One Year On*; and Bremer and Meese, *Defending the American Homeland.*

28 Project for the New American Century, *Rebuilding America's Defenses*, iv.

29 Meacher, "This War on Terrorism Is Bogus."

30 Austin, "War Hawks and the Ugly American," in Hamm, *Devastating Society*, 55.

31 Among the many publications that provide a brief evaluation of PNAC are Bryce, *Cronies*; Callinicos, *The New Mandarins of American Power*; Halper and Clarke, *America Alone*; Laurent, *Bush's Secret World*; Lind, *Made in Texas*; and Micklethwait and Wooldridge, *The Right Nation.* For a more

thorough discussion of PNAC's ties to the Bush administration, see Stelzer, *Neoconservatism*, 1–28.

32 Kristol and Kagan, "Toward a Neo-Reaganite Foreign Policy," 20, 23.

33 Interview with Gary Schmitt, 19 May 2004.

34 A former chief of staff to Vice-President Dan Quayle, William Kristol is also editor of the conservative magazine *The Weekly Standard*. Robert Kagan, author of the best-selling book *Of Paradise and Power*, is a senior associate at the Carnegie Endowment for International Peace.

35 Several journalists and scholars have also pointed to a letter written by PNAC to President Clinton on 26 January 1998 as evidence of their early support for the invasion of Iraq, a letter that many claim had a profound impact on President Bush's decision to overthrow Saddam Hussein. A copy of the letter, signed by several prominent conservative policy-makers, including Elliot Abrams (National Security Council), Richard Armitage (deputy secretary of state), John Bolton (US representative to the UN and former undersecretary, Arms Control and International Security), Richard Perle (Defense Policy Advisory Board), and Donald Rumsfeld (secretary of defense), can be found at www.theindyvoice.com.

36 Interview with Gary Schmitt, 19 May 2004.

37 Ibid.

38 Ibid.

39 Ibid.

40 Before becoming secretary of defense, Donald Rumsfeld chaired the Commission to Assess the Ballistic Missile Threat to the United States. The commission issued its final report on 15 July 1988.

41 Interview with Gary Schmitt, 19 May 2004.

42 Ibid.

43 Transcript, ABC News, transcript from *Nightline*, 5 March 2003, 2.

44 Ibid.

45 Ibid., 3.

46 Interview with Gary Schmitt, 19 May 2004.

47 Daalder and Lindsay, *America Unbound*, 2.

48 Bush was asked to identify the leaders of Chechnya, Pakistan, India, and Taiwan. He received partial marks for coming up with the Taiwanese leader's last name, Lee. For more on this subject, see Corn, "Bush Gets an F in Foreign Affairs," and Daalder and Lindsay, *America Unbound*, 17–19.

49 For more on Karen Hughes and her involvement in the Bush administration, see her autobiography, *Ten Minutes from Normal*. On Karl Rove, see Moore and Slater, *Bush's Brain*.

50 Associated Press, "Bush Turns to Foreign Policy Experts."

51 See Frum, *The Right Man.*

52 Daalder and Lindsay, *America Unbound,* 2.

53 For an interesting study on how commanders-in-chief have exercised their authority in foreign affairs, see DeConde, *Presidential Machismo.* Also see Johnson, *Overconfidence and War.*

54 Interview with Ivo Daalder, 20 May 2004.

55 Daalder and Lindsay, *America Unbound,*16.

56 Interview with Gary Schmitt, 19 May 2004.

57 In addition to giving speeches at AEI, President Bush has relied on several of its members in his administration. For example, John Bolton, whose appointment as US representative to the UN (until 2007) generated considerable controversy, previously worked at AEI. Morever, several of Bush's top officials, including Dick Cheney, Condoleezza Rice, and Donald Rumsfeld, have given speeches at the Council on Foreign Relations and at other think tanks. See Halper and Clarke, *America Alone,* 104–5.

58 Much has been made of the serious policy disagreements that have surfaced between George W. Bush and his father. For more on this subject, see Renshon, *In His Father's Shadow,* and Tanner, *The Wars of the Bushes.*

CONCLUSION

1 For useful insights into the minds of Kennan, Acheson, and Kissinger, see Kennan, *At a Century's Ending*; Chase, *Acheson*; and Kissinger, *Diplomacy.*

2 Steelman, Review of *Do Think Tanks Matter?* 165.

3 On the many challenges confronting think tanks, see McGann, *Scholars, Dollars and Policy Advice.*

Works Cited

ABC News. Transcript from *Nightline*, 5 March 2003.

Abelson, Donald E. *American Think Tanks and Their Role in US Foreign Policy.* London and New York: Macmillan and St. Martin's Press, 1996

– *Do Think Tanks Matter? Assessing the Impact of Public Policy Institutes.* Kingston and Montreal: McGill-Queen's University Press, 2002.

– "Policy Experts and Political Pundits: American Think Tanks and the News Media." *NIRA Review*, spring 1998, 28–32.

Abelson, Donald E., and Christine M. Carberry. "Following Suit or Falling Behind? A Comparative Analysis of Think Tanks in Canada and the United States." *Canadian Journal of Political Science* 31, no. 3 (1998): 525–55.

– "Policy Experts in Presidential Campaigns: A Model of Think Tank Recruitment." *Presidential Studies Quarterly* 27, no. 4 (fall 1997): 679–97.

Abouzeid, Pamela. "Hoover Institute: Stanford's Deep, Dark Secret?" *Oakland Tribune*, 18 July 1983.

Achenbach, Joel. "Wonk If You Love Clinton: Kennedy's They're Not: The Torch Has Been Passed to a Nerd Frontier." *Washington Post*, 8 November 1992.

Allen, Charles F., and Jonathan Portis. *The Comeback Kid: The Life and Career of Bill Clinton.* New York: Birch Lane Press, 1992.

Allison, Graham T. *The Essence of Decision: Explaining the Cuban Missile Crisis.* Boston: Little Brown, 1971.

Alterman, Eric. *Sound and Fury: The Washington Punditocracy and the Collapse of American Politics.* New York: Harper Collins, 1992.

Alterman, Eric, and Mark J. Green. *The Book on Bush: How George W. Bush (Mis) Leads America.* New York: Viking, 2004.

American Enterprise Institute. *Annual Report, 2003.* Washington, DC: American Enterprise Institute, 2003.

"America Withdraws from ABM Treaty." *BBC News,* 13 December 2001. Available at: www.news.bbc.co.uk/1/hi/world/americas/1707812.stm.

Anderson, Martin. *Impostors in the Temple.* New York: Simon and Schuster, 1992.

– *Revolution.* New York: Harcourt Brace Jovanovich, 1988.

– *Stanford and Hoover and Academic Freedom: A Collection of Published Reports on the Relationship between Stanford University and the Hoover Institution.* Stanford: Hoover Institution, 1985.

Associated Press. "Bush Turns to Foreign Policy Experts." 16 December 2000. Available at: http://quest.cjonline.com/stories/121600/gen_1216007443.shtml.

Babington, Charles. "Bush Names Zoellick as Trade Representative." *Washington Post,* 10 January 2000.

Baer, Donald. "A Network for the Nineties." *U.S. News and World Report,* 23 November 1992.

Balz, Dan, "Change Doesn't Come Cheap." *Washington Post,* 18 February 1993, A01.

Balzano, Michael P., Jr. "The Sacking of a Centrist." *Washington Post,* 6 July 1986.

Bandow, Doug. "New Democrats Lose Think-Tank War," *Wall Street Journal,* 18 March 1993.

Barnes, James A. "Will DLC Be a Lobbying Heavyweight?" *National Journal,* 23 October 1993.

Beers, David. "Button-Downed Bohemians." *San Francisco Chronicle,* 3 August 1986.

Beland, D., and A. Waddan. "From Thatcher (and Pinochet) to Clinton? Conservative Think Tanks, Foreign Models and U.S. Pensions Reform." *Political Quarterly* 71, no. 2 (April 2000): 202–10.

Bentley, Arthur F. *The Process of Government.* Chicago: University of Chicago Press, 1908.

Berman, Edward H. *The Influence of the Carnegie, Ford and Rockefeller Foundations on American Foreign Policy: The Ideology of Philanthropy.* New York: State University of New York Press, 1983.

Bernstein, Richard. *Out of the Blue: The Story of September 11th, 2001, from Jihad to Ground Zero.* New York: Times Books, 2002.

Bethell, Tom. "Liberalism, Stanford Style." *Commentary* 77, no.1 (January 1984): 42–7.

Bishop, Katherine. "Stanford and Hoover Institute at Odds." *New York Times,* 12 September 1985.

Blix, Hans. *Disarming Iraq.* New York: Pantheon Books, 2004.

Blumenthal, Sidney. *The Rise of the Counter-Establishment: From Conservative Ideology to Political Power.* New York: Harper and Row, 1988.

– "Think Tank Adrift in the Center." *Washington Post,* 26 June 1986.

Boese, Wade. "U.S. Withdraws from ABM Treaty; Global Response Muted." *Arms Control Today,* July/August 2002. Available at: www.armscontrol.org/act/2002_07-08/abmjul_aug02.asp.

Boston, T. "American Right-Wing Libertarians: the Opponents of Democracy, Ecology and Ethics." *Democracy and Nature* 6, no. 2 (July 2000): 199–210.

Bovard, James. *The Bush Betrayal.* New York: Palgrave Macmillan, 2004.

Bowman, Robert. *Star Wars: A Defense Insiders Case against the Strategic Defense Initiative.* Los Angeles: Tarcher; New York: Distributed by St. Martin's Press, 1986.

Brace, Paul, and Barbara Hinckley. *Follow the Leader: Opinion Polls and the Modern Presidents.* New York: Basic Books, 1992.

Braml, Joseph. *U.S. and German Policy Research Institutes' Coping with Influencing Their Environments.* Baden Baden: Nomos, 2004.

Brauer, Carl M. *Presidential Transitions: Eisenhower through Reagan.* New York: Oxford University Press, 1986.

Bremmer, L. Paul, III, and Edwin Meese III. *Defending the American Homeland.* Washington, DC: The Heritage Foundation, 2002.

Bremner, Robert H. *American Philanthropy.* Chicago: University of Chicago Press, 1988.

Breton, Albert, and Ronald Wintrobe. "An Economic Analysis of Bureaucratic Efficiency." *Law and Economic Workshop Series.* Toronto: University of Toronto, 1981.

Broad, William J. *Teller's War: The Top Secret Story behind the Star Wars Deception.* New York: Simon & Schuster, 1992.

Brookings Institution. *Annual Report 2003.* Washington, DC: The Brookings Institution, 2003.

– *Protecting the American Homeland: A Preliminary Analysis.* Washington, DC: Brookings Institution Press, 2002.

– *Protecting the American Homeland: One Year On.* Washington, DC: Brookings Institution Press, 2003.

Brown, Harold. "Is SDI Technically Feasible?" *Foreign Affairs* 64, no. 3 (1985): 435–54.

Brown, Seyom. *The Faces of Power: Constancy and Change in United States Foreign Policy from Truman to Clinton.* New York: Columbia University Press, 1994.

Brownlee, W. Elliot, and Hugh Davis Graham, eds. *The Reagan Presidency: Pragmatic Conservatism and Its Legacies.* Lawrence: University Press of Kansas, 2003.

Brownstein, Ronald, and Nina Easton. *Reagan's Ruling Class.* Washington, DC: Presidential Accountability Group, 1982.

Brock, David. *The Republican Noise Machine: Right-Wing Media and How It Corrupts Democracy.* New York: Crown Publishers, 2004.

Brummett, John. *High Wire: From the Backroads to the Beltway – The Education of Bill Clinton.* New York: Hyperion Press, 1994.

Bryce, Robert. *Cronies: Oil, the Bushes, and the Rise of Texas, America's Superstate.* New York: Public Affairs, 2004.

Bundy, W.M., ed. *The Nuclear Controversy: A Foreign Affairs Reader.* New York: Meridian, 1985.

Bush, George. *National Security Strategy of the United States: 1991–1992.* Washington: Brassey's (US), 1991.

Bush, George, and Brent Scowcroft. *A World Transformed.* New York: Knopf; Distributed by Random House, 1998.

Bush, George W. "A Period of Consequences." Speech delivered at the Citadel, Charleston, SC, 23 September 1999. Available at citadel.edu/r3/pao/addresses/pres_bush.

– Speech at the National Defense University, Washington, DC, 1 May 2001. Available at whitehouse.gov.

"Bush Marks End of ABM Treaty, with Call for Anti-Missile Shield," *Space Daily,* 13 June 2002. Available at: www.spacedaily.com/news/bmdo-02m.html.

"Bush to withdraw from ABM Treaty." *Guardian Unlimited,* 24 August 2001. Available at: www.guardian.co.uk/bush/story/0,7369,541845,00.html.

Butler, Stuart M., et al. *Mandate for Leadership II: Continuing the Conservative Revolution.* Washington, DC: Heritage Foundation, 1984.

Caldicott, Helen. *The New Nuclear Danger: George W. Bush's Military Industrial Complex.* New York: The New Press, 2002.

Callinicos, Alex. *The New Mandarins of American Power: The Bush Administration's Plans for the World.* Cambridge, UK: Polity; Malden, MA: Distributed in the USA by Blackwell Publishing, 2003.

Campbell, Colin. *Managing the Presidency: Carter, Reagan and the Search for Executive Harmony.* Pittsburgh: University of Pittsburgh Press, 1986.

Campbell, Colin, and Bert A. Rockman, eds. *The Clinton Presidency: First Appraisals.* Chatham, NJ: Chatham House Publishers, 1996.

Cannon, Lou. *President Reagan: The Role of a Lifetime.* New York: Simon and Schuster, 1991.

Carnegie, Andrew. *Autobiography.* Boston: Houghton Mifflin Co., 1920.

Carter, Jimmy. *Keeping Faith: Memoirs of a President*. Toronto, New York: Bantam Books, 1982.

– *Why Not the Best?* Nashville: Broadman Press, 1975.

Century Foundation. *Defeating the Jihadists: A Blueprint for Action*. New York: Century Foundation Press, 2004.

Chace, James. *Acheson: The Secretary of State Who Created the American World*. New York: Simon and Schuster, 1998.

Checkel, Jeffery T. *Ideas and International Political Change*. New Haven: Yale University Press, 1997.

Chisolm, Laura Brown. "Sinking the Think Tanks Upstream: The Use and Misuse of Tax Exemption Law to Address the Use and Misuse of Tax-Exempt Organizations by Politicians." *University of Pittsburgh Law Review* 51, no. 3 (1990): 577–640.

Cigler, Allen J., and Burdett A. Loomis, eds. *Interest Group Politics*. Washington DC: CQ Press, 1995.

Clarke, Richard. *Against All Enemies: Inside America's War on Terror*. New York: The Free Press, 2004.

Clinton, William Jefferson. *My Life*. New York: Alfred A. Knopf, 2004.

– "Remarks by the President on National Missile Defense." Gaston Hall, Georgetown University, Washington, DC, 1 September 2000. Available at: www.useu.be/ISSUES/nmd0901.html.

Clinton, William Jefferson, and Al Gore. President Clinton's New Beginning: The Complete Text of the Historic Clinton-Gore Economic Conference in Little Rock Arkansas. East Rutherford, NJ: Donald I. Fine, 1993.

Cohen, William S., and George J. Mitchell. *Men of Zeal: A Candid Inside Story of the Iran-Contra Hearings*. New York: Viking Press, 1988.

Coleman, William D., and Grace Skogstad, eds. *Public Policy and Policy Communities in Canada: A Structural Approach*. Toronto: Copp Clark Pitman, 1990.

Corn, David. "Bush Gets an F in Foreign Affairs." *Salon News*, 5 November 1999. Available at: http://www.salon.com/news/feature/1999/11/05/bush/.

– *The Lies of George W. Bush: Mastering the Politics of Deception*. New York: Crown Publishers, 2003.

– "Who's on PFIAB – A Bush Secret ... or Not?" *Nation*, 14 August 2002. Available at: http://www.thenation.com/blogs/capitalgames?bid=3&pid=97.

Council on Foreign Relations. *A Record of Fifteen Years: 1921-1936*. New York: Council on Foreign Relations, 1937.

– *The Council on Foreign Relations: A Record of Twenty-Five Years*. New York: Council on Foreign Relations, 1947.

– *1989 Annual Report*. New York: Council on Foreign Relations, 1989.

Critchlow, Donald T. *The Brookings Institution, 1916–1952: Expertise and the Public Interest in a Democratic Society*. DeKalb: Northern Illinois University Press, 1985.

Crotty, William J., ed. *The Politics of Terror: The U.S. Response to 9/11*. Boston: Northeastern University Press, 2004.

Crowley, Brian Lee. "How Can Think Tanks Win Friends and Influence People in the Media?" *Insider*, no. 264 (October 1999).

Daalder, Ivo H., and James M. Lindsay. *America Unbound: The Bush Revolution in Foreign Policy*. Washington, DC: Brookings Institution Press, 2003.

– "Bush: Still Needs Work on Foreign Affairs." *Newsday*, 8 December 1999.

Dahl, Robert A. *Who Governs? Democracy and Power in an American City*. New Haven: Yale University Press, 1961.

Dalby, Simon. *Creating the Second Cold War: The Discourse of Politics*. London: Pinter Publishers, 1990.

Dallek, Robert. *An Unfinished Life: John F. Kennedy, 1917–1963*. Boston: Little Brown and Company, 2003.

DeConde, Alexander. *Presidential Machismo: Executive Authority, Military Intervention, and Foreign Relations*. Boston: Northeastern University Press, 2000.

DeMuth, Christopher C. "President's Report: AEI's Mission." *Memorandum*, spring 1987.

Denham, Andrew. *Think-Tanks of the New Right*. Aldershot: Dartmouth, 1996.

Dickson, Paul. *Think Tanks*. New York: Atheneum, 1972.

Dolny, Michael. "What's in a Label? Right Wing Think Tanks Are Often Quoted, Rarely Labeled?" *Extra!* May/June 1998.

Domhoff, G. William. *The Bohemian Grave and Other Retreats: A Study in Ruling-Class Cohesiveness*. New York: Harper and Row, 1974.

– *The Higher Circles: The Governing Class in America*. New York: Vintage Books, 1970.

– *The Power Elite and the State: How Policy is Made in America*. New York: Aldine de Gruyter, 1990.

– *The Powers That Be: Processes of Ruling Class Domination in America*. New York: Vintage Books, 1978.

– *Who Rules America?* New Jersey: Prentice Hall, 1967.

– *Who Rules America Now? A View For the '80s*. New York: Simon and Schuster, 1986.

Domhoff, G. William, and Thomas R. Dye. *Power Elites and Organizations*. London: Sage, 1987.

Duignan, Peter. *The Hoover Institution on War, Revolution and Peace: Seventy-Five Years on its History*. Stanford: Hoover Institution Press, 1989.

Duignan, Peter, and Alvin Rabushka, eds. *The United States in the 1980s.* Stanford: Hoover Institution Press, 1980.

Draper, Theodore. *A Very Thin Line: The Iran-Contra Affairs.* New York: Hill and Wang, 1991.

Dye, Thomas R. "Oligarchic Tendencies in National Policy Making: The Role of Private Policy Planning Organizations." *Journal of Politics* 40 (1978): 309–31.

– *Who's Running America? The Conservative Years.* New Jersey: Prentice-Hall, 1986.

Easterbrook, Gregg. "Ideas Move Nations." *Atlantic Monthly* 257, no. 1 (January 1986): 66–80.

Edwards, Lee. *The Power of Ideas: The Heritage Foundation at 25 Years.* Ottawa, IL: Jameson Books, 1997.

Eisenstadt, Michael, and Eric Mathewson, eds. *U.S. Policy in Post-Saddam Iraq: Lessons from the British Experience.* Washington, DC: Washington Institute for Near East Policy, 2003.

Emery, Glenn, "New Troubles for an Old Think Tank." *Nation,* 7 April 1986, 26–7.

Evans, Peter B., Dietrich Rueschemeyer, and Theda Skocpol. *Bringing the State Back In.* Cambridge; New York: Cambridge University Press, 1985.

Everest, Larry. *Oil, Power and Empire: Iraq and the U.S. Global Agenda.* Monroe, ME: Common Courage Press, 2004.

Faupin, Alain. "How Thought Serves Action: The American Think Tanks." *Revue internationale et stratégique* 52 winter 2003–04: 97–105.

Feinsilber, Mike. "The Hoover-Reagan Campaign Resource: Stanford's Think Tank of the Right May Lead with Ideas in '80s." *Los Angeles Times,* 8 June 1980.

Feldman, Noah. *What We Owe Iraq: War and the Ethics of Nation-Building.* Princeton: Princeton University Press, 2004.

Feulner, Edwin J. "Ideas, Think Tanks and Government." *The Heritage Lectures,* 51. Washington, DC: The Heritage Foundation, 1985.

Fineman, Howard. "Clinton's Team: The Inner Circles." *Newsweek,* 26 October 1992.

Fischer, Frank. "Country Report: American Think Tanks: Policy Elites and the Politicization of Expertise." *Governance: An International Journal of Policy and administration* 4, no. 3 (1991): 343.

Flynn, Stephen E. *America the Vulnerable: How Our Government Is Failing to Protect Us from Terrorism.* New York: Harper Collins, 2004.

Ford, Patrick. "American Enterprise Institute for Public Policy Research." In Carol H. Weiss. *Organizations for Policy Analysis: Helping Government Think.* Newbury Park, CA: Sage Publications, 1992.

Friedman, Murray. *The Neoconservative Revolution: Jewish Intellectuals and the Shaping of Public Policy.* New York: Cambridge University Press, 2005.

Frost, Robert. *New Hampshire: A Poem with Notes and Grace Notes.* New York: Henry Holt and Co., 1923.

Frum, David. *The Right Man: The Surprise Presidency of George W. Bush.* New York: Random House, 2003.

Frum, David, and Richard Perle. *An End to Evil: How to Win the War on Terror.* New York: Random House, 2004.

Gardner, Lloyd C., and Marilyn B. Young, eds. *The New American Empire: A 21st Century Teach-In on U.S. Foreign Policy.* New York: The New Press, 2005.

Ghamari-Tabrizi, Sharon. *The Worlds of Herman Khan: The Intuitive Science of Thermonuclear War.* Cambridge: Harvard University Press, 2005.

Gedmin, Jeffrey. Presentation at the conference *"Think Tanks in the USA and Germany: Democracy at Work; How and Where Do Public Decision-Makers Obtain Their Knowledge?"* University of Pennsylvania, Philadelphia, 18–20 November 1993.

Germond, Jack W., and Jules Witcover. *Mad as Hell: Revolt at the Ballot Box, 1992.* New York: Warner Books, 1993.

Gill, Stephen. *American Hegemony and the Trilateral Commission.* New York: Cambridge University Press, 1990.

Glenn, John M., Lillian Brandt, and F. Emerson Andrews. *The Russell Sage Foundation, 1907–1946.* New York: Russell Sage Foundation, 1947.

Golding, Sue. *Gramsci's Democratic Theory.* Toronto: University of Toronto Press, 1992.

Goldman, Peter, Thomas M. De Frank, Mark Miller, Andrew Murr, and Tom Matthews. *Quest for the Presidency, 1992.* College Station: Texas A & M University Press, 1994.

Goldwin, Robert A., and Robert A. Licht, eds. *Foreign Policy and the Constitution.* Washington, DC: The American Enterprise Institute, 1990.

Goode, Stephen, and Ralph Z. Hallow, "Struggling Institute Fights to Survive." *Nation,* 21 July 1986.

Gordon, Phillip H., and Jeremy Shapiro. *Allies at War: America, Europe, and the Crisis over Iraq.* New York: McGraw-Hill, 2004.

Gorman, Siobhan. "Bush's Lesson Plan." *National Journal* 31, no. 32 (7 August 1999): 2230–2.

Graham, Daniel O. *We Must Defend America and Save the World from Madness.* Washington, DC: Regnery, 1983.

Greene, John Robert. *The Presidency of George Bush.* Lawrence: University Press of Kansas, 2000.

Grove, Lloyd. "Steering His Party toward the Center." *Washington Post*, 24 July 1992.

Guttman, Daniel, and Barry Willner. *The Shadow Government: The Government's Multi-billion-Dollar Giveaway of Its Decision-making Powers to Private Management Consultants, "Experts," & Think Tanks*. New York: Pantheon, 1976.

Haas, Peter M., ed. *Knowledge, Power, and International Policy Coordination*. Columbia: University of South Carolina Press, 1997.

Hager, George. "Bush Shops for Advice at California Think Tank: Ex-White House Stars Fill." *Washington Post*, 8 June 1999.

Hallow, Ralph Z. "Pines Quits as Heritage Senior VP." *Washington Times*, 14 April 1992.

Halper, Stefan A., and Jonathan Clarke. *America Alone: The Neo-Conservatives and the Global Order*. Cambridge; New York: Cambridge University Press, 2004.

Halperin, Morton H. *Bureaucratic Politics and Foreign Policy*. Washington, DC: Brookings Institution, 1974.

Hamm, Bernd, ed. *Devastating Society: The Neo-Conservative Assault on Democracy and Justice*. London: Pluto Press, 2005.

Harris, Michael. "Stanford-Hoover 'Divorce' Suggested." *San Francisco Chronicle*, 29 May 1985.

Harris, Roy J., Jr. "Peace Games: After the Cold War, Rand Remakes Itself as a Civilian Expert." *Wall Street Journal*, 18 June 1993.

Harrison, Kathryn, and George Hoberg. "Setting the Environmental Agenda in Canada and the United States: The Cases of Dioxin and Radon." *Canadian Journal of Political Science* 24, no. 1 (1991): 3–27.

Hart, John. *The Presidential Branch: From Washington to Clinton*. 2nd ed. Chatham, NJ: Chatham House Publishers, 1995.

Hartung, William D., and Michelle Ciarrocca. "Star Wars: The Next Generation." *Mother Jones Wire*, 31 January 2001. Available at: www.motherjones.com/reality_check/rumsfeld.html.

Hayward, Steven F. *The Real Jimmy Carter: How Our Worst Ex-President Undermines American Foreign Policy, Coddles Dictators and Created the Party of Clinton and Kerry*. Washington, DC: Regnery Publishing, 2004.

Healy, Patrick, and Sara Hebel. "Academics Start to Line Up behind Presidential Candidates." *Chronicle of Higher Education*, 28 May 1999.

Heatherly, Charles L., ed. *Mandate for Leadership: Policy Management in a Conservative Administration*. Washington, DC: Heritage Foundation, 1981.

– *Mandate for Leadership III: Policy Strategies for the 1990's*. Washington, DC: The Heritage Foundation, 1989.

Heclo, Hugh. "Issue Networks and the Executive Establishment." In Anthony King, ed., *The New American Political System*. Washington, DC: The American Enterprise Institute, 1978.

Hellebust, Lynn, ed. *Think Tank Directory: A Guide to Independent Nonprofit Public Policy Research Organizations*. Topeka, KS: Government Research Service, 1994.

Henri-Levi, Bernard. "In the Footsteps of Tocqueville." *Atlantic Monthly* 295, no. 4 (May 2005): 54–90.

Heritage Foundation. *1990 Annual Report*. Washington, DC: Heritage Foundation, 1990.

– *1998 Annual Report*. Washington, DC: Heritage Foundation, 1998.

– *2002 Annual Report*. Washington, DC: Heritage Foundation, 2002.

– *2003 Annual Report*. Washington, DC: Heritage Foundation, 2003.

– *Defending the American Homeland: A Report of the Heritage Foundation Homeland Security Task Force*. Washington, DC: Heritage Foundation, 2002.

Hess, Stephen. *Organizing the Presidency*. Washington, DC: Brookings Institution, 1988.

Hilsman, Roger. *The Politics of Policy-Making in Defense and Foreign Affairs: Conceptual Models and Bureaucratic Politics*. 3rd ed. Englewood Cliffs, NJ: Prentice-Hall, 1993.

Hinckley, Barbara. *Less than Meets the Eye: Foreign Policy Making and the Myth of the Assertive Congress*. Chicago: University of Chicago Press, 1994.

Hodgson, Godfrey. "The Establishment." *Foreign Policy* 10 (spring 1973): 3–40.

Hohenberg, John. *The Bill Clinton Story: Winning the Presidency*. Syracuse: Syracuse University Press, 1994.

Hollander, Paul. *Understanding Anti-Americanism: Its Origins and Impact at Home and Abroad*. Chicago: Ivan R. Dee, 2004.

Holsti, K.J. *International Politics: A Framework for Analysis*. Englewood Cliffs, NJ: Prentice-Hall, 1988.

Holwill, Richard N. *Agenda '83: A Mandate for Leadership Report*. Washington, DC: Heritage Foundation, 1983.

Hughes, Karen. *Ten Minutes from Normal*. New York: Viking, 2004.

Institute for Policy Studies. *Annual Report 2002*. Washington, DC: The Institute for Policy Studies, 2002.

Irving, Carl. "Stanford Faculty to Challenge Hoover Institution: Richly Funded Think Tank, Accused of Partisan Politics, Blames Criticism on Envy, Liberal Bias." *San Francisco Examiner*, 8 May 1983.

Ivins, Molly, and Lou Dubose. *Shrub: The Short but Happy Political Life of George W. Bush*. New York: Random House, 2000.

Jackson, Richard. *Writing the War on Terrorism: Language, Politics and Counter-Terrorism*. Manchester: Manchester University Press, 2005.

Jehl, Douglas. "Clinton, Others Begin 5-Day 'Thinking Party?' Retreat: Renaissance Weekend Is Casual in Tone, Intense in Discussion from Spiritual to Political." *Los Angeles Times*, 30 December 1992.

Johnson, Dominic D.P. *Overconfidence and War: The Havoc and Glory of Positive Illusions*. Cambridge: Harvard University Press, 2004.

Judis, John B. "Taking Care of Business." *New Republic*, 19 August 1999, 24–31.

Kagan, Robert. *Of Paradise and Power: America and Europe in the New World Order*. New York: Knopf, 2003.

Kagan, Robert, and William Kristol. *Present Dangers: Crisis and Opportunity in American Foreign and Defense Policy*. San Francisco: Encounter Books, 2000.

Kaplan, David A. *The Accidental President: How 413 Lawyers, 9 Supreme Court Justices, and 5,963,110 (Give or Take a Few) Floridians Landed George W. Bush in the White House*. New York: Morrow, 2001.

Kaplan, Lawrence, and William Kristol. *The War over Iraq: Saddam's Tyranny and America's Mission*. San Francisco: Encounter Books, 2003.

Kennan, George F. *At a Century's Ending: Reflections 1982–1995*. New York: Norton, 1996.

Kessler, Glenn. "Economic Advisor Has Knack for Translating Tough Issues." *Washington Post*, 4 January 2001.

Kingdon, John W. *Agendas, Alternatives, and Public Policies*. New York: HarperCollins, 1984.

Kissinger, Henry A. *Diplomacy*. New York: Simon and Schuster, 1994.

Kitfield, James. "Periphery Is Out, Russia and China, In." *National Journal* 31, no. 32 (7 August 1999): 2293.

– *War and Destiny: How the Bush Revolution in Foreign and Military Affairs Redefined American Power*. Washington, DC: Potomac Books, 2005.

Knickerbocker, Brad. "Heritage Foundation's Ideas Permeate Reagan Administration." *Christian Science Monitor*, 7 December 1984.

Kolakowski, Leszek. *Main Currents of Marxism*. Oxford: Clarendon Press, 1978.

Kraft, Joseph. "School for Statesman." *Harper's Magazine*, July 1958, 64–8.

Kramer, Martin. *Ivory Towers on Sand: The Failure of Middle Eastern Studies in America*. Washington, DC: The Washington Institute for Near East Policy, 2001.

Krasner, Stephen D. "Are Bureaucracies Important? (or Allison and Wonderland)." *Foreign Policy* 7 (summer 1972): 159–79.

– *Defending the National Interest: Raw Material Investment and U.S. Foreign Policy*. Princeton: Princeton University Press, 1978.

Kristol, William, and Robert Kagan. "Toward a Neo-Reaganite Foreign Policy." *Foreign Affairs* 75, no. 4 (July/August 1996): 18–32.

Kurtz, Howard. "Meese Helps Group to Raise Funds." *Washington Post*, 20 January 1982.

Laurent, Eric. *Bush's Secret World: Religion, Big Business, and Hidden Networks*. Cambridge, UK; Malden, MA: Polity, 2004.

Lawyers' Committee on Nuclear Policy and Western States Legal Foundation. "Judge Allows Bush's Withdrawal from ABM Treaty to Stand." *News Release*, 1 January 2003. Available at: www.lcnp.org/disarmament/ABMlawsuit/ABMdecisionpr.htm.

Ledeen, Michael A. *Tocqueville on American Character*. New York: St. Martin's Press, 2000.

Lieberman, Trudy. *Slanting the Story: The Forces That Shape the News*. New York: The New Press, 2000.

Lind, Michael. *Made in Texas: George W. Bush and the Southern Takeover of American Politics*. New York: Basic Books, 2003.

Lindblom, Charles E. "The Science of Muddling Through." *Public Administration Review* 19 (1959): 79–88.

Linden, Patricia. "Powerhouses of Policy." *Town and Country*, January 1987, 99–179.

Lindquist, Evert A. "Behind the Myth of Think Tanks: The Organization and Relevance of Canadian Policy Institutes. PhD dissertation, University of California at Berkeley, 1989.

– "Public Managers and Policy Communities: Learning to Meet New Challenges." *Canadian Public Administration* 35, no. 2 (1992): 127–59.

– "A Quarter-Century of Think Tanks in Canada." In Diane Stone, Andrew Denham, and Mark Garnett, eds., *Think Tanks across Nations: A Comparative Approach*. Manchester: Manchester University Press, 1998.

– "Think Tanks or Policy Clubs? Assessing the Influence and Roles of Canadian Policy Institutes." *Canadian Public Administration* 36, no. 4 (1993): 547–79.

Lipset, Seymour Martin. *Continental Divide*. New York: Routledge, 1990.

Lowi, Theodore J. *The End of Liberalism: Ideology, Policy, and the Crisis of Public Authority*. New York: Norton, 1969.

Lumpkin, John J. "Tests Put Off on Missile Defense Plan." *Associated Press*, 11 July 2005.

McCombs, Phil. "Building a Heritage in the War of Ideas." *Washington Post*, 3 October 1983.

McFarlane, Robert C., and Zofia Smardz. *Special Trust*. New York: Cadell & Davies, 1994.

McGann, James G. "Academics to Ideologues: A Brief History of the Public Policy Research Industry." *PS: Political Science and Politics* 24, no. 4 (December 1992): 739–40.

– *The Competition for Dollars, Scholars and Influence in the Public Policy Research Industry*. Lanham, MD: University Press of America, 1995.

– *Scholars, Dollars and Policy Advice*. Philadelphia: Foreign Policy Research Institute, 2004.

– *Think Tanks, Catalysts for Ideas in Action: An International Survey*. Tokyo: National Institute for Research Advancement, 1999.

– "Why Political Science? Think Tanks in a North American Perspective." Presentation delivered at the University of Passau, Germany, 3 December 2003.

McGann, James G., and Erik C. Johnson. *Comparative Think Tanks, Politics and Public Policy*. London: Edward Elgar Publishing, 2006.

McGann, James G., and R. Kent Weaver, eds. *Think Tanks & Civil Societies: Catalysts for Ideas and Action*. New Brunswick, NJ: Transaction Publishers, 2000.

McPherson, James M., ed. *To the Best of My Ability*. New York: DK Publishing, 2000.

Madison, James. "Federalist No. 10." In Clinton Rossiter, ed., *The Federalist Papers: Alexander Hamilton, James Madison, John Jay*. New York: New American Library, 1961.

Maggs, John. "Tax Cuts Big and Small." *National Journal* 31, no. 32 (7 August 1999): 2236.

Mann, James. *Rise of the Vulcans: The History of Bush's War Cabinet*. New York: Viking, 2004.

Maraniss, David. "Letter from Never-Never Land: Epiphany and Elbow-Rubbing at the Renaissance Weekend." *Washington Post*, 2 January 1993.

– "A Weekend with Bill & Friends Hilton Head's New Year's Tradition: Name Tags, Networking and Talk, Talk, Talk." *Washington Post*, 28 December 1992.

March, James, and Herbert Simon. *Organizations*. New York: John Wiley and Sons, 1958.

Marshall, Will, and Martin Schram. *Mandate for Change*. New York: Berkeley Books in cooperation with the Progressive Policy Institute, 1992.

Matlack, Carol. "Marketing Ideas." *National Journal*, 22 June 1991, 1552–55.

Meacher, Michael. "This War on Terrorism Is Bogus." *Guardian*, 6 September 2003. Available at: http://politics.guardian.co.uk/iraq/comment/0,12956,1036687,00.html.

Meese, Edwin, III. *The Transition to a New Administration*. Stanford: Hoover Institution, 1981.

– *With Reagan: The Inside Story.* Washington, DC: Regnery Gateway, 1992.

Menges, Constantine C. *Inside the National Security Council: The True Story of the Making and Unmaking of Reagan's Foreign Policy.* New York: Simon and Schuster, 1988.

Micklethwait, John, and Adrian Wooldridge, "For Conservatives, Mission Accomplished." *The New York Times,* 18 May 2004 (op-ed).

– *The Right Nation: Conservative Power in America.* New York: Penguin Books, 2004.

Miller, Steven E., and Stephan Van Evera. *Star Wars Controversy: An International Security Reader.* Princeton: Princeton University Press, 1986.

Mills, C. Wright. *The Power Elite.* New York: Oxford University Press, 1956.

Minutaglio, Bill. *First Son: George W. Bush and the Bush Family Dynasty.* New York: Three Rivers Press, 2001.

Mitchell, Elizabeth. *W: Revenge of the Bush Dynasty.* New York: Hyperion Press, 2000.

Mitrany, David. *A Working Peace System.* Chicago: Quadrangle Books, 1996.

Moore, James, and Wayne Slater. *Bush's Brain: How Karl Rove Made George W. Bush Presidential.* New York: Wiley, 2003.

Moore, Jim, and Rick Ihde. *Clinton: Young Man in a Hurry.* Fort Worth, Texas: The Summit Group, 1992.

Morgan, Dan. "Think Tank or Hired Gun?" *Sun Sentinel,* 13 February 2000.

Morin, Richard and Claudia Deane. "The Ideas Industry." *Washington Post,* 8 June 1999.

Mufson, Steven. "For Rice, a Daunting Challenge Ahead." *Washington Post,* 18 December 2000.

Muravchik, Joshua. "The Think Tank of the Left." *New York Times Magazine,* 27 April 1987.

Nash, George H. *Herbert Hoover and Stanford University.* Stanford: Hoover Institution Press, 1988.

National Commission on Terrorist Attacks upon the United States. *The 9/11 Commission Report.* New York: Norton, 2004.

Nelson, Craig. *The First Heroes: The Extraordinary Story of the Doolittle Raid – America's First World War II Victory.* New York: Viking Press, 2002.

Neustadt, Richard E. *Presidential Power.* New York: John Wiley & Sons, 1960.

Newsom, David D. *The Public Dimension of Foreign Policy.* Bloomington: Indiana University Press, 1996.

Nossal, Kim Richard. "Opening Up the Black Box." In David G. Haglund and Michael K. Hawes, eds., *World Politics: Power, Interdependence & Dependence.* Toronto: Harcourt Brace Jovanovich. Canada, 1990.

Nye, Joseph S. *The Paradox of American Power: Why the World's Only Superpower Can't Go It Alone*. Oxford and New York: Oxford University Press, 2002.

Oakland Tribune. "Reagan Team Consults Heritage Foundation Think-Tank." *Oakland Tribune*, 13 November 1980.

O'Connell, Brian, ed. *America's Voluntary Spirit*. New York: The Foundation Center, 1983.

Omang, Joanne. "The Heritage Report: Getting the Government Right with Reagan." *Washington Post*, 16 November 1980.

Orlans, Harold. *The Nonprofit Research Institute: Its Origin, Operation, Problems, and Prospects*. New York: McGraw Hill, 1972.

Osbourne, David E., and Ted Gaebler. *Reinventing Government: How the Entrepreneurial Spirit Is Transforming the Public Sector*. Reading, MA: Addison Wesley Publishers, 1992.

Otten, Allen L. "Campbell Comments on Hoover-Stanford Ties." *Stanford News*, 22 April 1988.

– "Faculty Senate Postpones New Study of Stanford-Hoover Ties." *Stanford News*, 17 November 1988.

– "On Stanford's Campus, a Partisan Think Tank Has Political Problems." *Wall Street Journal*, 15 June 1984.

– "Ronald Reagan's Presidential Papers May Come to the Hoover Institution at Stanford University." *Stanford News*, 7 November 1981.

Pal, Leslie A., and R. Kent Weaver, eds. *The Government Taketh Away: The Politics of Pain in the United States and Canada*. Washington, DC: Georgetown University Press, 2003.

Parmar, Inderjeet. *Think Tanks and Power in Foreign Policy*. London: Palgrave, 2004.

Parmet, Herbert S. *George Bush: The Life of a Lone Star Yankee*. New York: Scribner, 1997.

Pastor, Robert A. "The Carter Administration and Latin America: A Test Principle." In John D. Martz, ed., *United States Policy in Latin America: A Quarter Century of Crisis and Challenge*. Lincoln: University of Nebraska Press, 1988.

Pechman, Joseph A. *Setting National Priorities: Agenda for the 1980's*. Washington, DC: Brookings Institution, 1980.

Perloff, James. *The Shadows of Power: The Council on Foreign Relations and the American Decline*. Appleton, WI: Western Islands, 1988.

Peschek, Joseph G. "Free the Fortune 500! The American Enterprise Institute and the Politics of the Capitalist Class in the 1970s." *Critical Sociology*, summer-fall 1989, 165–80.

– *Policy Planning Organizations: Elite Agendas and America's Rightward Turn.* Philadelphia: Temple University Press, 1987.

Pfiffner, James P. *The Strategic Presidency: Hitting the Ground Running.* 2d ed, rev. Lawrence KS: University Press of Kansas, 1996.

Pillar, Paul. *Terrorism and U.S. Foreign Policy.* Washington, DC: Brookings Institution Press, 2001.

Piven, Frances Fox. *The War at Home: The Domestic Costs of Bush's Militarism.* New York: New Press; Distributed by W.W. Norton, 2004.

Pollack, Kenneth M. *The Threatening Storm: The Case for Invading Iraq.* New York: Random House, 2002.

Powell, S. Steven. *Covert Cadre: Inside the Institute for Policy Studies.* Ottawa, ILL: Green Hill, 1988.

Prados, John. *Hoodwinked: The Documents That Reveal How Bush Sold Us a War.* New York: The New Press, 2004.

Preble, Christopher. *Exiting Iraq: Why the U.S. Must End the Military Occupation and Renew the War against Al Qaeda.* Washington, DC: Cato Institute, 2004.

Pressler, Larry. *Star Wars: The Strategic Defense Initiative Debates in Congress.* New York: Praeger, 1986.

Project for the New American Century. "Letter from the Project for the New American Century to the Honorable William J. Clinton, President of the United States." *Indy Voice,* 26 January 1998. Available at: http://www.theindyvoice.com/index.blog?entry_id=417960.

– *Rebuilding America's Defenses: Strategy, Forces and Resources for a New Century.* Washington, DC: The Project for the New American Century, 2000.

Pross, A. Paul. *Group Politics and Public Policy.* Toronto: Oxford University Press, 1992.

Putnam, Robert. *Bowling Alone: The Collapse and Revival of American Community.* New York: Simon & Schuster, 2000.

Rampton, Sheldon, and John Stauber. *Weapons of Mass Deception: The Uses of Propaganda in Bush's War on Iraq.* New York: Jeremy P. Tarcher/Penguin, 2003.

RAND. *An Introduction to RAND: The Reach of Reason.* Santa Monica: RAND, 1999.

Raucher, Alan. "The First Foreign Affairs Think Tanks." *American Quarterly* 30, no. 4 (1978): 493–513.

Reagan, Ronald W. "Address to the Nation on Defense and National Security." 23 March 1983. Available at: http://www.learnworld.com/org/TX.002=1983.03.23.Reagan.html.

– *An American Life.* New York: Simon and Schuster, 1990.

– "Letter from President Reagan to General Daniel Graham." 25 November 1985. Available on High Frontier's Web site: www.highfrontier.org.

– "President Reagan's telephoned remarks on High Frontier's Tenth Anniversary." September 1991. Available on High Frontier's Web site: www.highfrontier.org.

Renshon, Stanley Allen. *In His Father's Shadow: The Transformations of George W. Bush*. New York: Palgrave Macmillan, 2004.

Ricci, David M. *The Transformation of American Politics: The New Washington and the Rise of Think Tanks*. New Haven: Yale University Press, 1993.

Rich, Andrew. "Think Tanks as Sources of Expertise for Congress and the Media." Paper presented at the annual meetings of the American Political Science Association, Boston, September 1998.

– *Think Tanks, Public Policy, and the Politics of Expertise*. New York: Cambridge University Press, 2004.

Rich, Andrew, and R. Kent Weaver. "Think Tanks, the Media and the Policy Process." Paper presented at the annual meetings of the American Political Science Association, Washington, DC, August 1997.

Robinson, William H. "Public Think Tanks in the United States: The Special Case of Legislative Support Agencies." Paper presented at the Conference "Think Tanks in the USA and Germany," University of Pennsylvania, Philadelphia, 1993.

Rockefeller, David. *Memoirs*. New York: Random House, 2002.

Rosenau, James N. *The Scientific Study of Foreign Policy*. New York: The Free Press, 1971.

Rosenbaum, David E. "Torrent of Free Advice Flows into Little Rock." *New York Times*, 15 November 1992.

Ross, Andrew, and Kristin Ross, eds. *Anti-Americanism*. New York; London: New York University Press, 2004.

Russo, Robert. "Bush Battling Questions of Brain Power." *London Free Press*, 13 December 1999.

Saloma, John S. *Ominous Politics: The New Conservative Labyrinth*. New York: Hill and Wang, 1984.

Sammon, Bill. *Fighting Back: The War on Terrorism from Inside the Bush White House*. Washington, DC: Regnery Publishing, 2002.

Sanders, Jerry Wayne. *Peddlers of Crisis: The Committee on the Present Danger and the Politics of Containment*. Boston: South End Press, 1983.

Santoro, Carlo Maria. *Diffidence and Ambition: The Intellectual Sources of U.S. Foreign Policy*. Boulder: Westview Press, 1992.

Sarder, Ziauddin, and Merryl Wyn Davies. *Why Do People Hate America?* Cambridge: Icon, 2002.

Satloff, Robert. *The Battle of Ideas in the War on Terror: Essays on U.S. Public Diplomacy in the Middle East.* Washington, DC: The Washington Institute for Near East Policy, 2004.

Saunders, Charles B. *The Brookings Institution: A Fifty-Year History.* Washington, DC: The Brookings Institution, 1966.

Savoie, Donald J. *Breaking the Bargain: Public Servants, Ministers, and Parliament.* Toronto: University of Toronto Press, 2003.

– *Thatcher, Reagan, Mulroney: In Search of a New Bureaucracy.* Toronto: University of Toronto Press, 1994.

Schlesinger, Arthur Meier. *The Imperial Presidency.* Boston: Houghton Mifflin, 1989.

Schneider, Mark, and Paul Teske. "Toward a Theory of the Political Entrepreneur: Evidence from Local Government." *American Political Science Review* 86 (1992): 737–47.

Schulzinger, Robert D. *The Wise Men of Foreign Affairs: The History of the Council on Foreign Relations.* New York: Columbia University Press, 1984.

Schweizer, Peter. *Reagan's War: The Epic Story of His Forty-Year Struggle and Final Triumph over Communism.* New York: Doubleday, 2002.

– *Victory: The Reagan Administration's Secret Strategy That Hastened the Collapse of the Soviet Union.* New York: Atlantic Monthly Press, 1994.

Seabrook, John. "Capital Gain." *Manhattan, Inc.,* March 1987, 71–9.

Sealander, Judith. *Private Wealth and Public Life: Foundation Philanthropy and the Reshaping of American Social Policy from the Progressive Era to the New Deal.* Baltimore, MD: Johns Hopkins University Press, 1997.

Seifert, Charlene S., and Molly Sturges Tuthill. "Scholarship and Public Policy: Ronald W. Reagan and the Hoover Institution." *Hoover Institution Internal Report,* September 1982.

Shoup, Laurence H. *The Carter Presidency and Beyond: Power and Politics in the 1980s.* California: Ramparts Press, 1980.

Shoup, Laurence H., and William Minter. *Imperial Brain Trust: The Council on Foreign Relations and United States Foreign Policy.* New York: Monthly Review Press, 1977.

Shultz, George Pratt. *Turmoil and Triumph: My Years as Secretary of State.* New York: Scribner's, 1993.

Simon, Herbert. *Administrative Behavior: A Study of Decision-Making Processes in Administrative Organization.* New York: The Free Press, 1965.

– *Models of Man: Social and Rational.* New York: John Wiley and Sons, 1957.

– *Models of My Life.* New York: Basic Books, 1991.

Simon, Steven, and Jonathan Stevenson. "Thinking outside the Tank." *National Interest* 78 (winter 2004–05): 90–8.

Sklar, Holly, ed. *Trilateralism: The Trilateral Commission and Elite Planning for World Management*. Boston: South End Press, 1980.

Smith, Bruce L.R. *The Rand Corporation: Case Study of a Non-profit Advisory Corporation*. Cambridge: Harvard University Press, 1966.

Smith, Hedrick. *The Power Game: How Washington Works*. New York: Random House, 1988.

Smith, James A. *Brookings at Seventy-Five*. Washington, DC: Brookings Institution, 1991.

– *The Idea Brokers: Think Tanks and the Rise of the New Policy Elite*. New York: The Free Press, 1991.

– *Strategic Calling: The Center for Strategic and International Studies; 1962-1992*. Washington, DC: Center for Strategic and International Studies, 1993.

Smith, Jean Edward. *George Bush's War*. New York: H. Holt, 1992.

Stairs, Dennis. "Public Opinion and External Affairs: Reflections on the Domestication of Canadian Foreign Policy." *International Journal* 33, no. 1 (winter 1977-78): 128–49.

Steelman, Aaron. Review of *Do Think Tanks Matter? Assessing the Impact of Public Policy Institutes*. *Cato Journal* 23, no. 1 (spring/summer 2003).

Stefancic, Jean, and Richard Delgado. *No Mercy: How Conservative Think Tanks Changed America's Social Agenda*. Philadelphia: Temple University Press, 1996.

Stein, Janice Gross, and Raymond Tanter. *Rational Decision-Making: Israel's Security Choices, 1967*. Columbus: Ohio State University Press, 1980.

Steinbruner, John D. *The Cybernetic Theory of Decision: New Dimensions of Political Analysis*. Princeton: Princeton University Press, 1974.

Stelzer, Irwin, ed. *Neoconservatism*. London: Atlantic Books, 2004.

Stern, Sheldon M. *Averting "the Final Failure": John F. Kennedy and the Secret Cuban Missile Crisis Meetings*. Stanford: Stanford University Press, 2003.

Stone, Diane. *Capturing the Political Imagination: Think Tanks and the Policy Process*. London: Frank Cass, 1996.

– "Recycling Bins, Garbage Cans or Think Tanks? Three Myths Regarding Policy Analysis Institutes." *Public Administration*, forthcoming.

Stone, Diane, and Andrew Denham, eds. *Think Tank Traditions: Policy Research and the Politics of Ideas*. Manchester: Manchester University Press, 2004.

Stone, Diane, Andrew Denham, and Mark Garnett. *Think Tanks across Nations: A Comparative Approach*. Manchester: Manchester University Press, 1998.

Struyk, Raymond J. *Reconstructive Critics: Think Tanks in Post-Soviet Bloc Democracies*. Washington, DC: Urban Institute Press, 1999.

Sussman, Edward. "Conservative Think Tank Comes Back from Brink of Financial Disaster, Leaning More to the Right." *Wall Street Journal*, 3 September 1987.

Swanson, J. "Brain Power: Bush Aligns with Hoover Think Tank." *Dallas Morning News*, 11 August 1999.

Tanner, Stephen. *The Wars of the Bushes: A Father and Son as Military Leaders.* Philadelphia: Casemate, 2004.

Tapper, Jake. *Down & Dirty: The Plot to Steal the Presidency.* Boston and London: Little, Brown, 2001.

Telgarsky, Jeffrey, and Makiko Ueno, eds., *Think Tanks in a Democratic Society: An Alternative Voice.* Washington: The Urban Institute, 1996.

Thomas, John N. *The Institute of Pacific Relations: Asian Scholars and American Politics.* Seattle: University of Washington Press, 1984.

Thunert, Martin. "Think Tanks in Germany." In Diane Stone and Andrew Denham, eds., *Think Tank Traditions: Policy Research and the Politics of Ideas.* Manchester: Manchester University Press, 2004.

Tocqueville, Alexis de. *Democracy in America.* Indianapolis, IN: Hackett Publishing, 2000.

Towell, Pat. "DLC Moves into Driver's Seat." *National Convention News: The Daily Newspaper for the 1992 Democratic National Campaign*, 13 July 1992.

Transparency. "War of the Worlds, Orson Wells, and the Invasion from Mars." Available at: www.transparencynow.com/welles.htm.

Truman, David B. *The Governmental Process: Political Interests and Public Opinion.* New York: Alfred A. Knopf, 1951.

Turner, Wallace. "Liberals at Stanford Protest Ties to Hoover Institute." *New York Times*, 24 May 1983.

Twentieth Century Fund. *Obstacle Course: The Report of the Twentieth Century Fund Task Force on the Presidential Appointment Process.* New York: The Twentieth Century Fund Press, 1996.

Tyman, Kathleen. "A Decade-Long Heritage of Conservative Thought." *Washington Times*, 4 October 1983.

Uhlmann, Michael M. "Reflections on the Role of the Judiciary in Foreign Policy." In Robert A. Goldwin and Robert A. Licht, eds., *Foreign Policy and the Constitution.* Washington, DC: The American Enterprise Institute, 1990.

Unger, Craig. *House of Bush, House of Saud: The Secret Relationship between the World's Two Most Powerful Dynasties.* New York: Scribner, 2004.

Union of Concerned Scientists. *Empty Promise: The Growing Case against Star Wars.* Boston: Beacon Press, 1986.

- *The Fallacy of Star Wars.* New York: Vintage Books, 1984.

Urban Institute. *30: The Urban Institute, 1968–1998.* Washington, DC: The Urban Institute, 1998.

"US House Democrats Sue Bush over ABM Treaty Withdrawl." *People's Daily*, 12 June, 2002. Available at: www.english.peopledaily.com.cn/200206/12/eng20020612_97666.shtml.

Van Slambrouck, Paul. "California Think Tank Acts as Bush 'Brain Trust.'" *Christian Science Monitor*, 2 July 1999.

Wall, Joseph Frazier. *Andrew Carnegie*. Pittsburgh: University of Pittsburgh Press, 1989.

Wallace, William. "Between Two Worlds: Think-Tanks and Foreign Policy." In Christopher Hill and Pamela Beshoff, eds., *Two Worlds of International Relations: Academics, Practitioners and the Trade in Ideas*, London: Routledge, 1994.

Wallison, Peter J. *Ronald Reagan: The Power of Conviction and the Success of His Presidency*. Bouder, CO: Westview Press, 2003.

Waltz, Kenneth N. *Theory of International Politics*. New York: Random House, 1979.

Weaver, R. Kent. "The Changing World of Think Tanks." *PS: Political Science and Politics* 22, no. 2 (September 1989): 563–78.

Weinberger, Caspar W. *Fighting for Peace: Seven Critical Years in the Pentagon*. New York: Warner Books, 1990.

Weinraub, Bernard. "Conservative Group's Blueprint for Reagan." *San Francisco Chronicle*, 11 December 1980.

Weisberg, Jacob. "Clincest: Washington's New Ruling Class." *New Republic*, 26 April 1993, 22–7.

Weko, Thomas J. *The Politicizing Presidency: The White House Personnel Office, 1948–1994*. Lawrence: University Press of Kansas, 1995.

Wheeler, Charles. "Heritage Chiefs Recall Decade of Growth, Power." *Washington Times*, 29 April 1987.

Whitaker, Ben. *The Foundations: An Anatomy of Philanthropy and Society*. London: Eyre Methuen, 1974.

Wolin, Sheldon S. *Tocqueville between Two Worlds: The Making of a Political and Theoretical Life*. Princeton: Princeton University Press, 2001.

Wood, Robert C. *Whatever Possessed the President? Academic Experts and Presidential Policy, 1960-1988*. Amherst: University of Massachusetts Press, 1993.

Woodward, Bob. *Bush at War*. New York: Simon & Schuster, 2002.

– *Plan of Attack*. New York: Simon & Schuster, 2003.

Workman, Bill. "Stanford Faculty Wants Review of Hoover Institute." *San Francisco Chronicle*, 27 May 1983.

Yoffe, Emily. "IPS Faces Life." *New Republic,* August 1977, 16–18.

Young, Lisa, and Joanna Marie Everitt. *Advocacy Groups.* Vancouver: UBC Press, 2004.

Index

Aaron, D., 28
Aaron, Henry, 28
Abelson, Donald E., 122, 123
Abrams, Elliot, 334n35
Abshire, David, 92. *See also* Center for Strategic and International Studies
Achenbach, Joel, 38
Acheson, Dean, 78, 229, 326n20
Adams, Tim, 41
Afghanistan, x, 16, 17, 41, 93, 172, 202, 203, 206, 210
Alchon, Guy, 66
Allen, Richard V., 33, 185, 194, 308n44, 309n51, 309n56; and foreign and defense policy groups, 31–2
Allison, Graham: and conceptual models of decision-making, 133, 136–9. *See also* rational actor model
American Association of Labor Legislation, 53
American Economics Association, 53

American Enterprise Association, 69, 80–1. *See also* American Enterprise Institute
American Enterprise Institute (AEI), xi, xiv, 17, 35, 40, 45, 69, 91, 93, 100, 125, 138, 143, 147, 149, 151, 155, 158, 159, 183, 195, 206, 207, 208, 210, 212, 222, 223; budget, 44, 83; and George W. Bush, xi, 223, 335n57; congressional testimony, 176–7; and Gerald Ford, 82; and Newt Gingrich, 4; history, 80–4; marketing strategies, 82; media exposure, 157, 172–3; and Reagan administration, 33, 82; research, 83; staff, 83
American Historical Association, 53
American International Group (AIG), 149
American Political Science Association, 59, 60
American Social Science Association (ASSA), 51

Anderson, Annelise, 36
Anderson, Martin, 19, 70,186, 194, 306n24; and Congressional Policy Advisory Board, 119; and domestic policy task forces, 31–2; and NORAD, 185; and Ronald Reagan, 30–3
Anti-Ballistic Missile (ABM) Treaty, 183, 185, 188, 190, 191, 194–5, 198
Armacost, Michael, 201, 205. *See also* Brookings Institution
Armitage, Richard, 41, 334n35
Arnold, General Henry H. ("Hap"), 75. *See also* RAND Corporation
Atlantic Institute for Market Studies (AIMS), 157
Austin, Andrew, 213

Babbitt, Bruce, 317n123
Ball, George, 326n20
Bark, Dennis, 78
Barnett, Richard, 95. *See also* Institute of Policy Studies

Baroody, William, Jr, 82–3, 125. *See also* American Enterprise Institute

Baroody, William J., Sr, 81–2. *See also* American Enterprise Institute

Bates, John, 192

Bendetsen, Karl, 186, 198

Bennett, Bill, 87

Benson, L.W., 29

Bentley, Arthur, xiii, 142

Bergsten, Fred C., 28

Berkowitz, Herb, 87

Bernstein, Carl, xii

Better America Foundation, 90–1. *See also* Dole, Bob

Bigelow, John, 58

Bigelow, Poultney, 314n47

bin Laden, Osama, 205, 208, 209, 210, 224

Blechman, Barry, 28–9

Blumenthal, Michael, 28

Blumenthal, Sidney, 81

Boeing, 158

Bohlen, Chip, 326n20

Bolton, John, 239, 334n35, 335n57

Boskin, Michael, 18

Bosworth, Barry, 29

Bowman, Isaiah, 72

Boyle, Patrick, 124

Brezhnev, Leonid: and ABM Treaty, 185

Brodie, Bernard, 75

Brookings, Robert S., 7, 60, 62–3, 64, 81, 114, 123. *See also* Brookings Institution

Brookings Institution, x, xiv, 6, 9, 12, 14, 40, 41, 46, 48, 51, 58, 61, 78, 79, 80, 91, 99, 100, 105, 112, 124, 128, 147, 149, 150, 151, 158, 159, 160, 183, 197, 200, 201, 208, 222; budget, 10, 44; and Jimmy Carter, 28–9; congressional testimony, 176–8; and corporate interests, 144; history, 62–4, 312–13n27, 313n30, 314n49; liberal

nature of, 63; media exposure, 7, 157, 172–5, 178, 199, 206; research programs, 11, 63; staff, 10. *See also* Institute for Government Research; Robert Brookings Graduate School of Economics and Government

Brown, David, 84

Brown, Harold, 28

Brown, Lewis H., 80–1

Brzezinski, Zbigniew, 78, 153, 204, 317n120; and Jimmy Carter, 25–8; and Center for Strategic and International Studies, 92; on policy experts and policy influence, 180–1; and Trilateral Commission, 25–8, 306n15

Buchanan, Pat, 317–18n123

Budget and Accounting Act, 1919, 61

Bundy, McGeorge, 78, 326n20

Bureau of Industrial Research, 53

bureaucratic politics model, 136–9

Burke, Arleigh, 92. *See also* Center for Strategic and International Studies

Burns, Arthur F., 32, 33, 307n28

Bush, George H.W., 39, 40, 88, 120, 219, 223, 330n23, 335n58; and Gulf War, 189; and Iraq, 104; and missile defense, 189; and neo-conservatives, 36; and Operation Desert Storm, 37; and think tanks, 4, 36, 309n56

Bush, George W., 83, 88, 105, 118, 180, 182, 190, 196, 197, 327–8n5, 335n58; and American

Enterprise Institute, xi, 223, 335n57; campaign 2000, 39–40, 191; and Center for Security Policy, 223; and Council on Foreign Relations, 223; as governor of Texas, 17; and Hoover Institution, 18, 40, 64, 311n72; and Iraq, 16, 109, 133, 211, 169; and missile defense, 16–17, 191–2, 195, 224, 331n37; and Project for the New American Century, 10, 14–16, 41, 93–5, 203, 204, 212–19, 221–4, 228, 333–4n31, 334n35; and think tanks, 39–41, 108, 183, 203, 204, 216, 220–3; and "the Vulcans," 40–1, 220; and war on terror, x, 201–4. *See also* Bush doctrine

Bush, Jeb: and Project for the New American Century (PNAC), 212, 213

Bush doctrine, 95, 173, 183, 207, 211, 216–17, 223; defined, 204

Butler, Nicholas Murray, 57

Butler, Stuart, 87

Caldicott, Helen, 195–6

Campbell, W. Glenn, 34, 315n84; and Hoover Institution, 69–70

Canadian Institute for International Peace and Security (CIIPS), 124

Carberry, Christine M., 122, 123

Carnegie, Andrew, 7, 52, 53, 56–8, 64, 81, 114, 123, 314n47. *See also* Carnegie Corporation; Carnegie Endowment for International Peace

Carnegie Corporation, 54, 62, 66, 124

Carnegie Endowment for International Peace, xiv, 12, 51, 54, 71, 89, 91, 99,

112, 124, 149, 150, 151, 152, 155, 183, 197, 200, 206, 207, 222; budget, 44, 59; history, 56–9, 312–13n27, 313n38; media exposure, 172–3; programs, 59; staff, 58

Carter, Jimmy, 30, 89, 120, 141, 180, 199, 306n19, 331n39; and Brookings Institution, 28–9; and Council on Foreign Relations, 28; and neoconservatives, 36; and think tanks, 4, 18, 23, 24–5, 29, 36, 37, 39; and Trilateral Commission, 25–8, 305n6, 306n14. *See also* Carter Center

Carter, Rosalynn, 89. *See also* Carter Center

Carter Center, 48; budget, 89; profile; 89–90; staff, 89. *See also* Carter, Jimmy; think tanks: legacy-based; think tanks: vanity-based

Cato Institute, xiv, 79, 87, 100, 138, 147, 151, 183, 195, 206, 305n3; budget, 44; congressional testimony, 176–7; media exposure, 172–3

Center for American Progress (CAP), 88

Center for National Policy, 305n3; budget, 10; staff, 10

Center for Responsive Politics, 90

Center for Security Policy (CSP), 8, 91, 144, 152, 155–6, 197, 222; budget, 44; and George W. Bush, 223; congressional testimony, 176–7; media exposure, 172–3, 199; and missile defense, 22, 93, 109, 182, 195–7, 198, 228; profile, 92–3; and Donald Rumsfeld; 93; staff, 92. *See also* Gaffney, Frank, Jr

Center for Strategic and International Studies (CSIS), 18, 35, 40, 91, 144, 149, 151, 158, 206, 208, 222; budget, 44, 92; congressional testimony, 176–8; media exposure, 172–3; profile, 92; and Reagan administration, 33; research, 92; staff, 92

Cheney, Lynne V., 40

Cheney, Richard (Dick), 15–16, 40, 41, 202, 335n57; and Project for the New American Century, 94, 180, 212, 213, 217, 223

Chicago Civic Federation (CCF), 52–3, 54

Choate, Joseph, 57

Citizens for a Sound Economy (CSE), 125

Clark, George T., 65

Clark, William, 309n51

Clarke, Richard, 209, 224

Clinton, Bill, 81, 88, 92, 105, 141, 199, 327–8n5; and Democratic Leadership Council, 37–8, 310n63, 310n66; and Economic Policy Institute, 4; and Heritage Foundation, 195; and Iraq, 15; and missile defense, 189–90; and Progressive Policy Institute, 4, 36–8, 310n66; and Project for the New American Century, 216, 334n35; and think tanks, 18, 36–9, 120, 135

Clinton, Hillary Rodham, 150

Collbohm, Frank, 75

Commission for Relief in Belgium (CRB), 64–6

Commission on US–Latin American Relations, 306n19

Committee on the Present Danger (CPD), 35; and

missile defense, 331n52; and Reagan administration, 33, 307–8n39

Commons, John R., 53–4

Concord Coalition, 149

Congressional Policy Advisory Board, 119

Congressional Research Service, 119

Coolidge, Calvin, 66

Coors, Joseph, 35, 84, 186, 198

Council on Foreign Relations, 14, 23, 51, 54, 78, 91, 105, 149, 150, 151, 155, 167, 183, 206, 222, 223; budget, 44; and George W. Bush, 223; and Jimmy Carter, 28; and corporate interests, 144; history, 71–4, 316n86, 316n98; media exposure, 172–4; members nationwide, 73

Crane, Philip, 85

Critchlow, Donald, 61

Crowley, Brian Lee, 157

Cuban Missile Crisis, 133, 137–9, 326n20

Curtis, Lionel, 72

Cutler, L.N., 29

cybernetic theory of decision-making, 140–1

Daalder, Ivo, 6, 41, 203, 219, 220, 221, 224

Dahl, Robert, 142–3

Dallek, Robert, 66

Davis, Karen, 28

Democratic Leadership Council (DLC), 310n63, 64, 310n67; and Bill Clinton, 37–8, 310n63. *See also* Progressive Policy Institute

DeMuth, Christopher, 83

Denham, Andrew, 5

Department of Homeland Security, 182, 211

Dickson, Paul, 49–51, 76

Dillon, Douglas, 326n20
Dodge, Cleveland H., 60
Dole, Bob, 48,
  317–18n123; and Better
  America Foundation,
  90–1; and Hoover
  Institution, 64
Domhoff, William, 51–2,
  98, 100, 144
Donaldson, Sam, 159
Donnelly, Thomas, 215
Donovan, Hedley, 25
Douglas Aircraft Company,
  75
Duignan, Peter, 67
Dutton, Samuel, 57
Dye, Thomas, 98, 144

Easley, Ralph, 52–3
Economic Council of
  Canada, 124
Economic Policy Institute,
  4; budget, 10; staff, 10
Eliot, Charles, 57
elite theory, 98–101
Ely, Richard, 53
Empower America, 87
Evers, Williamson, 40
Executive Committee
  (ExCom), 136–7, 326n20

Federal Election
  Commission (FEC), 91
Feldstein, Martin, 40
Feulner, Edwin, 84–5, 86,
  123, 152, 160, 308n44;
  and Ronald Reagan,
  33–4, 117, 180, 309n48,
  319n152. See also
  Heritage Foundation
Filene, Edward A., 52,
  312n16
Fisher, Sir Anthony, 124
Fisher, Harold, 66
Fletcher, James C., 188
Flynn, Stephen, 209, 211
Ford, Gerald, 24, 88, 92;
  and American Enterprise
  Institute, 82
Ford Foundation, 124
Foreign Policy Association,
  315n71

Foreign Policy Research
  Institute, xv
Forster, John W., 57
Foster, J.D., 40
Frankfurter, Felix, 60
Franklin, George S.
  ("Benji"), 25
Franklin Institute, 50
Fraser Institute, 124
Friedman, Milton, 24, 31,
  81, 307n28
From, Al, 310n66
Frum, David, xi, 83, 118,
  135, 210–11; and George
  W. Bush, 17, 220

Gaffney, Frank, Jr, 8, 93,
  195–7; and George W.
  Bush, 196. See also Center
  for Security Policy
Galston, Bill, 310n66
Gedmin, Jeffrey, 83
Gelb, Leslie, 149, 167, 170,
  227
General Accounting Office,
  119
General Dynamics, 158
Gilpatric, Roswell, 326n20
Gingrich, Newt, 4, 83, 91,
  151, 318n124
Golder, Frank H., 66
Goldwater, Barry, 331n39;
  and Trilateral
  Commission, 25–6
Good, James N., 61
Goodnow, Frank, 60
Gorbachev, Mikhail, 34–5
Gore, Al, 190, 214
Gorham, William, 77
Graham, Daniel: and Heri-
  tage Foundation, 192–3,
  228; and missile defense,
  186–8, 192–4, 198, 228;
  and Ronald Reagan,
  186–8, 192–4, 198, 228.
  See also High Frontier
"Grand Old Party" Action
  Committee (GOPAC), 91.
  See also Gingrich, Newt
Greene, Jerome D., 60
Greenspan, Alan, 32,
  307n28

Habib, Philip, 28
Haddad, Tammy, 159
Hadley, Arthur, 60
Halbouty, Michel T., 307n28
Hamre, John J., 92. See also
  Center for Strategic and
  International Studies
Harding, Warren, 61, 66
Harkin, Tom: and Institute
  for Policy Studies, 95
Harper, Edwin, 32
Harris, P.R, 28
Harrison, Carter, Sr, 52
Harrison, Kathryn, 123
Hart, Gary, 317–18n123
Hayward, Steven, 89
Heclo, Hugh, 106
Henriksen, Thomas, 79
Heritage Foundation, 7, 37,
  48, 79, 80, 83, 91, 93,
  100, 105, 123, 124, 138,
  141, 143, 147, 149, 151,
  152, 153, 155, 159, 160,
  180, 183, 197, 206, 208,
  212, 222; and ABM Treaty,
  194–5, 198; budget, xiv,
  10, 44, 86, 117; and Congress, 85, 117–18; con-
  gressional testimony,
  176–7; conservative
  nature, 63; fundraising,
  86, 318n124, 319n153;
  and Newt Gingrich, 4;
  history, 84–8; and High
  Frontier, 186; marketing
  strategies, 84–5; media
  exposure, 156–8, 172–4,
  199, 319n159; and missile
  defense, 22, 36, 87, 109,
  193–5, 198, 228; and
  Ronald Reagan, 33–6, 84,
  117, 180, 309n48,
  319n152; research, 11;
  staff, 10, 117
Hess, Stephan, 28
High Frontier, 229; and
  Heritage Foundation, 186;
  and missile defense, 22,
  186, 193–4, 197, 198,
  199; and Ronald Reagan;
  193–4, 199, 228. See also
  Graham, Daniel

Hill, James, 185
Hiller, Andy, 219
Hoberg, George, 123
Hoffman, Fred, 188
Holsti, K.J., 164–6, 168, 169, 227
Holt, Hamilton, 57
Honeywell, 158
Hoover, Herbert, 71, 315n76; and Commission for Relief in Belgium, 64–6; and Hoover Institution, 64–9. See also Hoover Institution on War, Revolution and Peace
Hoover Institution on War, Revolution and Peace, xiv, 12, 19, 24, 32, 35, 46, 54, 78, 91, 99, 119, 124, 143, 150; budget, 10, 44; and George W. Bush, 18; congressional testimony, 176–7; and Newt Gingrich, 4; history, 64–71, 312–13n27; media exposure, 172–3; and Ronald Reagan, 29, 33, 34, 64, 69, 70–1, 315nn83–4, 319n152, 327–8n5; staff, 10; and Stanford University, 64–71, 315n84; Washington Seminars, 154–5. See also Hoover War Library
Hoover War Library, 65–7. See also Hoover Institution on War, Revolution and Peace
House, Edward M., 316n88
Hubbard, R. Glenn, 40
Hudson Institute, 75, 138, 144, 151; congressional testimony, 176–7; media exposure, 172–4
Hughes, Karen, 17, 219, 334n49
Hussein, Saddam, x, 16, 169, 213, 217, 334n35

Inquiry, The, 72

Institute for Contemporary Studies, 79, 307n36
Institute for Defense Analyses, 33
Institute for Government Research, 54; history, 59–62, 313n30, 314n49. See also Brookings Institution
Institute for Naval Analysis, 144
Institute for Policy Studies, 7, 79, 91, 100, 105; budget, 44, 95; profile, 95; projects, 95; and Social Action and Leadership School for Activists (SALSA), 95; staff, 95
Institute for Research on Public Policy, 124
Institute for Research on the German Revolution, 66
Institute of Economics, 62, 313n30
Institute of Pacific Relations, 315n71
interest groups: and think tanks, 12–14
Internal Revenue Code, 13, 70
Iraq, x, xv, 15, 16, 41, 93, 104, 109, 133, 169, 172, 173, 177, 182, 203, 206, 210, 211, 212, 223, 224, 334n35. See also Bush, George H.W.; Bush, George W.; Operation Desert Storm; Persian Gulf War

Jackson, Henry ("Scoop"), 24
Jackson, Jesse, 317–18n123; and Institute for Policy Studies, 95
James Baker III Institute for Public Policy, 48
Johnson, Lyndon, 326n20; and Urban Institute, 76
Johnson, U. Alexis, 326n20

Kagan, Donald, 215

Kagan, Robert, 94, 214, 334n34
Kahn, Herman, 75
Kellogg, Paul U., 55
Kemp, Jack, 88, 307n28, 317–18n123, 318n124
Kennan, George, 78, 229
Kennedy, John F., 70, 76, 88, 95, 135, 138, 220, 307n26, 326n20
Kennedy, Robert, 326n20
Kerrey, Bob: and Institute for Policy Studies, 95
Kerry, John, 197
Keyworth, George, 186, 198
Khrushchev, Nikita, 138
Kingdon, John, 107, 108, 123
Kirby, Michael, 124
Kirkpatrick, Jeane, 31, 36, 45, 79, 81, 153
Kissinger, Henry, 78, 229, 317n120; and Center for Strategic and International Studies, 92
Kitfield, James, 40
Koppel, Ted, 217, 218
Kovner, Bruce, 83
Krasner, Stephen, 103–4, 108–9, 137, 221
Krieble, Robert H., 87
Kristol, Irving, 36
Kristol, William, 93, 94, 214, 217–18, 334n34
Kucinich, Dennis, 192
Kurtz, Howard, 158

Laird, Melvin, 82
Laura Spelman Rockefeller Memorial Fund, 66
Libby, Lewis ("Scooter"): and Project for the New American Century, 94, 212, 213
Lieberman, Joe, 149
Lindblom, Charles E., 325–6n15
Linden, Patricia, 81, 156
Lindquist, Evert, 106
Lindsay, James, 203, 219, 220, 221, 224

Lindsey, Lawrence, 18, 40, 83, 311n73
Linowitz, Sol, 306n19
Lovett, Robert, 326n20
Lowi, Theodore, xiii, 142
Lustick, Ian, 218
Lutz, Ralph H., 66
Lynn, James T., 307n28

McCain, John, 149
McCarthy, Joseph, 143
McCone, John, 326n20
McCracken, Paul, 307n28
McFarlane, Robert ("Bud"), 35, 309n51, 330n13
McGann, James G., xv, 5, 11, 43, 44, 77, 112
McGovern, George: and Institute for Policy Studies, 95
McHenry, Donald, 28
Machiavelli, Niccolò, 3
McNamara, Robert, 326n20
Macy, V. Everett, 52
Madison, James, 110–11
Manhattan Institute for Policy Research, 40
Marshall, Will, 310n66
Martin, Edward, 326n20
Meacher, Michael, 213
Mead, Edwin, 57
Meese, Edwin, III, 34, 86, 152, 185, 186, 308n44, 308n46, 318n124, 319n152; and Institute for Contemporary Studies, 307n36; and policy task forces, 31–2
Micklethwait, John, 182
Middle East Forum, 91
Miller, James, 32, 33
Mills, C. Wright, 109, 142, 143–4
Mitrany, David, 169
Mondale, Walter, 28; and 1984 election defeat, 38
Moore, Thomas, 32, 33
Morrow, Douglas, 185
Moulton, Harold G., 62
Munson, Lynne, 40

mutual assured destruction (MAD), 228; defined, 184

Nash, George, 65
National Bureau of Economic Research, 66
National Civic Federation (NCF), 52–3, 54
national missile defense (NMD), x, 8, 15, 16, 21–2, 36, 93, 109, 172, 182–200, 224, 227, 228; George H.W. Bush and, 89; George W. Bush and, 16–17, 191–2, 195, 224, 331n37; Center for Security Policy and; think tanks and, 192–200. See also Clinton, Bill; Reagan, Ronald; Star Wars; Strategic Defense Initiative (SDI); and individual think tanks
Neustadt, Richard, 4
Newsom, David, 101
Niskanen, William, 31, 32, 33
Nitze, Paul, 326n20
Nixon, Richard, 24, 30, 31, 82, 88, 92, 104; and ABM Treaty, 185; and Hoover Institution, 64, 69. See also Nixon Center for Peace and Freedom
Nixon Center for Peace and Freedom, 48; profile, 89–90; programs, 89; staff, 89. See also Nixon, Richard; think tanks: legacy-based; think tanks: vanity-based
Noble, Edward, 35
NORAD, 185, 198
Nossal, Kim Richard, 131

O'Donnell, Ken, 326n20
O'Hanlon, Michael, 7, 46
Olin Foundation, 83, 125
Operation Desert Storm, 37. See also Bush, George H.W.; Iraq; Persian Gulf War

organizational process model, 136–9
Owen, Henry D., 29

Panheuristics, 188
Paris Peace Conference, 72, 316n91
Pastor, Robert, 306n19
Penner, Rudolph, 32
Perkins, George, 52
Perle, Richard, 40, 83, 210–11, 332–3n15, 334n35
Perot, Ross, 48
Persian Gulf War, 15, 37, 104, 189, 205. See also Bush, George H.W.; Iraq; Operation Desert Storm
Peschek, Joseph, 14, 98, 127, 136, 166
philanthropic foundations, 54, 122, 124–5
Pillar, Paul, 201
Pines, Burton Yale, 84
Pipes, Sally, 124
Pitfield, Michael, 124
pluralism, 101–2
Podesta, John, 88
Podhoretz, Norman, 36
policy communities, 105–7, 167
policy cycle, 107
policy entrepreneurship, 122–5
political action committees (PACs): and think tanks, 12–14
Pollack, Kenneth, 211
Powell, Colin, 41, 202
Pritchett, Henry, 57
Progressive Policy Institute (PPI), 87, 149; and Bill Clinton, 4, 37–8, 310n66
Project for the New American Century, 15, 88, 91, 155, 180, 222, 229; budget, 10, 93; and George.W. Bush, 10, 14–16, 41, 93, 203, 204, 212–19, 221–4, 228, 333–4n31, 334n35; and Bush doctrine, 93–5, 173,

204, 216–17; congressional testimony, 176–7; media exposure, 172–4; profile, 93–95; staff, 10, 94
Putin, Vladimir, 192

Quayle, Dan, 334n34

RAND Corporation, xiii, 9, 46, 47, 50, 78, 91, 100, 105, 138, 143, 144, 149, 155, 183, 206, 208, 222; budget, xiv, 10, 44, 75, 115; congressional testimony, 176–7; and Department of Defense, 115; history, 75–6; media exposure, 172–4; research, 76, 317n109; staff, xiv, 76
Raskin, Marcus, 95. *See also* Institute for Policy Studies
rational actor model, 132–6; compared with bureaucratic politics model, 137–9
Ravitch, Diane, 40
Raymond, Arthur, 75
Reader's Digest Association, 83
Reader's Digest Foundation, 125
Reagan, Ronald, 30, 40, 41, 82, 83, 86, 93, 117, 120, 135, 143, 152, 160, 180, 183, 196, 199, 204, 210, 215, 218, 220, 222, 223, 227, 228, 306n20, 306n22; and American Enterprise Institute, 33, 82; and Center for Strategic and International Studies, 33; and Committee on the Present Danger, 33, 307–8n39; and Heritage Foundation, 33–6, 84, 117, 180, 309n48, 319n152; and High Frontier, 193–4, 199, 228; and Hoover

Institution, 29, 33, 34, 64, 69, 70–1, 315nn83–84, 319n152, 327–8n5; and missile defense, 21, 22, 36, 183–9, 193–4, 198, 200, 228, 330n13; and mutual assured destruction (MAD), 184, 228; and policy task forces, 31–2, 307n28; and think tanks, 4, 18, 23, 29–36, 37, 39
Reed, Bruce, 310n66
Reinsch, Paul S., 57–8
Ricci, David, x
Rice, Condoleezza, 40, 41, 191, 202, 219, 220, 224, 335n57
Rich, Andrew, 111, 115, 176
Richards, Anne, 17
Robert Brookings Graduate School of Economics and Government, 62, 313n30. *See also* Brookings Institution
Roberts, Paul Craig, 32
Robertson, Pat, 317–18n123
Rockefeller, David: and Jimmy Carter, 25–6, 28; and Trilateral Commission, 25–6, 28
Rockefeller Foundation, 54, 60, 66, 124
Rockwell, 158
Roosevelt, Franklin Delano, 4, 28, 67, 75, 220
Roosevelt, Theodore, 220, 313n37
Root, Elihu, 57, 71, 72, 313n37
Rosenthal, James, 35
Rove, Karl, 17, 219
Rudman, Warren, 328n5
Rumsfeld, Donald, 15, 16, 41, 150, 192, 196, 202, 220, 334n35, 334n40, 335n57; and Center for Security Policy, 93; and missile defense, 331n37; and Project for the New

American Century, 94, 180, 212, 213, 217, 218, 223
Rusk, Dean, 25, 78, 326n20
Russell Sage Foundation, 12, 54, 112, 124; history, 55–6, 312–13n27, 313n31
Russian Revolution Institute, 66

Sage, Margaret Olivia, 55, 64
Sage Foundation. *See* Russell Sage Foundation
Saloma, John, 98
Scaife, Richard, 35
Scalia, Antonin, 32
Schlesinger, Arthur, 4
Schlesinger, James: and Center for Strategic and International Studies, 92
Schmidlapp, J.G., 57, 58
Schmitt, Gary, 94, 214–18, 223. *See also* Project for the New American Century
Schultze, Charles L., 28
Science Council of Canada, 124
Scott, James Brown, 57
Scowcroft, Brent, 191, 219, 327–8n5
Shapiro, Robert, 310n66
Shepardson, Whitney H., 72
Shoup, Lawrence, 25, 26
Shultz, George, 18, 32, 40, 187
Simes, Dimitri, 89. *See also* Nixon Center for Peace and Freedom
Simon, Herbert, 134, 141
Simon, Steven, 113–14
Simon, William E., 307n28
Skocpol, Theda, 103
Smith, Alfred E., 66
Smith, Gerard C., 29
Smith, James, ix–x, 14, 51, 52, 53, 55–6
Smoot-Hawley Tariff, 67

Sorenson, Ted, 326n20
Spring, Baker, 193, 194–5
Sprinkel, Beryl, 32
Stairs, Dennis, 107
Stanford University, 64–6, 68–70. See also Hoover Institution on War, Revolution and Peace
Star Wars, 87, 183, 184, 195–6, 227, 331n52. See also national missile defense (NMD); Strategic Defense Initiative (SDI)
state theory, 102–5, 108–9
statist paradigm, 98, 102–5, 108–9
Steelman, Aaron, 103, 230
Stein, Herbert, 81
Steinbruner, John, 139–41
Sterling, Wallace, 69
Stevenson, Adlai, 326n20
Stevenson, Jonathan, 113–14
Stone, Diane, 5, 11, 106, 111
Strategic Defense Initiative (SDI), 87, 183, 184, 186–9, 194, 200, 330n13; criticisms of, 187–8. See also national missile defense (NMD); Star Wars
Straus, Oscar S., 57
sub-government: defined, 106
Sunley, Emil, Jr, 28
Swope, Gerard, 52

Taft, William Howard, 57
Taft, William Howard IV, 32
Taft Commission, 60
Talbott, Strobe, 63
Tax Foundation, 40
Taylor, John, 40
Taylor, Maxwell, 326n20
Taylor, William J., Jr, 158
Teeters, Nancy H., 29
Teller, Edward, 186, 198
think tanks: ability to influence policy, x–xvi, 8–9, 22, 197–200, 222–4; advocacy, 7, 47, 48–9,

77–88; assessing influence of, 8, 121–2, 160–81; budgets, 235–8; and the bureaucracy, 121–2; and George H.W. Bush, 4, 36, 309n56; and George W. Bush, 39–41, 108, 183, 203, 204, 216, 220–3; in Canada, 6, 47, 115, 318n126, 323n16; candidate-based, 47–8, 90–1; and Jimmy Carter, 4, 18, 23, 24–5, 29, 36, 37, 39; channels of influence, 147–60; and Bill Clinton, 18, 36–9, 120, 135; conceptual frameworks for, 97–109; conferences, workshops, and seminars, 207, 259–68; congressional testimony, 118, 176–8, 179–80, 207–8, 268–72, 278–81, 329nn10–11; defined, 10–11; development in Canada vs. United States, 122–4; evolution, 49–91; funding, 77, 79, 114, 122, 152, 318n124; in Germany, 6, 79, 111; as government contractors and specialists, 74–7; government positions held by staff, 239–58; in Great Britain, 6, 47, 115, 318n126; and interest groups, 12–14, 121, 128; legacy-based, 47–8, 88–90; media exposure, 7, 156–9, 170–6, 178, 273–8; and missile defense, 22, 182–4, 192–200; number in the United States, 128; number worldwide, 5, 43; and political parties, 79–80; and presidential advisory boards, 154, 327–8n5; and presidential campaigns, 18–19, 23–42, 154, 305n3; profiles,

235–7; proliferation after World War II, 74–7; proliferation in 1970s and after, 78–88; publications, 59, 73, 82, 92, 151, 282–302; and Ronald Reagan, 4, 18, 23, 29–36, 37, 39; relations with Congress, 102, 117–19; relations with the Executive, 102, 119–21; research-oriented, 45–6, 49–74; tax-exempt status, 13; typologies, 11, 45–8; vanity-based, 47–8, 88–90; and war on terror, 22, 149–50, 182, 183, 202–24. See also individual think tanks
Thompson, Dorothy, 205
Thompson, Fred, 83
Thompson, Llewellyn, 326n20
Tocqueville, Alexis de, 112
Trent, Darrell, 32, 33
Trilateral Commission, 25–8, 305n6, 306nn14–15. See also Carter, Jimmy
Trudeau, Pierre Elliott, 124
Truman, David, xii, 142, 145
Truman, Harry, 186
Ture, Norman, 32, 33
Turner, Stansfield, 28

Union of Concerned Scientists (UCS), 188, 197, 200
United Nations, 202, 211; Security Council, 169
United States Institute for Peace, 149
Urban Institute, 46, 47, 50, 138; budget, 76; and Department of Housing and Urban Development (HUD), 115; history, 76–7; research, 76; staff
USA PATRIOT Act: defined, 211

Vance, Cyrus, 27, 28
Van Kleeck, Mary, 56
Vietnam syndrome: defined, 229
Vietnam War, 24, 69, 79, 84, 144, 180, 229
Vilsack, Tom, 310n63. See also Democratic Leadership Council

Walker, Charles E., 307n28
Walker, Michael, 124
Wall, John Frazier, 57
Wallace, George, 24
war on terror, x, 8, 113, 182, 201–24, 227, 228; and 9/11, 201–2, 205; prior to 9/11, 208–9. See also Afghanistan; Bush doctrine; Iraq

Washington Institute for Near East Policy, 91
Watergate scandal, xii, 24, 84
Weaver, Kent, 5, 11, 19, 44–7, 79, 118, 176
Weidenbaum, Murray, 31, 32, 33, 307n28
Weinberger, Caspar, 32, 33, 187, 307n28; and Institute for Contemporary Studies, 307n36
Weinraub, Bernard, 35
Westinghouse, 158
Weyrich, Paul, 84, 85, 117
White, Andrew D., 57, 65
Wiarda, Howard, 121–2
Wilbur, Ray Lyman, 65

Willoughby, William F., 60–1
Wilson, Don, 326n20
Wilson, Woodrow, 4, 57, 60–1, 72, 316n88
Wisner, Frank, 149
Wolfowitz, Paul, 15–16, 40, 41, 202; and Project for the New American Century, 94, 212, 213, 217, 218, 223
Woodward, Bob, xii, 41, 203
Wooldridge, Adrian, 182
Wriston, Walter, 307n28

Zoellick, Robert, 18, 40